ROB TIDROW
JOE CASAD
MIKE WOLFE

MCSE
TRAINING GUIDE
WINDOWS® 95

MCSE Training Guide: Windows 95

By Rob Tidrow, Joe Casad, Mike Wolfe

Published by:
New Riders Publishing
201 West 103rd Street
Indianapolis, IN 46290 USA

Printed in the United States of America 1 2 3 4 5 6 7 8 9 0

Library of Congress Cataloging-in-Publication Data

CIP data available upon request

Warning and Disclaimer

This book is designed to provide information about **Windows 95**. Every effort has been made to make this book as complete and as accurate as possible, but no warranty or fitness is implied.

The information is provided on an "as is" basis. The author and New Riders Publishing shall have neither liability nor responsibility to any person or entity with respect to any loss or damages arising from the information contained in this book or from the use of the disks or programs that may accompany it.

Publisher	*Don Fowley*
Associate Publisher	*David Dwyer*
Publishing Manager	*Emmett Dulaney*
Marketing Manager	*Mary Foote*
Managing Editor	*Carla Hall*
Director of Development	*Kezia Endsley*

Acquisitions Editor
Nancy Maragioglio

Senior Editors
Sarah Kearns
Suzanne Snyder

Development Editor
Ami Frank

Project Editor
Theresa Mathias

Technical Editor
Michael J. Wolfe

Acquisitions Coordinator
Gretchen Schlesinger

Administrative Coordinator
Karen Opal

Manufacturing Coordinator
Brook Farling

Cover Designer
Karen Ruggles

Cover Production
Aren Howell

Book Designer
Gary Adair

Director of Production
Larry Klein

Production Team Supervisors
Laurie Casey
Joe Millay

Graphics Image Specialists
Kevin Cliburn
Sadie Crawford

Production Analyst
Erich J. Richter

Production Team
Kim Cofer, Tricia Flodder, Janelle Herber, Christopher Morris

Indexer
Chris Barrick

About the Authors

Rob Tidrow is a technical writer, Web site designer, trainer, and president of Tidrow Communications, Inc., a firm specializing in content creation and delivery. Rob has authored or co-authored more than 20 books on a wide variety of computer topics, including seven books on Windows 95. He authored *Windows 95 Registry Troubleshooting* and *Windows NT Registry Troubleshooting*, both published by New Riders, and *Windows 95, Deluxe Edition*, *Platinum Edition Using Windows 95*, *Inside the World Wide Web*, and *Windows 95 for Network Administrators*, all published by Macmillan Publishing. Rob lives in Indianapolis, Indiana, with his wife Tammy and their two sons, Adam and Wesley.

Joe Casad is a freelance writer and editor who specializes in programming and networking topics. He was the managing editor of the short-lived but well-received *Network Administrator Magazine*, a journal of practical solutions for network professionals. Mr. Casad received a B.S. in engineering from the University of Kansas in 1980 and, before becoming a full-time writer and editor, spent ten years in the computer-intensive areas of the structural engineering profession. He now lives in Lawrence, Kansas, with wife Barb Dinneen and a pair of pint-sized hackers named Xander and Mattie.

Mike Wolfe currently works for Chevron Information Technology Company as a member of the Common Operating Environment (COE) Team at the company campus in San Ramon, California. He provides top-level network software support, project management, and internal company consulting in an interesting and challenging workplace. Mike holds certifications as both a Novell Master CNE and a Microsoft MCSE. He is heavily involved in the corporate-wide deployment of Windows 95 and the eventual migration of network operating systems at Chevron from Novell NetWare to Windows NT Server. He was a mainframe applications developer for many years before switching to PCs and network computing. Mike lives in San Ramon, California, with his wife, Maggie. You can contact Mike at 73464,22@compuserve.com.

Trademark Acknowledgments

Dedication

From Rob Tidrow

This book is dedicated to my family.

Acknowledgment

I want to thank everyone involved with the creation of this book, including Don Fowley, Emmett Dulaney, Nancy Maragioglio, Ami Frank, Theresa Mathias, and Mike Wolfe. Thanks everybody!

—Rob Tidrow

Contents at a Glance

Table of Contents

Introduction

MCSE Training Guide: Windows 95 is designed for advanced end-users, service technicians, and network administrators who are considering certification as a Microsoft Certified Systems Engineer (MCSE) or as a Microsoft Certified Product (MCP) Specialist. The Windows 95 exam ("Exam 70-63: Implementing and Supporting Microsoft Windows 95") tests your ability to implement, administer, and troubleshoot systems as well as your ability to provide technical support to users of the Microsoft Windows 95 operating system.

Who Should Read This Book

This book is designed to help advanced users, service technicians, and network administrators who are working for MCSE certification prepare for the MCSE "Implementing and Supporting Microsoft Windows 95" exam (#70-63).

This book is your one-stop-shop. Everything you need to know to pass the exam is in here, and the book has been certified by Microsoft as study material. You do not *need* to take a class in addition to buying this book to pass the exam. However, your personal study habits may benefit from taking a class in addition to the book, or buying this book in addition to a class.

This book also can help advanced users and administrators who are not studying for the MCSE exam but are looking for a single-volume reference on Windows 95.

How This Book Helps You

This book takes you on a self-guided tour of all the areas covered by the MCSE Windows 95 exam and teaches you the specific skills you need to achieve your MCSE certification. You'll also find helpful hints, tips, real-world examples, exercises, and references to additional study materials. Specifically, this book is set up to help you in the following ways:

▶ **Organization.** This book is organized by major exam topics (12 in all) and exam objectives. Every objective you need to know for the "Implementing and Supporting Microsoft Windows 95" exam is covered in this book; we've include a margin icon, like the one in the margin here, to help you quickly locate these objectives. There are pointers at different elements to direct you to the appropriate place in the book if you find you need to review certain sections.

▶ **Decide how to spend your time wisely.** Pre-chapter quizzes at the beginning of each chapter test your knowledge of the objectives contained within that chapter. If you already know the answers to those questions, you can make a time-management decision accordingly.

▶ **Extensive practice test options.** Plenty of questions at the end of each chapter test your comprehension of material covered within that chapter. An answer list follows the questions so you can check yourself. These practice test options will help you decide what you already understand and what requires extra review on your part. The CD-ROM also contains a sample test engine that will give you an accurate idea of what the test is really like.

You'll also get a chance to practice for the certification exams using the test engine on the accompanying CD-ROM. The questions on the CD-ROM provide a more thorough and comprehensive look at what the certification exams really are like. The

CD-ROM includes the Microsoft Education and Certification Roadmap—a publication from Microsoft that provides a thorough outline of the certification process. The Roadmap Assessment Exam includes the best available examples of the kinds of questions you'll find on the certification exam. The Roadmap also includes the Planning Wizard, an online tool that helps you quickly map out a plan for achieving your certification goals.

 note

> For a complete description of New Riders' newly developed test engine, please see Appendix D, "All About TestPrep."
>
> For a complete description of what you can find on the CD-ROM, see Appendix C, "What's on the CD-ROM."

Most Roadmap Assessment Exams are based on specific product versions, and new elective exams are available on an ongoing basis. The Microsoft Education and Certification Roadmap is a quarterly publication. You can obtain updates of the Roadmap at any of the following locations:

Microsoft Education: Call (800) 636-7544

Internet: ftp://ftp.microsoft.com/Services/MSEdCert

World Wide Web: http://www.microsoft.com/train_cert/default.htm

CompuServe Forum: GO MSEDCERT

The enclosed CD-ROM also includes MCP Endeavor, an interactive practice test application designed exclusively for Macmillan Publishing that will help you prepare for the MCSE exams.

The CD-ROM also includes a white paper from Microsoft entitled "Comparing Windows 95 and Windows NT Workstation."

This book also can help you by serving as a desktop reference for information on Windows 95 and other computer networking topics, such as cabling, data transmission, protocols, and network technologies.

Understanding What the "Implementing and Supporting Microsoft Windows 95" Exam (#70-63) Covers

The "Implementing and Supporting Microsoft Windows 95" exam (#70-63) covers 12 main topic areas, arranged in accordance with test objectives. On the CD-ROM that comes with this book, you'll find document lpr70-63.doc, which is the exam preparation guide prepared by Microsoft. lpr70-63.doc describes what you will be tested on and suggests ways to prepare for the exam. The exam objectives, listed by topic area, are covered in the following sections.

Planning and Installation

▶ Identify appropriate hardware requirements for Microsoft Windows 95 installation

▶ Maintain program groups and user preferences when upgrading from Windows 3.1

▶ Determine when to use Windows 95 and when to use Microsoft Windows NT Workstation

▶ Configure a Windows 95 computer on a network using the appropriate protocol

▶ Select the appropriate security to meet various needs

▶ Determine the appropriate installation method for various situations

▶ Install the Windows 95 operating system

▶ Troubleshoot setup and system startup

▶ Set up files for network installation and for shared use

▶ Recognize files used in troubleshooting the installation process

Architecture and Memory

▶ Compare and contrast the memory usage of a Microsoft MS-DOS–based application, a 16-bit Windows-based application, and a 32-bit Windows-based application operating in Windows 95

Customizing and Configuring Windows 95

▶ Identify and explain the differences between the Windows 3.1 interface and the Windows 95 interface

▶ Set up a dual-boot system for Windows 95

▶ Install new hardware devices on various systems that support Plug and Play

▶ Given a specific bus configuration, identify areas of limitation for full Plug and Play

▶ Configure the Taskbar

▶ Configure shortcuts

▶ Add items to the Start menu

▶ Choose an appropriate method to accomplish a specified task using the user interface

▶ Customize the Desktop for a specified set of criteria

▶ Use the Windows 95 interface to create, print, and store a file

▶ Configure and use Windows Explorer

▶ Access the network through Network Neighborhood

▶ Configure the properties sheet for an object

▶ Define the purpose of the Windows 95 Registry

▶ Classify types of information in the Registry

▶ Determine where the Registry is stored

▶ Identify situations in which it is appropriate to modify the Registry

▶ Modify the contents of the Registry

▶ Choose the appropriate course of action when OLE information in the Registry becomes corrupted

Editing User and System Profiles

▶ Modify a user workstation to meet specified criteria

▶ Grant remote administration privileges on your computer

▶ Modify user profiles

▶ Set up user profiles

▶ Set up computer policies

▶ Define the System Policy Editor, and describe how it is used

▶ Create, share, and monitor a remote resource

▶ Administer a remote computer

Networking and Interoperability

▶ Configure a Windows 95 computer to access the Internet

▶ Configure a Windows 95 computer to use NetWare user-level security

▶ Configure a Windows 95 computer as a client or server in a NetWare network

▶ Identify the limitations of a Windows 95 NetWare server

▶ Configure a Windows 95 computer to use Windows NT Server user-level security

- ▶ Configure a Windows 95 computer as a client in a Windows NT Server domain

- ▶ Configure a Windows 95 computer as a client in a NetWare network

- ▶ Recognize how the UNC is used

- ▶ Configure Browse Master for Microsoft networks

- ▶ Configure Browse Master for NetWare networks

- ▶ Identify advantages and disadvantages of user-level and share-level security

- ▶ Identify elements of the Windows 95 operating system network architecture

- ▶ Install and configure TCP/IP for use with Windows 95

Managing Disk Resources and Utilities

- ▶ Manage long and short file names in a mixed environment

- ▶ Troubleshoot problems and perform disk compression

- ▶ Select the appropriate disk-management tool for a given situation

- ▶ Use Disk Defragmenter to optimize for speed

- ▶ Use ScanDisk in appropriate situations

- ▶ Use Backup in appropriate situations

Managing Printers

- ▶ Implement printers for Windows 95

- ▶ Identify situations in which metafile spooling is appropriate

- ▶ Set up Point and Print printing

- ▶ Access a printer through a NetWare network

▶ Create, reorder, and delete a Windows 95 print queue

▶ Set up and remove printer drivers in Windows 95

▶ Use Windows 95 to share a printer on the network

Running Applications

▶ Configure Windows 95 to run MS-DOS–based applications

▶ Predict potential problems when configuring 16-bit Windows-based applications

▶ Distinguish between MS-DOS Mode and the standard method for running MS-DOS–based applications

▶ Determine when an application should be run in MS-DOS Mode

▶ Resolve general protection faults

▶ Determine the appropriate course of action when the application stops responding to the system

Mobile Services

▶ Implement the appropriate level of security for use with Dial-Up Networking

▶ Choose applications that would be appropriate to run over Dial-Up Networking

▶ Configure Dial-Up Networking to be a client

▶ Configure Dial-Up Networking on a server

▶ Configure a modem to meet a specific set of user requirements

▶ Implement the various telephony options to meet a specific set of user requirements

▶ Use a Briefcase to transfer and synchronize data between two computers

Microsoft Exchange

▶ Share a fax

▶ Configure a fax for both stand-alone and shared situations

▶ Configure Microsoft Exchange to access the Internet

▶ Configure a Windows 95 computer to send and receive mail

▶ Configure a Windows 95 computer to access CompuServe mail

Plug and Play

▶ Explain how Windows 95 handles components that are not compatible with Plug and Play

▶ Explain hot docking and the potential consequences of the dynamic device changes

▶ Given a specific configuration, use Device Manager to manually reconfigure a Plug and Play device

Troubleshooting

▶ Resolve problems using appropriate resources

▶ Select appropriate tools for troubleshooting

▶ Monitor Windows 95 performance, and resolve performance problems

▶ Audit access to a Windows 95 local resource

▶ Optimize the system to use the Windows 95 drivers

▶ Optimize a computer for desktop performance

▶ Optimize a computer for network performance

▶ Optimize printing

▶ Discriminate between preemptive and cooperative multi-tasking

▶ Explain Windows 95 multitasking of 16-bit Windows-based applications and 32-bit Windows-based applications

▶ Discriminate between a process and a thread

▶ Discriminate between resource usage in Windows 3.1, Windows 95, and Windows NT

▶ Explain how Windows 95 performs memory paging as compared to Windows 3.x

▶ Choose the appropriate course of action when the installation process fails

▶ Use the startup disk to repair a faulty network setup

▶ Choose the appropriate course of action when an application fails

▶ Choose the appropriate course of action when a print job fails

▶ Choose the appropriate course of action when the boot process fails

▶ Choose the appropriate course of action when file system problems occur

▶ Choose the appropriate course of action when Dial-Up Networking problems occur

▶ Predict the consequences to the operating system when MS-DOS–based applications, 16-bit Windows-based applications, and 32-bit Windows-based applications fail to respond to the system while running under Windows 95

Hardware and Software Needed

As a self-paced study guide, much of the book expects you to use Windows 95 and follow along through the exercises while you learn. Microsoft designed Windows 95 to operate in a wide range of actual situations, and the exercises in this book encompass that range. Some of the exercises require only a single stand-alone computer running Windows 95. Others (those that explore some of the Windows 95 networking options) require a small Microsoft network. Some exercises refer to a pair of computers (one running Windows 95, and one running Windows 95 and Windows NT Server) configured as described in the following sections.

Computer 1

▶ Computer on the Microsoft Hardware Compatibility List

▶ 486DX 33-Mhz (or better) processor for Windows 95

▶ 8 MB of RAM (16 MB recommended) for Windows 95

▶ 200-MB (or larger) hard disk for Windows 95

▶ 3.5-inch 1.44-MB floppy drive

▶ VGA (or Super VGA) video adapter

▶ VGA (or Super VGA) monitor

▶ Mouse or equivalent pointing device

▶ Two-speed (or faster) CD-ROM drive

▶ Network Interface Card (NIC)

▶ Presence on an existing network, or use of a 2-port (or more) mini-port hub to create a test network

▶ MS-DOS 5.0 or 6.*x* and Microsoft Windows for Workgroups 3.*x* pre-installed

▶ Microsoft Windows 95 (CD-ROM version)

Computer 2

▶ Computer on the Microsoft Hardware Compatibility List

▶ 486DX2 66-Mhz (or better) processor for Windows NT Server

▶ 16 MB of RAM (minimum) for Windows NT Server

▶ 340-MB (or larger) hard disk for Windows NT Server

▶ 3.5-inch 1.44-MB floppy drive

▶ VGA (or Super VGA) video adapter

▶ VGA (or Super VGA) monitor

▶ Mouse or equivalent pointing device

▶ Two-speed (or faster) CD-ROM drive (optional)

▶ Network Interface Card (NIC)

▶ Presence on an existing network, or use of a 2-port (or more) mini-port hub to create a test network

▶ MS-DOS 5.0 or 6.x and Microsoft Windows for Workgroups 3.x pre-installed

▶ Microsoft Windows 95 (floppy version)

▶ Microsoft Windows NT Server (CD-ROM version)

Computers 1 and 2 should be running at least MS-DOS 5.0 and Windows for Workgroups 3.11 at the start. In fact, it is best if the computers have only MS-DOS 5.0 and Windows for Workgroups 3.11 at the beginning. Otherwise, you may be tempted to use a computer that contains real work and files that cannot be replaced easily. These computers should be test computers. You should not be afraid to format the hard drive and start over should it be necessary.

It is somewhat easier to get access to the necessary computer hardware and software in a corporate business environment. It is harder to allocate enough time within the busy workday to complete a self-study program. Most of your study time may occur after normal working hours, away from the everyday interruptions and pressures of your regular job. If you have access to only a single, non-networked computer, you will not be able to complete all of the networking exercises.

Tips for the Exam

Remember the following tips as you prepare for the MCSE certification exams:

▶ **Read all the material.** Microsoft has been known to include material not specified in the objectives. This book includes additional information not required by the objectives in an effort to give you the best possible preparation for the examination, and for the real-world network experiences to come.

▶ **Complete the exercises in each chapter.** They will help you gain experience using the Microsoft product. All Microsoft exams are experienced-based, and require you to have used the Microsoft product in a real networking environment. Exercises for each objective are placed at the end of each chapter.

▶ **Take each pre-chapter quiz to evaluate how well you know the topic of the chapter.** Each chapter opens with one essay question per exam objective covered in the chapter. Following the quiz are the answers and pointers to where in the chapter that objective is covered.

▶ **Complete all the questions in the "Review Questions" sections.** Complete the questions at the end of each chapter—they will help you remember key points. The questions are fairly simple, but be warned, some questions may have more than one answer.

▶ **Review the exam objectives in the Microsoft Education and Certification Roadmap.** Develop your own questions for each topic listed. If you can make and answer several questions for each topic, you should pass.

▶ **Complete the Roadmap Assessment Exam and visit the relevant topics in the MCP Endeavor application.** Do not make the mistake of trusting all the answers in the Assessment Exams—they're not always correct. Look at this not as a bug, but as a feature to test your knowledge; not only do you have to know you are right, you have to be sure about it, and you have to know why each of the answers is wrong.

Although this book is designed to prepare you to take and pass the "Implementing and Supporting Microsoft Windows 95" certification exam, there are no guarantees. Read this book, work through the exercises, and take the practice assessment exams.

When taking the real certification exam, make sure you answer all the questions before your time limit expires. Do not spend too much time on any one question. If you are unsure about an answer, answer the question as best you can and mark it for later review when you have finished all the questions. It has been said, whether correctly or not, that any questions left unanswered will automatically cause you to fail.

Remember, the object is not to pass the exam, it is to understand the material. Once you understand the material, passing is simple. Knowledge is a pyramid; to build upward, you need a solid foundation. The Microsoft Certified System Engineer program is designed to ensure that you have that solid foundation.

Good luck!

New Riders Publishing

The staff of New Riders Publishing is committed to bringing you the very best in computer reference material. Each New Riders book is the result of months of work by authors and staff who research and refine the information contained within its covers.

As part of this commitment to you, the NRP reader, New Riders invites your input. Please let us know if you enjoy this book, if you have trouble with the information and examples presented, or if you have a suggestion for the next edition.

Please note, though: New Riders staff cannot serve as a technical resource during your preparation for the MCSE certification exams or for questions about software- or hardware-related problems. Please refer to the documentation that accompanies Windows 95 or to the applications' Help systems.

If you have a question or comment about any New Riders book, there are several ways to contact New Riders Publishing. We will respond to as many readers as we can. Your name, address, or phone number will never become part of a mailing list or be used for any purpose other than to help us continue to bring you the best books possible. You can write us at the following address:

New Riders Publishing
Attn: Publisher
201 W. 103rd Street
Indianapolis, IN 46290

If you prefer, you can fax New Riders at (317) 817-7448.

You also can send e-mail to New Riders at the following Internet address:

edulaney@newriders.mcp.com

New Riders Publishing is an imprint of Macmillan Computer Publishing. To obtain a catalog or information, or to purchase any Macmillan Computer Publishing book, call (800) 428-5331.

Thank you for selecting *MCSE Training Guide: Windows 95*!

Test Yourself

Stop! Before reading this chapter, test yourself to determine how much study time you will need to devote to this section.

1. You are installing Windows 95 on a computer that currently has MS-DOS 5.0 and Windows 3.1. What is the lowest Intel processor you can have in this computer to install Windows 95?

2. Jill uses a computer running Windows 3.11 for Workgroups, with several 16-bit applications installed. She has program groups set up for these applications. When she installs Windows 95, what is one way she can be assured that her application program groups are maintained?

3. A law office with 15 desktop computers are networked using Windows NT Server on one server. The partners want to ensure that their new operating system for the 15 desktop computers (either Windows 95 or Windows NT Workstation) provides file-level security. Which operating system should the law office adopt?

4. Windows 95 includes networking features to make it easier for users to connect to existing networks or to build a network from the ground up. Which three networking protocols included with Windows 95 are Plug and Play–enabled? Which two protocols are installed by default by Windows 95?

5. Windows 95 supports share-level and user-level security. You want to set up Windows 95 on 10 workstations on a network to share printer and file resources, but you want to make sure pass-through authentication is used to validate users who access these resources. Which type of security must you set up?

6. Larry, a system administrator, must set up Windows 95 on 10 computers that are not connected to a network. He must perform a manual installation process on each machine, but he wants to automate the process as much as possible using a custom setup script. What is the name of the file on which Larry needs to base his setup scripts?

7. Windows' 95 installation process is modular. Name the four logical phases to the Windows 95 installation process.

8. Missy has Windows 95 installed on her computer. When she boots her computer, it usually starts Windows 95. One day, however, Windows 95 fails to start and her computer displays the Startup menu. Name the Start-up menu option Missy needs to select to start Windows and display each startup file line by line.

9. Windows 95 is being installed from a network server as a server-based setup. What is the name of the server-based setup program you must use to install Windows 95 source files on the network server?

10. Cindy encounters problems during the Windows 95 installation process and needs to troubleshoot the process. Name the three log files Windows 95 created when Cindy ran the Windows 95 Setup program.

Answers

1. 80386DX. See "Identifying Appropriate Hardware Requirements for Installation."

2. Jill should choose to install Windows 95 over her existing Windows 3.11 for Workgroups directory. See "How to Maintain Program Groups and User Preferences When Upgrading from Windows 3.1."

3. Windows NT Workstation running NTFS (NT File System) provides file-level security. See "Determine When to Use Windows 95 and When to Use Microsoft Windows NT Workstation."

4. IPX/SPX, NetBEUI, and TCP/IP are Plug and Play—enabled. Microsoft NetBEUI and IPX/SPX are installed by default. See "Configure a Windows 95 Computer on a Network Using the Appropriate Protocol."

5. User-level security. See "Select the Appropriate Level of Security to Meet Various Needs."

6. MSBATCH.INF. See "Manual, Customized, or Automated Setup?"

7. Startup and information gathering; hardware detection; file copy; and final system configuration. See "Installation Process."

8. Step-By-Step Confirmation. See table 1.7.

9. NETSETUP.EXE. See "Set Up Files for Network Installation and Shared Use."

10. SETUPLOG.TXT; DETLOG.TXT; and, DETCRASH.LOG. See "Recognize Files Used in Troubleshooting the Installation Process."

C h a p t e r

1

Planning and Installation

This chapter will help you prepare for the exam by covering the following objectives:

Test Objectives

- ▶ Identify appropriate hardware requirements for Microsoft Windows 95 installation

- ▶ Maintain program groups and user preferences when upgrading from Windows 3.1

- ▶ Determine when to use Windows 95 and when to use Microsoft Windows NT Workstation

- ▶ Configure a Windows 95 computer on a network using the appropriate protocol

- ▶ Select the appropriate security to meet various needs

- ▶ Determine the appropriate installation method for various situations

- ▶ Install the Windows 95 operating system

- ▶ Troubleshoot setup and system startup

- ▶ Set up files for network installation and for shared use

- ▶ Recognize files used in troubleshooting the installation process

Installation of Windows 95 requires careful planning, an understanding of the hardware and software requirements, an appreciation for the steps in the installation process, and the ability to troubleshoot any problems that arise. Although the Windows 95 Setup program is designed to handle most types of hardware configurations, you might be called upon to respond to many of the common problems. Experience in performing the Windows 95 installation is the best teacher.

This chapter is your guide to understanding the Windows 95 installation. In this chapter, you will learn about the following:

- ▶ Windows 95 installation media options

- ▶ Preparing for Windows 95 installation

- ▶ Windows 95 hardware and software requirements

- ▶ Installation decisions

- ▶ The four phases of the Windows 95 installation process

- ▶ Troubleshooting the Windows 95 installation

- ▶ Installing either locally or from the network

Windows 95 is positioned as the successor to Microsoft's *Disk Operating System* (DOS), Windows 3.*x*, and Windows for Workgroups 3.*x* products. It is part of the Microsoft Windows operating system family, which also includes Microsoft Windows NT. However, Windows 95 is intended to be the standard operating system for the general-purpose user, and runs only on an Intel-based computer. Windows NT is designed for leading-edge systems, running on Intel-based as well as RISC-based architectures. The key differences between Windows 95 and Windows NT are covered later in this chapter in the section "Making Installation Decisions." In that section, you learn when to use Windows 95, and when to use Windows NT Workstation.

If you are new to Windows 95, two other books from New Riders Publishing, *Inside Windows 95, Deluxe Edition* and *Windows 95 for Network Administrators*, offer greater detail about Windows 95 than this book, which primarily focuses on the certification process. Also, if you do not already own a copy of the *Windows 95 Resource Kit* from Microsoft Press, you should purchase one.

Microsoft Windows 95 Key Features

Within Windows 95, there are significant improvements. It is now a true operating system, by combining elements of DOS and Windows 3.*x*. Designed to become the desktop standard, Windows 95 is tuned to deliver the best performance from personal and business applications in either stand-alone computers or networked workstations. With millions of previously installed MS-DOS and Windows 3.*x* platforms existing today, Windows 95 is ideally suited as an upgrade product. The following sections describe key features of Windows 95 that explain why someone should upgrade.

A Better, More Intuitive User Interface

Microsoft conducted usability studies to improve the ease-of-use aspects of Windows 95. The *user interface* (UI) in Windows 95 had to meet certain requirements: it should be easy to set up, intuitively simple to learn, quick to use through the Start menu, and much better to manage and support. This simplicity should exist for both the novice or experienced user alike. Not only are the interface icons different, but the layout of the Desktop makes it easy to find and use resources.

32-Bit Operating System Architecture

The 32-bit architecture and superior resource handling within Windows 95 produce a more stable operating system environment. The 32-bit, protected-mode subsystems built into Windows 95 are more crash-resistant. A bad application, whether 16-bit or 32-bit, is less likely to stop the operating system. Even though the architecture is 32-bit, Windows 95 uses a combination of 32-bit and 16-bit code. The 32-bit code maximizes the performance of the system. The 16-bit code helps maintain compatibility with existing applications and drivers.

Preemptive Multitasking

The previous versions of Windows 3.*x* use cooperative multitasking, whereas Windows 95 uses preemptive multitasking. To the end user, the difference is subtle. Preemptive multitasking means that the Windows 95 operating system is tracking and preemptively allocating system resources. Cooperative multitasking means the operating system is relying on each application under Windows 3.x to cooperate in giving up control and system resources while running. This feature allows Windows 95 users to carry on several simultaneous computing tasks more smoothly than ever before.

Plug and Play Technology

Windows 95 is compatible with the Plug and Play (PnP) technology specification. Hardware devices written to this specification can identify themselves and their settings to Windows 95. When these hardware devices are added or re-configured, Windows 95 can adjust the computer's hardware configuration automatically to operate with those hardware device changes. It is a design philosophy that allows for automatic installation and configuration of new devices without any intervention by the user.

Integrated Networking Support

For the network administrator, Windows 95 is the perfect client workstation. Windows 95 comes with 32-bit networking components that allow it to work with all major networks, including Microsoft, Novell, and Banyan. These networking components include the redirector, the protocol, the network adapter, and various network services, such as file and print sharing. They are written for the multitasking environment, take up no real-mode memory, and offer fast, stable networking support.

Centralized Security and System Policies

Windows 95 supports "pass-through," server-based security for both Microsoft Windows NT and Novell NetWare networks. Users can be required to *log on* (Windows NT) or *log in* (NetWare) before they can use Windows 95 in a networked environment. This allows increased system security and control, which enables the network administrator to use existing user-based security rules to manage access rights. The use of system policies (new with Windows 95) allows further control over user access to the network. System policies also can be used to restrict a user's Windows 95 Desktop functionality. An administrator, for example, can set up a system policy so that a user cannot save changes made to the Desktop, such as wallpaper or color scheme changes. This way each time the user starts Windows 95, the same Desktop appears.

Support Built-In for Mail, Fax, and Telecommunications Functions

Mail, fax, and telecommunications functions are part of the Windows 95 operating system. A universal in-box is provided for all messaging services that support the *Messaging Application Programming Interface* (MAPI). Users need only go to one location to retrieve e-mail and fax information. The Microsoft Network and Internet Explorer allow users easy access to online services and the Internet.

Support for Mobile Services and Remote Access

Windows 95 supports the use of *PCMCIA* adapters as well as "hot" docking and undocking. This means users can add or remove a device, such as a PCMCIA card, while the computer is running. The computer automatically detects the change and adjusts the system settings accordingly. Windows 95 helps mobile computing by supporting dial-up network remote access and file synchronization.

Compatibility for Devices and Applications

Windows 95 was designed with backward compatibility in mind. Much of the existing hardware and software in use today will work with the new operating system. Windows 95 supports 32-bit applications and remains backward-compatible with existing DOS-based and 16-bit Windows-based applications.

Multimedia Capability

Windows 95 expanded the existing Windows multimedia capabilities, including built-in audio and video drivers and applications. No additional software is required to use most business and entertainment multimedia programs.

The video playback engine (Video for Windows) and CD-ROM file system (CDFS) are new 32-bit components of Windows 95 that deliver smoother video and sound reproduction.

Long File Names

A Windows 95 file name can be a total of 255 characters long. Windows 95 uses a new *Virtual File Allocation Table* (VFAT) system that allows file names with up to 255 mixed-case characters and spaces. Completely compatible with MS-DOS and Windows 3.1, VFAT writes two file names to disk for each file saved on a VFAT volume: one is an 8.3 short file name (an example would be bananas.doc for a Word document called bananas), also referred to as an *alias*, and the other a long file name. By creating two file names, the VFAT system allows users to create files with long file names using 32-bit Windows applications. Windows 95 opens files using the 8.3 file name in 16-bit Windows and DOS applications. Chapter 6, "Managing Disk Resources and Utilities," discusses long file names in detail.

New Tutorial and Help Files

Windows 95 includes a new tutorial called the "Windows Tour" as well as a new task-based help file. Very little actual written documentation comes with Windows 95. The hope is that using Windows 95 is very easy. So easy that between the new tutorial and the help file, little actual training will be required for new users.

Now that you know it will be worth your while to upgrade to Windows 95, the next step is to install it.

Microsoft Windows 95 Installation Options

Two versions of Windows 95 are available: a full version and an upgrade version. The upgrade version is used when the computer already contains a copy of DOS in combination with Windows 3.*x* or Windows for Workgroups 3.*x*, or the computer contains a copy of OS/2. The full version is intended for new computers that do not already have an operating system or for installing Windows 95 on a new, unpartitioned, unformatted hard drive. Except for new computer vendors and suppliers, often called *Original Equipment Manufacturers* or OEMs, most Windows 95 installations will be upgrades. The cost of a full version is roughly twice the cost of an upgrade.

The upgrade version checks for the existence of specific files to validate the installation. If you get stuck with a newly format- ted hard drive on a system that had both MS-DOS and Win- dows 3.*x* on it, follow these steps:

1. Format the drive with an MS-DOS 5.0 or better bootable disk using the FORMAT command.

2. Make the drive bootable by using the FORMAT /S command-line option to copy the system files after the format is completed.

3. Run the floppy disk upgrade version of the Windows 95 Setup program from MS-DOS to begin the restoration of the hard drive.

   If the computer has a CD-ROM, load enough of MS-DOS to get access to the CD-ROM drive; then run the CD- ROM version of the Windows 95 Setup program from MS-DOS to begin the restoration of the hard drive.

Windows 95 checks a valid setup disk from any upgrade- qualifying product listed on the Windows 95 box, which is either MS-DOS 3.31 or later in combination with Windows 3.0 or later, or OS/2 2.0 or later. This can be confusing. Just re- member MS-DOS AND Windows, OR only OS/2. An MS-DOS

setup disk will fail the upgrade check. Instead, use a valid
Windows 3.0 or later setup disk or an OS/2 2.0 or later installation disk.

If the hard drive has an existing Windows installation, the
Windows 95 Setup program checks for the following files to
determine whether the current installation is an upgrade from
Windows 3.x: WINVER.EXE, USER.EXE, WIN.COM, SYSTEM.
INI, and WIN.INI, plus PROTOCOL.INI in Windows for Workgroups 3.x. Version information is part of this check; false files
with the same names will not work. The first three files are the
key files being checked. Keep your upgrades legal.

You have three options by which to install Windows 95: CD-ROM,
floppy disks, or across a network. But, after learning to do the
"floppy shuffle" with 13 to 14 floppy disks, you quickly begin to
appreciate the value of a CD-ROM version. In addition, the floppy
disk version leaves some minor things out, such as the Online
Help Documentation (7.8 MB) and the Windows 95 Tour (2.5
MB). The CD-ROM version includes many useful administration
extras that can help you become certified.

Windows 95 installation is done through a program called Setup,
which is a Windows 3.1–based application. Setup is usually run
from within Windows, though it can be launched from MS-DOS.
When you start from MS-DOS, a stripped-down Windows 3.1 environment is loaded, with just enough functionality to activate the
Windows portion of the installation, beginning in real mode then
switching to protected mode. The entire installation process is
covered in greater detail in the section "Installation Process" later
in this chapter.

Using Floppy Disks

Windows 95 can be installed from floppy disks. The first disk
(Disk 1—Setup) is used to start the installation. Be aware that Disk
2 and those following are formatted with the new Microsoft *Distribution Media Format* (DMF), which allows more data to be stored
on one disk. This format means that MS-DOS disk commands,

such as COPY and DISKCOPY, will not work. For the average user, there is no way to make backup copies of these disks if needed.

> While Microsoft hasn't released a disk-formatting utility to duplicate the 1.68-MB DMF disks, some shareware utilities are now available that can. One such utility, WinImage, is available for download from the World Wide Web. One place to find it is to search the ClNet's Shareware.Com page with the keyword WinImage. Once you download WinImage, you can use it to make backup copies of your Windows 95 floppy disks.

Using CD-ROM

When using the CD-ROM to install Windows 95, the "floppy shuffle" goes away. It is the same procedure as the floppy disk installation, but easier. As mentioned before, the CD-ROM also contains additional components, including administration tools, that are not included with the floppy disk version. It would be worthwhile to browse the CD-ROM after your first installation to see exactly what it contains. One hidden jewel found on the CD-ROM is the *Windows 95 Resource Kit* help file.

> Although storing the Windows 95 installation files on the local hard drive is not one of the official installation methods, it might be the safest one, should the installation fail and either the CD-ROM or the network become unavailable. The Windows 95 installation files take up over 33 MB of space on the hard drive. The Hard Drive Usage Maxim states that "the amount of free space available is inversely proportional to the length of time the hard drive has been in service." For you as an installer, there might not even be enough hard drive space for Windows 95, let alone a copy of the installation files. Table 1.4 shows the approximate disk space requirements for Windows 95.

This method of storing the Windows 95 installation files locally is very sound for laptop users, who are often disconnected from the network and cannot afford to carry extra media around with them as they travel.

Using the Network

Windows 95 can be installed across a network. It can be installed from either a file server, such as Microsoft Windows NT Server, Novell NetWare Server, or from another network-shared resource.

The initial Windows 95 administrative setup option is done with a program called NETSETUP. This option is used to place the Windows 95 files on a network server. Do not try using the regular program used in the floppy disk or CD-ROM with the earlier administrative options of "/a" or "/n" because they are not available with Windows 95.

You must run NETSETUP from a Windows 95 workstation. The files can be written only to a mapped network drive on which you have full security rights. During a network setup, which must be done from a CD-ROM media version of Windows 95, all the necessary files are transferred to the mapped network drive, which configures these files as a server-based Setup copy.

Depending on the Windows 95 installation policy option selected while running NETSETUP, you can allow users to install to the local hard drive from the network, install a "shared copy" networked Windows version, or choose between the two. After completing the network setup, users can install Windows 95 from the server-based copy to either a stand-alone computer or as a shared Windows 95 copy that runs from the server, depending on the policy option.

As an exercise in Windows 95 installation, you will do an administrative setup later in this chapter.

In a networked environment, this installation offers the best performance overall. Storing 87 MB of the Windows 95 installation files on a network drive, and then making that drive readily available to all of the installers, gives you the most flexibility. However, do not neglect to have some backup media ready in case you get stuck and lose network connectivity on the Windows 95 computer near the end of the Windows 95 installation. The Windows 95 Setup program reboots your computer under Windows 95 and uses network (or CD-ROM) drivers to complete the installation. If Windows 95 is unable to make a connection to the network (or to your local CD-ROM), it cannot continue and complete the installation.

If needed, you can point to alternative sources for the installation files, so keep a copy of the floppy disks handy, just in case. The Iomega ZIP drive, which can attach to the parallel port of the computer as a guest drive and provide 100 MB of disk storage, provides another alternative source. All the Windows 95 installation files fit on a single Iomega ZIP disk.

Networked Windows

Microsoft refers to networked Windows as running a "shared copy" from a server. During this Windows 95 installation, the user simply connects to the server-based copy the network administrator has previously created and shared. In this installation option, the network administrator may have restricted the user to install only a shared copy of Windows 95. This restriction is set by selecting the Server radio button during the administrative setup. Selecting the Server radio button during the administrative setup sets this restriction.

The networked Windows 95 option installs the minimal files required into a temporary directory on the computer and starts Setup from that temporary directory. Therefore, most of the actual code remains on the server, not on the local computer. The advantages of this option include less disk space required on the local computer and better administrative control. The disadvantages are increased network traffic, shared space (approximately

87 MB) on the server, and slower load times for both Windows 95 and any shared applications.

> The networking world is split between those who believe Windows should be run locally on the stand-alone computer and those who believe it should be run as a shared, networked copy. There are many valid arguments, and both viewpoints have merit. The author firmly believes that network bandwidth is a critical resource. With both Windows and other applications getting larger and more complex, the extra network traffic generated by running a shared, network copy of Windows 95 is not worth the trouble. Save that bandwidth for multimedia and video, because those applications are going to need it in the near future.

Batch File Automation

The previous installation options discussed where to load the Windows 95 installation files before performing a network-based installation of Windows 95. Batch file automation offers the capability to use a batch script file to automate much, if not all, of the installation of Windows 95. A batch script file is used in either a CD-ROM, local hard drive, or a network setup.

The administrator can predetermine most of the settings required for Windows 95 installation. In an extreme case, depending upon your configuration and degree of standardization, installation could be wholly automated from start to finish. These batch script files (INF) can be called from Setup using the file name as a command switch, without the slash (/) leading character. It is best to leave the autodetect feature on during automated installations, so Windows 95 can detect the hardware devices installed on a computer.

> In the case of network drivers, especially Novell NetWare, Setup keeps any 16-bit real-mode network drivers, such as NETX or VLMs, instead of installing the 32-bit protected-mode
>
> *continues*

clients. A batch file can be used to force the installation of a new device driver, regardless of what was previously installed. Network drivers are covered in greater detail in Chapter 5, "Networking and Interoperability."

Preparing for Installation

Some activities can be done ahead of time to ensure the Windows 95 installation goes smoothly. The end-user of the computer can perform some of them, with guidance from you. For some activities, however, inexperienced end-users may not know how to conduct proper installation preparation procedures. You may need to conduct these preparations for them, or provide adequate training on how to perform these tasks. The following sections present questions that constitute a preparation checklist. Such a checklist produces several benefits:

▶ It forces careful consideration and planning.

▶ It involves the end-user in the process.

▶ It improves the chances of a trouble-free installation.

▶ It allows for easier troubleshooting and recovery in the event of installation failure.

Is the Hardware Supported?

The Microsoft Hardware Compatibility List (HCL) details whether your computer hardware is supported. Newer computer hardware might not appear on the list. If in doubt, check with the manufacturer. These Hardware Compatibility Lists are periodically updated, so contact Microsoft to obtain the latest list. Read the Windows 95 SETUP.TXT file on the installation disks; these are valuable sources of information. If you don't see the hardware component listed in the Add New Hardware wizard list, either select a close, emulated component or seek installation disks (INF) from the manufacturer directly.

Does the Computer Meet the Minimum Requirements?

Check table 1.1 (later in this chapter) for the minimum hardware requirements to run Windows 95. One design goal for Windows 95 is to have it run on computers capable of running Windows 3.*x*, but in reality, the minimum hardware requirement is much higher. Whereas Windows 3.1 will run on an Intel 286 computer, with 2 MB of RAM and an EGA monitor, Windows 95 needs more. The real published minimum hardware requirements for Windows 95 are an Intel 386DX computer, 20 Mhz (or higher) with 4 MB of RAM, and a VGA monitor.

Now the question becomes one of economics. Is it cheaper to upgrade older computers or simply replace them with new computers? Anything less than an Intel 486DX computer, 33 Mhz should be replaced. Non-standard hardware components also might need to be replaced to get away from having to run real-mode drivers within the CONFIG.SYS file.

There are useful utility programs that can test a computer to see if it will run Windows 95. A simple one, supplied by Microsoft, is called W95CHECK. It is available on CompuServe. This program scans a single machine for the following: processor, memory (RAM), disk space, and applications. It does a basic test and is not intended to serve as an all-inclusive diagnostic check for every known hardware and software compatibility issue with Windows 95. If something more complex is needed, the author recommends Touchstone Software's WIN'95 Advisor.

Backup Completed for Important User Document Files?

Always backup your files. Network Administrators harp on this theme, though most end-users do not listen. At a bare minimum, backup your key document files. The applications can always be re-installed, but the document files are difficult, if not impossible to replace. The single question you can use that drives home the point is, "If your hard drive were to crash tomorrow, what key files would you save today?"

Have TSRs and Virus Checking Been Disabled?

Terminate and Stay Resident (TSR) programs and Anti-Virus programs get loaded in the CONFIG.SYS and AUTOEXEC.BAT files, loaded and run from the WIN.INI file, and found in the Startup Group within Windows itself. These programs should all be disabled. Those that should not be disabled include the following: any required for partition or hard drive management, network drivers, video drivers, or devices (such as CD-ROMs and sound cards). The safest method, if possible, is to move both the CONFIG.SYS and AUTOEXEC.BAT aside by renaming them, and entering Windows without any other programs running.

Some motherboards also support BIOS anti-virus checking upon boot-up, which needs to be disabled. See the Windows 95 README file and SETUP.TXT on the installation disks for information on how to do this for specific anti-virus checking software. These files are valuable sources of information on specific software products.

Can Any Unused Programs Be Removed or Uninstalled?

Hard drives tend to collect programs, applications, and data like home owners store things in the garage. Soon there's barely enough room to park a car inside. Old, forgotten applications sit idle on the hard drive, taking up valuable space. Instruct users to do some spring cleaning by removing anything that is no longer needed. (You might provide a list of programs that need to remain on everyone's computer, such as networking programs, e-mail applications, and so on.) Most uninstall programs will help in this effort by tracking down all the various pieces of an application. Newer programs often include an uninstall program, while many older programs do not. Reclaim some of that space on the hard drive.

Is the Hard Drive Scanned and Defragmented?

Windows 95 will do a ScanDisk during the installation. *ScanDisk* does a quick check of the integrity of the hard drive where Windows 95 will be installed. Users might want to run earlier versions of this program that shipped with version 6.2*x* of MS-DOS, before the Windows 95 installation.

In addition, the Defrag utility is useful to defragment the hard drive. Over time, the performance of a hard drive can deteriorate as the files stored on the hard drive become fragmented and written to different portions of the hard drive.

Are All the Key System Files Backed Up?

There are key system files that should be backed up, as a precaution. You may want to instruct all end-users to make backup copies of these files, or perform these backups yourself on all computers. These are as follows:

- ▶ All initialization (INI) files in the Windows directory

- ▶ All Program Manager Group (GRP) files in the Windows directory

- ▶ The Registry (DAT) files in the Windows directory

- ▶ All password (PWL) files in the Windows directory

- ▶ The CONFIG.SYS and AUTOEXEC.BAT files in the root directory

- ▶ Any critical hardware drivers and support programs listed in either the CONFIG.SYS or the AUTOEXEC.BAT files

- ▶ Any batch files called from the AUTOEXEC.BAT

- ▶ All network configuration (NET.CFG) files (programs to connect with the network)

Is the Network Software Working Correctly?

Make sure the network connectivity is working properly before installing Windows 95. During setup, Windows 95 uses the settings to help configure itself. If there are problems with the network drop, the network interface card, the network configuration, access rights and privileges, and so on, they need to be resolved before the Windows 95 installation.

Understanding Hardware and Software Requirements

The hardware and software requirements for Windows 95 need to be clearly understood. These requirements are confusing (see the following section for specific requirements), especially with older hardware and software combinations. If, for example, you have an Intel 386 computer with 4 MB of RAM and at least 50 MB of hard drive space, and the only change being made to the computer is the installation of Windows 95, then the following applies: the performance should be the same, or even better, than Windows 3.*x* with the same hardware. This hardware configuration is what Microsoft labels a "minimal" computer for Windows 95. What is not said is that the performance of Windows 3.*x* on that minimal computer is poor in comparison to the standard Pentium computer in wide use today.

Identifying Appropriate Hardware Requirements for Installation

Table 1.1 details the minimum hardware requirements for running Windows 95 from the hard disk. Remember that Windows 95 is designed only to run on Intel-based 386DX or higher processors, such as 386, 486, Pentium, or Pentium Pro processors. For backward compatibility, this minimum hardware requirement is exactly the same as that recommended for Microsoft Windows for Workgroups 3.*x*. In reality, however, it should be considered the

bare minimum. A mouse or similar pointing device is listed as optional; however, you also should consider this a requirement due to the graphical nature of the Windows 95 user interface.

Table 1.1

Hardware Requirements

Component	Minimum for Windows 95
Computer	386DX, 20-Mhz (or higher) processor (see the following warning about the B-step 386 processor)
Memory	4 MB (or more)of RAM, 420 KB of conventional memory within Windows or 470 KB conventional memory from MS-DOS (600 KB total below 1 MB)
Floppy and Hard Drive	A high-density (HD) floppy-disk drive and a hard drive, if installing locally to the computer
Disk Space	Approximately 10 to 87 MB of hard drive space, depending on the installation options chosen; plus space for a swap file whose size is at least 14 MB (minus the RAM size installed on the computer)
Video Display	VGA (or better)
Optional	A mouse or similar pointing device, CD-ROM drive, modem, sound card, and Network Interface Card (NIC)

These minimum hardware requirements reflect computers that have been in broad scale use since the late 1980s. If you purchase a new computer, you will see that the Pentium processor has become the standard, with the computer having 8–16 MB of RAM and a hard drive of 1 GB or more. A basic rule of thumb when purchasing a new computer is to purchase the best computer you can afford, because the average corporate life-cycle before obsolescence is now only two to three years.

Windows 95 should not be loaded on a machine with a B1 (stepping) chip, which is the designator for Intel 386 microprocessors dated before April 1987. These chips introduce random math errors when performing 32-bit operations, making them incompatible with Windows 95.

If your 386 chip was manufactured before April 1987, or has a label on it that reads "For 16-bit operations only," contact your hardware manufacturer about a microprocessor upgrade. Several third-party companies offer 486 chip, Mhz clock-doubling upgrade processors that plug into the processor socket of a 386 motherboard. Rather than replacing the entire system, just upgrade the processor.

Before you purchase that Pentium Pro computer, be aware that its processor has been optimized for 32-bit operating systems, such as Windows NT. The Pentium Pro, often referred to as either the New Pentium or P6, is the latest processor from Intel. Windows 95 still contains 16-bit code and is not the ideal operating system for this processor. The performance difference between a Pentium and a Pentium Pro, both running at the same megahertz speed, is minimal when running Windows 95. The extra cost of a Pentium Pro computer over a Pentium computer generally is not worth the gain. However, if you are running mostly 32-bit applications under Windows 95, the 10–15 percent performance gain of a Pentium Pro computer may be justified.

These minimum hardware requirements often show up as a test question, if nothing other than to drive home the point that Windows 95 will actually run on an Intel 386 with 4 MB of RAM. The author loaded it on an IBM Thinkpad 701C laptop 486 processor that came standard with only 4 MB of RAM. After a few minor changes, including setting up a new 10+ MB swap file within Windows 3.1, it installed properly and worked surprisingly well.

Identifying Appropriate Software Requirements for Installation

You can install the retail version of Windows 95 as either a new install or as an upgrade over an existing operating system. You also can install Windows 95 over a number of different Microsoft operating systems, including MS-DOS, Windows 3.*x*, and Windows for Workgroups 3.*x*. It also can be installed over Novell DR DOS (or Novell DOS), IBM PC-DOS, and as a dual-boot operating system with either IBM OS/2 or Microsoft Windows NT.

The following lists the minimum operating system software required to install an upgrade version of Windows 95:

▶ MS-DOS version 3.2 or higher, or an equivalent version from the hardware manufacturer (such as Compaq version 3.31) that supports partitions greater than 32 MB; MS-DOS version 5.0 or better is recommended

▶ Windows 3.*x* (in combination with MS-DOS)

▶ Windows for Workgroups 3.*x* (in combination with MS-DOS)

▶ OS/2 2.*x*

▶ Dual-boot with OS/2 (with MS-DOS installed)

▶ Dual-boot with Windows NT (with MS-DOS installed)

You do not need to meet all these software requirements, merely a combination of either MS-DOS and Windows, or OS/2. The ability to dual-boot Windows 95 with either OS/2 or Windows NT requires you to install over a previously installed version of MS-DOS. Dual-boot with both OS/2 and Windows NT is discussed in greater detail in Chapter 3, "Customizing and Configuring Windows 95."

Windows 95 Setup checks the version of DOS as well as whether or not there is enough disk space to complete the installation. This space requirement is based on which

continues

Windows 95 components are selected for installation. If you are installing on a computer with partitions of 32 MB or less in size, you are better off using FDISK to delete the partitions. From that point, format the hard drive using the FORMAT command and install a new copy of MS-DOS. Use Microsoft DOS version 5.0 or better, because that will make the upgrade to Windows 95 run more smoothly and enable you to boot into the older version of DOS by pressing F8 during bootup, if necessary.

To check the DOS version installed on the computer, enter **ver** (version) at the command prompt.

To check the Windows version installed on the computer, enter **winver** (windows version) at the command prompt. From within Windows, choose Help, About, to display the Program Manager dialog box to check the version.

After you install Windows 95 on a machine, try these two commands, ver and winver, again. Compare the difference in the results. The ver command under MS-DOS gives its version; under Windows 95, it lists Windows 95. The winver command under the older versions of Windows gave an MS-DOS reply of the Windows version; while under Windows 95, it opens a dialog box. These differences highlight the fact that the new version of MS-DOS (version 7.0) has been incorporated directly into the Windows 95 operating system.

Many early versions of DOS were heavily modified by the Original Equipment Manufacturer to meet their specific hardware and tuning requirements. Even now, special utilities appear in the DOS directory of some laptops for such things like power management and hardware configuration. There are very subtle differences between the different companies' versions of DOS. Be aware that there might be problems with the installation because of these differences. Chapter 6 in the *Windows 95 Resource Kit* contains a Setup Technical Discussion that covers the installation of Windows 95 over different versions of DOS.

Setup Type and Hard Drive Space Requirements

Within the Windows 95 Setup, you can choose from several types of installation options. To a large degree, the choice you make will dictate the size of the Windows 95 installation on the computer. It also dictates the number of optional components installed, and the amount of control you will have in customizing the installation. Table 1.2 lists the setup types.

Table 1.2

Setup Types

Setup Type	Description
Typical	The default option, which Microsoft recommends for most users with desktop computers. This option performs most installation steps automatically for a standard Windows 95 installation with minimal user action. You need to confirm only the directory where Windows 95 files are to be installed, provide user and computer identification information, and specify whether to create a startup disk.
Portable	The recommended option for mobile users with portable computers. Installs the appropriate set of files for a portable computer. This includes installing Briefcase for file synchronization and the supporting software for direct cable connections to exchange files.
Compact	The option for users who have extremely limited disk space. Installs only the minimum files required to run Windows 95.
Custom	The option for users who want to select application and network components to be installed, and confirm the configuration settings for devices. Installs the appropriate files based on user selections. This type of Setup is recommended for advanced users who want to control all the various elements of Windows 95 Setup.

Table 1.3 compares many of the differences in the optional components installed for all four types of installation. The X means the component is pre-selected, and the O indicates that it is not pre-selected, but may be optionally selected. Notice that for Custom Setup, the options pre-selected by default are the same as for a Typical Setup. For the Portable Setup, the options pre-selected are designed to assist mobile users. For Compact Setup, no optional components are pre-selected, except for two disk utilities. Regardless of which setup type is initially selected, you have the choice to see the list of components and then can choose which to install.

Table 1.3

Optional Components Installed During Installation					
Optional Component	Typical	Portable	Compact	Custom	MB Size
Accessibility Options	X	X	O	X	0.3
Audio Compression	X	X	O	X	0.2
Backup	O	O	O	O	1.0
Briefcase	O	X	O	O	0.0
Calculator	O	O	O	O	0.1
CD Player	O	O	O	O	0.2
Character Map	O	O	O	O	0.1
Defrag	X	X	X	X	0.3
Desktop Wallpaper	O	O	O	O	0.6
Dial-Up Networking	O	X	O	O	0.4
Direct Cable Connection	O	X	O	O	0.5
Disk Compression Tools	X	X	X	X	1.0

Optional Component	Typical	Portable	Compact	Custom	MB Size
Document Templates	X	O	O	X	0.1
Games	O	O	O	O	0.6
Hyper-Terminal	X	X	O	X	0.4
Media Player	X	X	O	X	0.2
Microsoft Exchange	O	O	O	O	3.6
Microsoft Fax Services	O	O	O	O	1.7
Microsoft Fax Viewer	O	O	O	O	0.3
Microsoft Mail Services	O	O	O	O	0.6
Mouse Pointers	O	O	O	O	0.2
Net Watcher	O	O	O	O	0.1
Online User's Guide	O	O	O	O	7.7
Paint	X	O	O	X	1.2
Phone Dialer	X	X	O	X	0.1
Quick View	X	X	O	X	1.4
Screen Savers	X	X	O	X	0.1–0.2
Sound and Video Clips	O	O	O	O	0.4–6.5
Sound Recorder	X	X	O	X	0.2
System Monitor	O	O	O	O	0.1
The Microsoft Network	O	O	O	O	2.0
Video Compression	X	X	O	X	0.4

continues

Table 1.3   Continued

Optional Component	Typical	Portable	Compact	Custom	MB Size
Volume Control	X	X	O	X	0.1
Windows 95 Tour	O	O	O	O	2.4
WordPad	X	O	O	X	1.2

Note: X = installed by default; O = optional

For information about how Windows 95 Setup treats disk partitions created under other operating systems, see the *Windows 95 Resource Kit.* Table 1.4 discusses the approximate hard disk space requirements for Windows 95. This table does not indicate the maximum requirements, just the average requirements based on the default components installed. The actual space required depends on which options you choose to add during the Windows 95 installation. The bottom line, however, is Windows 95 requires more space than previous versions of both MS-DOS and Windows. The operating system and all of its programs are getting increasingly larger. If your hard drive is getting cluttered with unused programs and files, it might need cleaning up before the installation.

Table 1.4

Approximate Disk Space Requirements for Windows 95

Installation Base	Typical	Portable	Compact	Custom
New installation	47 MB	47 MB	44 MB	48 MB
MS-DOS upgrade	55 MB	55 MB	45 MB	55 MB
Windows 3.*x* upgrade	40 MB	40 MB	38 MB	40 MB
Windows for Workgroups 3.*x* upgrade	40 MB	40 MB	38 MB	40 MB

Setup Switches

Windows 95 Setup provides standard command-line options to control the installation process. These options, or *switches*, are specified on the command line as arguments for the setup command (such as setup /?). Similar to MS-DOS command arguments, the specific option is preceded by a forward slash (/) character, not the backslash character used to specify directory mappings.

Windows 95 Setup can be run with the setup command with the switches shown in table 1.5.

Table 1.5

Setup Switches

Switch	When Used
/?	Provides help for syntax and use of setup command-line switches. Available from both MS-DOS and Windows.

Troubleshooting Switches

Switch	When Used
/C	Instructs Windows 95 MS-DOS Setup not to load the SmartDrive disk cache.
/d	Instructs Windows 95 Setup not to use the existing version of Windows for the early phases of Setup. Use this switch if you have problems starting Setup that might be due to missing or damaged supporting DLL files within the existing version of Windows.
/in	Instructs Windows 95 MS-DOS Setup not to run the Network Setup module when installing Windows 95.
/im	Instructs Windows 95 Setup not to check for the minimum conventional memory required to install Windows 95.
/id	Instructs Windows 95 Setup not to check for the minimum disk space required to install Windows 95.
/iq	Instructs Windows 95 Setup not to perform the ScanDisk quick check when running Setup from MS-DOS.

continues

Table 1.5 Continued

Switch	When Used
	You probably want to use this switch if you use compression software other than DriveSpace or DoubleSpace. Also used from Windows in conjunction with /is not to perform the cross-linked hard disk check.
/is	Instructs Windows 95 Setup not to run the ScanDisk quick check. You probably want to use this switch if you use compression software other than DriveSpace or DoubleSpace.
/ih	Runs ScanDisk in the foreground so you can see the results. Use this switch if the system stalls during the ScanDisk check or if an error results.
/iL	Loads the Logitech mouse driver. Use this option if you have a Logitech Series C mouse.
/nostart	Instructs Windows 95 Setup to install the required, minimal Windows 3.x DLLs used by the Windows 95 Setup, and then to exit to MS-DOS without installing Windows 95. These files are copied in a :\WININST0.400 directory.

Administrative Switches

File.inf	Instructs Windows 95 Setup to use settings in the specified script file to install Windows 95 automatically; for example, executing **setup mybatch.inf** specifies that the Setup program should use the settings in the MYBATCH.INF script file.
/IW	This new switch enables you to bypass the license agreement screen. It is very useful when creating an automated script file that will run without stopping. The switch must be entered in capital letters.
/t:tempdir	Specifies the directory where Setup is to copy its temporary files. If the directory does not exist, it will be created. Be aware that any existing files in this directory will be deleted.

In a large corporate environment, if you can automate the Windows 95 installation by using script files, you will save yourself and your installers a lot of work. Murphy's Law states "what can go wrong, will." This exception processing approach to installing Windows 95 automatically enables you to focus on the real problem installations. Expect installation problems so you are not surprised when they occur.

> Hopefully, you will never need to use the Troubleshooting Switches for Setup, but it is important to know they are available and to know when to use them. Remember that /a and /n are no longer valid, use the NETSETUP program instead.

Making Installation Decisions

Some installation pre-planning is needed before starting the installation of Windows 95. There is plenty of material to help guide you in these efforts. The Windows 95 Resource Kit includes a Deployment Planning Guide that lays out a pretty detailed project plan for Windows 95. As a certified MCSE or MCP, you need to be knowledgeable about where to find the answers. This section of the chapter is devoted to helping you make some of these installation decisions.

What Setup Information Is Needed?

At a minimum, three pieces of information are needed for a successful Windows 95 installation. Most everything else can be automatically detected by the Windows 95 Setup program, including the current computer's hardware configuration. The following three pieces of information are unique to each Windows 95 installation:

▶ **Default User Name.** The initial user defined to the Windows 95 computer. User names are limited to 15 characters with no embedded spaces and can contain any of the following special characters including the period:

  ! @ # $ % ^ & ( ) - _ ' { } ~ .

This name should be unique and should correspond to your rules for user names in either the Windows NT domain environment or the Novell NetWare bindery/NDS environment, especially when using user-level access control. Although Windows NT and Novell NetWare allow longer names, most user names get no longer than eight characters. This is to allow mapping to the user's home directory on a file server.

▶ **Computer Name.** The Windows 95 computer name that is known on the network. The computer names also are limited to 15 characters, with no embedded spaces, and can contain any of the following special characters including the period:

! @ # $ % ^ & ( ) - _ ' { } ~ .

This name should be unique and should correspond to your rules for computer names for either the Windows NT domain environment or the Novell NetWare bindery/NDS environment. When you share computer resources on the network, other users reference that shared resource by using a combination of the computer name and the share name. For example, if your computer was named JACK-PC1 and the Windows 95 install directory was shared using the name of WIN95-INSTALL, then users would connect to \\JACK-PC1\WIN95-INSTALL.

Along with the computer name, you can have an optional *computer description*. This description can be up to 48 characters in length, and allows other information to be shared about the Windows 95 computer. Information such as the owner's full name, telephone number, building or room, and type of computer can be included. This description can contain embedded spaces but no commas. When browsing the Microsoft Network, both the computer name as well as the computer description are available. Using a good description makes the browsing easier.

▶ **Workgroup Name.** The logical grouping of computers with which the Windows 95 computer most often connects to share resources or data, or to exchange e-mail. The workgroup names also are limited to 15 characters, with no embedded spaces, and can contain any of the following special characters including the period:

! @ # $ % ^ & ( ) - _ ' { } ~ .

The workgroup name should be unique. A Windows 95 computer can freely join any peer-to-peer workgroup by simply changing the name. Instead of a workgroup name, you might need to specify a Windows NT domain name and/or a Novell NetWare preferred server. These last two names would be used to connect to either a Windows NT domain or to a Novell NetWare server/directory services network.

These three pieces of information, the user name, the computer name, and the workgroup name, are unique to each computer installation. Duplicate computer names can prevent the Windows 95 computer from joining the Microsoft Network. Wrong workgroup names affect the browse list generated when you open your Network Neighborhood. Incorrect or missing computer descriptions cause confusion to users wanting to share resources or data. In a corporate environment, it is important to agree on some standard naming convention that everyone adheres to and supports. It can make administration of the Windows 95 network much easier for all concerned.

The requirement for unique names stems from the way information is shared on a Microsoft Network. Try bringing up a second computer onto a Microsoft Network when the computer name is not unique. The second computer will not be allowed to join the Microsoft Network. No big deal, you might say, until it causes problems.

Suppose you are doing Windows 95 installations from the network, and the new Windows 95 computer will not connect to the Microsoft Network. If one of the network shares is the actual Windows 95 installation files from which you are installing, they will not be available because you are an isolated

continues

computer. Duplicate computer names can be very trouble-some to track down and resolve. A short-term fix is to use a temporary computer name, complete the Windows 95 installation, and then sort out the computer names later.

Standard naming conventions and naming provisions for multiple computers under each user's name should allow you to keep things unique and minimize this problem from happening. Good computer descriptions with accurate location information will help track down duplicate computer names.

How to Maintain Program Groups and User Preferences When Upgrading from Windows 3.1

Setup will detect whether Windows 3.1*x* or Windows for Workgroups 3.*x* is installed on the computer. Should it find one of them, it will offer to install Windows 95 in the same directory in order to upgrade the existing installation.

If you choose to install into the same directory, the Windows 95 Setup program takes the Windows 3.*x* or Windows for Workgroups 3.*x* Program Manager groups and converts them into folders in the Programs directory. This is so they can be displayed from the Windows 95 Start menu, under Programs. These folders can be opened or explored to find shortcuts to the applications previously contained within each Program Manager group. The Windows 3.*x* application icon converts into a Windows 95 shortcut. The Windows 95 Setup program also moves the configuration settings in SYSTEM.INI, WIN.INI, and PROTOCOL.INI, plus file associations from the Windows 3.*x* Registry, into the Windows 95 Registry. This enables all applications and networking settings to work automatically in the new Windows 95 environment.

If you don't want to reinstall all your applications, just upgrading the existing Windows environment to Windows 95 will save you a lot of work. This is a key exam question. Just remember, if you want to keep your old configuration, upgrade to Windows 95 on top of it.

There are several questions about this in the Microsoft Self-Assessment Windows 95 exam, so be open to other possible means of getting access to your Windows 3.1 environment.

You must choose to install Windows 95 in a new directory if you want to preserve the existing MS-DOS or Windows installation. When you do install into a new directory, you might have to reinstall most Windows-based applications before they can function properly in the new environment. If you are serious about setting up dual-boot capability, Chapter 3 will provide you with some experience.

Determine When to Use Windows 95 and When to Use Microsoft Windows NT Workstation

When should you use Windows 95 over Windows NT Workstation? The best answer at this time is, "It depends on what you're trying to do with the computer." Microsoft has published a white paper on the subject. A copy of that document is included on the CD-ROM. (An updated version for Windows NT 4.0 is available on the WWW at http://www.microsoft.com/windows/common/aa2699.htm.) But the criteria for determining when to use one instead of the other can be simplified into several key differences, which are discussed in the following sections.

Windows 95

The following points address when to use Windows 95 instead of Windows NT Workstation:

▶ Windows 95 is focused on making computing easier for anyone using a wide range of personal and business applications on desktop and portable computers. To protect their current investment, these Windows 95 users require the highest level of backward compatibility with today's applications and device drivers (32-bit Windows, 16-bit Windows, and MS-DOS).

▶ Windows 95 runs only on an Intel 386 and better platform, 4 MB or more RAM, 40 MB or more hard drive space.

▶ Windows 95 uses a new Windows (Next Generation) user interface.

▶ Windows 95 provides PnP technology support.

Windows NT Workstation

The following points address when to use Windows NT Workstation instead of Windows 95:

▶ Windows NT Workstation is focused on providing the most powerful desktop operating system for solving complex business needs. It delivers the highest level of performance to support the most demanding business applications for developers, technical, engineering, and financial users, and for critical line-of-business applications.

▶ NT Workstation will run some MS-DOS applications, 16-bit and 32-bit Windows applications, plus POSIX, and OS/2 1.x applications, but supports only 32-bit Windows device drivers.

▶ It will run on Intel 386 and better platforms, as well as PowerPC, MIPS, and DEC Alpha-based RISC systems with 12–16 MB RAM, 90–110 MB hard drive space.

▶ Windows NT Workstation supports symmetric multiprocessor (SMP) configurations for scaleable performance without changing the operating system or applications.

▶ Windows NT Workstation offers C-2 certifiable user-level security access to a stand-alone workstation. Files, folders, and applications on both the desktop and the server computers can be restricted to specific users.

▶ Windows NT Workstation has limited Power Management Support, which will be upgraded in a future release.

▶ Windows NT Workstation has limited Plug and Play technology Support, which will be upgraded in a future release.

For an exercise testing this information, see end of chapter.

You should understand the fundamental differences between Windows 95 and Windows NT Workstation. Although Microsoft endeavors to bring them closer in synchronization with each other, such as with the release of Windows NT Workstation Version 4.0 in the Fall of 1996, they are targeted to separate groups of users. Check the wording in each test question for clues as to which product would be best suited. If both seem likely, choose Windows 95, because the test you are taking covers Windows 95 certification.

New Microsoft joint licensing rules in 1996 for both Windows 95 and Windows NT Workstation in the corporate environment blurred these key differences even more. Users will be able to switch from one to the other, and back again, depending on their requirements.

Configure a Windows 95 Computer on a Network Using the Appropriate Protocol

Whenever someone mentions protocols, think of the language used for transporting data across the network. Often called either *transport protocols* or simply *networking protocols*, the word *protocol*, when used without an adjective, can be a bit confusing. The OSI model associates the networking protocol as a protocol driver, which is responsible for the routing of data and application messages in the Transport (Layer 4) and Network (Layer 3) layers. For the purposes here in Windows 95, the protocol is the language a computer uses to communicate. Different computers must use the same protocol, otherwise they will not be able to communicate. A Windows 95 computer can support multiple protocols running at the same time.

Protocols shipped with Windows 95 are implemented as 32-bit, protected-mode components. These protocols can be shared among the installed network clients. For example, a single TCP/IP protocol stack can be bound to both the Microsoft Client for Microsoft Networks as well as the Microsoft Client for NetWare Networks.

By default, Windows 95 installs both the Microsoft NetBEUI and IPX/SPX-compatible protocols.

Three of the protocols included with Windows 95 (NetBEUI, IPX/SPX, and TCP/IP) are Plug and Play–enabled. These protocols can sense when the network is not available and unload themselves after sending notification to any dependent applications. The following protocols are the most commonly used:

▶ **NetBEUI (NetBIOS Extended User Interface) Protocol.** A very fast protocol intended for small networks. It is not routable, which means it cannot pass through a larger network that uses routers to segment the network. The NetBEUI protocol stack included with Windows 95 is compatible with existing networks using NetBEUI. Windows for Workgroups, Windows NT Workstation and Server, LAN Manager, and the Workgroup Add-On for MS-DOS are some examples. NetBEUI's speed and ease-of-administration make it ideal for small local area networks.

▶ **IPX/SPX-Compatible (Internetwork Packet Exchange/ Sequence Packet Exchange) Protocol.** The standard protocol used in the Novell NetWare environment. Microsoft has written its own implementation of this protocol stack, which is compatible with the Novell NetWare IPX/SPX implementation. This protocol is routable, and will run on most larger networks that are designed for IPX/SPX routing. It also includes support for "packet burst," which offers improved network performance by reducing the number of packets required to send data. As a routable protocol, most users in medium- to large-sized networks prefer it over NetBEUI.

A big enhancement to Microsoft's implementation of the IPX/SPX-compatible protocol was Windows Sockets (WinSock) programming interface support. Because of this enhancement, any WinSock 32-bit applications can run on top of the IPX/SPX-compatible protocol using Windows 95. NetBIOS support also enables you to run NetBIOS applications.

▶ **TCP/IP (Transmission Control Protocol/Internet Protocol).** A standard protocol for connecting to the Internet and UNIX environments. This protocol stack is fully routable, offers standard connectivity to most networks, and is rapidly becoming the industry standard for many corporate wide-area networks. Within Windows 95, the TCP/IP protocol stack is implemented as a 32-bit, high-performance VxD. It includes most of the standard utilities such as ftp, telnet, arp, ping, route, netstat, and ipconfig. The TCP/IP protocol stack includes DHCP support for the automatic assignment of IP addresses. It also includes WINS support for IP address to NetBIOS name resolution and DNS support.

The TCP/IP protocol implementation includes Windows Sockets (WinSock) programming interface support and a WinSock DLL for both 16-bit and 32-bit applications. NetBIOS support also enables you to run NetBIOS applications.

There will be several test questions about the use of protocols within Windows 95. Remember that by default, Windows 95 installs both Microsoft NetBEUI and IPX/SPX-compatible protocols. You might be tempted to choose the TCP/IP protocol stack for Microsoft Networking, but the new Microsoft defaults for both Windows 95 and Windows NT are the IPX/SPX-compatible protocols (called NWLINK in Windows NT). These three protocols are not the only ones supported under Windows 95. Shipped with Windows 95 is support for the following: Banyan VINES, DEC Pathworks, IBM DLC, Microsoft DLC, Novell IPX ODI, and SunSoft PC-NFS. Other protocols can be added.

Select the Appropriate Level of Security to Meet Various Needs

Multiple levels of security are built into Windows 95. These levels include the security of the Windows 95 computer itself, the resources (folders, drives, printers, CD-ROMs) that are shared on the network in a peer-to-peer manner, and the file server security. While Windows 95 does not have the C2 level of security found in Windows NT, there are actions that can be done to keep your Windows 95 computer secure. Chapter 19 of the *Windows 95 Resource Kit* does a good job of explaining the security features of Windows 95. The following are some basic security procedures to understand:

► Unified logon process is where users on a Windows 95 computer can log on to all configured network clients and Windows 95 with a single prompt, providing they use the same user name and password. The initial logon prompt seen by the users when logging on to Windows 95 depends on the selection as the Primary Network Logon on the Network properties sheet. The same user name and password is sent to all configured network clients and Windows 95. If the user name or the password is different, the user will see additional prompts to log on.

► Windows 95 logon security is possible with the use of a system policy that prevents the user from easily logging on to Windows 95 if their Windows NT logon or Novell NetWare login is not validated. The user could still break in by either doing a re-boot and then PF8 to get to the Windows 95 boot menu, using a Windows 95 startup disk, or bypassing the logon prompt by using the Cancel button to get a default Windows environment. This is not as secure an operating system logon as the one used by Windows NT. To use this Windows 95 logon security feature you must enable the "Require Validation By Network For Windows Access" policy. See Chapter 4, "Editing User and System Profiles," for more information on the use-of-system policies.

► Share-level security is an access control level security that allows the user to assign passwords to shared resources on the Windows 95 computer. The computer running Windows 95 can allow both read-only or full access to a resource, with different passwords for each. Share-level security is normally used in small peer-to-peer networks, and is the default security access control when Windows 95 is installed. Share-level security is only available if you are running file and printer sharing for Microsoft with the Microsoft Client for Microsoft Networks. It is not available if you are running file and printer sharing for NetWare with the Microsoft Client for NetWare Networks.

▶ User-level security is an access control level security. It allows the user to base the access to shared resources on the Windows 95 computer on a user accounts list stored on one of the following: a Windows NT Workstation, a Windows NT Server, a Windows NT Domain Controller, or a Novell NetWare Server. What makes this work is the use of pass-through security, which passes the authentication requests to either Windows NT or Novell NetWare, so that the Windows 95 computer need not implement its own unique user-level security scheme. Instead, Windows 95 leverages off the network as a central security provider. This is normally used in larger networking environments that have some form of centralized security administration. The users attempting to access the resource are validated by the central security provider. The user's rights, once validated, remain defined on the Windows 95 computer.

▶ Password caching is the mechanism for saving the passwords when connecting to a password-protected resource. It is enabled by default when you install Windows 95. As you access a password-protected resource for the first time, you will be given the option to check a box to "save this password in your password list." The password list file (PWL) is encrypted and stored in the Windows directory on the Windows 95 computer. The Windows 95 logon opens this file, enabling the saved passwords to be given when connecting to the corresponding password-protected resource.

There are many levels of security within Windows 95. The unified logon process allows the user to log on once and use that same user name and password for all the configured networks. Share-level security requires that users themselves administer shared resources. User-level security makes use of user accounts already defined on another computer or file server to grant access to shared resources. This other computer or file server is responsible for administering user accounts and validating the passwords. Windows 95 logon security forces the user to be validated against the computer or file server providing user-level security. Finally, password caching allows the Windows 95 user's password to be used to save other passwords and to use those saved passwords when connecting to networked resources.

The password list file (PWL) is secured by each user's Windows 95 password. To cut down the number of different passwords a user must track and maintain, some network administrators advocate the use of a blank Windows 95 password. However, the use of a blank Windows 95 password along with password caching can expose your user's network resources to unauthorized use. This author recommends not using a blank Windows 95 password.

The Password List Editor, PWLEDIT, is used to edit a user's password list file. Use it to view the entries and remove specific password entries if problems are encountered using a cached password.

To install this tool on your local hard disk, use the following procedure:

1. Choose the Add/Remove Programs option in the Control Panel.

2. Select the Windows Setup tab.

3. Click on the Have Disk button.

4. Install the ADMIN\APPTOOLS\PWLEDIT directory from a Windows 95 CD-ROM.

Security is a very important issue, especially in a corporate environment. Windows 95 is leading the trend toward closer integration with Internet access. The Microsoft Network (MSN) optional component that comes with Windows 95 has easy links into the World Wide Web (WWW). Microsoft Plus! includes the Microsoft Internet Explorer (MSIE), which can be downloaded for free by any user. Peer-to-peer networking across this corporate environment opens many challenges for a network administrator.

Security and how to properly set it up under Windows 95 can be tricky. Using system policies is one way to keep your computer secure. The key point here is to understand the differences between user-level and share-level security, and how it relates to the sharing of a Windows 95 computer's resources.

A potential security problem exists with users running either Microsoft or NetWare file and print services with remote administration enabled. Microsoft has released updated drivers for both of these services to close any possible security breach. These security update files, Vservupd.exe and Nwservupd.exe, are available on CompuServe and Microsoft's World Wide Web site. They also are included in Service Pack upgrades to Windows 95.

Determine the Appropriate Installation Method (or Options)

As an advanced user or a network administrator, you can select various installation options for Windows 95. These options can be thought of as a series of choices that help determine the method you use for Windows 95 installations. The decision of which choice to use is yours. Chapter 3 of the *Windows 95 Resource Kit* covers this in greater detail.

The following sections discuss the options you should consider.

Run Setup from MS-DOS or Windows?

The Windows 95 Setup program can be run from either an MS-DOS command prompt or from within Windows 3.1 or Windows for Workgroups 3.1*x*. The preferred method is to run from within Windows. Run from the MS-DOS command prompt when neither

Windows 3.1 nor Windows for Workgroups 3.1x is installed on the computer, but MS-DOS, Windows 3.0, OS/2, or Windows NT is installed.

If either Windows 3.1 or Windows for Workgroups 3.1x is on the computer, the Windows 95 Setup program offers to install itself into the same directory to upgrade the existing Windows installation. If you choose to install into the same directory, the configuration settings in SYSTEM.INI and WIN.INI (and PROTOCOL.INI for Windows for Workgroups), plus any file associations from the Windows 3.x Registry, are moved into the Windows 95 Registry. In addition, the Windows 3.x Program Manager groups are converted into folders off the Start menu's Program selection. This upgrade allows programs and network settings to work automatically in the Windows 95 environment.

Whenever possible, run the Windows 95 Setup program from within Windows 3.1 or Windows for Workgroups 3.1x and install into the existing Windows directory. This minimizes any extra setup work needed to get all your applications to run properly under Windows 95. You will soon realize that the easy part was doing the Windows 95 installation; the hard part is getting all the various applications to function properly. You might have to reinstall each application again if you chose to install Windows 95 into a new directory.

Which Installation Type?

Within the Windows 95 Setup program, you can choose from four types of installation options. The choice you select affects the size of the Windows 95 installation, the computer, the components pre-selected for installation, and the amount of control you have in customizing the installation. You can install a typical compact or custom option for a desktop computer, or a portable option for a laptop computer.

The custom type of installation offers the most flexibility. Regardless of which type of installation you select, however, you can add any missing components later through the Add/Remove Programs icon in the Control Panel folder.

Local or Shared Windows?

You can choose to run Windows 95 from the local hard disk of the computer or as a shared copy from a network file server.

The Windows 95 installation files are available through the retail channels in three basic media versions:

▶ CD-ROM upgrade version

▶ 3.5-inch floppy disk upgrade version

▶ 3.5-inch floppy disk full version

All the upgrade versions check for valid upgrade files on the computer or qualifying setup disks and prompt for a serial number key. The full version allows for a formatted hard drive before starting the installation, and then prompts for a serial number key.

You can copy the Windows 95 source files (33 MB) to a shared network directory. Depending on your license agreement, such as Microsoft Select Licensing, any authorized licensed users can connect to this directory and run the installation from there. If you do a server-based setup to a network directory, the complete set of Windows 95 source code (87 MB) can be used to install either a local copy or a shared copy of Windows 95 to the computer.

If you choose to support installing and running a shared copy of Windows 95 from a file server, you can configure it in one of three ways:

▶ On a computer with a local hard drive, with system files stored on and running from the file server.

▶ On a computer with only a floppy disk drive, booting from the floppy disk, with system files stored on and running from the file server.

▶ From a Novell NetWare File Server that supports diskless workstations and an RIPL boot to a startup disk image stored on the file server, then using system files stored on and running from the file server.

For a shared copy of Windows 95, the system files reside on the file server and not on the local hard drive of the computer. The instructions for running a shared copy of Windows 95 can be found in Chapter 4 of the *Windows 95 Resource Kit*.

If possible, choose to run a local copy (one that is installed on the local computer) of Windows 95. The overall performance is better, and your users will thank you for it.

Manual, Customized, or Automated Setup?

You can choose to run the Windows 95 Setup program manually from each computer, configure a customized setup script, or automate the entire installation process to run remotely for many computers.

The manual method involves sitting down at each computer and running the Windows 95 Setup program. Depending on which setup type of installation you do, the installer might have to respond to only a few questions (Typical) or many questions (Custom). This manual method can take between 30 to 60 minutes for each installation.

To speed up the process of installing Windows 95, a custom setup script can be created. This script answers most, if not all, of the Windows 95 Setup program questions. These custom scripts are based on the MSBATCH.INF file format. Custom scripts can contain pre-defined options for all the Setup options and can be extended to contain instructions for installing additional software. A network administrator can use a customized setup script to standardize Windows 95 installations and reduce the support requirements. This method can significantly reduce installation time because few, if any, interruptions occur.

The automated method involves using both a customized setup script and an automated mandatory installation process for installing Windows 95 on multiple computers with the Windows 95 source code on a file server. Several different approaches can be used to automate installation:

▶ Use a login script to run Setup with a custom setup script, which is installed when each user logs onto the file server.

▶ Use the System Management Server (SMS) to distribute a mandatory Windows 95 Installation Package that runs Setup using a custom setup script.

▶ Use a network management software distribution package, such as Norton Administrator for Networks (NAN), to install Windows 95, automatically running Setup using a custom setup script.

An automated installation of Windows 95 saves a great deal of time when deploying Windows 95 within a large company, allowing the network administrator to focus on the few Windows 95 installations that might run into problems.

Repair Setup or Perform Maintenance?

Problems will arise during either the Windows 95 installation, normal operations, or the configuration of any hardware or software upgrades. You can choose among several troubleshooting methods to fix those problems. The Windows 95 Setup program or the maintenance applications in the Control Panel folder are available for your use.

The Windows 95 Setup program can be used to provide safe recovery during a failed installation or to repair a computer that has a damaged or corrupted installation. In addition, if after Windows 95 has been installed, you encounter missing, incorrect version, or damaged files within the operating system, the Windows 95 Setup program can replace, verify, or repair the files.

During the course of a Windows 95 installation, you have the option to create an emergency startup disk, which can be used to start the computer in case of configuration problems. You can also create an emergency startup disk from the Add/Remove Programs Properties sheet within the Control Panel folder. You should create at least one Windows 95 emergency startup disk for troubleshooting purposes.

Instead of running the Windows 95 Setup program, you can choose to run one of the various maintenance applications located within the Control Panel folder. The maintenance applications enable you to install and configure applications, hardware devices, the display monitor, printers, modems, and network services.

The System application within the Control Panel folder enables you to examine and repair your computer system configuration, and should be the first place you examine when hardware problems occur.

For an exercise testing this information, see end of chapter.

The best way to address this exam objective is by example. Exercise 1.4 at the end of the chapter is aimed at helping you determine the appropriate installation method to use for some given installations.

Make a list of the questions you would ask in order to determine the best method of installing Windows 95 at your location, then flowchart the process. Keep these queries in mind when you take the exam. Using CD-ROM is the best stand-alone method available. Using the network, along with a standard customized Setup script and a fully automated installation is the optimum method for doing whole-scale corporate-wide Windows 95 installations.

Installation Process

The Windows 95 Setup program is a Windows 3.1–based program. It will not run under Windows 3.0, but rather needs to be run under either Windows 3.1*x* or Windows for Workgroups 3.*x*. The Windows 95 Setup program can be started from DOS, if you have only Windows 3.0 or no version of Windows installed on your computer. The preferred method is to run the installation from within Windows.

If you start the Windows 95 Setup program from DOS, a minimal version of Windows 3.*x*, approximately 1 MB, will be copied to the hard drive into a temporary C:\WININST0.400 directory. This version requires about 600 KB of RAM (470 KB conventional memory) to launch the complete Windows 95 Setup program. It is often called *Minimal Windows* because it has only enough functionality to bring up the Windows portion of the Windows 95 installation. It starts in real mode and then switches to protected mode before beginning the hardware detection phase.

Microsoft realizes that the key ingredient to the successful installation of Windows 95 is the Windows 95 Setup program. It needs to handle the millions of different hardware and software combinations. It only needs to look easy to those users installing Windows 95 for the first time. It needs to be able to safely recover from most of the problems encountered during the installation. The Windows 95 Setup program uses a wonderfully complex installation process. As part of the certification process, you need to understand what is happening behind the scenes, and be able to troubleshoot any Windows 95 installation problems.

The Windows 95 installation process is extremely modular. The Windows 95 Setup program steps through this process, only running the modules either requested or needed. For example, the hardware detection phase will identify specific components on the computer, and the Windows 95 Setup program will run only those installation modules that match. Some of the modules used by the Windows 95 Setup program are standard wizards, such as the setup for network components, modems, printers, and display monitors.

There are four logical phases to Windows 95 installation:

- ▶ Startup and information gathering

- ▶ Hardware detection

- ▶ File copy

- ▶ Final system configuration

The next few sections explore the Windows 95 installation process in greater detail.

From the Computer Perspective

From the workstation perspective, the Windows 95 Setup program performs a series of steps when installing Windows 95. The first few steps depend upon from where the Windows 95 Setup program was started. At one point in the middle of the Windows 95 installation process, both the Windows 95 Setup program started from MS-DOS and the same Windows 95 Setup program started from within Windows 3.*x* end up running Windows in protected mode. This merge in the Windows 95 installation process occurs just before starting the hardware detection phase, as illustrated in figure 1.1.

Figure 1.1

The workstation perspective on the Windows 95 installation process.

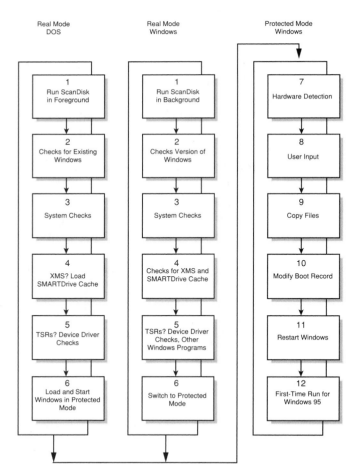

The Windows 95 Setup program automatically takes 12 steps during installation. You will not be aware that these steps are being performed; however, you should understand what is happening to the computer during installation. The 12 steps are as follows:

1. From DOS, the Windows 95 Setup program runs the ScanDisk version 7.0 program in the foreground.

   From Windows, the Windows 95 Setup program runs the ScanDisk 7.0 in the background, after displaying a message box about how long the process will take and asking the user to click on Continue to perform a routine check on the computer.

2. From DOS, the Windows 95 Setup program searches the local hard drives for a previous version of Windows 3.1 or better. If found, the Windows 95 Setup program suggests that the user start the existing version of Windows and then run the Setup program. You can bypass this suggestion and continue to run from DOS.

   From Windows, the Windows 95 Setup program checks the version number because it needs Windows 3.1 or better in order to run successfully. If you are trying to run from Windows 3.0, an error message should appear.

3. System checks are done to confirm the computer is capable of running Windows 95. These checks provide information on processor, amount of RAM memory, amount of disk space, and the MS-DOS version on the computer. If there is a problem, the Windows 95 Setup program will halt and inform the user.

4. The Windows 95 Setup program checks for extended memory (XMS) and installs an XMS provider if none is present. If there is not any existing disk caching loaded, the Windows 95 Setup program automatically loads SmartDrive.

5. Certain Terminate and Stay Resident (TSR) programs and Device Drivers can cause problems with the Windows 95 installation. Those known to cause problems are tested for

and either closed or unloaded. If unable to close or unload them, the Windows 95 Setup program halts and asks the user to disable or close them before re-starting.

From Windows, the program checks for any other processes running and asks the user to close those processes before continuing.

6. From DOS, the Windows 95 Setup program installs a minimal Windows 3.*x* environment and starts it with a shell=setup.exe command, running in protected mode.

   From Windows, the Windows 95 Setup program switches to protected mode. At this point, a Windows graphical user interface is shown to the user.

7. From this step onward, the Windows 95 Setup program runs the same, whether started from DOS or Windows. Certain user information gets gathered, such as where to install Windows 95, what setup option to use (typical, portable, compact, or custom), user name and company, and other related information.

   Hardware detection is accomplished, as the Windows 95 Setup program examines the computer for all installed hardware devices. The Registry gets created to contain the hardware configuration information for the computer.

8. The Windows 95 Setup program asks for user input on what components to install, how to configure the network, identification information, and whether to create a Windows 95 startup disk. If the Windows 95 Setup program cannot determine the hardware or configuration settings, the user is prompted to provide the information.

9. The required files are copied onto the computer's hard drive, according to where the Windows 95 Setup program was instructed to install them.

10. After all files have been copied, then the Boot Records are modified. This is where the computer is changed from its previous operating system to Windows 95.

11. Windows 95 restarts the computer.

12. There are some first-time run programs that run when Windows 95 is installed. These include the Plug and Play hardware configuration (if any of these hardware devices exist), plus any final system configuration: setting up the control panel, migrating existing program group settings, adding programs in the Start menu, creating Windows Help, MS-DOS program settings, and setting the time zone. A final reboot might be required to finalize any newly installed Plug and Play hardware devices.

From the User's Perspective

From a user's perspective, much of the Windows 95 installation process is automatic. Microsoft uses a Setup Wizard to guide you through the installation, prompting for information and requesting some decisions throughout the entire process. A lot of effort was expended in making the installation easy for the user. This section covers the typical interaction that you as a normal user will see during the Windows 95 installation.

As soon as you start the Windows 95 Setup program, a dialog box indicates that a routine check is being run on the system. During this earliest phase, several files needed to run Setup are copied to the local computer, and Setup runs ScanDisk to check the integrity of the hard disk. If successful, another dialog box appears as the Setup Wizard is being initialized.

The license agreement is shown. To continue with the installation, you must respond and agree to the licensing terms. If the licensing terms are declined, the Windows 95 Setup program terminates.

If the hard drive does not contain a copy of the software to be upgraded, you will be prompted to insert a disk to verify qualification for the upgrade. Usually this does not happen, because a previous, qualifying version of software is already installed on the hard drive.

The Setup Wizard, once loaded, divides the remaining activity in the Windows 95 installation into the following three parts:

▶ **Gathering User and Computer Information.** You are prompted for information that the Windows 95 Setup program needs to complete the setup. This part includes the hardware detection done when analyzing your computer.

▶ **Copying Windows 95 Files.** The Windows 95 Setup program copies those files to your computer that are required based on your hardware configuration and the components you have chosen to install.

▶ **Restarting the Computer and Finishing Setup.** Windows 95 starts up and completes the final settings needed to run properly.

The Setup Wizard initial screen, shown in figure 1.2, and the steps it follows to complete the Windows 95 installation reinforce this user perspective. This initial screen appears again at each of the three parts of the process, with the current part highlighted in bold type, and with a small triangular arrow pointing to it on the screen. This allows you to follow along in the Windows 95 installation process.

Figure 1.2

The user's perspective on the Windows 95 installation process.

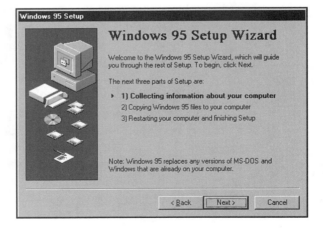

Gathering Information

The first part of the Windows 95 installation process gathers information about the computer.

This begins only after the following has been done:

- ▶ The startup process has been completed.

- ▶ A routine check has been run on the system.

- ▶ The Windows 95 Setup Wizard has loaded.

- ▶ You have approved the Microsoft Windows 95 license agreement by entering OK.

To navigate through the Windows 95 Setup program, click on the Next or Back buttons. Click on the Next button or press Enter to accept the choices you have made on the current screen and to continue forward to the next screen. Click on the Back button to return to the previous screen to review or make changes.

Choosing the Windows Directory

If a previous installation of Windows 3.1*x* or Windows for Workgroups 3.*x* exists, the Windows 95 Setup program asks you to confirm the directory where Windows 95 is to be installed. The directory containing the existing Windows installation is selected, by default (see fig. 1.3).

If you choose to install Windows 95 in a new directory, you might need to reinstall all the Windows-based applications. This is because Windows 95 uses the Registry rather than initialization (INI) files in Windows 3.*x* for storing configuration information. It is also because application support (DLL) files normally found in the Windows 3.*x* System directory will be missing from the new Windows 95 directory.

Figure 1.3

Choose the directory in which to install Windows 95.

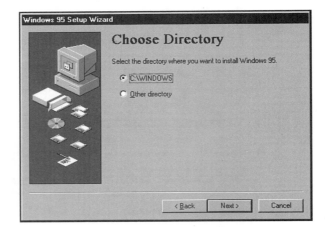

The Windows 95 Setup program checks next for previously installed components and whether or not there is sufficient disk space on the computer. If the Windows 95 Setup program thinks there is not enough disk space, you will get a warning. As a general rule, pay close attention to any warnings while running the Windows 95 installation.

Selecting the Type of Setup

The Windows 95 Setup program asks you to select the type of setup you want. For a description of these options, refer to table 1.2 in the "Setup Type and Hard Drive Space Requirements" section. By default, the Typical Setup Option is selected.

Figure 1.4 shows the Setup Options dialog box where you choose the type of setup you want to install.

The Typical Setup Option is the default, and it is usually the easiest, fastest, and safest way to install Windows 95. The detection process is much simpler, because most hardware gets automatically detected and configured with default settings.

However, for network administrators and service technicians, the Custom Setup Option offers the most flexibility and control over the detection process and the configuration settings. This option is used when the computer's hardware components are not using the normal default settings. It also is used when the Windows 95

Setup program needs to be told about hardware it will not automatically recognize during hardware detection.

Figure 1.4

Choosing the type of setup option.

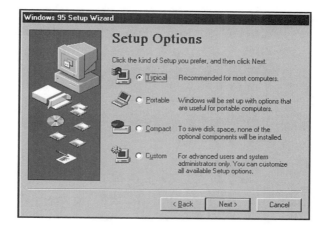

Providing User Information

Whatever setup option is selected, you will be asked to supply user information (see fig. 1.5). Windows 95 uses this information to identify both the user's name and company. This information will show up in the Windows 95 Help About dialog boxes and the FAX configuration dialog box. The user name also gets truncated and is used to populate the Computer Name and Description fields on the Computer Identification screen later in the Setup process.

Figure 1.5

Entering user information.

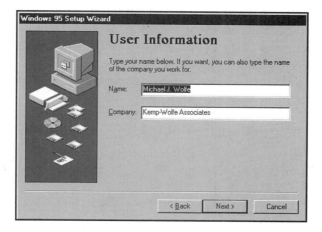

You must type and verify a response for Setup to continue.

Windows 95 Setup next requests a product identification number. You must type and verify a response for Setup to continue, or just choose Next to continue. If no product identification number is entered, a warning message appears; choose Ignore to continue. The Product ID dialog box might not appear if you are installing Windows 95 from the network, depending on the license agreement at your site. The product ID number can be found on your Windows 95 floppy disks, CD-ROM jacket, or on your Certificate of Authenticity.

Analyzing Your Computer

After you enter the user information, the Windows 95 Setup program prepares to analyze your computer. This is the hardware detection phase. Setup will search automatically for the all basic system components such as disk drives and controllers, display devices, pointing devices, and keyboards. The detection process involves a series of approaches to detect these hardware devices.

The first approach determines whether the computer is already running Windows 95. If so, any Plug and Play components are identified and noted.

The second approach is called *safe detection*. This involves methodically searching the computer for software clues that can indicate the presence of certain devices. The CONFIG.SYS, AUTOEXEC.BAT, and all Initialization (INI) files are checked. Certain memory locations are checked for installed drivers. If these safe methods suggest the presence of a device, then it gets configured.

If some devices cannot be identified during this safe detection, you will be prompted for the existence of certain classes of devices (see fig. 1.6). These classes of devices are the following:

▶ CD-ROM drives (Proprietary Cards)

▶ Sound, MIDI, or Video Capture Cards

> ► Network adapters

> ► SCSI devices

Figure 1.6

*Analyzing your
computer.*

The third approach involves interactive query routines to spot any additional devices. This process of examining specific memory locations, testing values and return codes, and actively probing for devices can cause the computer to lockup during hardware detection. If the computer should fail during this detection process, you will need to re-boot, and restart the Windows 95 Setup program once again. The Setup Failure and Recovery process will avoid the trouble area, and continue from that point. Troubleshooting is discussed later in this chapter in the section "Troubleshooting Setup and System Startup."

For information about specific device types supported in Windows 95, see the Manufacturers and Models lists in the Add New Hardware Wizard, as well as the Windows 95 README and SETUP.TXT files.

Hardware Detection

The hardware detection process can take several minutes. The progress indicator shows what portion of hardware detection has been completed (see fig. 1.7). Note that this is also the point at which Windows 95 Setup can stall if hardware detection fails for a particular system component.

Figure 1.7

The hardware detection phase.

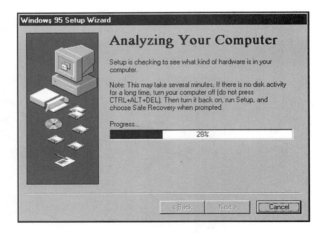

Getting Connected

After the hardware detection completes, the Windows 95 Setup program asks whether or not you want to install a variety of tools that enable you to access various services. The three choices included in the Windows 95 installation are the following:

▶ **The Microsoft Network.** Installs files required to access the Microsoft Network (MSN). MSN is an online server run by Microsoft that enables electronic mail, bulletin board access, chat sessions online, file library information, and Internet connectivity. When you select this, you do not automatically sign-up, that must be done later. In order to have access, you must have a modem.

▶ **Microsoft Mail.** Installs files that enable connectivity to a Microsoft Mail Post Office running on a local area network file server. This component is only the service provider portion, which is to distinguish it from the Microsoft Exchange client application, which enables it.

▶ **Microsoft FAX.** Installs files that enable you to use your computer to send and receive faxes from the computer. In order to use this, you must have a fax modem.

If any of these three choices are selected by you, the Microsoft Exchange client application is installed as well (see fig. 1.8). This extra component requires another 4.6 MB of hard disk space, plus a minimum of 8 MB of RAM to operate properly.

Figure 1.8

*Getting
connected
components.*

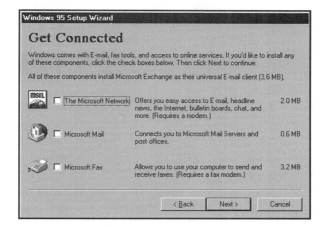

Windows Components

The Windows Components screen is a key screen. The Windows
95 Setup program asks you whether you want to install the common components. This is based on the Setup option (Typical,
Portable, Compact, or Custom) that was selected previously. As
stated before, the Custom Setup Option gives you the most control over the Windows 95 installation process. Under the Custom
Setup Option, you will not even see this screen. However, whatever the Setup Option selected, you will get a chance to select from
the various components (see fig. 1.9).

Figure 1.9

*Windows
components
decision.*

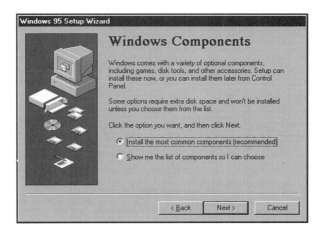

If you trust the components that Microsoft has recommended for installation under each of these Setup Options, then accept the default selection and Continue. If you know, however, that there are some components you want to add during installation that are optional (refer to table 1.3 in the "Setup Type and Hard Drive Space Requirements" section earlier in the chapter), select the Show Me the List of Components So I Can Choose radio button.

If you choose the option for customizing the list of components to be installed, or selected the Custom Setup type of installation, the Select Components dialog box appears (see fig. 1.10). This is the one place where you will see actual information about the amount of cumulative disk space required for the Windows 95 installation. As each component is either selected or deselected, the space needed by the Windows 95 Setup program will change.

Figure 1.10

Selecting Windows components.

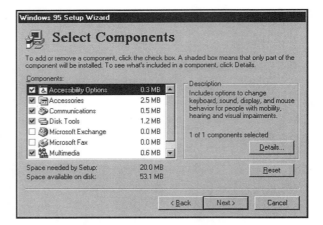

Within the Select Components dialog box, use the following instructions to select or deselect components:

▶ From the Components list, select a component category, and then click the Details button. A dialog box appears, listing the components in the category.

▶ Select the component you want to install, and then click OK. To add a component, make sure the component is checked.

▶ To prevent a component from being installed, make sure the component is not checked.

You can install or remove any of these components after Windows 95 is installed. You can achieve this by using the Add/Remove Programs option in Control Panel, which will be discussed in Chapter 4.

Network Connection

The Windows 95 Setup program allows you to specify network components and settings. With a Typical Setup Option installation, this will be done for you if you have a network adapter or choose to install Dial-Up Networking. The Network Wizard will allow you to configure these settings. Because this is covered in greater detail in Chapter 5, "Networking and Interoperability," this discussion is bypassed for the moment.

The Windows 95 Setup program provides appropriate settings based on the hardware and software detection for the network components running when you start Setup. You should accept the default settings unless you know that particular settings need to be changed. Those settings can always be changed later.

Identification

The Windows 95 Setup program, after configuring network components and settings, will prompt for a unique identifier for your computer. The rules for naming were covered earlier in the section "What Setup Information Is Needed?" In the Identification screen, you are asked for a computer name, a workgroup if you plan to use Microsoft Networks, and an optional computer description (see fig. 1.11).

Figure 1.11

Identification for Microsoft networking.

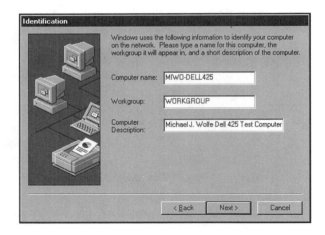

Creating the Startup Disk

A startup disk is a Windows 95 bootable floppy disk that contains utilities you can use to troubleshoot a malfunctioning system. The startup disk loads the operating system and presents an MS-DOS command line. It is strongly recommended that you create a startup disk for Windows 95. You can create a Windows 95 startup disk during the file copy phase of Windows 95 Setup (see fig. 1.12). You can also create or update a disk after the Windows 95 installation by using the Add/Remove Programs option in Control Panel.

Figure 1.12

Creating a Windows 95 startup disk.

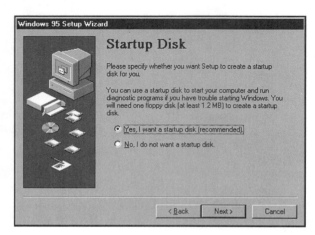

To create a startup disk, Windows 95 formats the floppy disk in drive A, and then copies files to the disk in drive A. These 16 files take up 948 KB of space on a 1.44-MB floppy disk. Table 1.6

describes the files that are copied. Other programs and files need to be added to support access to CD-ROM drives, the network, or any other special requirements.

Table 1.6

Files Found on the Startup Disk

File	Description
attrib.exe	File attribute utility
chkdsk.exe	Disk check utility
command.com	Core operating system file
debug.exe	Debug utility
drvspace.bin	Disk compression utility
ebd.sys	Utility for the startup disk
edit.com	Text editor
fdisk.exe	Disk partition utility
format.com	Disk format utility
io.sys	Core operating system file
msdos.sys	Core operating system file
regedit.exe	Real-mode Registry Editor
scandisk.exe	Disk status and repair utility
scandisk.ini	Disk status utility configuration file
sys.com	System transfer utility
uninstal.exe	Uninstall utility

For recovery purposes, you might also want to copy the following files into a subdirectory on the startup disk: SYSTEM.DAT, CONFIG.SYS, AUTOEXEC.BAT, WIN.INI, and SYSTEM.INI, plus any CD-ROM or other device drivers. If you do not place these files into a subdirectory, you'll have to rename them to prevent problems with the startup disk.

It is strongly recommended that you create at least one start-up disk during a Windows 95 Setup. If you want to create a startup disk after Windows 95 has been installed, you can use the Add/Remove Programs option in Control Panel to create one. Because there is nothing special about a Windows 95 Startup Disk, you can save some time during Windows 95 installations by not creating extras.

After hardware detection is complete and Windows 95 Setup has obtained all required information, the next phase of Windows 95 Setup begins. During this phase, the Windows 95 files are copied to the destination drive and directory.

Copying Windows 95 Files

This second part of the Windows 95 installation process uses the information gathered in the first part to start copying all the files it needs. The source for these files are the Windows 95 Cabinet (CAB) files. If you are installing from floppy disks, here comes the floppy shuffle. Installing from CD-ROM or from the network is a lot faster. Depending upon the speed of your computer and where the Windows 95 installation files are coming from, this part can take anywhere from 20 minutes to an hour (see fig. 1.13).

Figure 1.13

Copying Windows 95 files.

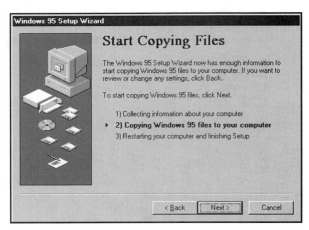

The first group of files copied are those used to create a startup disk. At about the 20 percent stage, if you had chosen to have the

Windows 95 Setup program create a startup disk, Setup asks you to insert a floppy disk into drive A. The disk does not need to be formatted or empty, but any information you have stored on the disk will be permanently deleted. After you insert the disk, click OK to create the startup disk. The Windows 95 Setup program formats the disk and copies the appropriate files (refer to table 1.6). This disk will be useful when troubleshooting problems with Windows 95.

When the copying of Windows 95 files is completed, the Windows 95 Setup program updates the configuration files. This process can take a couple of minutes. Finally, the Windows 95 Setup program asks you to remove any disks from the floppy disk drives (see fig. 1.14). After you click on Finish the computer is restarted and the third and final part of the installation process begins.

Figure 1.14

Restarting for final Windows 95 installation.

Preparing the Computer to Restart

Just before actually restarting the computer, the Windows 95 Setup program renames existing MS-DOS boot files, copies a new IO.SYS and MSDOS.SYS, and modifies the boot records and the boot track to point to the new IO.SYS file.

Up to this point in the Windows 95 installation, your old operating system was still available should the Windows 95 installation fail. The Safe Recovery feature of Windows 95 would allow you to simply restart the Windows 95 Setup program in your old operating system. Now you are running Windows 95. Beyond this point, if the Windows 95 Setup program should fail, you'll need to re-start in Windows 95 to complete the installation. For most cases, the remainder of the Windows 95 installation goes easily.

Restarting Your Computer and Completing Setup

This initial boot-up of Windows 95 is called First-Time Run, be-cause it is the first time that Windows 95 has been started on this computer. The standard Windows 95 bitmap is displayed, with the lower banner indicating that this the first time startup. This is the third and final part of the Windows 95 installation.

Windows 95 might prompt you to log on to the computer. The user ID and password entered can optionally be saved into a Pass-word List (PWL) file.

Windows 95 sets up the hardware configurations and recognizes any Plug and Play devices.

Finally, Windows 95 asks you to complete several configuration options. These are the run-once options that Windows 95 starts the first time it is run. These run-once options are the following:

- ▶ **Control Panel Configuration.** Sets up the control panel icons and programs.

- ▶ **Programs on the Start Menu Configuration.** Builds the Start menu shortcut, converts old Program Manager Groups into folders and menu selections.

- ▶ **Windows Help File Configuration.** Builds the Help File index for search capability.

- ▶ **MS-DOS Program Settings.** Creates the default MS-DOS shortcut.

- ▶ **Time Zone Configuration.** You are asked to select the time zone appropriate to your location, and whether the clock should automatically adjust to Daylight Savings changes. This is a nice graphic map representation where you can click on a location on the map and it selects the appropriate time zone for you. You can adjust both date and time later from either the Control Panel or from the Task Bar.

▶ **Printer Configuration.** You can use the Printer Wizard to
define either a local or network printer. You can add printers
later using the Printers folder located in My Computer. This
configuration option might not always appear. If printers
were set up under an earlier version of Windows that was
updated to Windows 95, the previous printer configuration
is used.

Completing Windows 95 Setup

Depending on which options you selected during Setup, the hardware devices you have, or the computer you have, additional run-
once options might need to be completed. One example is the
wizard for configuring MIDI devices. After all the run-once options are completed, all of the files are installed, and the computer is ready to run Windows 95. Some hardware devices, including
PnP-enabled hardware devices, might require yet another reboot
of the computer before they are fully configured.

Setup Failure Detection and Recovery

Windows 95 has been designed to install without problems. However, Murphy's Law states that "whatever can go wrong, will."
Hardware and software can cause problems during a Windows 95
installation. So Microsoft has wisely built in mechanisms for the
Windows 95 Setup program to detect failure and to recover automatically. It might not be a very sophisticated process, but it does
ensure a high percentage of successful Windows 95 installations.

The Windows 95 Setup program maintains a setup log
(SETUPLOG.TXT) during the installation and can determine
where failures have occurred. The most likely place for failure is
during hardware detection. A detection log (DETLOG.TXT)
keeps track of what the Windows 95 Setup program discovers during the hardware detection phase. These files will be covered in
the next section.

If any previous attempt to install Windows 95 has failed, Windows
95 Setup provides you with an option to use the Safe Recovery
feature or to simply run a full new Setup process (see fig. 1.15). If
the Safe Recovery dialog box appears when you start the Windows

95 Setup program, you should always select the Use Safe Recovery option. When you select this option, Windows 95 Setup can use various built-in methods to avoid the problems that occurred previously.

Figure 1.15

Using Safe Recovery.

The following are basic Safe Recovery rules for you to know in case a failure happens:

▶ Before hardware detection begins, the Windows 95 Setup program uses SETUPLOG.TXT to determine the point of failure when you restart. The Windows 95 Setup program then knows what to redo and what it can skip.

▶ During hardware detection a DETCRASH.LOG is created. When the Windows 95 Setup program is restarted, it finds this file and uses it to determine which detection module was running at the point of failure. In a Safe Recovery mode, the Windows 95 Setup program reads the Registry to verify all the devices detected already, and skips any detection modules up to the point of failure. It also skips any detection modules that caused the failure, or any previously logged failure. Safe Recovery then proceeds to the next detection module. When the hardware detection phase finishes, the DETCRASH.LOG is deleted.

▶ After hardware detection phase finishes, the Windows 95 Setup program recognizes that the hardware detection is successfully completed, and will skip past this point. It assumes that all the necessary hardware information is stored in the Registry.

The Safe Recovery process depends on where in the Windows 95 installation process the Windows 95 Setup program reached before encountering problems. It continues from that point onward, attempting to bypass the problems. Although this approach enables the Windows 95 Setup program to complete the Windows 95 installation, it might leave these problems for you to resolve later.

To continue if Windows 95 Setup stops during hardware detection, do the following:

1. Press F3, or click on the Cancel button to quit Setup.

   If the computer does not respond to the Cancel button, restart the computer by turning it off and then back on again. Do not just warm boot or hit the Reset button.

2. Run Setup again. The Windows 95 Setup program prompts you to use Safe Recovery to recover the failed Windows 95 installation.

3. Choose Use Safe Recovery (should be the default), and then click on the Next button.

4. Repeat your installation choices. Hardware detection then runs again, but the Windows 95 Setup program skips the portion that caused the initial failure.

5. If the computer stops again during the hardware detection process, repeat this procedure until the hardware detection portion of Setup completes successfully.

Your most likely point of failure will occur during the hardware detection phase. With the millions of Intel computers in use today, the countless number of hardware configurations, old legacy hardware, and the new PnP hardware available, this is where you are going to see most of the problems. Only a limited number of Interrupts (IRQs), DMA channels, I/O address assignments, and upper memory space allocations are available. There might be conflicts—especially if you add multimedia capability, CD-ROMs, Network Interface Cards, SCSI adapters, and other hardware devices to your computer.

These resource conflicts might already be resolved before you begin the installation of Windows 95. If your computer is running successfully, and no hardware changes are made, you can reasonably expect that simply upgrading to Windows 95 will not create any problems. If the computer is being upgraded with new hardware devices at the same time as the upgrade to Windows 95, however, conflicts might occur. It is much easier to resolve these conflicts if the new hardware devices are added after Windows 95 is installed.

Safe Recovery helps you blow safely past the hardware detection conflicts. It does not solve them. You'll need to be knowledgeable about the computer configuration in order to uncover the conflicts and fix them. As you install Windows 95 across a variety of computers, you will very likely get this opportunity.

If the Windows 95 Setup program fails after the boot records have been modified, you would simply restart Windows 95 to complete the installation. There is no need to start the Windows 95 Setup program from the beginning.

Recognize Files Used in Troubleshooting the Installation Process

The Windows 95 Setup program creates several log files— SETUPLOG.TXT, DETLOG.TXT, DETCRASH.LOG—during hardware detection failure, and others—NETLOG.TXT and BOOTLOG.TXT—as Windows 95 starts up the first time. Some of these have been mentioned previously, but several are new. The following list looks at these files in detail:

▶ **SETUPLOG.TXT.** This is an ASCII text file that contains the Windows 95 Setup information created during installation. As Windows 95 is being installed, entries are written into this text file for each step in sequence. This file will show any error conditions encountered. It is used by the Windows 95 Setup program in case of setup failure, and you can also use it to troubleshoot errors during the installation process.

The Windows 95 Setup program uses the information contained within SETUPLOG.TXT to ensure that the Windows 95 installation program does not fail twice on the same problem. When you restart the Windows 95 Setup program after a failure, the contents are reviewed to see which process started, but did not complete successfully. These processes are skipped, and the next process in sequence is run. The DETLOG.TXT and DETCRASH.LOG files, which are discussed next, are used to skip any hardware detection modules that failed.

Buried on the CD-ROM version of Windows 95 is a helpful program called LOGVIEW.EXE, which enables you to examine all the text files mentioned in this list in a manner similar to the SYSEDIT.EXE program found in earlier versions of Windows. To find this program, look in the OTHER\MISC\LOGVIEW directory.

SETUPLOG.TXT is stored as a hidden file on the computer's root directory. Information is added to this file in the same order as the installation process. If you need to determine what caused the Windows 95 Setup program to fail, look at the entries at the bottom of this file before restarting again.

▶ **DETLOG.TXT.** This is an ASCII text file that contains a record of all devices found during the hardware detection phase of installation. If a device is found, the detected parameters are identified and recorded.

If the hardware detection phase should cause the computer to stall or lock up, a binary file named DETCRASH.LOG is created. While DETLOG.TXT is an ASCII file for you to read, the Windows 95 Setup program reads the binary information in DETCRASH.LOG to determine what steps successfully completed.

DETLOG.TXT is stored as a hidden file on the computer's root directory. Information is added to this file in the same order as the hardware detection phase. If you need to determine what caused the Windows 95 Setup program to fail or lockup, look at the entries at the bottom of this file before restarting again.

▶ **DETCRASH.LOG.** This is a binary file that only exists during the hardware detection phase. It tracks the entire process in case of errors for the Windows 95 Setup program. You need to be aware of its existence, but you would use the DETLOG.TXT ASCII file to do any troubleshooting.

▶ **NETLOG.TXT.** This is an ASCII text file that contains a record of all detected network components found during installation. There are four parts to the network detection phase. These correspond with the four class types of network configuration: network clients; network protocols; network adapters; and network services, such as file and print sharing.

This file is stored as a non-hidden file on the computer's root directory. Information is added to this file in the same order as the network detection phase. If you need to determine what caused the Windows 95 Setup program to not communicate across the network, look at the entries in this file.

▶ **BOOTLOG.TXT.** This is an ASCII text file that contains a record of the current startup process when starting Windows 95. As Windows 95 is started for the first time, this file gets created automatically. This file records the Windows 95 components and drivers as they are loaded and initialized, and also records the status of each step.

The information in BOOTLOG.TXT is written in sequence during startup. You might need to examine it closely to determine which error occurred. The Windows 95 Resource Kit has a good description of the sections within this file. You can also create this file by pressing F8 during the "Starting Windows 95" startup and selecting menu option 2—normal with a boot log.

This file is stored as a hidden file on the computer's root directory. Information is added to this file during the Windows 95 startup process. If you need to determine what caused the Windows 95 to fail or lockup, look at the entries within this file before restarting again.

The three key files used to troubleshoot the Windows 95 installation process are the SETUPLOG.TXT, DETLOG.TXT, and BOOTLOG.TXT ASCII text files. The *Windows 95 Resource Kit* provides code for a batch file you can create that looks at these key files and extracts the information. This batch file has been created and placed on the CD-ROM under the file name of ATTEMPT.BAT, should you need it.

Troubleshooting Setup and System Startup

The Windows 95 installation is usually successful. But on occasion there can be problems. These problems are usually due to hardware configuration and software difficulties. This section is directed toward helping you troubleshoot both the Windows 95 installation and normal system startup. Some basic troubleshooting techniques are also discussed in much finer detail in the chapter of the *Windows 95 Resource Kit* on general troubleshooting. You should review it.

The author uses a simple approach to problem solving, which you can adopt (or adapt) for your own use as well. This simple approach can be characterized as making the solution "FIT" the problem. The following details how this particular problem-solving approach works:

▶ **F.** Find the problem by drawing a box around it. Collect the symptoms of the problem, under what conditions it occurs, and when it happens. Draw a box around the problem to determine and narrow the scope. Consult any technical resources to see if it is a known problem. If the problem is a known problem, it might already have a known solution or work-around.

▶ **I.** Isolate and diagnose the problem. Make an assumption about what is causing the problem. Don't overlook the obvious. Ask what has recently changed, and why.

▶ **T.** Test the solution to the problem. By eliminating recent changes or controlling the number of variables, you can methodically test each modification to see if it solves the problem. Return the computer to the original state after each test. If you change three things and this somehow fixes the problem, which change was the effective one? Document your solution for the next time, or for the next person.

Troubleshooting Aids for Setup and Startup

Windows 95 has many troubleshooting aids to assist you in fixing problems that occur during either the setup or the startup process. The following troubleshooting aids are available:

▶ Safe Recovery during Windows 95 Setup

▶ Windows 95 Startup Disk

▶ Installed Components Verification

▶ Startup Menu Options and Safe Mode

▶ WIN.COM switches

Because both Safe Recovery and the Windows 95 Startup Disk have been discussed previously, please review those earlier sections of this chapter. The remaining three troubleshooting aids are covered in this section.

Installed Components Verification

Windows 95, like the previous versions of Windows and DOS, is comprised of many system programs and files. The loss, data corruption, or incorrect replacement of a single system program or file could result in problems when running Windows 95. The system program or file might have been inadvertently deleted, become corrupted because of an errant application, been infected by a virus, or been updated to a different version that will not work with all applications or devices. There can be many likely causes.

Windows 95 provides a setup option for verification of installed components when the Windows 95 Setup program detects an existing Windows 95 installation. Figure 1.16 illustrates the screen that is displayed when running the Windows 95 Setup program on a computer that has Windows 95 already installed.

Figure 1.16

Verifying Windows 95 installation.

When you run the verify option, the Windows 95 Setup program reads SETUPLOG.TXT for the installed components and then reruns the Setup process to verify all system components. If verify finds a missing or damaged file, the Windows 95 Setup program reinstalls that file. As part of the verification, VMM32.VXD also gets rebuilt.

Startup Menu Options and Safe Mode

Should the system fail to start and need to be re-booted, Windows 95 will display a Startup menu. Table 1.7 outlines the menu items on the Startup menu. You can also invoke this Startup menu yourself if you immediately press the F8 key when you see the message at boot-up saying "Starting Windows 95."

Table 1.7

Microsoft Windows 95 Startup Menu	
Menu Item	Description
Normal	Start Windows, loading all normal startup files and Registry values.
Logged	Runs system startup, creating a startup (\BOOTLOG.TXT) log file named BOOTLOG.TXT on the boot directory.
Safe Mode	Start Windows, bypassing startup files and using only basic system drivers. You can also start this option by pressing F5 or typing **win /d:m** at the command prompt.
Safe Mode with Network Support	Start Windows, bypassing startup files and using only basic system drivers, including basic networking. You can also start this option by pressing F6 or typing win /d:n at the command prompt.
Step-By-Step Confirmation	Start Windows, confirming startup files line by line. You also can start this option by pressing F8 when the Startup menu is displayed.
Command Prompt Only	Starts the operating system with startup files and Registry, displaying only the command prompt.
Safe Mode Command Prompt Only	Starts the operating system in Safe Mode and displays only the command prompt, bypassing startup files. You also can start this option by pressing Shift+F5.
Previous Version MS-DOS	Starts the version of MS-DOS previously installed on this computer. You also can start this option by pressing F4. This option is only available if BootMulti=1 is in the MSDOS.SYS file.

Safe Mode

Sometimes Windows 95 does not start properly in the normal way. The opening graphical screen freezes, and the computer does not respond. The Windows 95 Registry might even be corrupted.

Whatever the reason, Windows 95 automatically selects Safe Mode when the computer is re-booted because it detects that system startup has failed. The Windows 95 Startup menu is displayed, and Safe Mode is the default selection.

Select Safe Mode from the Startup menu to conduct troubleshooting. Safe Mode bypasses all the startup files, including the Registry, CONFIG.SYS, AUTOEXEC.BAT, and both the [Boot] and [386Enh] sections of the SYSTEM.INI file. It does provide you access to the Windows 95 configuration files, where you can make some corrective changes and then restart Windows 95.

When you start Windows 95 in the Safe Mode, only the mouse, keyboard, and VGA device drivers are loaded. Little Safe Mode messages are posted on each corner of the Windows 95 Desktop as reminders that you are running in Safe Mode. Not all the System Properties information will be available when running in Safe Mode, but at least you have access to make some changes. You cannot, for example, use Super VGA device drivers for screen resolutions above 640 × 480.

Often the best course of action when forced to troubleshoot your computer in Safe Mode is to remove the suspected problem hardware device using the System Properties, Device Manager tab within the Control Panel folder. Although the Registry information is not available to resolve conflicts, removing the hardware device might enable you to restart Windows 95. Then the hardware device can be added back again through the Add New Hardware application in the Control Panel folder. Be sure to let Windows 95 perform a complete hardware detection.

Using incorrect display drivers can also force you into starting Windows 95 in Safe Mode, which loads only a default VGA driver. This is similar to starting Windows NT in VGA Mode, since both startup methods allow you to make corrections to the display drivers.

WIN.COM Switches

When you start the computer at the command prompt, you can use switches with the win command to control the Windows 95 startup for troubleshooting purposes (see table 1.8).

Table 1.8

WIN.COM Command Switches	
Switch	Description
/d:f	Turns off 32-bit disk access. This is equivalent to 32BitDiskAccess=False in the SYSTEM.INI file.
/d:m	Starts Windows 95 in Safe Mode.
/d:n	Starts Windows 95 in Safe Mode with networking support.
/d:s	Tells Windows 95 not to use the ROM space between F000 and 1 MB for a break point. This is equivalent to SystemROMBreakPoint=False in the SYSTEM.INI file.
/d:v	Tells Windows 95 to use the ROM routine to handle interrupts from the hard disk controller. This is equivalent to VirtualHDIRQ=False in the SYSTEM.INI file.
/d:x	Excludes all the upper memory area (UMA) from being used by Windows 95. This is equivalent to EMMExclude=A000-FFFF in the SYSTEM.INI file.

Windows 95 System Startup Files

Table 1.9 describes the old files used in pre-Windows 95 DOS and the new files used in Windows 95 for system startup. There are not many obvious differences; however, now under Windows 95 the two older MS-DOS system files (IO.SYS and MSDOS.SYS) are replaced by a new IO.SYS. IO.SYS is a real-mode operating system file containing the information needed to start the computer. The new MSDOS.SYS is a text file containing special information for Windows 95. It was kept around for backward compatibility because certain applications require this file to be present before they will install successfully. The CONFIG.SYS and AUTOEXEC.BAT are mostly optional files under Windows 95, because certain settings are incorporated directly into either the IO.SYS or the MSDOS.SYS files (see table 1.10).

Table 1.9

System Startup Files

Pre-Windows 95 DOS	Windows 95
IO.SYS	IO.SYS
MSDOS.SYS	MSDOS.SYS (text file)
COMMAND.COM	COMMAND.COM
CONFIG.SYS	CONFIG.SYS (optional)
AUTOEXEC.BAT	AUTOEXEC.BAT (optional)

Table 1.10

Default Settings for Windows 95

Setting	Description
HIMEM.SYS	Enables access to High Memory Area (HMA). Loads and runs the real-mode Memory Manager.
DOS=HIGH	Specifies MS-DOS should be loaded into the HMA.
DOS=UMB	If EMM386.EXE is loaded in CONFIG.SYS, the Upper Memory Blocks (UMB) are set to allow both DeviceHigh and LoadHigh settings in the CONFIG.SYS and AUTOEXEC.BAT.
SETVER.EXE	Included for compatibility reasons. Some MS-DOS applications require specific versions of MS-DOS to be running. This TSR-type device responds to those applications that query for version number by responding directly from an internal table.
IFSHLP.SYS	Installable File System (IFS) Helper, which loads device drivers that allow Windows 95 to make calls to the file system.
FILES=60	Specifies number of file handle buffers to create for files opened by MS-DOS calls. Not required by Windows 95. Included for back-ward compatibility. Default value is 60.

continues

Table 1.10 Continued

Setting	Description
BUFFERS=30	Specifies number of file buffers to create. Used by applications using IO.SYS calls. Not required by Windows 95. Default value is 30.
LASTDRIVE=Z	Specifies the last drive letter available for assignment. Not required by Windows 95, but included for backward compatibility. If the Windows 95 Setup program finds this value, it is moved into the Registry. Default value is z.
FCBS=4	Specifies the number of file control blocks that can be open at the same time. Older programs might require such a setting in the CONFIG.SYS file. Default value is 4.
STACKS=9,256	Specifies the number and size of stack frames. Not required by Windows 95, but included for backward compatibility. Default value is 9,256.
SHELL= COMMAND.COM	Indicates what command process to use. Adds the /p switch by default to make the command process permanent.
PATH=<*windir*>; <*windir*>\command	Default path statement points to the Windows 95 directory and the Windows 95 command directory.
TMP= <*windir*>\TEMP	Temporary working directory default.
TEMP= <*windir*>\TEMP	Temporary working directory default.
PROMPT= rent pg	Default MS-DOS prompt option shows cur-drive and path followed by the greater-than character (>).
COMSPEC= <*windir*>\command \command.com	Another default reference to the command process.

These Windows 95 default settings make it possible to not have either a CONFIG.SYS or an AUTOEXEC.BAT file. In fact, one good method of improving your Windows 95 installation success ratio is renaming both these files just before running the Windows 95 Setup program.

Chapter 35 on general troubleshooting in the *Windows 95 Resource Kit* is a good source of information. As part of your preparation in this exam area, study it carefully.

Troubleshooting Scenarios

The *Windows 95 Resource Kit* lists many of the errors you might encounter with Windows 95. The following are some of the more common situations, and possible problem-solving steps:

- ▶ **The Windows 95 Setup program fails to start.** Check if there is enough free RAM; conventional memory, upper memory, and expanded (XMS) memory—use **mem /c/p** at the DOS command prompt. Check for viruses. Check and disable extra lines in both the CONFIG.SYS and the AUTOEXEC.BAT files.

- ▶ **The Windows 95 Setup program starts but reports an error.** These errors usually have an error message, which describes what caused the error. Check for viruses. See the SETUPLOG.TXT and DETLOG.TXT files.

- ▶ **The Windows 95 Setup program reports a B1 error.** The older Intel 386 processors are not supported. Upgrade the processor and re-install.

- ▶ **The Windows 95 Setup program has problems during the file copy phase.** There could be problems with virus detection software or virus protection BIOS setups. Either unload or disable BIOS virus protection and re-install.

- ▶ **The Windows 95 Setup program cannot find a valid boot partition.** A valid MS-DOS partition must exist. Either there is an actual partition error, or disk compression software or network components are mapping over the boot drive. Use FDISK to verify that a valid, active MS-DOS partition exists.

- ▶ **The Windows 95 Setup program stalls during the first restart of Windows 95.** Legacy hardware might be incorrectly configured before the Windows 95 installation. Remove settings in the CONFIG.SYS and AUTOEXEC.BAT files. Ensure all SCSI devices are properly terminated. The ISA enumerator (device=ISAPNP.386) in the [386Enh] section of the SYSTEM.INI might need to be commented out by adding a semicolon in front of the line.

▶ **At Windows 95 Startup, bad or missing file name.** Where the file name is the actual file causing the problem, check the existence, location, version number, and integrity of the file named. You might need to restart the Windows 95 Setup program with the Verify option to replace missing or damaged files.

▶ **At Windows 95 Startup, the System Registry File is missing.** The Windows 95 System Registry file is actually two files, SYSTEM.DAT and USER.DAT, which are backed up after each successful startup of Windows 95. These copies are called SYSTEM.DA0 and USER.DA0, and will be used to attempt a recovery. This is very similar to the "Last Known Good Boot" process of Windows NT. See Chapter 4 for more information about troubleshooting the System Registry.

▶ **At Windows 95 Startup, the wrong programs are running.** The WIN.INI is still processed, as well as the converted Startup Group, which is now the Start Menu Startup folder. You also might have previously designated an alternate Startup Group in the PROGMAN.INI file. Check all these locations and modify as needed. To correct this last item, you will need to alter the Registry, see the *Windows 95 Resource Kit* for details.

▶ **At Windows 95 Startup, not all devices are available.** The hardware detection phase and subsequent first run configuration of Plug and Play devices might still leave some hardware devices not working correctly. See Chapter 12, "Troubleshooting," for further information about troubleshooting your hardware configuration.

Because the Windows 95 Registry plays such an important role in the operation of Windows 95, it is a good idea to always make backup copies of your Registry files (SYSTEM.DAT and USER.DAT) before making any modifications.

If you create a Windows 95 Startup disk, verify it works before you have to use it. Always add backup copies of the Windows 95 configuration files, including the Registry. A good time for backing up these files and updating the Windows 95 Startup disk is after you have installed new hardware devices or applications, and you have a good working computer configuration.

Another recent book from New Riders Publishing is *Windows 95 Registry Troubleshooting*. You might want to add that to your Windows 95 library.

Installation Steps

The following section is designed to run you through the process of installing Windows 95 on your computer using a variety of methods. You should have access to at least two computers, one for Windows 95 and the other for Windows NT Server. (You can get by with only a single computer, but the networking example will not be possible.)

Install the Windows 95 Operating System: Windows 95 CD-ROM Setup

The following steps should be treated as a normal installation, so run this from the CD-ROM on Computer 1. The end result will be to have Computer 1 running Windows 95.

Install Windows 95 on Computer 1 using a CD-ROM drive. This is a hands-on example that requires about 60 minutes. Walk through the following steps:

1. Reboot Computer 1, loading MS-DOS and Windows for Workgroups. Access the Windows 95 CD-ROM from the File, Run option in Program Manager and start the Windows 95 setup.exe program.

   A routine check of the system is done, followed by the preparation of the Setup Wizard.

2. The software license appears. After reading it, tab or click on the Yes button to continue.

3. The Setup Wizard appears to start collecting information about your computer. Click on Next to continue.

4. When prompted for a location to install Windows 95, take the default, which is C:\WINDOWS. Click on Next to continue.

5. Windows 95 will prepare the directory, check for installed components and check for available disk space.

6. Because you upgraded from Windows for Workgroups, you will be prompted whether or not to Save System Files. With these files saved, you could easily uninstall Windows 95, if desired. These files take up approximately 6 MB of disk space. If you want to be able to cleanly uninstall Windows 95, as if it were another software application, click on the Yes button and then click Next to continue.

7. Choose the type of installation, the default is Typical. Click on Next to continue.

8. For User Information, enter your full name and the name of your organization or company. Click on Next to continue.

9. For Product Identification, enter the product key code from the CD-ROM cover.

   Setup will analyze your computer, searching for all hardware devices available.

10. If asked to check for specific hardware such as CD-ROM drive or Sound Cards, check the appropriate boxes, and then click on Next to continue.

11. After hardware detection, a Getting Connected dialog box will appear. Do not select any of these components.

12. You will be prompted to install the default components, as determined by your setup option. Accept the defaults, and click on Next to continue.

13. Verify your network configuration, if prompted. For a stand-alone installation, you will not see these screens.

14. If asked to identify your computer and workgroup, enter the appropriate information. Ensure that computer name is unique. Click on Next to continue.

15. When asked whether you want to create a Startup Disk, accept the default. Choose Yes, I want a startup disk. Click on Next to continue.

16. The Setup Wizard begins copying files to your computer. Click on Next to continue.

17. The copy process might take a while, enter a Startup Disk floppy, when prompted.

18. The Setup Wizard reappears to finish the Windows 95 installation on your computer. Click on Finish to continue.

19. Windows 95 starts and prompts you for your name and password. The Control Panel, Start menu, and Help system will be configured.

20. When prompted for Time Zone, click on your approximate location on the world map, which helps select the correct time zone. Choose Close when done to continue.

21. If you have a printer, ignore this setting and continue. You will install printers in Chapter 7, "Managing Printers."

22. The Welcome to Windows 95 screen appears. Click on the buttons to take both the Windows 95 Tour and to see What's New in Windows 95.

The Windows 95 Setup program is very automated and modular. In most cases, very little information is required in order to install Windows 95.

Set Up Files for Network Installation and Shared Use: Windows 95 Server-Based Setup

 The following steps should be treated as a network (or server-based) installation. Run this from the CD-ROM on Computer 1. This requires access to either a mapped, shared drive on Computer 2 or a new separate directory on Computer 1 if using only one computer. Warning: This installation requires up to 87 MB of hard disk storage.

Ensure Computer 2 is running Microsoft Networking under Windows for Workgroups and that both computers are in the same workgroup name. Each computer should be able to see the other before proceeding.

Use Netsetup.exe to install Windows 95 source files on a network server, and to prepare for either network installations or shared installations of Windows 95. (This tool replaces SETUP /A used in earlier versions of Windows.)

It is recommended that you run NETSETUP from the CD-ROM.

For more information about server-based setup, see Chapter 4 of the *Windows 95 Resource Kit*. To execute a server-based, network installation, use the following steps:

1. From Computer 1, with CD-ROM drive, start Windows 95. On Computer 2, install both DOS and Windows for Workgroups. In this case, the server-based install can be to either Computer 2, as a network shared drive, or to a Windows NT Server or a Novell NetWare Server.

   For the purposes of this example, use Computer 2. If you only have one computer, install to a new directory.

2. Establish an Install directory share with full rights on Computer 2. If using a Windows NT Server or a NetWare Server, be sure to grant sufficient privileges or rights if required.

3. Run NETSETUP from the ADMIN\NETTOOLS\NETSETUP directory on Computer 1 from the Windows 95 CD-ROM. The server-based setup program can only be run from a computer that is already running Windows 95.

4. The Server Based Setup dialog box appears (see fig. 1.17). Click on the Set Path button to specify the server path where the Windows 95 installation files will be installed. Click on OK when done. If the server path was previously defined, the button name is Change Path.

Figure 1.17

Server-based setup.

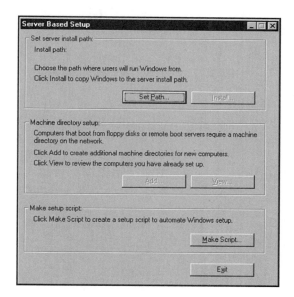

5. Click on the Install button to start the installation.

6. You will be presented with a series of dialog boxes. These boxes will confirm the paths to install from and to. The dialog boxes will also specify how the users can install Windows 95 from the server to a local hard drive as a shared copy or user's choice. Make it user's choice for the purposes of this exercise. Click on OK to continue.

7. Click on Don't Create Setup Batch Scripts because you will be doing this in the next exercise.

8. Enter the Product Identification number when prompted. Click on OK to continue with the server-based setup.

9. You will receive a dialog box when the server-based setup is complete. Click on OK, but do not close the Window. You want to examine a batch file script in the next exercise.

The Windows 95 server-based setup program is simple, and makes it easy to install Windows 95 on a server. With the Windows 95 installation files on a server, installations are much faster.

Automated Setup Using Batch Files: Windows 95 Batch File Creation

One of the command-line switches for the Setup program allows the reference to a batch script file that contains the setup options. There are several ways to create this text file. You will use one in the following steps:

1. From Computer 1, with CD-ROM drive, start Windows 95.

2. If the server-based Setup program is still running, then go to step 2. If, however, you are beginning anew, run NETSET-UP from the ADMIN\NETTOOLS\NETSETUP directory on Computer 1, from the Windows 95 CD-ROM. The server-based setup program can only be run from a computer already running Windows 95.

3. The Server Based Setup dialog box will appear (refer to fig. 1.17). Click on the Make Script button to specify that you want to create a batch script.

4. Select the MSBATCH.INF file from the server-based setup directory. A Properties sheet will appear, which enables you to graphically create a batch script file for use in automating your Windows 95 installations (see fig. 1.18).

5. See the *Windows 95 Resource Kit* for full explanation behind each field and check mark. Set a few values, save by clicking on OK, then Exit.

6. Start the Notepad application by choosing Start, Programs, Accessories, Notepad and open the text file MSBATCH.INF in your server-based setup directory. You will see how the

information gathered in the previous step is translated into options, fields, and values that the Windows 95 Setup program can read and understand.

Figure 1.18

Batch file server-based setup.

Many ways are available to create a custom script file for a Windows 95 installation. As you did in the preceding steps, you can use the server-based setup (Netsetup.exe) program. This program also enables you to install source files and create machine directories for a shared network installation. There is another Windows-based program called Batch Setup (Batch.exe) that makes it easy to create custom scripts. Finally, you can use a text editor, such as Notepad (Notepad.exe) to directly edit the custom script file.

See Chapter 5 on custom, automated, and push installations in the *Windows 95 Resource Kit* for further reference material. It is a good idea to read and understand all the basics surrounding automated installation of Windows 95.

Removing Windows 95 from a Computer

If you upgraded from Windows 3.1*x* or Windows for Workgroups 3.*x*, then you will be presented with an option to Save System Files. This saves the existing MS-DOS–based and Windows-based system files and enables you to easily uninstall Windows 95 from the computer if required, such as if mission-critical applications do not properly run under Windows 95. These system files you save require about 6 MB of hard disk space.

> The following steps work properly only if you selected the Save System Files during the Windows 95 installation. Otherwise, you need to follow a longer series of steps, as described in Chapter 6 of the *Windows 95 Resource Kit* under "Removing Windows 95 with Your Previous Operating System."

To remove Windows 95, use the Windows 95 Startup Disk's Uninstall (Uninstal.exe) program. Use the following steps to uninstall Windows 95:

1. From Computer 1, place your Windows 95 Startup disk in the floppy drive.

2. From the Start menu, choose Run. Type **a:\uninstal.exe** and press Enter.

3. From the Windows 95 Uninstall dialog box, click Yes to begin the uninstall process.

   Windows 95 will then shut down, and the uninstall will continue automatically.

Your previous configuration will be restored. When finally prompted, remove the Windows 95 startup disk from the floppy drive, and press Enter to re-boot your computer.

> The preceding steps will remove Windows 95 from the computer. To continue with the remaining exercises in this study guide, please either do a standard Windows 95 install to Computer 1, as previously outlined in the "Install the Windows 95 Operating System" section, or a clean Windows 95 install to Computer 1, as outlined in the next section.

Clean Windows 95 Installation

How do I load Windows 95 on the hard drive of a computer after formatting the hard disk? This is the key question that many network administrators would like to know the answer to.

Currently, there is no easy way to format a computer's hard drive and copy down an "image" of another standard Windows 95 computer. When used in this context, the word image refers to a backup copy of an entire computer's hard drive that is stored on a network file server.

Under MS-DOS and Windows 3.*x*, it is possible to take a standard computer and create an image that could be downloaded on top of a newly formatted hard drive on one or more computers. As long as the computers were roughly identical, this strategy could save you a significant amount of time conducting many installations. Otherwise, you could easily take a day per computer to reinstall and test, on a clean hard drive, the operating system, Windows, and all the applications. This time estimate also assumes you have easy access to all the license software setup disks, and backups of key data files.

This same strategy of creating a Windows 95 image is not very practical. The Registry plays a much more important role under Windows 95. The Registry entries of each machine are different. This makes creating a usable image extremely difficult. What can be done is to format the hard drive and then install Windows 95. After Windows 95 is installed, there are automated processes that you can use to load the rest of the applications.

There are several workable approaches to this clean Windows 95 installation process that work, and they all follow a set pattern:

1. Use a Windows 95 Startup disk to boot the computer to a Windows 95 command prompt:

   ▶ If installing from floppy disk, continue.

   ▶ If installing from CD-ROM, ensure that the CD-ROM is accessible to the system by adding references to both the CONFIG.SYS and AUTOEXEC.BAT files.

▶ If installing from the network, load network drivers and map the Windows 95 installation drive.

2. Fdisk and format the hard drive(s), adding Windows 95 system files to the C:\ drive.

3. Access the Windows 95 Setup program and run. If installing from the network, ensure that the network configuration is set up correctly.

The floppy version of Windows 95 that is for computers without Windows already includes a Boot Disk. This version runs an OEMSETUP.EXE program to accomplish the task. Upgrade versions of Windows 95 will prompt you for setup of disk 1 of Windows 3.x or Windows for Workgroups 3.x, or an OS/2 2.x installation disk in order to verify that you qualify for running the upgrade.

While the procedure in the following steps installs a clean copy of Windows 95 on the computer, it still leaves the network administrator with the arduous task of reinstalling all the applications. A better approach might be to create a clean MS-DOS and Windows 3.x image with all the applications already installed, download that image, and then upgrade the computer to Windows 95.

The procedure in the following steps uses either the floppy disk or CD-ROM version of Windows 95 to do a clean installation. Here are the steps for doing an installation with the floppy disk version. If you have removed Windows 95 in the previous section, please complete this exercise as well.

1. From Computer 1, boot with the Windows 95 Startup Disk, format the hard drive, and add the Windows 95 system files to the boot drive (Format c: /s).

2. Insert disk 1 of the floppy version of the Windows 95 installation disks into the floppy drive and run Setup.exe from the command prompt.

3. Complete the Windows 95 installation (see the example shown in the previous section called "Install the Windows 95 Operating System").

If you have only the CD-ROM version of Windows 95, you have to boot the computer with an earlier version of MS-DOS that has all the files required to access the CD-ROM drive, or create a modified Windows 95 Startup disk that adds the equivalent files to allow access to the CD-ROM drive. Here are the steps for doing an installation with the CD-ROM version:

1. From Computer 1, boot with either the Windows 95 Startup disk or an equivalent MS-DOS boot disk. The boot files on the disk, CONFIG.SYS and AUTOEXEC.BAT, must be able to allow access to the CD-ROM drive. Format the hard drive and add the Windows 95 system files to the boot drive (Format c: /s).

2. Insert the CD-ROM version of the Windows 95 installation disks into the CD-ROM drive and run Setup.exe from the command prompt.

3. Complete the Windows 95 installation (see Exercise 1.6).

Exercises

Exercise 1.1: Choosing Between Windows 95 and Windows NT

Exercise 1.1 will help you make the choice between a Windows 95 or Windows NT operating system. In each of the following cases, indicate which Windows operating system should be used, either Windows 95 or Windows NT:

1. Office environment with general tasks, such as word processing, spreadsheet analysis, and e-mail, running on an installed base of Intel-based personal computers, where management wants to maximize their existing investment.

2. Engineers, scientific researchers, statisticians, and other technical users who often use processing-intensive applications for data analysis and design activities.

3. Employees who spend a lot of their working hours away from their office (at a customer site, in a hotel, or out in the field) and rely on personal laptop computers to help them perform their jobs.

4. Banking and defense workers who need to protect sensitive data or application files with high levels of security.

5. Home-based users who find computers challenging and unfriendly. They want to be able to take advantage of new capabilities, such as multimedia and easily accessible online information services.

6. Experienced computer users who require very high levels of availability and performance, and cannot afford downtime, regardless of the application that they are running.

Exercise 1.2: Choosing a Protocol

In Exercise 1.2, you select the protocol that is most appropriate for a variety of situations. In each of the following cases, determine which protocol should be used—either NetBEUI, IPX/SPX, or TCP/IP:

1. A local area network, running against both a Novell NetWare Server and a Windows NT Server.

2. A small office network with only Windows 95 computers, plus some Windows for Workgroup computers that have not been upgraded yet.

3. A wide area network, connecting to UNIX Servers and the Internet.

Exercise 1.3: Selecting a Security Level

In Exercise 1.3, you choose the optimal level of security for a variety of situations. In each of the following cases, select the appropriate level of security: user-level, share-level, or no (no file and printer sharing) security:

1. A local area network, running against both a Novell NetWare Server and a Windows NT Server.

2. A small office network, only Windows 95 computers, plus some Windows for Workgroup computers that have not been upgraded.

3. A wide area network, connecting to UNIX Servers and the Internet.

Exercise 1.4: Choosing an Installation Method

Exercise 1.4 is aimed at helping you determine the appropriate installation method to use for some given installations. For each of the cases listed, choose from the following list the letter that corresponds to the correct response:

a. Setup from MS-DOS

b. Setup from Windows 3.*x*

c. Typical, Compact, or Custom Setup type

d. Portable setup type

e. Local Windows

continues

Exercise 1.4: Continued

    f. Shared Windows

    g. Manual install

    h. Customized Setup Script install

    i. Automated install

    j. Repair install

    k. Maintenance applications

1. A key Windows 95 system file has become corrupted, how would you fix it?

2. A computer with MS-DOS 5.0 and Windows 3.0 needs to be updated to Windows 95. Where would you start setup?

3. If the computer is running Windows 95 from the local hard drive of the computer, it is said to be running what kind of Windows?

4. What Setup type of Windows 95 installation should you use to heavily customize both components and settings during installation?

5. An installation of a home computer without a CD-ROM drive that needs to be updated with Windows 95 is an example of which kind of installation?

6. If a computer with MS-DOS 6.22 and Windows for Workgroups 3.11 needs to be updated to Windows 95, where do you start setup?

7. What Setup type of Windows 95 installation should you use for a laptop computer on which you want to run Windows 95 mobile computing components?

8. A computer running Windows 95 from a file server rather than its local hard drive is running which kind of Windows?

9. A batch file, such as MSBATCH.INF, that is used to pre-select Windows 95 installation settings is an example of which kind of installation?

10. If a Windows 95 component is not installed during the Windows 95 installation, how might you add it later?

11. A Windows 95 installation program that can be set for a mandatory start during the network logon is an example of which kind of installation?

The correct responses are as follows:

1. j	5. g	9. h
2. a	6. b	10.k
3. e	7. d	11.i
4. c	8. f	

Exercise 1.5: Determining Hard Disk Space Required for Installing All Optional Components

In Exercise 1.5, you calculate the disk space required to install every optional hardware component. While doing an actual Windows 95 installation (see Exercise 1.6), determine how many megabytes of additional hard disk space are required to install every component listed above and beyond the hard disk space required for the base Windows 95 operating system. Use the Reset button to return to the original pre-selected components.

If you add up all the greatest numbers in the Size column of table 1.3 (see the "Setup Type and Hard Drive Space Requirements," section), the total for all the components listed is approximately 36 MB.

Exercise 1.6: Windows 95 CD-ROM Setup

Install Windows 95 on Computer 1 using a CD-ROM drive. This is a hands-on exercise that requires about 60 minutes. Walk through the following steps:

1. Reboot Computer 1, loading MS-DOS and Windows for Workgroups. Access the Windows 95 CD-ROM from the File,

continues

Run option in Program Manager and start the Windows 95 setup.exe program.

A routine check of the system is done, followed by the preparation of the Setup Wizard.

2. The software license appears. After reading it, tab or click on the Yes button to continue.

3. The Setup Wizard appears to start collecting information about your computer. Click on Next to continue.

4. When prompted for a location to install Windows 95, take the default, which is C:\WINDOWS. Click on Next to continue.

5. Windows 95 will prepare the directory, check for installed components and check for available disk space.

6. Because you upgraded from Windows for Workgroups, you will be prompted whether or not to Save System Files. With these files saved, you could easily uninstall Windows 95, if desired. These files take up approximately 6 MB of disk space. If you want to be able to cleanly uninstall Windows 95, as if it were another software application, click on the Yes button and then click on Next to continue.

7. Choose the type of installation, the default is Typical. Click on Next to continue.

8. For User Information, enter your full name and the name of your organization or company. Click on Next to continue.

9. For Product Identification, enter the product key code from the CD-ROM cover.

Setup will analyze your computer, searching for all hardware devices available.

10. If asked to check for specific hardware such as CD-ROM drive or Sound Cards, check the appropriate boxes, and then click on Next to continue.

11. After hardware detection, a Getting Connected dialog box will appear. Do not select any of these components.

12. You will be prompted to install the default components, as determined by your setup option. Accept the defaults, and click on Next to continue.

13. Verify your network configuration, if prompted. For a stand-alone installation, you will not see these screens.

14. If asked to identify your computer and workgroup, enter the appropriate information. Ensure that computer name is unique. Click on Next to continue.

15. When asked whether you want to create a Startup Disk, accept the default. Choose Yes, I want a startup disk. Click on Next to continue.

16. The Setup Wizard begins copying files to your computer. Click on Next to continue.

17. The copy process might take a while, enter a Startup Disk floppy, when prompted.

18. The Setup Wizard reappears to finish the Windows 95 installation on your computer. Click on Finish to continue.

19. Windows 95 starts and prompts you for your name and password. The Control Panel, Start menu, and Help system will be configured.

20. When prompted for Time Zone, click on your approximate location on the world map, which helps select the correct time zone. Click on Close when done to continue.

21. If you have a printer, ignore this setting and continue. You will install printers in Chapter 7.

22. The Welcome to Windows 95 screen appears. Click on the buttons to take both the Windows 95 Tour and to see What's New in Windows 95.

The Windows 95 Setup program is very automated and modular. In most cases, very little information is required in order to install Windows 95.

Exercise 1.7: Windows 95 Server-Based Setup

This exercise should be treated as a network (or server-based) installation. Run this from the CD-ROM on Computer 1. This requires access to either a mapped, shared drive on Computer 2 or a new separate directory on Computer 1 if using only one computer. You need up to 87 MB of hard disk storage.

1. From Computer 1, with CD-ROM drive, start Windows 95. On Computer 2, install both DOS and Windows for Workgroups. In this case, the server-based install can be to either Computer 2, as a network shared drive, or to a Windows NT Server or a Novell NetWare Server.

    For the purposes of this example, use Computer 2. If you only have one computer, install to a new directory.

2. Establish an Install directory share with full rights on Computer 2. If using a Windows NT Server or a NetWare Server, be sure to grant sufficient privileges or rights if required.

3. Run NETSETUP from the ADMIN\NETTOOLS\NETSETUP directory on Computer 1 from the Windows 95 CD-ROM. The server-based setup program can only be run from a computer that is already running Windows 95.

4. The Server Based Setup dialog box will appear (refer to fig. 1.17). Click on the Set Path button to specify the server path where the Windows 95 installation files will be installed. Click OK when done. If the server path was previously defined, the button name is Change Path.

5. Click on the Install button to start the installation.

6. You will be presented with a series of dialog boxes. These boxes will confirm the paths to install from and to. The dialog boxes will also specify how the users can install Windows 95 from the server to a local hard drive as a shared copy or user's choice. Make it user's choice for the purposes of this exercise. Click on OK to continue.

7. Click on Don't Create Setup Batch Scripts because you will be doing this in the next exercise.

8. Enter the Product Identification number when prompted. Click on OK to continue with the server-based setup.

9. You will receive a dialog box when the server-based setup is complete. Click on OK, but do not close the Window. You want to examine a batch file script in the next exercise.

The Windows 95 server-based setup program is simple, and makes it easy to install Windows 95 on a server. With the Windows 95 installation files on a server, installations are much faster because the files are stored on the hard disk of the server, not on the CD-ROM (hard disks are much faster than CD-ROM drives).

Exercise 1.8:   Windows 95 Batch File Creation

The following exercise walks you through creating a batch script file.

1. From Computer 1, with CD-ROM drive, start Windows 95.

2. If you left the server-based Setup program running at the end of Exercise 1.7, then go to step 2. If, however, you are beginning anew, run NETSETUP from the ADMIN\ NETTOOLS\NETSETUP directory on Computer 1, from the Windows 95 CD-ROM. The server-based setup program can only be run from a computer already running Windows 95.

3. The Server Based Setup dialog box will appear (refer to fig. 1.17). Click on the Make Script button to specify that you want to create a batch script.

4. Select the MSBATCH.INF file from the server-based setup directory. A Properties sheet will appear that enables you to graphically create a batch script file for use in automating your Windows 95 installations (refer to fig. 1.18).

5. See the *Windows 95 Resource Kit* for full explanation behind each field and check mark. Set a few values, save by clicking on OK, then Exit.

6. Start the Notepad application by choosing Start, Programs, Accessories, Notepad and open the text file MSBATCH.INF in your server-based setup directory. You will see how the

continues

Exercise 1.8:   Continued

information gathered in the previous step is translated into options, fields, and values that the Windows 95 Setup program can read and understand.

Exercise 1.9:   Removing Windows 95

The following exercise, which shows how to remove Windows 95 from a computer, works properly only if you selected the Save System Files during the Windows 95 installation. Otherwise, you need to follow a longer series of steps, as described in Chapter 6 of the *Windows 95 Resource Kit* under "Removing Windows 95 with Your Previous Operating System."

1. From Computer 1, place your Windows 95 Startup disk in the floppy drive.

2. From the Start menu, choose Run. Type **a:\uninstal.exe** and press Enter.

3. From the Windows 95 Uninstall dialog box, click on Yes to begin the uninstall process.

   Windows 95 will then shut down, and the uninstall will continue automatically.

Your previous configuration will be restored. When finally prompted, remove the Windows 95 startup disk from the floppy drive, and press Enter to re-boot your computer.

Exercise 1.9 will remove Windows 95 from the computer. To continue with the remaining exercises in this study guide, please either do a standard Windows 95 install to Computer 1, as previously outlined in Exercise 1.6, or a clean Windows 95 install to Computer 1, as outlined in the next exercise, Exercise 1.10.

Exercise 1.10:   Windows 95 Clean Install

While the procedure in Exercise 1.10 installs a clean copy of Windows 95 on the computer, it still leaves the network administrator with the arduous task of reinstalling all the applications. A better approach might be to create a clean MS-DOS and Windows 3.*x* image with all the applications already installed, download that image, and then upgrade the computer to Windows 95.

This exercise uses either the floppy disk or CD-ROM version of Windows 95 to do a clean installation. Here are the steps for doing an installation with the floppy disk version. If you have removed Windows 95 in the previous exercise, please complete this exercise as well.

1. From Computer 1, boot with the Windows 95 Startup Disk, format the hard drive, and add the Windows 95 system files to the boot drive (Format c: /s).

2. Insert disk 1 of the floppy version of the Windows 95 installation disks into the floppy drive and run Setup.exe from the command prompt.

3. Complete the Windows 95 installation (refer to Exercise 1.6).

If you have only the CD-ROM version of Windows 95, you have to boot the computer with an earlier version of MS-DOS that has all the files required to access the CD-ROM drive, or create a modified Windows 95 Startup disk that adds the equivalent files to allow access to the CD-ROM drive. Here are the steps for doing an installation with the CD-ROM version:

1. From Computer 1, boot with either the Windows 95 Startup disk or an equivalent MS-DOS boot disk. The boot files on the disk, CONFIG.SYS and AUTOEXEC.BAT, must be able to allow access to the CD-ROM drive. Format the hard drive and add the Windows 95 system files to the boot drive (Format c: /s).

2. Insert the CD-ROM version of the Windows 95 installation disks into the CD-ROM drive and run Setup.exe from the command prompt.

3. Complete the Windows 95 installation (refer to Exercise 1.6).

continues

Review Questions

The following questions will test your knowledge of the information in this chapter. For additional questions, see MCP Endeavor and the Microsoft Roadmap/Assessment Exam on the CD-ROM that accompanies this book.

1. Windows 95 provides compatibility with many of today's existing computers. Before installing Windows 95 on a computer, make sure it has a processor that can run it. The lowest Intel processor recommended to run Windows 95 is _____.

   A. 80286

   B. 80386SX

   C. 80386DX

   D. 80486

   E. Pentium

2. Shirley uses a computer at work that runs Windows 95. Her computer at home does not have Windows 95 installed yet; she asks you how much Random Access Memory she needs in her computer to install Windows 95. You tell her the minimum amount of RAM that Windows 95 requires is _____.

   A. 2 MB

   B. 4 MB

   C. 8 MB

   D. 14 MB

   E. 16 MB

3. Graphics Unlimited is upgrading its five computers to Windows 95. The company must decide which media type to purchase to be able to upgrade all its computers. Which three of the following installation options are available for Windows 95?

A. From 5.25-inch floppy

B. From 3.5-inch floppy

C. From CD-ROM

D. From the network

E. From optical disk

4. On the "minimal" computer, as defined by Microsoft, the performance of Windows 95 should be _____ and _____ using Windows 3.1 with the same hardware (choose two).

A. worse than

B. about the same as

C. possibly improve over

D. much faster than

E. twice as fast as

5. When putting together a company report for upgrading to Windows 95, you must list those computers in the company that will not run Windows 95. Windows 95 will not run on which two of the following types of Intel 386 processors?

A. 386SX (with 16-bit I/O buffers)

B. 386DX B-Step Processor

C. 386DX Non-B-Step Processor

D. 386DX with ID 0303

E. 386DX with ID other than 0303

6. The minimum amount of RAM recommended for running either Microsoft Exchange Inbox, Microsoft Network, or multiple 32-bit Windows-based applications is _____.

A. 2 MB

B. 4 MB

C. 8 MB

D. 14 MB

E. 16 MB

7. Windows 95 uses swap files as virtual memory storage. As a rule of thumb, the amount of RAM on a Windows 95 computer and the amount of free space needed for a swap file should total at least _____.

A. 2 MB

B. 4 MB

C. 8 MB

D. 14 MB

E. 16 MB

8. Markus upgrades his MS-DOS computer to Windows 95. When installing over an MS-DOS–based operating system, Windows 95 will only install on a computer with an operating system equivalent to _____ or later.

A. MS-DOS 3.2

B. MS-DOS 3.3

C. MS-DOS 4.0

D. MS-DOS 5.0

E. MS-DOS 6.0

9. You are manning a technical support phone line and receive a call asking about partitions supported by Windows 95. Which of the following two types of partitions does Windows 95 support?

A. HPFS

B. NTFS

    C. CDFS

    D. FAT

    E. Unformatted

10. Windows 95 provides different installation types. Which one of the following is not a Windows 95 Setup type of installation?

    A. Custom

    B. Compact

    C. Express

    D. Typical

    E. Portable

11. Tracy is running Windows NT and wants to install Windows 95 on the same computer. She also has MS-DOS, Windows 3.*x*, and OS/2 installed on the same computer in different partitions. The Windows 95 Setup program can be run from which two of the following places?

    A. Within OS/2

    B. Within Windows NT

    C. From within Windows

    D. From a Windows DOS box

    E. From DOS

12. The preferred method for running the Windows 95 Setup program is from within _____ and _____ (choose two).

    A. MS-DOS

    B. MS Windows 3.1*x*

    C. an MS-DOS window inside Windows

    D. MS Windows for Workgroups 3.*x*

    E. a bootable floppy

13. Steve runs several 32-bit applications at the same time under Windows 95. What is the name of the type of multitasking that Windows 95 uses?

    A. cooperative

    B. cohabitive

    C. preemptive

    D. presumptive

    E. shared

14. You create a file in Windows 95 Explorer named Budget For This Year.XLS. This is a long file name. Long File Name (LFN) support on a Windows 95 computer works because it uses the _____ file system.

    A. FAT

    B. HPFS

    C. NTFS

    D. CDFS

    E. VFAT

15. You are setting up Windows 95 in a school's computer lab, which does not have a CD-ROM drive available. You know there are extra files on the CD-ROM version of Windows 95 and want to persuade the school administration to purchase a new CD-ROM drive. From the following list, choose the three differences in the Windows 95 upgrade between the floppy version of Windows 95 and the CD-ROM version.

    A. Windows Tour

    B. What's New

    C. Full online help

    D. Accessibility options

    E. Administrative extras

16. Windows 95 is a large program and includes many files (more than 1,000 files). To squeeze these files on the 3.5 inch floppy disks, Microsoft uses which of the following formats for most of the Windows 95 installation disks?

    A. FAT

    B. VFAT

    C. DMF

    D. CDFS

    E. NTFS

17. You are installing Windows 95 as a server-based setup from a computer that has Windows 95 installed. The Windows 95 Administrative Setup is done by running the _____ program (and parameters).

    A. Setup /a

    B. Setup /n

    C. Setup /as

    D. Netsetup

    E. Batch

18. A batch script file can be used in which three of the following Windows 95 installations?

    A. From the Windows 95 3.5-inch floppy disks

    B. From CD-ROM

    C. From the network

    D. From the local hard drive

    E. From 5.25-inch floppy disk

19. A coworker sends you e-mail telling you he has Windows 3.1 installed on his laptop at home, but cannot remember the laptop's hardware specifications. To help him, you tell him that the minimum hardware requirements for Windows 95 are _____ the minimum needed for Windows 3.1.

A. lower than

B. the same as

C. higher than

D. no different than

E. approximately the same as

20. Not all processors available can run Windows 95. Windows 95 will run on the _____ processor.

A. Intel 286

B. Intel 386 and higher

C. DEC Alpha

D. PowerPC

E. MIPS

21. The B1 error that can happen on a Windows 95 installation is the result of _____.

A. step B1, hardware detection, generating an error on the second floppy drive

B. the processor being an SX type, without a math coprocessor

C. the processor being a 386 B1 stepping chip, which can generate random math errors, making it incompatible with Windows 95

D. failure of the network configuration

E. corruption of the boot sector

22. Lynn wants to upgrade to Windows 95, but also needs to boot into MS-DOS (her existing operating system) at times. The Windows 95 option to boot into the previous version of MS-DOS is only available if upgrading from which version of MS-DOS or better?

A. MS-DOS 3.2

B. MS-DOS 3.3

C. MS-DOS 4.0

D. MS-DOS 5.0

E. MS-DOS 6.0

23. Before you begin upgrading the computers in your company, you send an e-mail asking all users to check the version of MS-DOS on their computers and to report back to you their findings. To check the version of DOS on their computers, you tell them to execute the _____ command at the DOS prompt.

A. Setver

B. Winver

C. Dosver

D. Ver

E. Getver

24. Hard drive space is at a premium at the Cycle Shop company. They want to upgrade to Windows 95, but they're not sure they have enough hard drive space to accommodate it. The approximate disk requirements for Windows 95 in a Typical Setup upgrade of Windows is _____.

A. 20 MB

B. 30 MB

C. 40 MB

D. 47 MB

E. 55 MB

25. Adam starts Windows 95 from the command prompt and uses WIN.COM command switches to control the way Windows 95 starts. What three of the following command switches can Adam use with the Windows 95 Setup program?

A. /?

B. /B

C. /ID

D. /D

E. /IS

26. The naming standards for _____ are all the same: limited to 15 characters, no embedded spaces, and can contain these special characters:

! @ # $ % ^ & ( ) - _ ' { } ~ .

A. user's full name

B. default user's name

C. computer name

D. workgroup name

E. computer description

27. Stacey chooses to keep program groups and system settings from her previous Windows 3.1 installation when upgrading to Windows 95. To migrate program groups and system settings when upgrading from Windows 3.x to Windows 95, which of the following should Stacey do?

A. Upgrade into a new Windows 95 directory.

B. Upgrade into an existing Windows directory.

C. Copy group and initialization files into a new Windows 95 directory.

D. Copy older DLL files into the new Windows 95 directory.

E. Run GRPCONV to convert older program groups into folders.

28. The Windows 95 Setup program will not run from Windows 3.0, but instead wants to run from MS-DOS. How much conventional memory is required to run from MS-DOS?

    A. 370 KB

    B. 420 KB

    C. 470 KB

    D. 512 KB

    E. 640 KB

29. Windows 95 performs four logical phases during the Windows 95 Setup routine. Which one of the following is not a logical phase in the Windows 95 installation?

    A. Startup and information gathering

    B. Hardware detection

    C. Software detection

    D. File copy

    E. Final system configuration

30. Alex is running the Windows 95 Setup program from MS-DOS. You know there are differences running Setup from DOS and from Windows. Which three of the following are differences between starting the Windows 95 Setup program in MS-DOS versus starting it in Windows?

    A. ScanDisk running in the foreground rather than the background

    B. Searching for Windows version 3.0 versus checking Windows version 3.1 or better

    C. Checking for TSRs versus checking for TSRs and other Windows programs running

    D. System checks done in DOS versus Windows

    E. DOS graphical interface versus Windows graphical interface after starting protected mode

31. You are prompted for user name and company name during which part of running the Windows 95 Setup program?

    A. initial startup and Setup Wizard load

    B. gathering user and computer information

    C. copying Windows 95 files

    D. restarting the computer and finishing Setup

    E. after Windows 95 is completely installed

32. The Startup disk is used in case you experience problems with your Windows 95 installation. You are asked to remove the newly created Startup disk during which part of running the Windows 95 Setup program?

    A. initial startup and Setup Wizard load

    B. gathering user and computer information

    C. copying Windows 95 files

    D. restarting the computer and finishing Setup

    E. after Windows 95 is completely installed

33. TSRs are known to cause problems when you install Windows 95. You are asked to unload any detected TSRs during which part of running the Windows 95 Setup program?

    A. initial startup and Setup Wizard load

    B. gathering user and computer information

    C. copying Windows 95 files

    D. restarting the computer and finishing Setup

    E. after Windows 95 is completely installed

34. The time zone option is used to set up your computer's clock and maintain proper settings during the spring and fall. You are asked to enter a time zone for the computer during which part of running the Windows 95 Setup program?

    A. initial startup and Setup Wizard load

    B. gathering user and computer information

    C. copying Windows 95 files

    D. restarting the computer and finishing Setup

    E. after Windows 95 is completely installed

35. You can ask to run the verify option for the computer during which part of running the Windows 95 Setup program?

    A. initial startup and Setup Wizard load

    B. gathering user and computer information

    C. copying Windows 95 files

    D. restarting the computer and finishing Setup

    E. after Windows 95 is completely installed

36. Tom is setting up Windows 95 on his laptop. He wants to use the Portable setup option, but doesn't know which option is the default setup type. Which one of the following is the default Windows 95 setup type of installation?

    A. Custom

    B. Compact

    C. Express

    D. Typical

    E. Portable

37. Windows 95 enables you to create a Startup disk to help you recover from problems. The Startup disk contains all the following files except _____.

    A. IO.SYS

    B. MSDOS.SYS

    C. COMMAND.COM

    D. CONFIG.SYS

    E. REGEDIT.EXE

38. The Startup disk, when created by the Windows 95 Setup program, contains 16 files and uses _____ of disk space?

    A. 640 KB

    B. 948 KB

    C. 1.0 MB

    D. 1.20 MB

    E. 1.44 MB

39. During a training session you are asked to describe the Start-up disk. Which two of the following statements are true about the Windows 95 Startup disk?

    A. It can be created only during a Windows 95 installation.

    B. It needs a pre-formatted floppy disk at the start.

    C. It enables you to boot to the Windows 95 command prompt.

    D. It includes CD-ROM drivers, if needed.

    E. It enables you to troubleshoot your Registry files.

40. Windows 95 includes several networking protocols. Which three of the following networking protocols included with Windows 95 are Plug and Play–enabled?

    A. Ethernet

    B. TCP/IP

    C. NetBEUI

    D. Token Ring

    E. IPX/SPX

41. You are asked to set up a stand-alone computer for several different people to access at different times during the day. Which level of security would be used for a stand-alone computer with multiple users, each of whom has different Windows 95 preferences and Desktops?

    A. Windows 95 access control

    B. Unified logon process

    C. Windows 95 logon security

    D. Share-level security

    E. User-level security

42. Which level of security would be used to base the access rights to shared resources on the Windows 95 computer using a user accounts list stored on a Novell NetWare Server?

    A. Windows 95 access control

    B. Unified logon process

    C. Windows 95 logon security

    D. Share-level security

    E. User-level security

43. Which level of security would be used to base the access rights to shared resources on the Windows 95 computer on a password-assigned basis?

    A. Windows 95 access control

    B. Unified logon process

    C. Windows 95 logon security

    D. Share-level security

    E. User-level security

44. You run the Windows 95 Setup program and get to the hardware detection phase. The computer stops responding and you let it sit for 30 minutes. If the hardware detection fails at a certain point in the process, what can you do?

    A. You cannot do anything.

    B. Restart the Windows 95 Setup program in Safe Recovery.

C. Restart the Windows 95 Setup program and run the entire hardware detection repeatedly until it clears up.

D. Call technical support to test your computer.

E. If you are technical support, call Microsoft.

45. Beverly upgrades to Windows 95 but does not install the Microsoft Exchange component during the Windows 95 installation process. She asks you if she can, now that she has Windows 95 running, install Exchange. You tell her she can, but she will have to _____.

A. restart the Windows 95 Setup program again to add a component

B. restart the Windows 95 Setup program in verify mode and then add the component

C. use the Add/Remove Programs option in Control Panel

D. use the Install Components Wizard from My Computer

E. restart the Windows 95 Setup program from scratch and reinstall Windows 95

46. Log files are ASCII text files you can use to help troubleshoot problems encountered during installation. Which one of the following log files is not used during the Windows 95 installation?

A. SETUPLOG.TXT

B. HARDWARE.TXT

C. DETLOG.TXT

D. NETLOG.TXT

E. BOOTLOG.TXT

47. Jack experiences problems with his laptop computer during the Windows 95 installation process, and cannot get Windows 95 to install. You advise him to examine which three of

the following key files to troubleshoot the Windows 95 installation process?

    A. SETUPLOG.TXT

    B. HARDWARE.TXT

    C. DETLOG.TXT

    D. NETLOG.TXT

    E. BOOTLOG.TXT

48. You want to boot your computer and have the Windows 95 Startup menu display. Which Function Key allows you to see the Startup menu when Windows 95 is first booting?

    A. F1

    B. F4

    C. F5

    D. F6

    E. F8

49. A device is not working when you boot Windows 95, so you decide to run the Safe Mode option when you boot Windows 95. In Safe Mode, Windows 95 only loads which three of the following device drivers?

    A. CD-ROM

    B. Mouse

    C. Keyboard

    D. Sound

    E. VGA

50. At Windows 95 Startup, you receive an error message saying there is a bad or missing file, and giving you the file's name. Which three of the following can you do to track down this error?

A. Check for the existence and location of the file.

B. Check for the version and integrity of the file.

C. See if the applications all still running.

D. Restart the Windows 95 Setup program with the Verify option to replace missing or damaged files.

E. Call Microsoft technical support.

Review Answers

1. C	11. C E	21. C	31. B	41. A
2. B	12. B D	22. D	32. C	42. E
3. B C D	13. C	23. D	33. A	43. D
4. B C	14. E	24. C	34. D	44. B
5. B D	15. A C E	25. A C E	35. E	45. C
6. C	16. C	26. B C D	36. D	46. B
7. D	17. D	27. B	37. D	47. A C E
8. A	18. B C D	28. C	38. B	48. E
9. D E	19. C	29. C	39. C E	49. B C E
10. C	20. B	30. A B C	40. B C E	50. A B D

Test Yourself

Stop! Before reading this chapter, test yourself to determine how much study time you will need to devote to this section.

1. Sally likes to run multiple applications simultaneously under Windows 95. She has one 32-bit application running, one MS-DOS application running, and two 16-bit applications running. How many virtual machines is Windows 95 running? Explain.

Answers

1. Two. Windows 95 has one virtual machine running for the Windows 95 program and for the 16-bit and 32-bit applications, and one virtual machine running for the MS-DOS applications. See "Windows 95 Virtual Memory" and "Architectural Evaluation."

C h a p t e r

2

Architecture and Memory

This chapter will help you prepare for the exam by covering the following objectives:

Test Objectives

> ▶ Compare and contrast the memory usage of a Microsoft MS-DOS–based application, a 16-bit Windows-based application, and a 32-bit Windows-based application operating in Windows 95

You might recall the old wives' tale that a bride should wear "something old, something new, something borrowed, something blue" to ensure a happy marriage. Windows 95 is similar to that bride's wedding apparel. It has features and capabilities of the older versions of both DOS and Windows. Windows 95 includes many great new features that were not present in previous versions of either DOS or Windows. Windows 95 borrows heavily from the 32-bit architecture of Windows NT. Finally, Windows 95 will not make you blue when you're trying to run most of your older DOS and 16-bit Windows applications.

This chapter gives you an overview of the architecture of Windows 95, and how Windows 95 manages memory. In this chapter, you will learn about the following:

- ▶ Windows 95 System Services
- ▶ Windows 95 virtual machines
- ▶ Windows 95 virtual memory
- ▶ Windows 95 task scheduling and multitasking
- ▶ Windows 95 internal messaging
- ▶ Application memory usage comparison

Understanding Ring 0 and Ring 3

Windows 95 uses an Intel 386 or better processor to support multiple privilege levels for executable code. Of the four levels, or "rings," in the Intel 386 protection model, Windows 95 uses Rings 0 and 3. These rings provide different levels of protection and privileges. The lower the ring number, the higher the levels of protection and privileges.

Figure 2.1 illustrates the layout of the ring architecture for Windows 95. Components of Windows 95 are divided between Ring 0 and Ring 3 code. Each ring offers a different level of system protection. The Ring 0 code is protected by the Intel processor architecture and consists of all the low-level operating System Services, such as the File Management subsystem and the Virtual Machine Manager subsystem. The Ring 3 code is protected from other running processes by protection services provided in the operating system. The Ring 3 code runs the System Virtual Machine and any Virtual DOS Machines.

Figure 2.1

The ring architecture of Intel 386 or better processors.

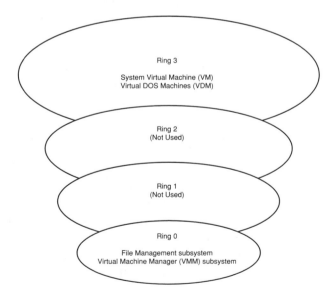

Ring 0 components are protected by the processor architecture. The processor prevents the component code from writing over another existing component's code. These Ring 0 components are the core elements of Windows 95. They can run all privileged operations, including direct communication with the hardware components. They have access to the entire computer system. A bad component in Ring 0 can bring down the computer system; therefore, every component running in Ring 0 needs to be extremely reliable. All of the low-level Windows 95 core components run in Ring 0.

Ring 3 components have no processor protection; the operating system must provide protection for Ring 3 components. Ring 3 components cannot write to the hardware components. They must communicate to a Ring 0 process to write to a hardware component. A bad application component in Ring 3 does not necessarily bring down the computer system. Usually you can recover from any problems associated with a Ring 3 component by simply closing that component. Applications and non-critical System Services of Windows 95 components run on Ring 3.

Windows 95 Components

Understanding how the various components of an operating system, such as Windows 95, fit together can be difficult. The *Windows 95 Resource Kit* and the New Riders book *Inside Windows 95* provide better reference material on this subject. This section provides some perspective on Windows 95 components.

Figure 2.2 contains a diagram of the Windows 95 components that run in both Ring 0 and Ring 3 of the Intel 386 protection model.

Ring 3 hosts the virtual machines (VMs) in which MS-DOS, Windows 16-bit, and Windows 32-bit applications execute. The MS-DOS applications all run in separate VMs, known as *Virtual DOS Machines* (VDMs). All Windows applications, whether Windows 16-bit or 32-bit, execute in the System VM. The System VM allows multiple concurrent applications to run. Whereas all Windows 32-bit applications are isolated in private address spaces, all the active Windows 16-bit applications share a single, common address space. These applications are managed by the Virtual Machine Manager (VMM) in Ring 0. As a result, the Windows 16-bit applications operate much as they do under Windows 3.1, where they are cooperatively multitasked. Windows 32-bit and MS-DOS applications are preemptively multitasked. (See Chapter 1, "Planning and Installation," for a discussion of cooperative and preemptive multitasking.) The central components of the Windows graphical environment also run as System Services. These include Kernel, GDI, and User. The next section looks at these System Services in greater detail.

Figure 2.2

Windows 95 system architecture.

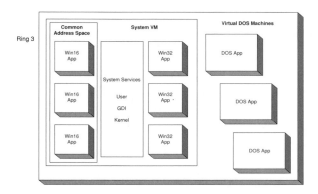

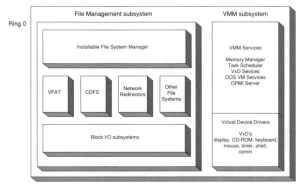

Ring 0 hosts both the VMM subsystem and the File Management subsystem. The VMM subsystem provides the resources needed for each application and system process running on the computer, including memory management and task scheduling. Virtual Device Drivers (VxDs) are 32-bit, protected-mode drivers that manage a system resource, such as a hardware device or installed software. They allow more than one application to use the resource at the same time. The File Management subsystem features an Installable File System Manager, which supports multiple file systems, such as VFAT, CDFS, and Network redirectors. The

Installable File System Manager also supports an open file system architecture, so future file systems can be added later. The Block I/O subsystems are responsible for the interaction with the physical storage devices.

Windows 95 System Services

Much of the code within Windows 95 is either new 32-bit code or older Windows 3.*x* code rewritten as 32-bit code, rather than 16-bit code. Windows 95, however, is not completely a 32-bit operating system. Windows 95 strikes a balance between three requirements: delivering compatibility with existing applications and drivers, decreasing the size of the operating system to run on 4 MB of RAM, and offering improved system performance. To provide this balance, Windows 95 uses a combination of both 32-bit and 16-bit code.

Windows 95 employs 32-bit code wherever 32-bit code significantly improves performance without sacrificing application compatibility. Existing 16-bit code is retained where it is required to maintain compatibility, or where 32-bit code would increase memory requirements without significantly improving performance. All of the I/O subsystems and device drivers in Windows 95, such as networking and file systems, are fully 32 bit. All memory management and scheduling components, such as Kernel and Virtual Memory Manager, are 32 bit as well. Figure 2.3 depicts the relative distribution of 32-bit code versus 16-bit code present in each of the Windows 95 System Services. The sizes of the boxes in the figure illustrate the number of lines of code for each 16-bit and 32-bit version of the three System Services files.

Three sets of files constitute the Windows 95 System Services: Kernel, Graphics Device Interface (GDI), and User:

▶ The Kernel (KRNL386.EXE and KERNEL32.DLL) provides base operating system functions, including file I/O services, virtual memory management, application management, and task scheduling.

▶ The GDI (GDI.EXE and GDI32.DLL) controls the graphics operations that create images on the system display and other devices, such as printers.

▶ The User (USER.EXE and USER32.DLL) creates and maintains windows on-screen and carries out all requests to create, move, size, or remove a window. The User also handles requests regarding the icons and other components of the user interface. It also directs input to the appropriate application from the keyboard, mouse, and other input sources.

Figure 2.3

Ring 3 System Services.

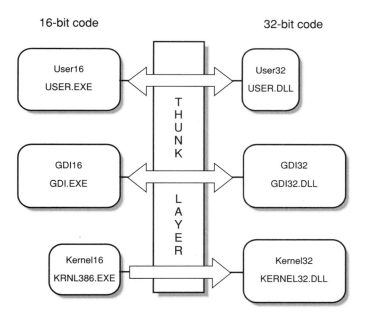

As illustrated, most of the System Services provided by the operating system Kernel are provided as 32-bit code. The remaining 16-bit code consists of hand-tuned assembly language, delivering performance that rivals the 32-bit code. Many functions provided by the GDI have been moved to 32-bit code, including the spooler and printing subsystem, the font rasterizer, and the drawing operations performed by the graphics DIB engine. Roughly half of all GDI calls are handled in the 32-bit code. The 16-bit code for GDI contains most of the drawing routines. Much of the window management User code still remains 16-bit to maintain Windows 16-bit application compatibility.

The *Thunk Layer*, shown in figure 2.3, makes reference to the term *thunking*. This special term describes how 16-bit code components communicate with their 32-bit code component counterparts. The thunking process translates memory addresses between 32-bit calls and 16-bit calls. A slight performance degradation occurs in the translation, although it is hardly noticeable.

In general, the 32-bit code is provided in Windows 95 to maximize the performance and reliability of the system. The 16-bit code balances the requirements for reducing the size of the operating system while maintaining compatibility with existing applications and drivers.

Windows 95 Virtual Machines

All applications and dynamic link library (DLL) programs run in Ring 3. They execute in a *virtual machine* (VM), which looks like a separate computer from the application's perspective. A VM is an environment created by Windows 95 to simulate a complete computer, with all the resources available to a physical computer, such as hard disk controllers and a timer. The VMM creates and maintains the virtual machine environments and provides each application the system resources needed to run the system.

The System VM runs the System Services as well as all Windows 32-bit and 16-bit applications. The 16-bit Windows applications all run in a shared, common address space. Each 32-bit Windows application runs in its own private address space. Each MS-DOS application runs in its own separate VDM. The Virtual Machine Manager, in addition to creating and maintaining these virtual machines, provides several key services:

> ▶ **Memory Management.** Controls the 4 GB of addressable virtual memory, paging from RAM to the hard disk, and performs memory address translation. This is discussed in the following section, "Windows 95 Virtual Memory."

> ▶ **Task Scheduling and Multitasking.** Allocates system resources and time to the applications and other processes running on the computer. These are discussed in the section

"Windows 95 Task Scheduling and Multitasking" later in this chapter.

▶ **MS-DOS Mode support.** For MS-DOS applications that need exclusive access to system resources. This special mode of Windows 95 operations should not be confused with the VDM. It is a separate and exclusive MS-DOS operating environment, and is discussed further in Chapter 8, "Running Applications."

Windows 95 Virtual Memory

Windows 95 uses two types of memory: physical and virtual. Most users are familiar with the amount of RAM, or physical memory, on the computer itself. As mentioned in Chapter 1, the minimum requirement for RAM on a computer running Windows 95 is 4 MB. The recommended amount of RAM is at least 8 MB. The author even suggests 16 MB of RAM for Windows 95. With Windows 95, the operating system uses all of the available physical memory on the computer. You can overcome hardware memory limitations through the use of virtual memory.

The Windows 95 operating system uses a *flat memory model*, which leverages off the Intel 386 or greater processor's capability to handle 32-bit addresses. This flat memory model provides a logical address space range of up to 4 GB. Although current computer hardware does not yet handle up to 4 GB of physical memory, some file servers can now run with up to 1 GB of RAM. Virtual memory bridges the gap between physical memory and logical memory.

The 4 GB of addressable space used as virtual memory under the flat memory model is implemented through the use of RAM and a swap file. The Windows 95 operating system performs memory management, called *demand paging*, whereby code and data are moved in 4-KB pages between physical memory and the temporary Windows 95 swap file on the hard drive. The Virtual Memory Manager controls paging and maintains a page table. The page table tells which pages are swapped to the hard drive, which remain in RAM, and to which system process or application they belong.

Application programs are allocated a virtual memory address space, which is the set of addresses available for use by that program. Both 32-bit Windows and MS-DOS–based programs are allocated private virtual memory address space. All 16-bit Windows-based programs share a single, common virtual memory address space. Figure 2.4 shows how Windows 95 allocates the 4 GB of virtual memory to each address space. Each process is allocated a unique virtual address space of 4 GB. The upper 2 GB is shared with the system, whereas the lower 2 GB is private to the application.

Figure 2.4

Virtual memory address space allocation.

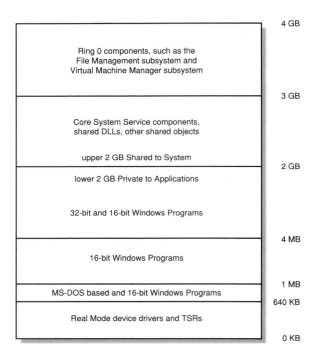

The virtual memory is allocated as follows:

▶ **0–640 KB.** If not used for a Virtual DOS Machine (VDM), this memory is made available for any real-mode device drivers and terminate-and-stay-resident (TSR) programs.

▶ **0–1 MB.** In a VDM, this memory is used to execute MS-DOS programs. If a shared, common, 16-bit Windows VM is used, then 16-bit Windows applications operate much as they do under Windows 3.1.

- ▶ **1–4 MB.** Normally this memory is unused. Windows 95 does not use this space, nor do Windows 32-bit applications. If this memory is needed by 16-bit Windows applications, it is available.

- ▶ **4 MB–2 GB.** This memory is used by 32-bit Windows applications and some 16-bit Windows applications. Each Windows 32-bit application has its own address space, whereas Windows 16-bit applications all share a common address space.

- ▶ **2–3 GB.** This memory is used to run all Core System Service components, shared DLLs, and other shared objects. Those components are available to all applications.

- ▶ **3–4 GB.** This memory is reserved for all Ring 0 components, such as the File Management subsystem and the VMM subsystem. Any VxDs are loaded in this address space.

Virtual memory and virtual addresses enable you to have more memory available to programs than actually exists on the computer in physical RAM. The Windows 95 swap file implementation is much improved over that from Windows 3.1.

With Windows 3.1, you can have either a temporary or permanent swap file. Windows 3.1 recommends how much hard disk memory to allocate to the swap file. If the hard-disk controller is compatible with 32-bit disk access, running 32-bit disk access will improve performance. A temporary swap file that does not need to be on contiguous hard disk space is created when Windows 3.1 starts. This same temporary swap file is released when the user exits Windows. Although a permanent, contiguous swap file provides better performance than a temporary swap file, because it is a static file, hard disk space is not freed up when the user exits Windows.

In Windows 95, the swap file configuration is much easier. The best features of temporary and permanent swap files are combined through improved virtual memory algorithms and 32-bit access methods. By default, Windows 95 uses a dynamic swap file, which shrinks and grows based on the needs of the operating system and the available hard disk space. A permanent swap file has little benefit in Windows 95.

The best way to ensure swap file performance is to put the swap file on a hard disk that has ample free space so the swap file can shrink or grow as required. If you have multiple hard drives, select the one with the fastest access time as well as the most free space.

Windows 95 Task Scheduling and Multitasking

Windows 95 uses a task scheduler to determine the order and priority of processes running on the computer. These processes run as threads. A *thread* is a unit of executable code. Each thread has a base priority, which is the priority the thread normally wants to run.

MS-DOS applications and 16-bit Windows applications usually have a single thread. Newer 32-bit Windows applications can take advantage of running multiple threads to improve performance. Some tasks within the 32-bit Windows application can be spun off as separate threads that run concurrently.

Windows 95, like Windows NT, uses priority levels to help schedule processes. There are 32 priority levels, ranging from the lowest priority level of 0 to the highest of 31. A thread may have its base priority altered by as much as two levels higher or lower than the original priority level. Applications have low priority; critical system tasks (such as I/O) have high priority.

Figure 2.5 illustrates how the two parts of the scheduler process, the primary and secondary scheduler, work. The primary scheduler evaluates all thread priorities and gives the thread with the highest priority a time slice of execution time. If two or more threads have the same priority, they're stacked. Each stacked thread is granted a time slice of execution in sequence until no threads have the same priority. The actual length of a time slice depends on the configuration of the computer.

Figure 2.5

*Scheduling
threads to run.*

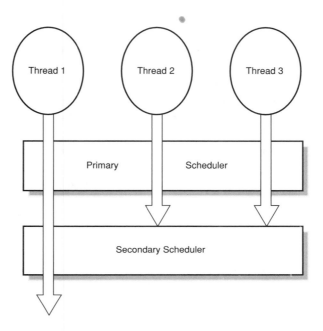

The secondary scheduler can boost the priority of non-executing threads. This priority boost helps prevent threads that have a lower base priority from being blocked from receiving execution time. The secondary scheduler also adjusts the priority of threads over time to smooth the execution of programs. Windows 95 adjusts threads as follows:

▶ Threads waiting for user input (in the foreground) get a priority boost, making the system more responsive.

▶ Threads completing a voluntary wait get a priority boost.

▶ All threads periodically receive a priority boost to prevent them from locking shared resources needed by higher priority threads.

▶ Compute-bound threads get a priority decrease, so that I/O operations are not blocked.

The task scheduler is the Windows 95 component responsible for providing system resources to the applications and other processes. It also schedules processes in a way that enables multiple applications to run concurrently. This method of concurrent process scheduling is called *multitasking*. Windows 95 uses cooperative multitasking as well as preemptive multitasking.

With Windows 3.1, applications run concurrently using cooperative multitasking. Cooperative multitasking requires the application to periodically check the message queue and cooperatively release control of the system to other applications that are running. Applications that do not check the message queue regularly can "hog" CPU cycles and prevent other applications from running. For backwards compatibility, Windows 95 cooperatively multitasks Windows 16-bit applications.

For Windows 32-bit applications, Windows 95 uses preemptive multitasking, which allows the operating system to take control of the processes running at any time. Preemptive multitasking is a more efficient means of multitasking. The task scheduler decides which processes acquire control of the system, preemptively allocating system resources. The priority of the process itself is used to help the scheduler allocate enough execution time for each process.

Windows 95 Internal Messaging

Windows applications use a *message-passing* model to help control programs. An event (such as a keyboard entry, mouse movement or click, the receipt of data by a hardware buffer, and so on) generates an interrupt. Events are converted by the interrupt handler into messages. Windows applications generate messages to request the operating system to perform a function or to pass data to another Windows application.

One bottleneck for Windows 3.1 is that it uses only a single message queue for all applications. If only one application fails to retrieve its messages, the system becomes unstable and hangs because the other applications are blocked from retrieving their messages. As a result, the computer locks up and you must reboot your system.

This bottleneck does not exist in Windows 95. Although a single message queue exists for all Windows 16-bit applications for backwards compatibility (that is, for applications designed for previous versions of Windows), each Windows 32-bit application thread has its own private message queue. Figure 2.6 illustrates this new internal messaging structure. The Windows 95 operating system takes messages from the raw input queue and passes them to the appropriate Windows 32-bit application thread or, if the message is for a Windows 16-bit application, to the Windows 16-bit subsystem. Therefore, if one of these processes or applications hangs and no longer receives its incoming messages, the other processes are unaffected.

Figure 2.6

Windows 95 message-passing queue structure.

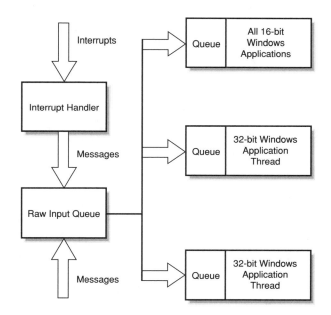

For study purposes, remember the following:

▶ Windows 32-bit applications have a message queue for each thread.

▶ Windows 16-bit applications share a common message queue. If a Windows 16-bit application fails, messages are blocked for all running Windows 16-bit applications until the failed program is cleared.

▶ MS-DOS applications do not use the message-passing design nor do they have a message queue.

Because WIN16 applications share a common memory address space and a common message queue, if a WIN16 process hangs while in the foreground, all other WIN16 processes cease to receive messages from the operating system and appear hung. This is due to a flag that is set for WIN16 processes, known as the *WIN16 mutex* (Mutually Exclusive). Because 16-bit code is considered non-reentrant (it cannot be used by more than one process at a time), a system must be in place to ensure that no two processes attempt to use the same piece of 16-bit code simultaneously. Under Windows 95, this is done by enforcing the rule that only the process that currently owns the rights to the WIN16 mutex is able to make requests to 16-bit API functions. When the given process is finished using the 16-bit code, it hands the mutex to the next process.

You learn more about the mutex in Chapter 8, "Running Applications."

Architectural Evaluation

This topic area has only one exam objective. To properly address the objective, however, you need a clear understanding of the Windows 95 system architecture.

Table 2.1 compares and contrasts the memory usage of a Microsoft MS-DOS–based application, a 16-bit Windows-based application, and a 32-bit Windows-based application operating in Windows 95.

Table 2.1

Comparing Memory Usage

Application	Memory Usage
MS-DOS	Each runs in a private Virtual DOS Machine. No message queue. Loaded in the lower 1 MB of virtual memory.
Windows 16-bit	All run in a common address space and share a single message queue. Loaded in the lower 2 GB of virtual memory.
Windows 32-bit	Each runs in a private address space, and each thread has its own message queue. Loaded in the 4 MB to 2 GB range of virtual memory.

To see how Windows 95 runs applications, see Chapter 8. You also might want to perform Exercise 2.1 to see how different applications affect the number of virtual machines that execute under Windows 95.

Exercises

Exercise 2.1:   Counting Virtual Machines

To illustrate the point about how Windows 95 manages virtual machines, follow Exercise 2.1 to count the number of virtual machines running on your Windows 95 computer.

1. From your computer, start Windows 95.

2. If you installed Windows 95 on your computer with the Typical Setup option, the System Monitor program might not be installed, because it is an optional component.

   To determine whether the System Monitor utility program is installed, from the Start menu, choose Programs, Accessories, System Tools, and then System Monitor. If System Monitor is not available, you must add it to your computer by following these steps:

   a. From the Start menu, choose Settings, Control Panel. From the Control Panel program group, choose the Add/Remove Programs icon.

   b. Click on the Windows Setup tab, double-click on Accessories, and add a check mark to the System Monitor check box. Press Enter or choose OK. Press Enter or choose OK again to install the System Monitor.

3. From the Start menu, choose Programs, Accessories, System Tools, System Monitor. The System Monitor utility program displays key system information in either a Line Chart, Bar Chart, or Numeric Chart format.

4. Any items previously selected are displayed when the System Monitor utility program starts. When you run the System Monitor utility program for the first time, the Kernel Processor Usage (%) appears in a Line Chart.

5. You must remove all current items to run this exercise. Highlight any items you want to remove, and then from the Edit menu, choose Remove Item.

6. Choose Edit, Add Item to open the Add Item dialog box. From the Category list, click on Kernel to display the list of Kernel items.

7. Choose Virtual Machines from the Item list. If you need an explanation of each item, choose Explain to see that this shows the number of virtual machines present in the system. Press Enter or choose OK to add the item Virtual Machines as a selection.

8. Choose View, Numeric Charts to obtain the number of virtual machines that currently are active. Normally this value is 1, because the Windows 95 computer has just been started. It could be higher.

9. Open some Windows program applications or the Windows Explorer. Has the number of virtual machines changed? The number of active virtual machines should not change when Windows programs are started.

10. Start an MS-DOS command prompt by choosing Start, Run to open the Run dialog box, or choose Start, Programs, then MS-DOS Prompt. Has the number of virtual machines changed? It should change, because each MS-DOS application will start another virtual machine.

11. Start another MS-DOS command prompt, and then a third. What happens to the count of virtual machines after you start each new MS-DOS command prompt? Each time another MS-DOS command prompt is started, the number of virtual machines should increase by a count of 1. If the initial count was 1, then starting three MS-DOS command prompts increases the number to 4.

12. Close all three MS-DOS command prompts. How many virtual machines are currently active? The count of virtual machines should be back down to 1, or the starting number in step 8.

Based on what you know about virtual machines, explain why the count changes during the exercise.

continues

Exercise 2.1: Continued

All of the Windows 16-bit and 32-bit applications run in a single system virtual machine. But each MS-DOS application runs in its own Virtual DOS Machine. Opening a new MS-DOS command prompt causes the virtual machine count to increase by one.

13. When you finish viewing the System Monitor utility information, close the System Monitor.

Review Questions

The following questions will test your knowledge of the information in this chapter. For additional questions, see MCP Endeavor and the Microsoft Roadmap/Assessment Exam on the CD-ROM that accompanies this book.

1. The ring architecture of Intel 386 processes provide different levels of protection and privileges. Windows 95 executes in which two of the following rings of the Intel 386 protection model? Select the two best answers:

    A. Ring 0

    B. Ring 1

    C. Ring 2

    D. Ring 3

    E. Ring 4

2. Windows 95 is an advanced operating system that takes advantage of the Intel ring architecture. To understand how Windows 95 uses the ring architecture, you need to understand the rings themselves. Which one of the following rings of the Intel 386 protection model offers the most privileges, including direct communication with the hardware components?

    A. Ring 0

    B. Ring 1

    C. Ring 2

    D. Ring 3

    E. Ring 4

3. You are asked to present an overview of the Windows 95 system architecture, including rings. You draw a diagram that points out each ring and its protection level. Which of the following rings of the Intel 386 protection model offers no processor protection, but instead needs the operating system to provide processor protection?

A. Ring 0

B. Ring 1

C. Ring 2

D. Ring 3

E. Ring 4

4. On the diagram you create for the presentation in Question 3, you need to point out where applications run. In which of the following rings of the Intel 386 protection model do the MS-DOS, Windows 16-bit, and Windows 32-bit applications run?

A. Ring 0

B. Ring 1

C. Ring 2

D. Ring 3

E. Ring 4

5. Within its System Services, Windows 95 uses a combination of 32-bit and 16-bit code to run applications. In which of the following rings of the Intel 386 protection model do the System Services run?

A. Ring 0

B. Ring 1

C. Ring 2

D. Ring 3

E. Ring 4

6. Windows 95 runs applications in Virtual Machine. The Virtual Machine Manager is used to manage these applications. In which of the following rings of the Intel 386 protection model does the Virtual Machine Manager run?

A. Ring 0

B. Ring 1

C. Ring 2

D. Ring 3

E. Ring 4

7. Which of the following components make up System Services? Select the three best answers:

A. User

B. Thunk

C. GDI

D. GUI

E. Kernel

8. John runs several applications at once on his Windows 95 computer. Which of the following applications do not run in separate, private, virtual machines?

A. Windows 32-bit

B. Windows 16-bit

C. MS-DOS

D. All of the above

E. None of the above

9. The Virtual Machine Manager provides several services, including memory management, task scheduling, and DOS mode support. Every time you open an MS-DOS application, the count of the number of virtual machines running under Windows 95 _____.

A. decreases by two

B. decreases by one

C. stays the same

D. increases by one

E. increases by two

10. Windows 95 uses two types of memory: physical and virtual. Virtual memory is comprised of which two of the following components? Select the two best answers:

   A. ROM

   B. RAM

   C. VMM

   D. A swap file

   E. A page table

11. For what is the 16-bit Windows mutex used?

   A. It protects a non-reentrant area of code from being preempted by a 16-bit process at potentially disastrous points.

   B. It provides a layer between the virtual memory space and between MS-DOS and 16-bit applications.

   C. It provides system resources for the applications and other processes.

   D. It hosts the virtual machines in which MS-DOS, Windows 16-bit, and Windows 32-bit applications run.

Review Answers

1. A D	6. A	11. A
2. A	7. A C E	
3. D	8. B	
4. D	9. D	
5. D	10. B D	

Test Yourself

Stop! Before reading this chapter, test yourself to determine how much study time you will need to devote to this section.

1. Wendy migrated from Windows 3.1 to Windows 95. To open documents in Word for Windows, Wendy used to double-click on the document file in Windows' 3.1 File Manager. Name three ways, besides using Word for Windows, that Wendy can launch her document in Windows 95.

2. John is upgrading to Windows 95 on a computer that currently has MS-DOS 6.11 and Windows 3.1. After he installs Windows 95, he wants to be able to boot into either Windows 95 or Windows 3.1. Can he do this? If so, what must he do to enable this to happen?

3. Name the three major components a computer system needs to be specified as Plug and Play–compatible under Windows 95.

4. Although Plug and Play promises to aid users in setting up and configuring hardware devices, you can still encounter problems setting up devices. Name the Windows 95 system utility you can use to help set up devices and see which IRQs, I/O port addresses, and DMA channels are assigned to which devices.

5. Bill runs an application under Windows 95 that he wants to display so that the application window covers the entire screen. What are the steps he can take to hide the Windows 95 Taskbar from view?

6. Roger's Windows 95 Desktop includes a shortcut to a file he wants to delete from his computer. He selects the shortcut and deletes the shortcut. Does the file associated with the shortcut delete as well? If not, explain why it doesn't.

7. Brenda has three items she wants to add to the Windows 95 Start menu. What is the quickest way to do this if she has the Windows Explorer open?

8. When Kathy upgrades to Windows 95 and installs a shareware program called PICTURE.EXE, an icon for the program is not placed on the Start menu's Program folder. How can Kathy locate the PICTURE.EXE application using the Find option on the Start menu?

9. After you install Windows 95, you see a number of different icons and objects displayed on the Desktop. Name at least five common icons and objects that display on the Desktop after you install Windows 95.

10. A common task that Jackie performs under Windows 95 is creating a text file using Notepad and then printing the text to a printer. Describe the steps Jackie must perform to complete this task.

11. What is the command you use to launch the Windows Explorer from the command line and open a new Windows Explorer double-pane view?

12. Sharon uses the Network Neighborhood to access network resources. She wants to view the Network Properties sheet to see which workgroup name is displayed. How can she do this from the Desktop using the Network Neighborhood icon?

13. In Windows 95, you need to configure the properties sheet for a shared folder named DOCUMENTS. After you display the properties sheet for that folder, what are three attributes you can set on the General tab, and what is the name of the option you specify on the Sharing tab to enable sharing?

14. Windows 95 uses the Registry to store configuration information. It does this by organizing the information in a tree-like, _____ database structure. (Fill in the blank with the correct word.)

15. Amber uses Windows 95 and wants to know more about the Registry. She asks you which files comprise the Registry and you tell her what? Name at least two of the three files.

16. As a help desk operator in your company, you advise users to use the Device Manager and applications in the Control Panel to make changes to the Windows 95 Registry. However, if a user must modify the Registry directly, you tell him to use which application?

17. Tim is advised to add a new entry to the HKEY_LOCAL_MACHINE\System\CurrentControlSet\control\FileSystem subkey. What application does he use to locate this subkey, and which menu option does he use to add the new entry?

18. OLE information is stored in the Registry. Name the Registry subkey that stores OLE information.

Answers

1. Double-click on a document file in Windows Explorer; double-click on a document file in My Computer; and double-click on a shortcut to the document file. See, "Identify and Explain the Differences Between the Windows 3.1 and Windows 95 Interfaces."

2. Yes, as long as he installs Windows 95 in a different directory from the one that contains Windows 3.1. See "Setting Up a Dual-Boot System."

3. Devices must be able to identify themselves and declare their resource requirements; a Plug and Play BIOS that accepts and responds to resource requirements communicated from Plug and Play devices; and a Plug and Play operating system. See "Installing New Hardware Devices."

4. Device Manager. See "Limitations for Full Plug and Play" and "Installing New Hardware Devices."

5. Right-click on the Taskbar and select Properties. On the Taskbar Properties sheet, choose the Auto Hide option. Click on OK. See "Configuring the Taskbar."

6. No, because the shortcut represents a link to the original file, not the original file itself. See "Configuring Shortcuts."

7. Select the three items in Explorer, click and hold down the left mouse button, and drag and drop the items on the Start menu. See "Adding Items to the Start Menu."

8. Click on the Find option and select Files or Folders from the submenu. In the Named field on the File: All Files dialog box, enter **PICTURE.EXE** and click on Find Now. See "Using the Windows 95 User Interface."

9. Possible answers include: My Computer, Network Neighborhood, Inbox, Recycle Bin, My Briefcase, Microsoft Network, the Taskbar, and the Start menu. See "Customizing the Desktop."

10. Right-click on the Desktop and select Text Document from the context-sensitive menu. Enter a file name for the document. Double-click on the new text document icon to display Notepad. Use Notepad's features to create the new document and to save the file. Choose File, Print to print the document. See "Using the Windows 95 Interface to Create, Print, and Store a File."

11. Enter **explorer /e** in the Run dialog box. See "Windows Explorer Command-Line Switches."

12. Right-click on the Network Neighborhood icon and choose Properties. See "Accessing the Network Through Network Neighborhood."

13. Read-only, Archive, and Hidden. Shared As. See "Configure the Properties Sheet for an Object."

14. Hierarchical. See "Using the Registry."

15. Possible answers include: SYSTEM.DAT, USER.DAT, and CONFIG.POL. See "Determining Where the Registry Is Stored."

16. The Registry Editor. See "Deciding When It Is Appropriate to Modify the Registry."

17. The Registry Editor. Choose Edit, New, Key. See "Modifying the Contents of the Registry."

18. HKEY_LOCAL_MACHINE\SOFTWARE\Classes. See "When OLE Information in the Registry Becomes Corrupted."

Chapter

3

Customizing and
Configuring Windows 95

This chapter will help you prepare for the exam by covering the following objectives:

Test Objectives

- ▶ Identify and explain the differences between the Windows 3.1 interface and the Windows 95 interface

- ▶ Set up a dual-boot system for Windows 95

- ▶ Install new hardware devices on various systems that support Plug and Play

- ▶ Given a specific bus configuration, identify areas of limitation for full Plug and Play

- ▶ Configure the Taskbar

- ▶ Configure shortcuts

- ▶ Add items to the Start menu

- ▶ Choose an appropriate method to accomplish a specified task using the user interface

- ▶ Customize the Desktop for a specified set of criteria

- ▶ Use the Windows 95 interface to create, print, and store a file

- ▶ Configure and use Windows Explorer

- ▶ Access the network through Network Neighborhood

- ▶ Configure the properties sheet for an object

- ▶ Define the purpose of the Windows 95 Registry

- ▶ Classify types of information in the Registry. Determine where the Registry is stored

- ▶ Identify situations in which it is appropriate to modify the Registry

- ▶ Modify the contents of the Registry

- ▶ Choose the appropriate course of action when OLE information in the Registry becomes corrupted

Making Windows 95 work the way you want it to work involves knowing how to customize and configure Windows 95. This requires you to be very knowledgeable about how the Windows 95 user interface can be adjusted to suit your style, improved to offer better ease of use, and protected against configuration errors. Experience in making these type of changes is the best teacher. This chapter is your guide to understanding how to customize and configure Windows 95. In this chapter, you will learn how to do the following:

- ▶ Configure dual-boot computers

- ▶ Configure the Taskbar

- ▶ Configure shortcuts

- ▶ Customize the Windows 95 Desktop

- ▶ Get your work done using Windows 95

- ▶ Configure and use the Windows Explorer

- ▶ Understand what makes up the Windows 95 Registry

- ▶ Fix errors in the Windows 95 Registry

For many Windows 3.x users, Windows 95 represents a big change. The new Windows 95 graphical user interface (GUI) has significantly changed over the user interface within the Windows 3.x or Windows NT 3.x versions. Windows 95 also features improvements in ease of use, performance, compatibility, and built-in support for networking and communications. These same improvements have contributed to making Windows 95 the new choice as the standard desktop operating system for upgrading either Windows 3.*x* or Windows for Workgroups 3.*x* running on top of MS-DOS.

This chapter looks at ways to customize and configure Windows 95 to work the way you want it to work. You should expect a lot of questions on the test in this topic area. To help you better understand how to make Windows 95 work for you, most of the exam objectives covered in this chapter contain hands-on exercises.

Making Windows 95 Work for You

The Windows 95 Project Team worked hard to ensure that Windows 95 was easy to use for both novices and experienced users. Novice users are people who have never used a computer before, or who have used one infrequently. Novices have trouble navigating the user interface and need more information or coaching, so an online help system is provided. Experienced users make more use of the operating system than novice users, and they want it to easily allow them to configure and customize the computer to meet their requirements. The goal for Windows 95 is to make it easy to work the way you want to work.

The Windows 95 user interface design centers around answering one basic question: how can the user interface in Windows 3.1 be improved? Through usability tests, focus groups, educator feedback, and a suggestion database, the Windows 95 Project Team gathered input. The end result was an operating system with a user interface that incorporates the following:

▶ **Ease of use.** Most of the common and essential features of Windows 95, such as launching an application, task switching, and finding a file, are easily discoverable through the Taskbar, with its Start menu and push-button task switching.

▶ **Speed and power.** Windows 95 promotes efficiency, control, and easy customization via the use of shortcuts, secondary mouse clicks, properties sheets, and the new Windows Explorer.

▶ **Compatibility.** The user interface has features and online help files that make Windows 95 easy to learn, especially for those already familiar with previous versions of Windows 3.*x.*

Windows 95 employs an object model as a mechanism to define and use hardware devices, programs, and other resources. Although Windows 95 is not a true object-oriented operating system, users have a better grasp of how Windows 95 works if everything is represented as an object.

Working with Windows 95 Objects

An object has a form (icon) and attributes (properties) that the user can easily understand. In general, objects can be opened or explored by clicking on an icon, and objects have properties that can be viewed. These properties define what the object can do, or what can be done to the object. Object behavior is consistent— once you know how to work with one object, other similar objects work the same way.

The properties of an object, its settings and parameters, are found on the object's properties sheet. These properties can be changed or adjusted as required. The properties sheet provides a consistent and convenient way to view an object's properties. To view the properties sheet for an object, highlight the object with a single click of the right mouse button. A context-sensitive menu appears, from which you select Properties. Again, the specific properties shown on an object's properties sheet depend on the type of object itself.

An optional mouse or similar pointing device becomes almost a requirement to use the Windows 95 user interface effectively. Which button becomes the left mouse button and which becomes the right mouse button depends on how you have configured the mouse. If you are right-handed, the left mouse button is usually the left mouse button, making the right mouse button the right mouse button. If you are left-handed, you want to configure the mouse buttons in the opposite way.

continues

To configure the Windows 95 mouse buttons, use the Mouse icon in the Control Panel. Be sure to remember the differences in primary versus secondary mouse button assignments when preparing for the exam. For right-handed users, the primary button is usually the left mouse button and the secondary button is the right mouse button. For left-handed users (who have changed the left and right mouse assignments), the right mouse button is the primary button and the left mouse button is the secondary button.

Improving the Windows 95 User Interface

In trying to make Windows 95 a more intuitive operating system, the Windows 95 Project Team put extra effort into several user interface design areas that seemed to cause Windows 3.x users the most problems. These areas include the following:

▶ **Windows management.** The Desktop was confusing. Open windows overlapped each other, or were minimized out of sight on the Desktop. Some users would open numerous windows and then become overwhelmed or lose track of running programs. Windows 95 provides the Taskbar, which enables quick access to all active programs by maintaining a title button for each open program on the Taskbar itself.

▶ **Hierarchical views.** File Manager hierarchies of storage were confusing. The concept of storing one object in another, in yet another, caused users problems in knowing where to look to find their favorite programs or utilities. Files were lost in the catacombs of subdirectories. Information in Windows 95 is stored in folders (directories) and files. The Windows 95 Explorer lets users view a hard disk in a consistent manner, whether the local hard drive or a mapped network drive.

▶ **Double-clicking.** The action of double-clicking to launch an application was not discoverable. Single-clicking would not always open programs nor produce the desired results within the confines of an active window. Most actions in Windows 95 now can be accomplished with a single click. Double-clicking still exists, but it is used to start or open from a shortcut, plus a few odd backward-compatible events, such as closing a window using the icon in the upper-right corner.

▶ **Task switching.** The way to switch from one active task to another was not discoverable. Many users never ran multiple applications because they did not know how to task switch. The Windows 95 Taskbar now makes it easy to switch between open programs or start new ones.

▶ **Overlapping functionality.** There was too much overlap among the Windows middle-management functions of Program Manager, File Manager, Print Manager, Windows Setup, and Control Panel under Windows 3.*x*. This is streamlined in Windows 95.

▶ **Short 8.3 file names restrictive.** The MS-DOS 8.3 file and directory naming limitation often led to cryptic and easily forgettable names. Windows 95 supports the use of Long File Names (LFNs) that can be up to 255 characters long. The length of a file name might be less, because the maximum length for both the path and file name cannot exceed 258 characters. The longer the path, the shorter the file name allowed.

▶ **User interface not customizable.** This limitation created an active market for third-party software companies to improve the look and feel of and capability to customize the Windows 3.*x* Desktop. The Windows 95 Desktop is neat, clean, and logical. Users start with a default Desktop, but are not restricted in how to customize their Windows 95 Desktop.

▶ **Network and connectivity integration.** This integration was poor under Windows 3.*x*, depending on which network operating system was in use. Windows 95 has been called the perfect network client because of its great network integration features. Remote access also is built-in to the Windows 95 operating system.

Configuring and Customizing Windows 95

Windows 95 is extremely easy to customize and configure. This is great for the end-user; however, this same strength can cause serious headaches for support staff, who need to respond to any end-user problems. The following are three basic rules for the customization and configuration of Windows 95:

▶ Use properties sheets to configure objects. From the context-sensitive menu for an object, select Properties.

▶ If you need help, ask for it. From the Start menu, choose Help. Always install the full Online Help file, and add the *Windows 95 Resource Kit* Help file for good measure.

▶ Never play with the Windows 95 Registry. It's like running through the house with open scissors—very dangerous. Use Control Panel functions to safely change the Windows 95 Registry values.

> Two excellent books for your Windows 95 bookshelf are the Que book, *Windows 95 Installation and Configuration Handbook*, and New Riders' *Inside Windows 95*.

One of the first impressions you will form about Windows 95 is that it is significantly different than Windows 3.*x* in both look and behavior. When Windows 95 first installs, the default Windows 95 Desktop is presented. The Windows 95 Desktop is the most significant change as well as the most significant advancement. The Windows 95 Desktop can be used to launch applications, store files and folders, maintain shortcuts to files or programs, and provide easy access to your Windows 95 configuration settings.

No two computer systems are entirely the same. Each is unique. Each has its own setup and configuration. Even if two computers are the same make and model, they may start out alike, but that rapidly changes as hardware and software changes are made to the computers. Windows 95 must be both flexible enough to handle these differences and still be simple enough to configure. You can configure Windows 95 to suit your own needs. This tweaking (making minor adjustments) to the standard Windows 95 setup is needed often.

Windows 95 can be easily configured to make it your own in terms of how it operates, shortcuts, and the settings and attributes of objects. The following sections cover the key differences between Windows 3.*x* and Windows 95, installing Plug and Play hardware devices, and configuring the various components of the Windows 95 user interface. How to configure a printer is covered in Chapter 7, "Managing Printers."

Windows 95 also can be easily customized to make it your own in terms of ease of use, flexibility, and Desktop appearance. This section also covers setting up a dual-boot system, the fundamentals of Plug and Play, adding items to the Start menu, and customizing your Windows 95 Desktop. Both configuring and customizing Windows 95 are important topics you need to understand to pass the "Implementing and Supporting Microsoft Windows 95" exam.

Identify and Explain the Differences Between the Windows 3.1 and Windows 95 Interfaces

 What are the differences between the Windows 3.*x* interface and the Windows 95 interface? If you think about the interface of Windows 3.*x* and then try to draw comparisons to the interface of Windows 95, you are well on the way to understanding this exam objective—there is no single correct answer. Many of the key concepts found in the interface for Windows 95 have historical connections to the previous versions of Windows, like Windows for Workgroups 3.*x* and Windows NT. Table 3.1 compares the two interfaces to highlight the key differences.

Table 3.1

Interface Differences Between Windows 3.x and Windows 95	
Windows 3.x	Windows 95
Program Manager	Explorer runs the Desktop, and the Start menu launches programs. Program Manager (PROGMAN. EXE) is still included as an optional interface at installation time.
Program Groups (grp); no nested groups allowed.	Converted into Start menu folders; nested folders allowed.
Minimized programs show as the icons on the Desktop, or might be hidden behind open windows.	All active programs appear on the Taskbar, which itself can be hidden at the edge of the screen using the Auto Hide feature. Some active programs might be hidden.
Close programs through the menu or by double-clicking on the command bar on the upper-left side of the screen.	Close programs through the menu, by double-clicking on the program icon, or by clicking on the Close button on the upper-right side of the screen.
Maximize, Minimize buttons; up and down arrow heads.	Maximize, Minimize buttons; full windows and Taskbar line.
Icons in Program Manager	Shortcuts
File Manager	Explorer and My Computer programs; File Manager (WINFILE. EXE) is still included, if needed.
Directories, subdirectories	Folders
File extensions shown	Known file extensions not shown. Use the View menu options on the View tab to see all file extensions.
Short 8.3 file names	Long File Names, up to 255 characters; maximum 258 characters for both path and file name.
Connect network drives through File Manager	Use Network Neighborhood to see available network resources, or Explorer to connect network drives.

Windows 3.*x*	Windows 95
DOS delete/undelete	Recycle Bin
Control Panel	Control Panel folder opened by choosing Start, Settings, Control Panel; or opened from My Computer folder.
Print Manager	Printer Folder and Printer Wizard, opened by choosing Start, Settings, Printers; or opened from My Computer folder.
Task list (CTRL-ESC)	Taskbar; Task Manager (TASKMAN.EXE) is still included, if needed.
Clock must be started.	Clock part of Notification Area. Can turn off display of clock from the Taskbar Properties sheet.
MS-DOS Prompt	Start menu, Programs, MS-DOS Prompt; or Run command program.
Run command in File Manager	Start menu, Run command

You can find other sources of information about the differences between Windows 3.*x* and Windows 95 in the Windows 95 Help File Contents, "If you've used Windows before" section. Also, in the small manual that comes with the Windows 95 operating system, called *Introducing Windows 95*, look in the Welcome section, "If you've used Windows before."

Setting Up a Dual-Boot System

 Many users are hesitant to jump into Windows 95 without a safety net that permits them to continue to get work done using their previous operating system while they adjust to the new operating system. Larger corporate sites will experience a long transition to either Windows 95 or Windows NT Workstation and might need to operate in multiple, mixed environments. One way to accomplish both these objectives is to enable dual-booting.

Dual-booting is a generic term for having multiple operating systems on the computer at the same time and using a menu-system front-end to select the operating systems with which to boot the computer.

It is possible to operate Windows 95 in a dual-boot mode. Table 3.2 outlines useful information about installing Windows 95 as an upgrade to other pre-existing operating systems, and which of the operating systems combinations can support dual-boot with Windows 95.

Table 3.2

Installing Windows 95 with Pre-Existing Operating Systems

Operating System	Upgrade to Windows 95?	Dual-boot?
MS-DOS 3.2 versions or greater	Yes, if Windows 3.1x or Windows for Workgroups 3.x is on the computer, it is recommended to install from within Windows.	Yes (with MS-DOS 5.x or 6.x)
Novell (DR) DOS	Yes	No
PC-DOS versions	Yes	Yes (with PC-DOS versions 5.x or 6.x)
Windows 3.0	Yes, must install from MS-DOS	Yes, by installing to a different directory with version 5.x or 6.x of MS-DOS or PC-DOS.
Windows 3.1x	Yes	Yes, by installing to a different directory with version 5.x or 6.x of MS-DOS or PC-DOS.
Windows for Workgroups 3.x	Yes	Yes, by installing to a different directory with version 5.x or 6.x of MS-DOS or PC-DOS.

Operating System	Upgrade to Windows 95?	Dual-boot?
Windows NT	No	Yes, with MS-DOS already installed. Must install Windows 95 to a different directory, with a FAT partition.
OS/2 2.*x*	Yes, install from MS-DOS	Yes, with MS-DOS already or greater installed. Must install Windows 95 to a different directory, with a FAT partition.

Upgrading to Windows 95 over Existing Operating Systems

You can install Windows 95 as the only operating system on the computer, which represents a clean install. More likely, however, you will install Windows 95 as an upgrade. As discussed in Chapter 1, "Planning and Installation," Windows 95 is primarily designed to be an upgrade to either Windows 3.1*x* or Windows for Workgroups 3.*x* in combination with MS-DOS. Windows 95 can be installed over other operating systems (refer to table 3.2). This section explains your upgrade options.

You can install Windows 95 over most versions of DOS, which might have an existing Windows 3.*x* or Windows for Workgroups 3.*x* installation. During installation, the Windows 95 Setup program detects whether Windows 3.1*x* or Windows for Workgroups 3.*x* is already installed on the computer. If found, the Windows 95 Setup program offers to install Windows 95 into the same directory to upgrade the existing Windows installation.

Installing into the Existing Windows Directory

If you choose to install into the existing Windows directory, the Windows 95 Setup program uses any existing configuration settings to configure Windows 95. This includes configuration settings in SYSTEM.INI, WIN.INI, and PROTOCOL.INI, plus file associations from the Windows 3.*x* Registry. These configuration settings are moved into the Windows 95 Registry so applications and networking settings automatically work in Windows 95. Windows 3.x Program Manager groups are also converted into folders in the Programs folder (directory), which enables them to be displayed from the Windows 95 Start menu, under Programs.

The Windows 95 Setup program deletes some of the old DOS files, replaces the compression programs such as DBLSPACE or DRVSPACE with Windows 95 versions, and renames the boot files. For the best detailed reference on these changes to both DOS and Windows, see Chapter 6, "Setup Technical Discussion," of the *Windows 95 Resource Kit*. Please note that some of the old DOS files are deleted only if you install Windows 95 into the existing Windows directory.

Installing into a New Windows 95 Directory

If you choose to install Windows 95 into a new directory, or to not upgrade an existing Windows installation, you can dual-boot to your previous version of DOS and Windows if you are running version 5.x or 6.x of either MS-DOS or PC-DOS. The Windows 95 MSDOS.SYS file is automatically updated to include the entry BootMulti=1, which enables dual-boot capabilities with your previous version of DOS.

Windows NT cannot be upgraded to Windows 95; you must install Windows 95 to a new directory. The Windows NT computer must already be configured to dual-boot between Windows NT and MS-DOS before you install Windows 95. The Windows NT installation documentation outlines the details of how to configure the dual-boot between Windows NT and MS-DOS. Windows 95 needs to be installed from an MS-DOS prompt, so start the Windows NT computer using MS-DOS, then run the Windows 95 Setup program.

Depending on how Windows NT was initially installed, if you try to install Windows 95 into the same directory as Windows NT there might be some problems. Both Windows 95 and Windows NT have DLL names in common between the two operating systems, and both store these DLLs in the SYSTEM directory. Thus, if Windows 95 were installed to the same directory, one or both of the operating systems would not run properly. Windows 95 needs to be installed in a FAT partition, which has enough room for Windows 95 and its swap file. NTFS, or even HPFS, partitions are not available from within Windows 95.

Although OS/2 2.*x* qualifies as an operating system that can be upgraded to Windows 95, you must install Windows 95 in a new directory. The Windows 95 Setup program cannot migrate any of the Desktop or other configuration settings from OS/2. Any Windows-based applications have to be re-installed to run under Windows 95. The OS/2 computer must already be configured to dual-boot between OS/2 and MS-DOS before you install Windows 95. The OS/2 installation documentation outlines the details of how to configure the dual-boot between OS/2 and MS-DOS. Windows 95 needs to be installed from an MS-DOS prompt, so start the OS/2 computer using MS-DOS, then run the Windows 95 Setup program.

The OS/2 operating system supports either dual-boot or an OS/2 Boot Manager. If your computer has the OS/2 Boot Manager, the Boot Manager will be disabled by the Windows 95 Setup program in order to complete the Windows 95 installation. All the OS/2 files are kept intact. To restore the OS/2 Boot Manager, make the OS/2 Boot Manager partition active again by using OS/2 Boot disks, and then running the OS/2 version of the FDISK utility. Windows 95 needs to be installed in a FAT partition, which has enough room for Windows 95 and its swap file. HPFS partitions are not available from within Windows 95.

Dual-Booting Windows 95 with Existing Operating Systems

You can install Windows 95 with existing operating systems on the computer. This type of installation typically represents an upgrade install. If you choose to install Windows 95 into a different directory, most Windows applications need to be reinstalled to update the WIN.INI, SYSTEM.INI, and the Registry, as well as reload any application files (DLLs) into the Windows 95 WINDOWS/SYSTEM and WINDOWS directories. Table 3.2 lists the dual-boot options for Windows 95 and existing operating systems. This section explains your dual-boot options.

Dual-Boot with DOS and Windows 3.x

The versions of MS-DOS supported for upgrading Windows 95 are versions 3.2 or higher, or an equivalent version from a hardware manufacturer (such as Compaq version DOS 3.31) with partitions greater than 32 MB. Other versions of DOS include IBM's PC-DOS and Novell's DR-DOS. However, due to conflicts with DOS naming standards in Windows 95, Novell's DR-DOS cannot be dual-booted with Windows 95. You would need to first update Novell's DR-DOS to MS-DOS 6.*x*, and then upgrade to Windows 95 in order to dual-boot.

To install dual-boot capabilities for DOS, the computer must be running version 5.*x* or 6.*x* of MS-DOS or PC-DOS. Previous versions of DOS often were heavily modified by manufacturers, so the Windows 95 Setup program checks both the type and version number. The controlling factor in configuring dual-boot is the pre-existing operating system. If Windows 3.1*x* or Windows for Workgroups 3.*x* is detected on the computer, you must choose to install Windows 95 in a different directory to enable dual-boot.

Dual-boot needs the Windows 95 install to be made into a new directory that does not contain a version of Windows 3.*x*. The Windows 95 Setup program makes all the changes needed to preserve your existing version of DOS, Windows 3.1*x*, or Windows for Workgroups 3.*x*, and your current CONFIG.SYS and AUTOEXEC.BAT files. The older DOS files are not deleted, enabling you to dual-boot and start the computer using the older version of DOS.

Several original MS-DOS boot files are renamed for future use, and have DOS extension (see table 3.3). When you press F8 at the Windows 95 Startup and choose the option to start the previous version of MS-DOS, or press F4 at Windows 95 Startup, the Windows 95 versions of these same files are renamed with W40 extensions (except for IO.SYS), and the DOS files are renamed with their original extensions. In dual-boot mode, regardless of the previous choice at boot-up, Windows 95 starts each time.

Table 3.3

MS-DOS or Windows 95 Files Renamed During Dual-Boot

Boot Files	MS-DOS Versions	Windows 95 Versions
IO.SYS	IO.DOS	WINBOOT.SYS
MSDOS.SYS	MSDOS.DOS	MSDOS.W40
COMMAND.COM	COMMAND.DOS	COMMAND.W40
CONFIG.SYS	CONFIG.DOS	CONFIG.W40
AUTOEXEC.BAT	AUTOEXEC.DOS	AUTOEXEC.W40

To illustrate how dual-booting between MS-DOS and Windows 95 works, during the Windows 95 installation the Windows 95 Setup program renames existing MS-DOS boot files and creates a new set of Windows 95 boot files. All the old MS-DOS boot files are given a file extension of DOS. While the computer boots into Windows 95, there are only two sets of boot files: the Windows 95 boot files and the renamed MS-DOS version. When you choose to start the previous version of DOS, the Windows 95 boot files are renamed with the file extension W40, though IO.SYS is renamed WINBOOT.SYS. The old MS-DOS boot files are renamed to their original names, and then the computer is rebooted. While the computer boots into the old version of DOS there are still only two sets of boot files: the older MS-DOS boot files and the renamed Windows 95 boot files. These sets of boot files are renamed back and forth, depending on which of the two operating systems is actually booting the computer.

To set up dual-boot capabilities after Windows 95 is installed, follow the directions in the section "Installing Windows 95 for Dual-booting with Windows 3.*x*" in Chapter 6, "Setup Technical Discussion," of the *Windows 95 Resource Kit*.

To take advantage of Windows 95 dual-boot capabilities with versions 5.*x* or 6.*x* of MS-DOS or PC-DOS, the entry `BootMulti=1` must be set in the Windows 95 MSDOS.SYS file

continues

> in the root directory. If you are installing Windows 95 to a different directory that does not contain a copy of Windows 3.*x*, dual-boot is automatically enabled.

Dual-booting to a down-level operating system (for example, MS-DOS 6.22 or earlier) can cause long file name problems when certain commands, such as MOVE, COPY, REN, MD, RD, DE-FRAG, and ScanDisk, are used. Furthermore, almost any third-party or shareware file-maintenance utility that uses the same APIs as these commands likely causes long file name errors when the utility is used under the down-level operating system. Be aware of this problem. Long file names are discussed in Chapter 6, "Managing Disk Resources and Utilities."

DriveSpace (disk compression) drives are accessible under Windows 95. However, if you're using MS-DOS 5.*x*, and you decide to compress your drive in Windows 95 with DriveSpace, you will not be able to dual-boot because both DriveSpace (DRVSPACE) and DoubleSpace (DBLSPACE) file-compression utilities are specific to MS-DOS version 6.*x*.

If you choose to install Windows 95 to a non-boot hard drive, approximately 8 MB of space is required on the root of the host boot drive.

Dual-Boot with Windows NT

Windows NT has a built-in multi-boot capability called the *Windows NT Boot Loader* (NTLDR). When you first boot your computer, if MS-DOS was loaded when you initially installed Windows NT, the Windows NT Boot Loader appears and lets you choose between Windows NT and MS-DOS. Windows 95 must be installed to a FAT partition big enough to hold Windows 95 and its swap file. NTFS, as well as HPFS, partitions are not available for Windows 95 to install into.

To install Windows NT on a computer on which Windows 95 is already installed, switch to the directory containing the Windows NT installation files and type **winnt /w**. This starts the MS-DOS–based Windows NT setup, but allows the Windows NT Setup program to run under Windows. Otherwise, you are forced to exit to an MS-DOS 7.0 prompt and start from there. The 32-bit Windows version of the Windows NT Setup program, WINNT32.EXE, does not run under Windows 95.

To install Windows 95 on a computer already configured to use the Windows NT Boot Loader for Windows NT (as well as MS-DOS), you need to start the computer using the MS-DOS operating system. The FAT partition must be large enough to accommodate both Windows 95 and the swap file (between 50–55 MB of empty space is recommended). Where you install Windows 95 depends on where Windows NT was installed, and whether or not there was a copy of Windows 3.*x* on the computer. Your options are as follows:

▶ **Windows NT only, no MS-DOS.** Boot MS-DOS from a floppy disk to install Windows 95. Install Windows 95 to a different directory than Windows NT. The Windows NT Boot Loader will be disabled, so restore it using the Windows NT emergency repair disk and select the Repair option. You will need to manually add the Windows 95 option to the BOOT.INI file if the Repair option does not recognize Windows 95 as another Windows NT boot option.

▶ **Windows NT and only MS-DOS.** Run the Windows 95 Setup program from an MS-DOS prompt. Install Windows 95 to a different directory than Windows NT. The Windows NT Boot Loader still might reference MS-DOS, so modify the BOOT.INI file as described in Exercise 3.2, so it reads Windows 95 rather than MS-DOS.

▶ **Windows NT and Windows 3.*x* sharing a directory.** If both Windows NT and Windows 3.*x* are installed in the same directory, you cannot update the existing copy of Windows 3.*x* to Windows 95. Install Windows 95 to a different directory. You need to re-install each of your Windows applications to run them under Windows 95.

▶ **Windows NT and Windows 3.*x* in different directories.** If Windows NT is installed in a different directory than the existing copy of Windows 3.*x*, you have the option of updating Windows 3.*x* to Windows 95. However, you can choose to install Windows 95 into a third directory, which requires you to re-install each of your Windows applications to run them under Windows 95.

To complete the Windows 95 installation, the computer might need to reboot once or twice, depending on the presence of Plug and Play devices. If the Windows NT Boot Loader is still working, select the MS-DOS option each time the computer is rebooted until the Windows 95 installation is successfully completed.

As a general rule, do not install Windows NT and Windows 95 into the same directory. They share common DLLs, which are stored in the same location in the directory. The last install over-writes the former and causes serious problems for one, if not both, of the operating systems. For example, Windows 95 replaces the Windows 3.*x* DLLs in the Windows System sub-directory to support both 16-bit and 32-bit Windows applications. Windows NT depends on the old Windows 3.*x* DLLs to run 16-bit Windows applications.

Dual-Boot with OS/2

OS/2 has several built-in multi-boot options, one called *dual-boot* and the other the O*S/2 Boot Manager*. The dual-boot option uses a BOOT.COM program to switch between the key boot files of either OS/2 or MS-DOS and then reboot the computer. The last boot selection is the one that runs when you start the computer. The OS/2 Boot Manager is like the Windows NT Boot Loader in that a menu front-end is displayed at system startup and the user selects which partition on the computer to make active at the start-up. See your OS/2 documentation for details. New Riders' *OS/2 Certification Handbook* outlines both of these multi-boot options.

Remember that Windows 95 must be installed to a FAT partition that is big enough to hold the Windows 95 and the swap file. HPFS partitions are not available for Windows 95 to install into.

If installing OS/2 after Windows 95, follow the standard OS/2 installation instructions. If installing OS/2 with Windows support built-in, you should not impact the Windows 95 setup. If, however, you have the version of OS/2 that needs an existing copy of Windows 3.*x*, you should have both Windows 3.*x* and Windows 95 installed into separate directories. OS/2 then uses the existing Windows 3.*x* programs to run 16-bit Windows applications.

To install Windows 95 on a computer in which OS/2 has already been installed, switch to DOS before beginning the installation. The Windows 95 Setup program warns you that the OS/2 Boot Manager is disabled. After Windows 95 is installed, run the OS/2 Fdisk utility from the OS/2 boot disk to reactivate the OS/2 Boot Manager.

Dual-boot is a very useful feature that allows you to run multiple operating systems on the same computer. As a support person, you might be asked to help set up dual-boot capability. Expect some questions, especially about running either previous versions of DOS/Windows or in conjunction with running Windows NT.

Installing New Hardware Devices

One of the toughest areas for you to configure in Windows 95 is hardware. Computer owners are finding that new applications are demanding more—more RAM memory, more hard disk space, more speed in quicker video refresh rates, more display size and better resolution, more modem speed, and so on. Although Windows 95 does not require you to make any system changes and hardware upgrades, it does encourage you to seriously consider them.

Any user who has previously chosen to add hardware devices to his or her computer knows how difficult it can be to reconfigure the operating system and get all the software to work correctly with the new hardware. A new operating system upgrade also might force you to spend a considerable amount of valuable time getting all the hardware devices to work correctly. It makes you wonder if all the pain is worth the gain. Windows 95 hopes to change this through support for the Plug and Play (PnP) specification.

Chapter 11, "Plug and Play," covers PnP in greater detail. However, for the purpose of addressing this exam objective, this section looks at the many ways to configure Windows 95 using PnP hardware devices.

To fully support the PnP specification, a computer system needs three major components:

▶ PnP hardware devices and device drivers capable of identifying themselves and declaring their resource requirements. For ISA bus hardware, this capability requires a new generation of modified hardware devices, because the current generation is not capable of communicating this information. To dynamically activate a newly inserted PnP device, the corresponding device drivers for that device must also be able to be dynamically loaded and unloaded from memory. Removing the driver from memory when the device is not present or not active enables Windows 95 to make more efficient use of memory.

▶ A PnP computer BIOS that can accept and respond to the resource requirements communicated from PnP hardware devices.

▶ A PnP operating system that orchestrates all hardware components in the system by loading and configuring PnP device drivers, and by responding to hardware changes and automatically reconfiguring the system without any user intervention.

Not all three major components are necessary to enjoy some of the benefits of PnP. The Windows 95 operating system supports PnP hardware devices. Older computers usually have a BIOS version that does not support PnP, as well as older installed hardware devices that are not PnP capable. So the only component that does support PnP may be the Windows 95 operating system itself. Older computers and hardware devices that do not support PnP are called *legacy hardware*. The Windows 95 operating system auto-detects many of your hardware devices and automatically sets them up properly. But beware, sometimes Plug and Play performs more like Plug and Pray. Chapter 11 covers this in much greater detail.

Many newer hardware devices that might be used to upgrade the hardware on older computers support PnP. You can configure PnP hardware devices in one of the four following ways:

- ▶ **Use the Windows 95 Setup program.** PnP hardware devices are automatically detected (default) during the hardware detection phase of the Windows 95 installation.

- ▶ **Add new Hardware Wizard.** The Windows 95 Control Panel can run through the same automatic detection of PnP hardware devices (default) as is done during Windows 95 installation.

- ▶ **During the normal boot process.** Windows 95 loads the Registry Databases according to the user information (USER.DAT) and system information (SYSTEM.DAT) on your computer. If a new PnP hardware device is discovered, it is set up automatically.

- ▶ **During warm- or hot-docking situations.** Windows 95 tests for PnP hardware devices, such as a docking station or even PC Cards in laptop computers. *Warm-docking* refers to docking or undocking a laptop computer in suspended mode (minimum power); whereas *hot-docking* refers to docking a laptop computer running at full power. PC Cards can be detected at boot or when inserted into the computer.

Depending on the hardware configurations of your computers, you might have several new hardware devices that now support PnP. The newer Network Interface Cards (NICs) from companies like 3Com, which makes the 3C509B Ethernet Adapter, all support PnP. Check the hardware device specifications or talk to the manufacturer's technical support staff to be sure that what you have supports PnP applications.

Updating to the Windows 95 operating system may provide you with your first encounter with PnP hardware devices. Newer computers are fully PnP compatible. You may have seen this PnP configuration occur during the installation exercises in Chapter 1, or again earlier in this chapter in the dual-boot installation exercises.

> What separates promise from reality is the experience you must acquire to properly configure hardware devices under Windows 95. PnP promises installations that are simple and fail-safe. For hardware devices, the installation would be automatic: plug in the device, turn on the computer, and it just works. The reality of the situation is you need to be aware of IRQs, I/O port addresses, DMA channels, and memory ranges assigned to the various hardware components of your computer. The Device Manager tab on the System Properties sheet can help you ferret out the problems; however, experience is the greatest teacher.

Limitations for Full Plug and Play

Plug and Play is discussed in much greater detail in Chapter 11. The goal of PnP is to enable changes to be made to the computer's configuration without requiring any active intervention by the user. You simply plug in the hardware device, and it works. PnP is a standard set of industry specifications, developed by a group of hardware and software companies, for new computer hardware devices. With all the legacy hardware and software in existence, however, full PnP implementation is limited in some computers in use today. The goal of this exam objective is that you understand the various computer bus configurations and the limitations these bus configurations have under the PnP specification.

A bus configuration refers to the types of bus architecture used on the computer. The bus configurations in the following list have been improved and have matured over time as the Intel-based personal computer has evolved. (These bus configurations are not limited to only Intel-based computers, but because Intel is the predominant computer architecture, the two are often linked.)

The standard bus configurations are as follows:

▶ **Industry Standard Architecture (ISA).** The bus design of the 1984 IBM PC/AT computer. The bus supports the original 8-bit or 16-bit edge adapter cards, configured through the use of jumper pins and dip switches. These adapter cards are often called legacy adapter cards, because of their age and the appearance of newer hardware bus designs. New generation ISA adapters now fully support PnP. The ISA bus design can be found along with either the VL local bus or PCI local bus configurations on many newer computers.

▶ **Micro Channel Architecture (MCA).** A bus design created by IBM in 1987. MCA improved on the ISA bus, but was too closely associated with the IBM PS/2 line of computers. The bus supports 32-bit edge adapter cards, which were configured through software. Stiff royalties and licensing rules by IBM discouraged wide-scale use by IBM clone manufacturers.

▶ **Enhanced Industry Standard Architecture (EISA).** A bus design by non-IBM companies in the late 1980s that competed with MCA. It offers the same features as MCA. The bus supports 32-bit edge adapter cards, which are configured through software. EISA often is found in high-end Intel computers used as network servers. For the individual computer user, EISA offered few advantages over ISA and did not justify the increased cost.

▶ **Video Electronic Standards Association or VESA Local bus (VL).** A bus design produced in 1992 by a standards group responsible for creating display and monitor specifications. The original goal was to improve the video throughput, achieve higher display resolutions, and faster display refresh scan rates (kilohertz). This local bus enables high-speed connections to peripheral hardware devices, not just video adapters, and is used with the ISA bus configuration.

▶ **Peripheral Component Interconnect bus (PCI).** A bus design produced by Intel in 1993 that competes with VL. PCI is a local bus design being promoted as the logical successor to VL. It enables high-speed connections to peripheral hardware devices. The PCI bus design can be found with ISA bus configurations on many Pentium computers.

▶ **Small Computer Standard Interface (SCSI).** A bus design that supports chaining multiple hardware devices together. Usually a SCSI bus can support up to seven hardware devices, such as hard disk drives and CD-ROM drives. Each hardware device is assigned a number from zero to seven for communication with the SCSI controller, and is often configured through software. This specification has been improved to support faster speeds across the bus, and even double the number of hardware devices.

▶ **Personal Computer Memory Card International Association or the new name, PC Card (PCMCIA).** A bus design standard originally developed to support adding memory expansion cards to portable computers. This specification has expanded to include a wide range of credit-card-sized interface cards for portables, docking stations, and regular desktop computers.

Table 3.4 outlines the bus configurations in the preceding list and identifies their key Plug and Play limitations:

Table 3.4

Bus Configuration Plug and Play Limitations	
Bus	Plug and Play Limitation
ISA	Legacy cards. You can mix and match PnP ISA and standard ISA adapter cards. Windows 95 polls the card or asks the user to supply values. Static data is stored in the Registry. Hardware resources are assigned before other PnP hardware devices, and have priority.
EISA	Meets most PnP requirements. Bus enumerator used to query nonvolatile RAM on adapter card for resource requirements. Cannot be reconfigured by Windows 95.
MCA	Meets most PnP requirements, such as EISA, but OEM (IBM) must provide the bus enumerator used to query nonvolatile RAM on card for resource requirements. Cannot be reconfigured by Windows 95.

Bus	Plug and Play Limitation
SCSI	Multiple-device chained interface, which does not currently support PnP. Like ISA in some regards. Difficult to configure due to both host adapter configuration and the SCSI bus termination, in addition to other issues.
VL\PCI	Secondary bus, used for high-speed video or other devices. PnP compatible, but dependent on primary bus architecture. VL bus enumerators provided by OEM. PCI can also share IRQs, whereas ISA devices cannot. BIOS must be set to prevent IRQ overlaps.
PCMCIA	PC Card standard. Card and socket services allow dynamic configuration. Supports all the PnP functionality, plus hot docking, which allows PC Card insertion with the power on.

Many of these bus configurations are compatible with the PnP specifications. Windows 95 groups hardware devices and the various bus configurations into classes for purposes of installing and managing device drivers as well as allocating the computer's resources. Not every bus configuration is 100 percent compliant with PnP. Windows 95 deals with each differently, gathering as much needed information as possible before prompting the user to supply additional information.

The Windows 95 hardware tree is a record of the current system configuration, based on the configuration information for all classes in the Hardware Branch of the Registry. The hardware tree is created in RAM each time the computer is started and can be dynamically modified. Some changes require a reboot of the computer before they become effective.

Although PnP solves many of the hardware configuration issues, you occasionally need to manually change device settings. For example, in the dual-boot setup of Windows for Workgroups 3.*x* and Windows 95, or Windows 95 and Windows NT, the network interface card settings might prevent you from connecting to the network. Non-PnP operating systems have default settings for the cards, whereas Windows 95 allows a PnP adapter to select its own settings. In these cases, you might need to disable the PnP features of the network interface card and manually set them.

You use the Device Manager to view the computer's hardware tree. If some hardware device on your computer is not working correctly, the Device Manager tab on the System Properties sheet will display either a yellow or red icon on top of the hardware device icon. Keep in mind, however, that the Device Manager is only the second step in your hardware troubleshooting. The first step to any type of computer hardware troubleshooting can be summarized by three Cs: connection, current, and configuration. Exercise 3.5 at the end of the chapter shows how to use the Device Manager.

Connection refers to ensuring that the hardware device is properly connected to the computer. The simple act of re-seating an adapter card can often restore a connection that has worked itself loose through constant use. *Current* refers to verifying that the hardware device has power. Make sure the power is turned on at the power strip, check that the power cable is properly inserted, or plug in the secondary power converter to a socket for a device that needs power. *Configuration* refers to reading the device manual and using any utilities or vendor-supplied INF files to ensure the hardware is properly configured. Make sure you take note of any special resource requirements, such as I/O ports, Interrupts, or DMA channels. You may need to use these resource values to configure the hardware device.

If you eliminate the obvious sources of your hardware problems, and the problem still exists, the Device Manager is the next best place to look.

The Device Manager allows you to change the configuration of most devices located on the computer. You can view devices by type or connection. Problems with the hardware configuration on the computer show up in the Device Manager tab of the System Properties sheet.

Configuring the Taskbar

The Windows 95 Taskbar is new in the Windows interface. It provides quick access to all your active programs by maintaining a set of buttons that represent the programs' title boxes. The Taskbar is always available to easily let you switch between active programs by clicking the programs' buttons. Or you can use the Start menu to open programs. A notification area displays the clock and status information. Figure 3.1 shows the Windows 95 Taskbar.

Figure 3.1

The Windows 95 Taskbar.

The Windows 95 Taskbar comprises three sections, shown in figure 3.1 from left to right: the Start menu, Taskbar active program buttons, and the Notification Area. The Notification Area is used for the clock, and space exists for status information. The status information displays small icons for programs running in the background. The background programs can be printers, modems, and sound cards. The Microsoft Plus! package includes a System Agent that also displays a small icon if any scheduled events are pending. Many Windows 95 applications also use this notification area.

By default, the Taskbar sits at the bottom of the screen. You can reposition the Taskbar by dragging it to either side or to the top of the screen. Just grab the Taskbar with your mouse pointer and drag it to another location on-screen. The Taskbar sits only on the four edges of the display: left or right side, top or bottom. You can resize the Taskbar to take up more or less room on-screen. Move the mouse pointer over the inner edge of the Taskbar. When the mouse pointer changes to a double-sided arrow, press and hold your left mouse button and drag the Taskbar to size it as you like.

You can use the Taskbar Properties sheet to adjust several options for the Taskbar. To open the Taskbar Properties sheet, right-click on a clear section of the Taskbar and select Properties, or choose Start, Settings, Taskbar. Figure 3.2 shows the Taskbar Properties sheet.

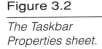

Figure 3.2

The Taskbar Properties sheet.

Taskbar options include the following:

▶ **Always on Top.** This option keeps the Taskbar visible, even when using a full-screen program. When Always on Top is used with Auto Hide, the Taskbar reappears over any full-screen program when activated.

▶ **Auto Hide.** This option leaves the screen vacant by automatically hiding the Taskbar to the side of the screen where it is placed. It reappears when the cursor is moved to that edge of the screen.

▶ **Show Small Icons in Start Menu.** This option changes the default large icons used in the Start menu to smaller icon versions. This option also reduces the size of the Start menu when you click on the Start menu.

▶ **Show Clock.** This option displays a digital clock with the computer's time in the notification area. Not displaying the clock does not remove the entire notification area. Having the cursor pointer positioned over the clock displays the date. Double-clicking on the clock opens the Date/Time Properties sheet of the Control Panel.

For an exercise testing this information, see end of chapter.

It is important for the exam objective to know the various options available to you and what each option enables you to do when you configure the Windows 95 Taskbar. Exercise 3.6 at the end of the chapter shows you how to configure the Taskbar.

> If you have a lot of active programs or open windows, the Taskbar can become busy, and the size of each button can be reduced to the point that it is difficult to determine what is what. The best solution is to position the Taskbar on one side of the screen, resize the width to a usable size to read each button, and use the Auto Hide feature to have the Taskbar appear only when you need it. The Auto Hide feature is less useful if you make use of the Taskbar to quickly switch from one active program to another. Plus, if you use a full-screen application with scroll bars near the edge of the screen, you occasionally activate the Taskbar, which gets in your way and covers the scroll bar until it finally disappears again after a few seconds of inactivity.

Configuring Shortcuts

Windows 95 introduces the concept of shortcuts. A *shortcut* is a connection or pointer between an icon and the physical location of an object. It is a virtual mapping. The shortcut itself is an object that points to the original object. The shortcut object has an LNK extension, or link extension, and this object's file type appears as shortcut in file folder details.

Shortcuts give you an easy way to make commonly used programs, folders, or files readily available. It does not matter where the original object is actually located, the shortcut makes it appear to exist where the shortcut object is located. To start or open a shortcut, simply double-click on the shortcut.

You can distinguish between the original object and the shortcut to that object by the small arcing arrow box in the lower-left corner of the icon. You can add shortcuts directly onto your Windows 95 Desktop, place them inside a folder, or add them to the Start menu.

To create a shortcut, you can use any one of several methods:

▶ Secondary mouse-click from an open spot on the Windows 95 Desktop and choose New, Shortcut. Type the path and file name in the command line, or browse to find the object. You can change the name of the shortcut before you finish.

▶ Drag and drop from Windows Explorer to the Windows 95 Desktop. If you use the primary mouse button, the object is moved. However, if the object is an application, dragging and dropping will create a shortcut. If you use the secondary mouse button to drag and drop the object, a context-sensitive menu opens, giving you the option to move, copy, or create a shortcut.

▶ Secondary mouse-click on the object to open a pop-up context-sensitive menu, then choose Create Shortcut to directly create a shortcut. A new shortcut then is created in the same folder. You will be repositioned on the newly created shortcut, and you can then drag and drop the new shortcut where you like.

Creating a shortcut is different than just copying or moving an object. If you need to make changes to the properties of the original object, go to the object rather than the shortcut. The best analogy is an icon in a Windows 3.1 Program Manager group that points to the file. Shortcuts are just pointers to the original object. Changing or deleting the shortcut does not affect the original object. A copy command creates two separate objects, and a move command relocates the object.

A shortcut object has properties that include the location of the original object. To view a shortcut's properties sheet, click the shortcut with the right mouse button. From the context-sensitive menu, choose Properties. In the following steps, you create a shortcut that you will use later in the chapter.

1. From the Start menu, choose Programs, Windows Explorer, to open the Windows Explorer program.

2. Explore the Windows 95 directory and locate the Registry Editor (REGEDIT.EXE) application.

3. Highlight the REGEDIT object using the primary mouse button. With the button held down, drag and drop a shortcut onto the Windows 95 Desktop.

4. Exit Windows Explorer.

5. Click on the shortcut's name field below the icon titled "Shortcut to Regedit.exe" and change it to read "Registry Editor."

6. Right-click on the newly created shortcut and select Properties from the context-sensitive menu to display the Registry Editor Properties sheet. Assign the shortcut a hot key combination of Ctrl+Alt+R. The shortcut opens when you enter those keys (see fig. 3.3). Choose OK to save the change.

Figure 3.3

A Windows 95 Shortcut Properties sheet.

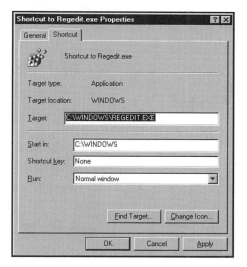

What happens to the original object when you make changes to the shortcut's settings? Nothing, because the shortcut's properties apply only to the shortcut itself.

A shortcut points to the original object through a one-way pointer link. This link can break if the original object is moved or deleted. Windows 95 attempts to automatically update a shortcut if the original object has been moved, but if Windows

continues

> 95 is unsuccessful, this might cause an orphaned shortcut. If this occurs, you need to find the moved file and re-enter the full path name to the file in the target text box, or delete the shortcut object.

Shortcuts can make your Windows 95 Desktop much easier to use. A shortcut icon usually has a small arcing arrow box in the lower left-hand corner of the icon, except when the shortcut is added to the Start menu. If you look closely at the Start menu folder under Windows 95, you will notice that all the programs listed are actually shortcuts.

Adding Items to the Start Menu

On the Windows 95 Taskbar, you use the Start menu to initiate most of your computer activity. The Start menu is the main starting point for running applications. Click on the Start menu to see a list of key menu features and functions:

▶ **Programs.** Corresponds to the Windows 3.*x* concept of program groups within Program Manager. If you install Windows 95 in an existing Windows 3.*x* directory, all your groups are converted into folders, and those application shortcuts are displayed with this menu selection.

▶ **Documents.** Displays a list of the most recently edited or saved files. This list is kept in a hidden folder called Recent, which stores shortcuts to the actual documents themselves.

▶ **Settings.** Enables you to open the Control Panel, the Printers folder, and the Taskbar Properties sheet.

▶ **Find.** Locates a folder or a file on your computer, a shared resource on the network, or a location on The Microsoft Network.

▶ **Help.** Provides information from the extensive Windows 95 Help System. Installing the optional Online User's Guide component makes this menu selection the best method for users to get information, especially with the new help index and find features. You also can use the F1 key to open the Windows 95 Help System.

▶ **Run.** Enables you to launch applications directly from the Start menu. You can specify the name of an executable file, folder, document, or shared folder from the command line. A list of previously used commands are cached and can be retrieved from a drop-down list.

▶ **Shut Down.** Offers you the choice to shut down, restart, restart in MS-DOS Mode, close all programs and, if you are on a network, to log on as a different user. You should always use the Shut Down option before turning off your computer. Following this practice ensures that all programs and files are closed properly before you actually turn off the power.

▶ **Suspend.** Can be added to the Start menu (for laptops with advanced power management) by selecting a check box on the Taskbar Properties sheet. Suspend puts the computer in suspended or sleep mode. This choice is available only on computers that support this feature.

▶ **Eject PC.** Allows a controlled undocking of laptops from a docking station that supports hot docking. This choice is present only on computers that support this feature.

To add items to the Start menu you can either drag and drop the item onto the Start menu, or open the Taskbar Properties sheet. To open the Taskbar Properties sheet, either right-click on an open area of the Taskbar and select Properties, or choose Start, Settings, Taskbar.

There is a limit to the number of programs that can be placed on the first level of the Start menu. Depending on the icon size used to display the Start menu and your display resolution, you can have approximately 13 to 17 menu selections available. More than that will not be displayed. The Advanced button on the Taskbar Properties sheet allows you to view all the various Start menu levels at one time. You then can drag and drop, or copy between the folders, which can be found within the Start menu folder under the Windows folder on the computer.

You can use your keyboard and cursor keys to access the Start menu. Press Ctrl+Esc to bring up the Start menu and show the Taskbar (if it is hidden). The Microsoft Natural keyboard, as well as some of the newer Windows 95–ready keyboards, include special Windows keys that enable single keystroke access to the Start menu.

Customizing the Desktop

The Windows 95 Desktop consists of several different components with a much different user interface than previous versions of Windows. For most users, the Windows 95 Desktop represents their first view of the new operating system.

Users initiate most actions from the Windows 95 Desktop, and they may organize the objects on the Desktop to suit their needs. The Windows 95 Desktop can contain icons, shortcuts, folders, files, windows, and the Taskbar. These are all objects and they can be manipulated as objects. Favorite folders and files can be left on the Windows 95 Desktop, where they are easily accessed. Several objects common to most Windows 95 Desktops include the following:

▶ **My Computer.** Represents the computer object, and loosely corresponds to the File Manager in previous versions of Windows. My Computer is a folder that gives you quick access to your entire computer, as well as to the Control Panel folder, Printers folder, and Dial-Up Networking folder. All objects stored on your computer can be accessed through the My Computer folder.

▶ **Network Neighborhood.** Represents the network object; it exists only if the computer is on a network. Network Neighborhood is a folder that gives you access to computer icons that represent members of your workgroup and an icon that represents the entire Network. Chapter 5, "Networking and Interoperability," discusses the Network Neighborhood in greater detail.

▶ **Inbox.** Represents a built-in universal inbox for Windows 95, which is used to send, receive, and organize e-mail, faxes, items from online services, and other information. Although it refers to Microsoft Exchange when started, it is not the full client that comes with Microsoft's Exchange server. See Chapter 10, "Microsoft Exchange," for more information.

▶ **Recycle Bin.** Represents a trash-bin object. Any folders and files you delete are automatically moved to this folder. Recycle Bin provides you with an opportunity to recover deleted files by opening the Recycle Bin icon, selecting the files you want to recover, and then choosing File, Restore. You can purge any deleted files by selecting File, Empty Recycle Bin.

▶ **My Briefcase.** Represents a briefcase object that contains files and folders you want to keep current. The Briefcase is very useful for working with files off-site, perhaps on a portable computer. It is a special folder that you can use to synchronize files between two computers, or between your computer and a network file server to help ensure that the files are up-to-date. See Chapter 9, "Mobile Services," for more information.

▶ **Microsoft Network.** Represents the Microsoft Online Service object, which is used to connect to the Microsoft Network (MSN) service. You can use the Microsoft Network to exchange messages; read the latest news, sports, weather, and financial information; download programs; and connect to the Internet. It is similar to CompuServe, America Online, and Prodigy.

▶ **The Taskbar.** Represents a list of all active programs by maintaining a title button for each active program. The Taskbar allows you to quickly switch between programs. At the far right of the Taskbar is the notification area, which is used for status information. By default, the notification area contains the clock, but it can also show battery status on your portable computer, print job status, modem status, speaker volume status, and so on. At the far left of the Taskbar is the Start menu.

▶ **The Start menu.** Represents the Start program menu. Most computer activities can be initiated from the Start menu. You also can use the Start menu to start any application.

To customize the Windows 95 Desktop, start with the Display Properties sheet. To open the Display Properties sheet, either right-click in an open area of the Windows 95 Desktop and select Properties from the context-sensitive menu; or choose Start, Settings, Control Panel, and then choose the Display icon. Figure 3.4 shows the Display Properties sheet.

Figure 3.4

The Display Properties sheet.

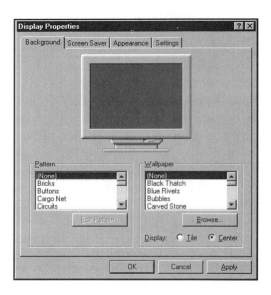

The Windows 95 display parameters are divided into four tabs if Microsoft Plus! is not installed, and five tabs if it is installed. The following tabs are available:

▶ **Background.** Use the Background tab to establish settings for the background pattern and wallpaper. Both are mutually exclusive, with wallpaper taking precedence over the background pattern. You can select your own bitmap (BMP) file to use as the wallpaper by using the Browse button. Depending on the size of the bitmap, you can tile or center it.

▶ **Screen Saver.** Use the Screen Saver tab to add a Windows 95 screen saver. The default screen saver is Flying Windows. Other Windows 95 screen savers are included, and you also can add additional ones with Microsoft Plus!. Each installed screen saver has settings that control its appearance. You can also password-protect your computer, and the screen saver password can be different from your other passwords. You change the screen-saver password through the Screen Saver tab on the Display Properties sheet.

▶ **Appearance.** Use the Appearance tab to configure the look of all the various components of your windows and Desktop. You can choose from pre-defined color schemes or create one of your own.

▶ **(Microsoft) Plus!.** The Plus! tab is an optional fifth tab on the Display Properties sheet. You can use it to change the standard icons, mouse pointer, folder icons, and so on using Desktop Themes. Several new features can dramatically improve the look and feel of your Windows 95 desktop, all of which come with the Microsoft Plus! package. One option allows you to stretch the desktop wallpaper to fit the screen resolution.

▶ **Settings.** The Settings tab contains configuration options for the monitor. You can make changes to the color palette, desktop area resolution (if supported by your display driver), font size and type, and specification of both the display driver and monitor type.

One of the Display settings you most likely will want to change is font size, especially when running at higher resolutions for the display. At 800×600 or higher display resolutions, you can change the font size. Larger fonts can make text easier to read as your display resolution increases. Windows 95 enables you to dynamically change the display resolution by adjusting the slider bar (which appears only if your adapter and monitor can support the higher resolutions).

The higher the display resolution, the slower the display refreshes. If you dynamically change your resolution setting using the Display Properties sheet, Windows 95 gives you the following warning message:

```
Windows will resize your desktop. This could take a few
minutes, during which your screen might flicker. If Windows
does not reappear correctly, wait 15 seconds, and your
original settings will be restored.
```

If your screen changes to the newer resolution without problems, you receive a second message, as follows:

```
You resized your desktop. Do you want to keep this setting?
```

You can choose either Yes to accept the change, or No (default) to return to the previous setting. However, if your screen does not change properly, or turns black, you need to reboot into Safe Mode, which loads a standard VGA driver, then shut down again and restart Windows 95 to restore your earlier settings. Make sure you choose an adapter and monitor type for the display that matches the equipment installed on your computer.

The Windows 95 Desktop is yours to customize to the way you work. Learn how the objects on the Windows 95 Desktop function and what changes can be made to the various properties sheets.

Configuring and Using Windows Explorer

Whereas the Start menu presents an easy way to launch applications, the Windows Explorer offers you a hierarchical view of folders and files shown in the context of the entire computer system. The Windows Explorer provides a structured path to your computer, where you can view and manage your files, plus other objects. Although similar to the Windows 3.*x* File Manager, the Windows Explorer gives you much greater functionality and flexibility.

The Windows Explorer is tightly integrated into the Windows 95 user interface. The Windows 95 Desktop itself is managed by the

Windows Explorer. If you examine in detail the workings of the Windows Explorer, you will discover that the Windows 95 Desktop is nothing more than an expanded Windows Explorer contents pane view using large icons. The Windows Explorer is always running in the background, helping to manage your Windows 95 Desktop.

To illustrate the point that the Windows Explorer is always running in Windows 95, right-click on the My Computer icon to open a context-sensitive menu. Select Explore to open the Windows Explorer program (see fig. 3.5). From the left side tree pane, click on the Desktop folder. The right side contents pane displays the contents of the Desktop folder. The contents of the top-level Desktop folder are the same as the objects located on your Windows 95 Desktop.

Figure 3.5

The Windows Explorer.

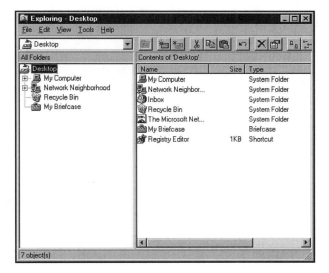

Opening Versus Exploring

In Windows 95, objects allow you to either open them or explore them. The difference between opening and exploring is subtle, but the results of each action are much different. Knowing about these differences will help you understand the results of both opening and exploring.

You open an object by either double-clicking the object with the left mouse button, or single-clicking the object with the right mouse button and selecting Open from the context-sensitive menu. The results of opening an object depend on what the object does. Opening a program starts the program. Opening a folder or a system folder, such as My Computer, provides a window with a single-pane view of the objects contained inside the folder. By default, opening an object produces a new window, either starting the program or showing the object's contents.

Every successive new window opened on-screen can cause confusion, especially if the title bar on the window is truncated due to the size of the window. Some objects, like My Computer or Network Neighborhood, allow you to specify view options that close the previous window when a new window is opened. To set this view option, choose View, Options and select the option Browse Folders by Using a Single Window that Changes as You Open Each Folder. This view option greatly reduces the number of open windows. To move up through the hierarchy of folders, use the backspace key.

You explore an object by right-clicking on the object and selecting Explore from the context-sensitive menu to open a Windows Explorer double-pane window. The left pane contains the object's files and folders displayed in a hierarchical tree that includes all the objects in the system. The right pane displays the object's contents, the same view produced if the object were opened.

Every time you select another object within Windows Explorer, the double-pane window displays the new object's contents. As you transverse the hierarchical structure during a search, the left pane shows your last-opened level, and the right pane displays the contents. This makes it easy to keep track of where you are without cluttering your screen with open windows.

Unlike the Windows 3.x File Manager, the Windows Explorer allows access to both local and network resources from the same system view. You can scroll directly to the appropriate resource and view its contents without having to open another window.

Objects in the Windows Explorer tree contain a small plus sign (+) in front of them if they contain additional folders. To expand a folder to show the next level of subfolders, either click on the plus sign, or double-click on the object. The small plus sign changes to a small minus sign (–) as you expand the folder. Collapsing folders can simplify the tree view and speed up your search.

Configuring Windows Explorer

The Windows Explorer can be used with most objects and configured by the user. You can use the View menu to customize Windows Explorer. The View menu contains the following options:

▶ **Toolbar.** Adds a toolbar to the top of the Windows Explorer. The toolbar contains a series of buttons that duplicate menu selections and make using the Windows Explorer even easier.

▶ **Status Bar.** Adds a message bar at the bottom of the Windows Explorer. This message bar displays information about the various parts and functions of a Windows Explorer session.

▶ **Large Icons.** Shows the contents of the folder as large icons with a description under each icon.

▶ **Small Icons.** Shows the contents of the folder as small icons with a description to the right of each icon.

▶ **List.** Shows the contents of the folder as a list. This view is very similar to the Small Icons view except that the scroll bar appears below the list rather than to the right of it.

▶ **Details.** Shows the contents of the folder as a detailed list. The detailed list contains the name, size, type, and date of most recent modification.

▶ **Arrange Icons.** Leads to another menu that allows the contents to be sorted alphabetically by name, by size, by type, or by modification date. If either Large Icons or Small Icons is selected, then the contents can be set by default to be automatically arranged.

▶ **Line up Icons.** If either Large Icons or Small Icons is selected, this option is used to arrange the icons. The Line up
Icons option is unnecessary if the Auto Arrange option is set.

▶ **Refresh.** Refreshes the contents of the folder. The Refresh
option can be helpful if you are exploring a series of floppy
disks or removable media drives.

▶ **Options.** Leads to a dialog property box that can set what
types of files are displayed, whether certain file extensions
are visible, and what extensions are associated with certain
programs.

Other options might be available in Windows Explorer, depending on the type of object. For example, the Windows 95 Fonts
folder replaces the Small Icons option with a List Fonts by Similar-
ity option.

Of all the Windows Explorer view options, the Toolbar option is
the most powerful. It contains a number of tools you can use
to select a new current folder, move to the current folder's
parent folder, connect or disconnect a network drive, manipulate the contents of the folder, or change the contents pane
view. The Toolbar option is not selected as a default. If selected, you can quickly determine a toolbar button's function by
holding the cursor over the toolbar button briefly and reading
the tooltip description.

Windows Explorer Command-Line Switches

The Windows Explorer, EXPLORER.EXE, has several command-
line switches you can use to add flexibility to how a window or
folder is viewed. These command-line switches are not available
when you open the Windows Explorer by choosing Start, Programs, Windows Explorer. Instead, you add these command-line
switches by choosing Start, Run to open the Run dialog box, and
then entering **explorer.exe**. The syntax for the Windows Explorer
command line is as follows:

explorer [/n] [/e] [,/ *root,object*] [[,/ *select*] ,*subobject*]

Each of the command-line switches is explained in table 3.5. Experiment with the various combinations to properly use the Windows Explorer.

Table 3.5

Windows Explorer Command-Line Switches

Switch	Function
/n	Opens a new window. Opens a single pane view for each item selected, even if doing so duplicates an already open window.
/e	Opens a new Windows Explorer double-pane view for each item selected. This is the default view.
/root,object	Specifies the object to use as the root in the tree view. The default is the normal name space root (the Desktop). Whatever object is specified for the root is where the window begins the display. If a subobject is also specified (optional) without the use of /select, that subobject is opened in the contents view.
/select	Specifies the folder or object to receive the initial focus.
subobject	Specifies the object to open in the contents pane. If used with /select, the parent folder is opened and the specified subobject is only selected or highlighted, rather than opened.

If you use the Windows Explorer often, you might want to either create a shortcut on the Windows 95 Desktop or move the Windows Explorer to the top level of the Start menu. This will be easier than always running Explorer by choosing Start, Programs, Windows Explorer. The Windows Explorer always appears last in the Programs list, and depending how crowded your menu selections are, might be cascaded to a second column and therefore be difficult to locate and run quickly.

Configuring the Mouse

The Windows 95 user interface is designed to be used with a mouse or a similar pointing device. With Windows 95, both the left and right mouse buttons provide expanded features and capabilities. You can use the Mouse Properties sheet to configure the mouse buttons, customize the mouse cursor appearance, set the mouse speed, and so on (see fig. 3.6). Different functions might be available, depending on the pointing device being used with your computer.

Figure 3.6

The Mouse Properties sheet.

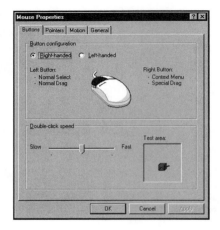

It is important for you to understand the differences between the primary (left) and secondary (right) mouse buttons, and how you can use the mouse to manipulate multiple objects in the same manner as a single object.

Primary Mouse Button

The primary mouse button, usually the left button for right-hand users and the right button for left-hand users, is used in the traditional mouse activities of selecting, pointing at, or dragging an object. The usual functionality associated with selecting and dragging a file is to move a file on a single drive, create a copy of a file on another drive, or create a shortcut to an executable file. Most drag-and-drop functions default to the left mouse button.

Secondary Mouse Button

The secondary mouse button, usually the right button for right-hand users and the left button for left-hand users, is now used as an object menu button. Clicking on an object with the right mouse button presents a context menu, offering choices of actions you can take with the object. Depending on the object, these choices commonly include the following:

- ▶ Open
- ▶ Explore
- ▶ New
- ▶ Send To
- ▶ Create Shortcut
- ▶ Print
- ▶ Quick View
- ▶ Cut
- ▶ Copy
- ▶ Delete
- ▶ Rename
- ▶ Properties

When you use the right mouse button to drag and drop an object, a menu of options appears. The following options are the most common:

- ▶ Move Here
- ▶ Copy Here
- ▶ Create Shortcut(s) Here
- ▶ Cancel

Manipulating Multiple Objects

You also can use the mouse to manipulate multiple objects at one time. You may select a series of objects by drawing a box around them or use the left mouse button to click a series of objects while holding down the Ctrl key. Once selected, you can manipulate all the objects as if they were a single object.

Configuring the Properties Sheet for an Object

Throughout the earlier exercises in this chapter, you had the opportunity to configure several properties sheets for objects within Windows 95. An object's properties, the settings and parameters, are found on the object's properties sheet. These properties might be different from one object to another object, depending on the type of object. The properties sheet provides a standard way to view an object's properties. When you want to view the properties sheet for an object, highlight the object with a single click of the right mouse button. A context-sensitive menu appears, from which Properties can be selected. For a selected file or a folder, the File menu also has an option named Properties.

These properties can be configured as required by using the object's properties sheet. The use of a properties sheet is a convenient and consistent way to review, change, or adjust the settings and parameters of an object. Figure 3.7 shows a sample file properties sheet, which shows when the file was first created, last modified, and last accessed.

Figure 3.7

A file properties sheet.

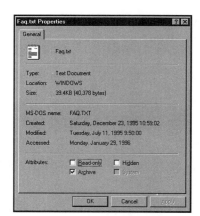

It is important for you to understand the use of properties sheet information, and how this information might be different between one object type and another. As with the properties sheets for DLL and EXE programs, useful information can be gained by viewing the properties sheet for the object.

Using the Windows 95 User Interface

Using the Windows 95 user interface to get your work accomplished is the whole purpose behind your customization and configuration efforts. The following sections cover different ways of using the Windows 95 user interface; creating, printing, and storing documents; and accessing your Network Neighborhood.

Using the User Interface to Accomplish Specific Tasks

The Windows 95 graphical user interface (GUI) is significantly different from the Windows 3.*x* interface. Accomplishing tasks is easier in Windows 95. This exam objective is targeted toward helping you understand and become familiar with using the Windows 95 user interface. Common questions judge your experience in getting your work done in Windows 95. You should focus on the following tasks:

- ▶ Work with the Windows Explorer

- ▶ Find something on your computer

- ▶ Get help

- ▶ Change system settings

- ▶ Organize files and folders

- ▶ Install software

- ▶ Install hardware

- ▶ Set up your computer to use a network

- ▶ Optimize your computer

Each task is described in more detail in the following sections.

Along with using this book to study for the exam, use the *Introducing Microsoft Windows 95* manual you receive with Windows 95. This manual is available in the Windows 95 software box. Read through this 80-odd page manual in detail.

Also, this chapter covers how you might customize and configure Windows 95 to get your work done. However, working with Windows 95 is by far the best way to prepare for the Windows 95 exam. One of the best references on Windows 95 is the New Riders book *Inside Windows 95.*

Work with the Windows Explorer

In the "Configuring and Using Windows Explorer" section earlier in this chapter, you learn how to use and configure the Windows 95 Explorer. Refer to that section to help you study for this part of the exam.

Find Something on Your Computer

Windows 95 provides an expanded find feature, the Find tool, to help you locate files or folders on your computer and on the network, as well as locate computers on a network. You also can save your search results and search criteria to use later.

To use Find to locate files or folder, use the following steps:

1. From the Start menu, choose Find, Files or Folders. The Find: All Files dialog box appears (see fig. 3.8).

Figure 3.8

The Find: All Files dialog box.

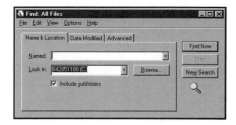

2. Enter your search criteria in the Named field. You can type the complete file or folder name for which you are searching, or type just part of the name. You can use the wildcard character * to help locate items if you are not sure of their complete name. If, for example, you search for a file named TEAM-BUDGET.XLS, but you are not sure of its complete name, enter TEAM-*.XLS. Windows locates all files that begin with TEAM- and that have an XLS extension. If you want to find all files of a specific type, such as text files (with an TXT extension), enter *.TXT in the Named field.

3. Choose the drive on which you want the search to occur from the Look In drop-down list. If you want to search on all local drives, select My Computer from the drop-down list. Click on the Browse button to specify a different location, such as a network drive from Network Neighborhood.

4. Make sure the Include Subfolders check box is selected if you want Windows to search through all the subfolders in a folder. If this check box is not selected, Windows searches in only the folder you specify.

5. Click on the Date Modified tab to specify date parameters for the search. By default, the All files option is specified to tell Windows to search for all files regardless of saved or modification date. On the other hand, you can narrow your search criteria find files that have been saved within a specific date. The following are the options you can choose from here:

   ▶ **Between *n* and *n*.** Use this option when you want to find a file that has a saved date between two dates you specify. Enter specific dates for the *n* parameters, such as 3/3/97 and 3/25/97.

   ▶ **During the Previous *n* Month(s).** Use this option when you want Windows 95 to find a file that has been saved within a specific number of months. Specify a number for the *n* parameter, such as 2.

▶ **During the Previous *n* Day(s).** Use this option when you want Windows 95 to find a file that has been saved within a specific number of days. Specify a number for the *n* parameter, such as 5.

6. Click on the Advanced tab to further narrow your search criteria. From the Of Type drop-down list, you can specify the type of file Windows should search for. This drop-down list contains all the file types installed on your computer, such as Bitmap Image, Briefcase, Movie Clip (AVI), and so on. Use this drop-down list when you may not know a file's name, but you know what type of file it is. In the Containing Text field, you can enter a text string that appears in the content of the file you are searching for. Finally, use the Size Is field to specify a minimum and maximum file size that Windows should search for. File sizes are in KB (kilobytes).

Choose File, Save Search to save your search criteria for this search.

7. Click on the Find Now button to begin the search. When Windows finds all the files matching your search criteria, the files are listed at the bottom of the Find dialog box. If you want to stop the search, click on the Stop button. If no files are found that match your criteria, no files are listed and the status bar of the Find dialog box says 0 file(s) found.

After the search results display, you can save them by choosing Options, Save Results from the Find dialog box.

8. Choose File, Close to close the Find dialog box; or, click on New Search to create a new search.

The Find feature also can search for items on the Microsoft Network (MSN). To do this, you must have an MSN account, a modem, and a phone line connected to the modem.

Get Help

Windows' 95 Help feature is a drastic improvement over the previous Windows 3.1 Help feature. With Windows' 95 Help feature, you can search by topic, by key words, or by full text search. Help provides not only textual help, but also assists the user in performing a task. A user, for example, who does not know how to install a modem can look up the help item Install Your Modem. The help topic includes a button the user clicks on to start the Install New Modem Wizard. From there, the user walks through the wizard to finish the installation process.

To start Help, use the following steps:

1. From the Start menu, choose Help. The Help Topics: Windows Help dialog box appears (see fig. 3.9).

Figure 3.9

The Help Topics: Windows Help dialog box.

2. Double-click on a topic or book on the Contents tab. If, for example, you want to locate the help topic on troubleshooting, double-click on the Troubleshooting book; then click on a topic in the book and click on the Display button.

3. Choose the Index tab to locate help topics by keyword. You can enter a word or the first few letters of a word to locate the help topic; or, scroll through the list of index entries to find what you're looking for.

4. Choose the Find tab to search for specific words in the help topics. When you first use this option, you need to create a database of words from the help files. You can select to minimize the database size, maximize the search capabilities of the database, or customize the search capabilities.

5. Choose Cancel to close the Help Topics: Windows Help dialog box.

Windows 95 provides the Help feature as the primary documentation for Windows 95. If you have a problem using Windows 95, look in Help first, then consult another resource.

Organize Files and Folders

The primary way to organize files and folders in Windows 95 is to use the Windows Explorer or the My Computer folder. With these two tools, you can move, copy, rename, and delete folders and files.

To move a file using the Explorer, use the following steps:

1. Open the Explorer.

2. Locate the file you want to move.

3. Perform one of the following actions:

   ▶ Right-click on the file and choose Cut from the context-sensitive menu. Open the folder in which you want to move the file and right-click on the folder. Choose Paste from the context-sensitive menu to move the file.

   ▶ Click on the file and hold down the mouse button. Drag the file from its original folder to its new location. Drop the file into the new folder. For this method to work well, you should have both the file to move and the new folder displaying in the Explorer at the same time. If the file is an executable file (one with an EXE or COM extension), use the next method to drag and drop the file.

► Right-click on the file and hold down the mouse button. Drag the file from its original folder to its new location. Drop the file into the new folder. A context-sensitive menu appears; choose Move from the menu.

You can use the preceding steps to move a folder from one folder to another; or to move a subfolder to the root folder.

To copy a file from one folder to another, use the following steps:

1. Open the Explorer.

2. Locate the file you want to copy.

3. Perform one of the following actions:

   ► Right-click on the file and choose Copy from the context-sensitive menu. Open the folder in which you want to copy the file and right-click on the folder. Choose Paste from the context-sensitive menu to copy the file.

   ► Press and hold down the Ctrl key on the keyboard. Next, click on the file and hold down the mouse button. Drag the file from its original folder to the location where you want to copy it. Drop the file into the folder and release the Ctrl button. For this method to work well, you should have both the file to copy and the new folder displaying in the Explorer at the same time.

   ► Right-click on the file and hold down the mouse button. Drag the file from its original folder to the location where you want to copy it. Drop the file into the new folder. A context-sensitive menu appears; choose Copy from the menu.

You can use the preceding steps to copy a folder from one folder to another; or to move a subfolder to the root folder.

Windows 95 enables you to rename a file or folder by using the Windows Explorer or My Computer. Unlike File Manager in Windows 3.1, Windows 95 enables you to change a file or folder name within the Explorer or My Computer window. You do not have to use menu commands from the menu bar. This makes managing your files and folders easy.

To rename a file or folder, use the following steps:

1. Open Explorer.

2. Locate the file or folder you want to rename and click once on it. Do not double-click on it.

3 Press F2. A dotted line appears around the selected file or folder name. You also can right-click on the file or folder and choose Rename from the context-sensitive menu.

4. Enter a new name for the file or folder.

5. Press Enter to finish the renaming procedure. If you change the extension of a file name, Windows displays a warning asking if you are sure you want to change the extension.

Another organization task you can perform with files and folders is to delete them. When you delete a file or folder, Windows places it in the Recycle Bin in case you want to undelete it later. Use the following steps to delete a file from your system (use the same steps for deleting a folder):

1. Open Explorer or My Computer.

2. Locate the file you want to delete and click on it.

3. Press Delete. You also can right-click on the file and choose Delete from the context-sensitive menu.

4. Choose Yes in the Confirm File Delete dialog box, which asks if you're sure you want to send the selected file to the Recycle Bin.

Choose Edit, Undo Delete if you want to immediately undelete a file or folder. Or, open the Recycle Bin, select the file or folder to undelete, and choose File, Restore. This restores the deleted file or folder back to its original location.

Install Software

Windows 95 provides two primary ways to install software. First, applications distributed on CD-ROM can be written to automatically launch its installation program when you insert the CD-ROM in your computer. This method is designed to help new users immediately understand how to install a program under Windows 95. For more advanced or experienced users, you can use the second method to install a program. This is done by running the Add/Remove Programs tool from Control Panel.

To use the Add/Remove Programs tool to install software under Windows 95, use the following steps:

1. From the Start menu, choose Settings, Control Panel to open the Control Panel window.

2. Double-click on the Add/Remove Programs icon to open the Add/Remove Programs Properties sheet (see fig. 3.10).

Figure 3.10

The Add/Remove Programs Properties sheet.

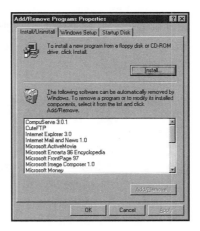

3. Choose the Install button to start the Install Program from Floppy Disk or CD-ROM Wizard. This wizard walks you through installing your new software.

4. Insert the installation disk or CD-ROM for the new program in your computer.

5. Choose Next. Windows automatically searches for the new software. If Windows does not locate it, you are prompted to enter the path and name for the setup program. If you need to search for the installation program, click on the Browse button and locate the setup file. This is handy if the setup program is located on a network drive.

6. Choose Finish to start the installation program for the software.

After the installation program for the new software begins, you need to follow the instructions on-screen to complete the install process. Because every program has different installation instructions, those instructions cannot be covered here. You must refer to the instructions that come with the specific program you are installing.

Install Hardware

In the past, installing hardware under Windows 3.1 was difficult and intimidating for new users. Even experienced users dreaded installing or upgrading a piece of hardware. With Windows 95, however, many of the complications with installing hardware are minimized. The key to minimizing the hassles with hardware installation is the Add New Hardware Wizard. This wizard walks users through the process of detecting the new hardware and then installing the proper device driver for it.

Another feature of Windows 95 that is instrumental in helping users install new hardware is the PnP feature. PnP is a hardware specification that enables Windows 95 to automatically detect the hardware device (usually during the boot process) and set up the proper resources for that device. Although you can use the Add New Hardware Wizard to install PnP devices, you usually do not need to unless you experience problems with installing the new device. For more information on Plug and Play, read Chapter 11.

To install new hardware under Windows 95, use the following steps:

1. From the Start menu, choose Settings, Control Panel to open the Control Panel window.

2. Double-click on the Add New Hardware icon to open the Add New Hardware Wizard (see fig. 3.11).

Figure 3.11

The Add New Hardware Wizard.

3. Choose the Next button to begin the wizard. A new wizard screen appears.

4. To have Windows search for your new hardware, keep the Yes option clicked. To specify the type and name of the device you are installing, choose No. Although the Yes option is handy for new users, most experienced users use the No option and specify the new hardware manually. This usually is the fastest way as well. The following steps assume you choose the No option.

5. Choose Next. On the next screen, select the type of hardware to install, such as CD-ROM controllers, Modem, Mouse, and so on. The next wizard screen that displays depends on the device type you select here. The following steps assume you click on the Mouse type.

6. Choose Next. A screen displays showing you manufacturer and model names. If your new mouse manufacturer and model name appear, click on them. If not, click on the Have Disk button and select the path for the hardware installation disk that comes with your device. Choose OK after entering this information.

7. Choose Next. The final wizard screen appears.

8. Choose Finish to have Windows install your new hardware. You may be prompted to insert the Windows disks or CD-ROM, as well as disks from the hardware manufacturer.

After Windows installs the hardware drivers, you may need to shut down and restart Windows for the new device to be active.

Set Up Your Computer to Use a Network

Windows 95 makes it easy to set up a computer to be connected to a network. You can connect two or more computers running Windows 95 together, connect Windows 95 to a Windows NT server, or connect Windows 95 to a server running Novell NetWare. Chapter 5 covers Windows' 95 networking features in detail.

To set up your computer to use a network, you first need to have a few required items, which are described in the following list:

▶ **Network adapter.** This is a hardware device you add to your computer to which you attach a networking cable, which is attached to another computer to form a network. You must purchase the adapter separately from Windows 95. Refer to the preceding section to install the network adapter. When you purchase a network adapter, make sure it's compatible with Windows 95 (look at the product packaging or ask your dealer for this information).

As you learn in Chapter 9, Windows 95 includes the Dial-Up Adapter for connecting to remote servers, such as an Internet service provider. Although the Dial-Up Adapter is considered a network adapter, it is not a piece of hardware you need to install. It is only software you install.

▶ **Network client software.** Client software is the software that Windows 95 uses to communicate over the network with other computers and the network server. Windows 95 includes support for Banyan, Microsoft, Novell, and SunSoft networking clients. For example, if you're connecting Windows 95 to another Windows 95 computer, use the Microsoft

Client for Microsoft Networks software; however, if you want to connect Windows 95 to a Novell NetWare server, install the Client for NetWare Networks software.

▶ **Network protocol.** The protocol is the language a network uses so all computers connected to that network can communicate with each other. Windows 95 includes a number of different protocols, including TCP/IP, IPX/SPX, and Net-BEUI. You must make sure all computers on the network use the same protocol. Also, your network adapter must support the protocol you choose.

▶ **Network cable.** The network cable physically connects the computers to the network. The network cable is analogous to the television cable that links your television inside your home to the main cable company to display the shows you watch. The cable used most often for computer networks is coaxial and twisted-pair cable. *Coaxial cable* is the same type of cable used in homes for cable television. *Twisted-pair cable* is similar to the cabling used in standard telephone lines. You must make sure the cable you select works with the network adapter you purchase.

▶ **Network services.** Services enable a computer on the network to share files, printers, and perform other services with other computers on the network. Windows 95 includes backup services, HP JetAdmin printer services, and file and printer sharing service. You must make sure the services you select are compatible with the protocol and client software you install.

For more information about the preceding topics and for coverage on how to install and configure Windows 95 for networks, see Chapter 5.

Optimize Your Computer

Windows 95 includes tools to help you optimize your computer. These tools help you increase your computer's disk space, defragment your hard drive, and check your files and hard drive for errors. The following are the tools you can use:

▶ **DriveSpace.** Compresses the data on your computer's hard disk to make more space on the disk. Running DriveSpace can give you from 50 percent to 100 percent more space on your hard drive.

▶ **Disk Defragmenter.** Defragments your files so they are read from and written to in a more efficient and faster way. Files become defragmented because parts of the file are stored in different locations (called *clusters*) on your hard drive. For your hard drive to be optimized, files should occupy contiguous clusters, which is how Disk Defragmenter sets up your hard drive.

▶ **ScanDisk.** Checks and fixes files and folders on your hard disk for data errors and physical surface problems. ScanDisk is an upgrade to the ScanDisk utility included with MS-DOS 6.*x*. Windows 95 includes both a graphical ScanDisk utility and a DOS-command prompt utility.

You learn how to run and use all of these tools in Chapter 6.

Using the Windows 95 Interface to Create, Print, and Store a File

This exam objective covers the fundamental tasks of creating a file, printing its contents, and saving the file. The file can be either textual, graphical, or both. Windows 95 comes with several applications for working with both text files and graphics files. Table 3.6 lists these applications.

Table 3.6

Windows 95 Applications	
Application	Description
Notepad	Automatically installed. Notepad is limited in the size of text file that it can open. Windows 95 will open a file in WordPad if it is too large for Notepad.

Application	Description
WordPad	A mini-version of the Microsoft Word program. Replaces both Windows 3.*x* Write and Notepad. A 32-bit text editor that supports OLE and MAPI. An optional Windows 95 component.
Paint	A mini-version graphics program, replaces Windows 3.*x* Paintbrush. A 32-bit graphical editor that supports OLE and MAPI. An optional Windows 95 component.

WordPad and Notepad are discussed in detail in Chapter 8, "Running Applications." See that chapter for instructions on starting and using these applications.

You can create, view, and edit images in Windows 95 using Paint. Paint enables you to create or edit bitmap files in BMP, PCX, or RLE formats. *Bitmap files* are images made up of individual pixels. The BMP file format is the standard Windows bitmap format, whereas the PCX format has become the de facto graphics file standard. *PCX* is a format developed by Z-Soft for a product called PC Paintbrush, not to be confused with Windows Paint or the Paintbrush application included with prior versions of Windows. *RLE* is a compressed bitmap graphics format that generally occupies less space than BMP files of the same resolution.

To use Paint to display an image, follow these steps:

1. From the Start menu, choose Programs, Accessories, Paint. The Paint window appears (see fig. 3.12).

2. Choose File, Open from the Paint menubar.

3. In the Open dialog box, open the Windows folder. This folder contains a number of BMP files bundled with Windows 95.

If you did not install all of the Desktop Wallpaper components during the Windows 95 installation process, you should do so now so you can follow along. Or, select a different BMP file than the one selected here.

4. From the Open dialog box, select the CLOUDS.BMP file and choose Open. Paint displays the CLOUDS.BMP file.

Figure 3.12

The Paint window.

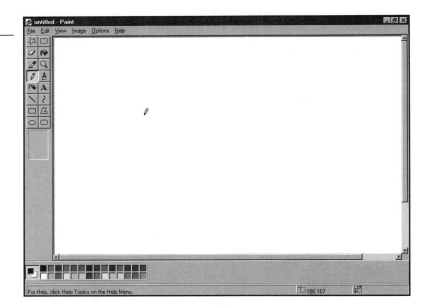

You now can edit the image using the Paint tools. These tools are located in the Paint Toolbox on the left side of the Paint window. You also can choose to change the colors of objects using the Color palette at the bottom of the Paint window. Finally, the Image menu contains several image attribute options you can choose, such as Flip, Rotate, Invert Colors, and more.

When you finish creating or editing an image, you save it by choosing File, Save, which saves it to its previous file name. To provide a new name, choose File, Save As and fill out the File Name field of the Save As dialog box.

Accessing the Network through Network Neighborhood

The Network Neighborhood is a new concept in Windows 95. Chapter 5 discusses networking and interoperability in greater detail. This exam objective, however, covers using the Network Neighborhood to access network resources.

If your computer is set up to use a network, the Network Neighborhood icon appears on your Windows 95 Desktop. When you double-click on the Network Neighborhood icon, you see the computers in your workgroup or any NetWare servers to which you are connected. If your workgroup name happens to match a Microsoft domain name, then your Microsoft network browsing capability is enhanced. You can see other computers on the network, those not in your workgroup, by double-clicking on the Entire Network icon, which appears in the Network Neighborhood.

Windows 95 is a good networking client. Network configuration is simple and straightforward. Setting up your computer to use a network requires two major steps: setting up hardware and setting up software. First, your computer hardware needs to be correctly installed, which includes the network interface card (NIC), cabling, and hubs. Second, the network configuration of network clients, adapters, protocols, and services needs to be performed. For Microsoft networking, several key pieces of information need to be supplied: default user name, the computer name, and workgroup name. The access control security level needs to be established, whether share-level (default) or user-level security. You also might need to install or configure some other supporting networking components, such as pass-through file server security, mobile dial-up networking, agents for backup and remote administration, and support for system policies and user profiles.

Chapter 5 discusses setting up your computer on the network. Another good reference book from New Riders is *Windows 95 for Network Administrators*. If you are a network administrator, your Windows 95 library should include a copy.

To quickly display the Network Properties sheet in the Control Panel, right-click on the Network Neighborhood icon on the Windows 95 Desktop, and select Properties. If you have trouble seeing other computers in your browse list, check the workgroup name on the Identification tab of the Network Properties sheet.

Using the Registry

The key to Windows 95 is the Windows 95 Registry. First, a word of caution is in order. If you can avoid making Windows 95 Registry changes using the Windows 95 Registry Editor, do. If you must make Windows 95 Registry changes using the Windows 95 Registry Editor, be careful. The Windows 95 Registry contains all your Windows 95 configuration information. If it gets corrupted, your Windows 95 computer will not run properly.

The nearest analogy is working with electricity. Precautions should always be taken. Never deal with it lightly. Be careful. Know what you are doing because this is one area where you can seriously mess up. You might have a margin for error, but it is a slim one.

This section covers the Windows 95 Registry. There are many other good references available, including the Microsoft *Windows 95 Resource Kit* and the New Riders book, *Windows 95 Registry Troubleshooting*.

Defining the Purpose of the Registry

In Windows 3.*x*, the Registry Database is a single file, named REG.DAT, that contains only file associations and Object Linking and Embedding (OLE) registration information. The remainder of the system information for Windows 3.*x* was scattered in various INI files. This caused problems for configuration management due to the following:

▶ Information was stored in several different locations, including CONFIG.SYS, AUTOEXEC.BAT, WIN.INI, SYSTEM.INI, PROTOCOL.INI, and other INI and GRP files.

▶ The INI files were text-based, limited to 64 KB in size, and used APIs that allowed only simple get/write operations.

▶ The INI file information was non-hierarchical (flat) and supported only two levels of information: key names by section. It did not support multiple configurations for a specific key value.

▶ Configuring the INI files properly was complicated, they stored little or no user information, and they could not be administrated remotely with ease.

To solve these problems, the Windows 95 Registry was designed with the following purposes in mind:

▶ To centralize all the configuration information

▶ To utilize a tree-structured, hierarchical database structure, rather than text-based, limited capability INI files

▶ To provide a means to store user, application, and computer-specific information

▶ To simplify the support burden and allow both local and remote access to configuration information

Rather than a single file, the Windows 95 Registry is stored in two files. The SYSTEM.DAT file contains the computer hardware configurations, and the USER.DAT file contains user-specific settings. Together these two files are the central repository of information for the Windows 95 operating system. Windows 95 needs a clean Registry to boot properly. After each successful boot of Windows 95, copies of both files are saved as SYSTEM.DA0 and USER.DA0 (The "T" in the file extension is replaced with a zero "0"). This is very much like Windows NT's "last-known good configuration," though not as simple to recover from if a problem occurs.

Some Windows 95 references include a third file, CONFIG.POL, that stores administrative policies that are setup on a network server. CONFIG.POL is not a required component of the Windows 95 Setup, and when implemented, it is stored on the network server rather than the local computer.

> Microsoft provides the REGEDIT utility to view and change the contents of the Windows 95 Registry. Before you make changes to the Windows 95 Registry, first make a backup copy of the two Registry files—SYSTEM.DAT and USER.DAT. Both of these files are hidden in the Windows folder.

For backward compatibility, the older Windows 3.*x* configuration files, such as CONFIG.SYS, AUTOEXEC.BAT, WIN.INI, SYSTEM.INI, PROGMAN.INI, CONTROL.INI, and PROTOCOL.INI, still exist. The 16-bit Windows APIs used to update the INI files also still exist; however, developers of WIN32 applications are encouraged to use the Registry APIs to load application-specific information into the Registry.

Classifying Types of Information in the Registry

The Windows 95 Registry is a database created during Windows 95 startup. It is a front-end for all your Windows 95 configuration information, including system configuration, hardware configuration, the setup information for 32-bit Windows-based applications, and user preferences. The actual files in which this configuration information is stored are called USER.DAT, SYSTEM.DAT, and, optionally, CONFIG.POL. These files are not in readable format. To view and change your current user and system configurations, you need to run REGEDIT.EXE, the Windows 95 Registry Editor. Figure 3.13 shows the hierarchical tree-like structure of the Windows 95 Registry database.

Figure 3.13

The Windows 95 Registry Editor.

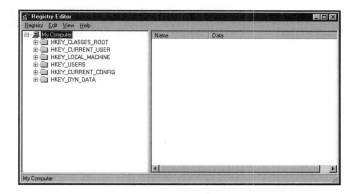

The Windows 95 Registry is made up of six root keys. Although more complex than the simple registry in Windows 3.*x*, the Windows 95 Registry is not as comprehensive as the Windows NT registry. The following sections describe the six root keys.

HKEY_CLASSES_ROOT

This key contains the same type of data as the simple REG.DAT registry file in Windows 3.*x* and provides backward compatibility for OLE and DDE support. It also contains OLE and association mapping information to support drag-and-drop operations, Windows 95 shortcuts (that are, in fact, OLE links), and core aspects of the Windows 95 user interface. The association mappings allow Windows 95 to run or print from an application when a specific file type is selected.

This key merely points to the Registry branch within another root key, HKEY_LOCAL_MACHINE\SOFTWARE\Classes. The three basic key types within HKEY_CLASSES_ROOT are file extensions, file associations, and OLE2 objects.

HKEY_CURRENT_USER

This key contains user-specific settings for applications, desktop configurations, and user preferences, in much the same way that WIN.INI does under Windows 3.*x*. This key is created at run time (when the user logs on to Windows 95) from information stored in the user's entry under HKEY_USERS. If the user does not already exist, the .DEFAULT information is used.

These user-specific settings are copied back into the HKEY_USERS branch when you shut down Windows 95. There are several different key types: events, schemes, user-specific Control Panel settings, most recently used (MRU) location of installation files, keyboard layout, network, dial-up networking settings, and software settings.

HKEY_LOCAL_MACHINE

This key contains computer-specific information about the type of hardware installed, drivers, and other system settings. This information is used for all users that log on to the computer. It is the same information stored within the SYSTEM.DAT configuration file and is required to properly run the hardware.

Multiple hardware configurations are listed under the Config key, in the case of a laptop computer with a docking station and both docked and undocked configurations. Much of the device manager information can be found under the Enum key, though this information is easier to view through the System icon in the Control Panel. There are several different key types: hardware configurations (usually only one), device manager information, network-specific security information, installed software information, and system settings.

HKEY_USERS

This key contains information about all users who log on to the computer, including the .DEFAULT generic user settings. The generic program and system settings act as a template for any new users on the computer. See the earlier section "HKEY_CURRENT_USER" for the list of user information stored under this key. It is the same information stored within the USER.DAT configuration file and is required to properly run the system.

HKEY_CURRENT_CONFIG

This key contains information about the current running hardware configuration. It is used when multiple hardware configurations are available to the computer. The prime example of multiple hardware configurations is a laptop computer that can be either docked or undocked in a docking station. The information for this key is directly copied from the various configuration information contained in the HKEY_LOCAL_MACHINE key.

HKEY_DYN_DATA

This key contains the dynamic status information for various devices as part of the Plug and Play configuration. It is regenerated every time the system starts up. This information can change as hardware devices are added to or removed from the computer. The information kept for each hardware device includes the associated hardware key, any problems, and current status. This key also contains information on system monitoring being performed using the System Monitor tool. This key is not part of either registry file and is always dynamically created.

The Windows 95 Registry Editor program is not available from the Start menu for a very good reason. The Registry is self-maintaining and should only be modified in extreme cases. Any modifications to the system are best done through the appropriate user interface, such as the System icon, Device Manager tab, or with the other Control Panel icons.

If you need to change the Registry, make a backup copy first.

Determining Where the Registry is Stored

The Windows 95 Registry contains all the Windows 95 system and user information. It is an ASCII database that pulls information from the three files listed in table 3.7. These files are not in readable form, so you can view or change their contents only by using a Windows application, such as the Windows 95 Registry Editor program, the Control Panel icons, or the System Policies Editor (for the optional CONFIG.POL file). The USER.DAT and SYSTEM.DAT files are stored on the local computer's hard drive. If the CONFIG.POL file exits, it is stored on a network file server to be downloaded when a user logs onto the network.

Table 3.7

Files in the Windows 95 Registry

Registry File	Description
SYSTEM.DAT	Contains hardware-related and computer-specific settings.
USER.DAT	Contains user-specific information found in user profiles, such as user rights, Desktop settings, and so on.
CONFIG.POL (Optional)	Contains policy information related to the system and user settings. The information in the system policies file can override information in both SYSTEM.DAT and USER.DAT files. This is an optional file.

Always make backup copies of your Windows 95 Registry files before you make any changes. In the Windows 95 Registry Editor program, choose Registry, Export Registry file to create a REG file. This exported REG file represents the contents of the DAT files at a given point in time. The Windows 95 CD-ROM includes two other useful utilities, found in the Other\Misc subdirectory. The first is an Emergency Recovery Utility (ERU.EXE), which saves key Windows 95 files to either a floppy drive, a local drive, or a network drive. The second is a Configuration Backup (CFGBACK.EXE) utility that can save and restore up to nine configurations of your Windows 95 Registry. Periodically, you can also run a simple batch file to save copies of both the SYSTEM.DAT and USER.DAT files.

Deciding When It Is Appropriate to Modify the Registry

In general, the Windows 95 Registry is not where you should make your changes. Most of the configuration information you can modify in the Windows 95 Registry can be changed using a GUI front-end; however, some configuration information cannot. Only in these situations is it appropriate to modify the Registry using the Registry Editor program.

The best advice that can be given for when to modify the Registry directly using the Registry Editor is only as the last resort. There are times when a value in the Registry must be manually set by a user or system administrator. The following are some of these situations:

▶ You may need to edit the Registry via the Registry Editor because of data not deleted from the Registry from an application or device you have removed. Sometimes you'll remove an application and the application or Windows does not remove all traces of the application. If a setting left behind interferes with another process, application, or device, you may experience problems. You'll need to hunt down and remove these stray Registry settings. Usually, you won't know about these situations unless you read about them from bug reports or updates from the software manufacturer.

▶ You might read about a bug fix from Microsoft that you need to use the Registry Editor to fix. Often Microsoft posts bug fixes or Knowledge Base articles on their World Wide Web site that instruct you to modify the Registry directly. This might be the case to fix a network protocol issue, remove a Desktop icon, or other fix.

▶ You might want to enhance a feature using the Registry Editor. A number of feature enhancements or customization options are available by modifying the Registry directly. One of these is to remove the Microsoft Network icon from your Desktop. You cannot simply delete this icon; you must use the Registry Editor and locate its setting to disable it.

Modifying the Contents of the Registry

The only modification to the Windows 95 Registry that this author has seen that might be of worth is tweaking the 8.3 naming conventions when using long file names in Windows 95. The tilde character (~) and a number are tacked onto the short version of your long file names. This can differ from the default long file naming that Novell NetWare servers follow when using OS/2 Name Space to support long file names.

In the following steps (and again in Exercise 3.16 at the end of the chapter), you make a very minor modification to the Windows 95 Registry. This modification changes the naming behavior so that unique, auto-generated, DOS 8.3 names do not use tilde-type tails (see fig. 3.14). Remember to make a backup first. See the earlier section, "Determining Where the Registry Is Stored," for instructions on how to make a backup copy of your Registry.

Figure 3.14

Add Registry Entry.

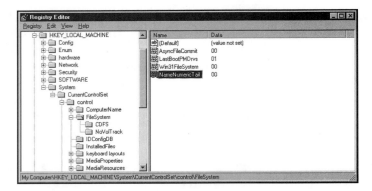

1. If you have not backed up your Registry files on your computer already, please do so now.

2. From your computer, start the Windows 95 Registry Editor program. The shortcut created on your Windows 95 Desktop uses the key combination of Ctrl+Alt+R. Use the key combination or double-click on the shortcut itself.

3. Locate the following Windows 95 Registry entry:

   HKEY_LOCAL_MACHINE\System\CurrentControlSet\control\ FileSystem

4. Add a binary value with the name NameNumericTail and value 00 by choosing Edit, New, Binary Value.

5. Exit from the Windows 95 Registry Editor.

If you get into trouble changing the Registry, restore by following these steps:

1. From the Start menu, choose Shut Down.

2. Choose Restart the Computer in MS-DOS Mode, and then choose Yes.

3. Change to your Windows directory. For example, if your Windows directory is C:\Windows, type the following:

   cd c:\windows

4. Type the following commands, pressing Enter after each one (note that System.da0 and User.da0 contain the number zero):

   attrib —h —r —s system.dat

   attrib —h —r —s system.da0

   copy system.da0 system.dat

   attrib —h —r —s user.dat

   attrib —h —r —s user.da0

   copy user.da0 user.dat

5. Restart your computer.

Following this procedure restores your Registry to the state it was in when you last successfully started your computer.

When OLE Information in the Registry Becomes Corrupted

In the previous section, "Classifying Types of Information in the Registry," you learned that all the OLE information is stored in HKEY_LOCAL_MACHINE\SOFTWARE\Classes. This includes both OLE1 and OLE2 support. The *Windows 95 Resource Kit*, Chapter 22, "Application Support," discusses using OLE to share data between applications. When this data becomes corrupted, your OLE operations no longer function. You have several courses of action to fix the corruption:

▶ Restore the Registry files from a backup copy. This action assumes that the previous versions have non-corrupted OLE information.

▶ Import into the Registry from a REG ASCII file containing the entries to correct the corrupted OLE information. This action assumes that correct information was exported prev-iously.

▶ Reinstall the application whose OLE information was corrupted. This action assumes that the reinstall updates the corrupted OLE information.

▶ Compare Registry OLE information between the corrupted computer and one in which the OLE operation is working. This task is laborious, and it might or might not fix the problem. Keep in mind that every problem you discover might hide several more problems.

Whatever course of action you take, talking with a Microsoft help desk representative will improve your chances of finding and fixing the problem. Remember that the rules for working with the Windows 95 Registry are like the rules for working with electricity. Precautions should always be taken.

Exercises

Exercise 3.1:   Explain Windows 3.1 and Windows 95 Differences

Exercise 3.1 makes use of two computers to compare and contrast the differences between Windows 3.*x* and Windows 95. It will be helpful to you in this exercise to visually compare the two versions of Windows. If you have only a single dual-boot computer, run down each column before dual-booting between the two versions of Windows.

Dual-boot Computer 1 to Windows for Workgroups, and leave Computer 2 running Windows 95. Go through each entry in table 3.4 and compare the user interfaces between the two computers. How do you start an application program in Windows 3.1 versus Windows 95?

Exercise 3.2:   Dual-Boot with DOS and Windows 3.1

Exercise 3.2 leads you through the process of dual-booting with DOS and Windows 3.1.

Treat this dual-boot exercise as a custom installation to Computer 2; run this from the shared CD-ROM on Computer 1 or from a CD-ROM drive on Computer 2. If Computer 2 still has the network-based Windows 95 directory from Exercise 1.7, the Windows 95 installation also can be run from there.

Computer 2 should still be running both MS-DOS and Windows for Workgroups. The end result will have Computer 2 running Windows 95 in a dual-boot configuration. This is a hands-on exercise, with a 60-minute duration. Walk through the following steps:

1. Reboot Computer 2, loading MS-DOS and Windows for Workgroups. From a Windows 95 installation directory, start the Windows 95 SETUP.EXE program by one of the following means:

   ▶ Shared CD-ROM on Computer 1

   ▶ CD-ROM on Computer 2 itself

continues

Exercise 3.2: Continued

> ▶ Server-based Setup of the Windows 95

> ▶ A routine check of the system, followed by the preparation of the Setup Wizard

2. The software license appears. Read it, then choose Yes to continue.

3. The Setup Wizard appears to start collecting information about your computer. Choose Next to continue.

4. When prompted for a location to install Windows 95, do not take the default, C:\WINDOWS. Instead, select to install to an Other directory. Choose Next to continue.

5. Install into a new Windows 95 directory, C:\WIN95. Choose Next to continue.

6. A Setup warning message appears, which tells you that installing Windows 95 to a new directory requires the reinstallation of all your Windows-based programs to make them work properly under Windows 95. Choose Yes to continue.

7. Windows 95 prepares the directory. Check for installed components and available disk space.

8. Choose the type of installation—the default is Typical. Choose Custom and then choose Next to continue.

9. For User Information, enter your full name and the name of your organization or company. Choose Next to continue.

10. For Product Identification, enter the product key code from the CD-ROM cover.

    Setup analyzes your computer, searching for all hardware devices available.

11. If asked to check for specific hardware, such as a CD-ROM drive or Sound Card, check the appropriate boxes, and choose Next to continue.

12. After hardware detection, a Getting Connected dialog box appears. Do not select any of these components.

13. You are prompted to install the default components, as determined by your setup option. Choose the options you will most likely use, and choose Next to continue.

14. Verify your network configuration, if prompted by the Windows 95 Setup program. With a Windows for Workgroups connected computer you might not see these prompts.

15. If asked to identify your computer and workgroup, enter the appropriate information. Make sure the computer name is unique. Choose Next to continue.

16. The Computer Settings screen appears. Verify all your computer settings, and choose Next to continue.

17. When asked whether you want to create a startup disk, accept the default; that sets the radio button to Yes, I Want a Startup Disk. Choose Next to continue.

18. The Setup Wizard begins to copy files to your computer. Choose Next to continue.

19. The copy process might take a while; enter a Startup Disk floppy when prompted.

20. The Setup Wizard reappears to finish the Windows 95 installation on your computer. Choose Finish to continue.

21. Windows 95 starts and prompts you for your user name and password. The Control Panel, Start menu, and Help system are configured.

22. When prompted for the time zone, choose your approximate location on the world map to help select the correct time zone. Choose Close to continue.

23. If you have a printer, ignore the printer wizard and continue. Chapter 7 discusses printer installation.

continues

Exercise 3.2:   Continued

24. The Welcome to Windows 95 screen appears. From the Start menu, run Notepad.exe and open the MSDOS.SYS file on the root of drive C. Verify MSDOS.SYS contains the entry for enabling dual-boot, `BootMulti=1`. Close the application.

25. Be aware that network Plug and Play adapters might not always configure themselves properly, so network browsing might be impacted. Check Hardware Configuration if any errors are encountered.

The Windows 95 Setup program should automatically enable dual-boot because Windows 95 is installed into a new directory, and the version 5.*x* or 6.*x* of MS-DOS was installed on the computer.

Exercise 3.3:   Dual-Boot with Windows NT

In Exercise 3.3, you install Windows NT in a dual-boot configuration. Treat this exercise as a routine installation of Windows NT 3.51 Server to Computer 2. Run the exercise from the shared CD-ROM on Computer 1 or from a CD-ROM drive on Computer 2. Computer 2 must meet the hardware requirements for a Windows NT Server. If you are new to Windows NT Server, two other good books from New Riders Publishing are recommended: *Inside Windows NT Server* and *Windows NT Server Professional Reference*. MCSE candidates must master Windows NT Server as part of the core operating system requirements.

The installation process for Windows NT Server 4.0 is more Windows 95–like. The new user interface update is the most significant improvement in the new version of Windows NT. If you are installing Windows NT Server 4.0, rather than the older Windows NT Server 3.51, review this exercise for the appropriate settings only. Be aware that the Microsoft certification exam objectives and test questions usually reflect the newer versions of software after four to six months.

Computer 2 should still be dual-booting both MS-DOS/Windows for Workgroups and Windows 95 (following Exercise 2.1). The end result has Computer 2 running Windows 95 in a multiple, dual-boot configuration. This is a hands-on exercise with a 60-minute duration. Walk through the following steps:

1. Reboot Computer 2, loading Windows 95. From a Windows NT Server installation directory (either on a shared CD-ROM on Computer 1 or a CD-ROM on Computer 2), start the Windows NT Server Installation (WINNT.EXE) program. Please have four pre-formatted, 1.44-MB HD 3.5-inch floppies handy to create the Windows NT boot disks and an emergency repair disk.

2. Use the winnt /w option from either within Windows 95 after it has finished rebooting or during reboot, press F8 at Windows 95 Startup, choose the option to start the command prompt only, and then run winnt.

3. Confirm when you are prompted that the current directory is the one on which the Windows NT Server installation files reside.

4. Insert disk 3 into the floppy drive and follow the Windows NT Server Setup program instructions.

   The three bootable Windows NT disks are created in reverse order, and the files are copied.

5. Restart the computer with disk 1, the Windows NT Boot Disk in drive A.

6. Choose where to install Windows NT, select a hard drive, as suggested by the Windows NT Server Setup program. All hard drives are displayed, showing available free space.

7. Leave the current file system intact (no changes). Do not convert to NTFS.

8. Choose the directory name for the Windows NT Server install. Accept the suggested default.

continues

Exercise 3.3: Continued

9. The Windows NT Server files are copied, and the computer is restarted with zero time at the Windows NT Boot Loader in order to complete the installation. Enter name and company information.

10. Make this computer a Primary Domain Controller. You have to re-install Windows NT Server to change this selection.

11. Enter a computer name, following the same naming rules as for Windows 95 computer names (see Chapter 1).

12. Accept the language default—English.

13. Skip the Printer setup.

14. For the network card, accept the default protocols, NWLINK (IPX/SPX compatible) and NetBEUI.

15. Assign the Primary Domain Controller a domain name, which you can use later. Keep the name simple.

16. For the default user-id-named administrator, choose OK to use a blank password.

17. Select the appropriate time zone for the computer.

18. Test the screen display, then choose OK.

19. Restart Windows NT Server.

20. Create an emergency repair disk when prompted.

21. Modify the Windows NT Boot Loader menu selection. Go to Control Panel, System, and choose MS-DOS as the default startup, rather than Windows NT Server Version 3.5x, which is the original default. Choose OK to save your changes.

22. Using Windows NT File Manager, change the properties of the BOOT.INI file on the root to remove the Read-Only property so the file can be edited. Using Notepad, change MS-DOS line to read "Windows 95" rather than "MS-DOS"

and then save the file. Change the properties of the BOOT.INI file back to Read-Only.

23. Shut down and then restart the computer.

Exercise 3.4:   Configuring a Plug and Play Hardware Device

In Exercise 3.4, you add a Plug and Play hardware device. You can either re-install a Plug and Play hardware device already on your computer (if one exists) or add a new Plug and Play hardware device.

1. If adding a new Plug and Play hardware device, shut down the computer and install the device, then go to step 5.

2. If reinstalling an existing Plug and Play hardware device, choose Start, Settings, Control Panel, and double-click on the System icon. The System Properties sheet appears (refer to fig. 3.1).

3. Select the Device Manager tab on the System Properties sheet to view the hardware configuration.

4. Find a Plug and Play hardware device, highlight the device, and click on the Remove button to remove the Plug and Play hardware device that you want the system to automatically detect in the next step. Shut down the computer.

5. Restart the computer. The normal Windows 95 boot process should recognize the Plug and Play hardware device and add it to the system configuration.

6. If the Plug and Play hardware device is not automatically added, you must choose Start, Settings, Control Panel, and double-click on the Add New Hardware icon to run the hardware detection process.

What happens during the automatic detection of Plug and Play hardware devices? The hardware devices should be automatically recognized by Windows 95. Are you prompted for any configuration information? If the hardware device has Plug and Play enabled, you should not be prompted for any configuration information.

Exercise 3.5: Viewing the Hardware Tree

In Exercise 3.5 you examine the hardware configuration of your computer

1. From a Windows 95 computer, choose Start, Settings, Control Panel, and double-click on the System icon. The System Properties sheet appears.

2. Select the Device Manager tab on the System Properties sheet to view the hardware configuration (see fig. 3.15).

Figure 3.15

The Device Manager tab of the System Properties sheet.

Which of the bus configurations listed in table 3.3 can be found on your computer? The most common workstation bus configuration is an ISA bus, followed by a combination of either ISA and VL, or ISA and PCI.

Exercise 3.6: Configuring the Taskbar

In Exercise 3.6 you configure the Windows 95 Taskbar.

1. On your computer, run Windows 95.

   Drag the Taskbar to each of the four sides of the screen display. Leave the Taskbar on the side that makes the most sense to you; the default is the bottom of the screen.

2. Resize the Taskbar by placing the tip of the mouse pointer on the inner edge of the Taskbar until a double-sided arrow appears. With the left mouse button depressed, drag the inner edge to resize the Taskbar. Leave the Taskbar at a comfortable size for your needs.

3. From the Start menu, choose Settings, Taskbar to open the Taskbar Properties sheet (refer to fig. 3.2).

4. Select Auto Hide and choose OK. The Taskbar all but disappears. It is still there, but the only visible sign is a thin line of pixels on the side of the screen. Move the mouse pointer to the very edge of the screen where the Taskbar currently resides. The Taskbar will reappear.

5. Move the mouse pointer away from the edge of the screen where the Taskbar currently resides. The Taskbar automatically hides again.

6. Experiment with various combinations of Taskbar options and select one that works best for you.

Exercise 3.7: Configuring a Shortcut

In Exercise 3.7, you are shown how to create a shortcut to the Registry Editor.

1. From the Start menu, choose Programs, Windows Explorer, to open the Windows Explorer program.

2. Explore the Windows 95 directory and locate the Registry Editor (REGEDIT.EXE) application.

3. Highlight the REGEDIT object using the primary mouse button. With the button held down, drag and drop a shortcut onto the Windows 95 Desktop.

4. Exit Windows Explorer.

5. Click on the shortcut's name field below the icon titled "Shortcut to Regedit.exe" and change it to read "Registry Editor."

continues

Exercise 3.7: Continued

6. Right-click on the newly created shortcut and select Properties from the pop-up menu to display the Registry Editor Properties sheet. Assign the shortcut the key combination of Ctrl+Alt+R. The shortcut opens when you enter those keys (refer to fig. 3.3). Choose OK to save the change.

What happens to the original object when you make changes to the shortcut's settings? Nothing, because the shortcut's properties apply only to the shortcut itself.

Exercise 3.8: Adding a Program to the Start Menu

In Exercise 3.8, you add one of your favorite programs to the Start menu. If you do not have a program in mind, add the program WORDPAD.EXE, which, if installed, can be found in the Accessories folder of the Program Files subdirectory. The quotes around the path to a particular program are required if the path includes a long file name with embedded spaces.

1. From Computer 1, open the Start menu and choose Settings, Taskbar to open the Taskbar Properties sheet.

2. Select the Start Menu Programs tab on the Taskbar Properties sheet (see fig. 3.16).

Figure 3.16

The Start Menu Programs tab of the Taskbar Properties sheet.

3. Click on the Add button. The Create Shortcut Wizard appears. In the command-line box, enter **"C:\Program Files\Accessories\Wordpad.exe"** or click on the Browse button to find a different program. The double quotes are necessary for the Wordpad.exe program because the Program Files folder includes a space in its name between the words "Program" and "Files."

4. Choose a location in the Start menu to place the new shortcut. Choose to put the shortcut into the Start menu folder. Give the shortcut an appropriate long file name, such as "Wordpad Program." Select Finish when done. Choose OK to close the Taskbar Properties sheet.

5. Open the Start menu to display all the key menu features and functions. Where in the Start menu does the program appear? Usually you will see the new program at the top of the Start menu. Be aware there is a limit on the number of items in the Start menu, depending on whether you are using large or small icons.

Exercise 3.9:   Customizing Your Windows 95 Desktop

In Exercise 3.9, you experiment with the look and feel of your Desktop by making changes to the Display Properties sheet.

1. From the Start menu, choose Settings, Control Panel, and then choose the Display icon. The Display Properties sheet opens (refer to fig. 3.4).

2. Select the Background tab. Click on the scroll box in the Wallpaper field to select a bitmap (BMP) file, or choose Browse to select your own file.

3. Explore the various tabs on the Display Properties sheet and change your display settings as desired.

4. When you finish, choose OK to close the Display Properties sheet.

continues

Exercise 3.9: Continued

What happens when you make changes to the Desktop settings? The changes are shown first to the Display Properties sheet's display monitor, and are applied only when you click on the Apply button or choose OK to close.

Exercise 3.10: Running Explorer from the Command Line

Exercise 3.10 will help you understand the impact of using the various command-line switches with the Windows Explorer. A shortcut can be created on the Windows 95 Desktop to the Windows Explorer using these command switches. This enables you to quickly open an Explorer window.

1. From the Start menu, choose Run. In the Run dialog box, enter the following series of Windows Explorer commands, as detailed in steps 2 through 7. Each command opens a new Windows Explorer instance.

2. Run Explorer with the /n option by entering **explorer /n**.

3. Run Explorer with the /e option by entering **explorer /e**.

4. Run Explorer with the /root option by entering **explorer /root,c:\windows**.

5. Run Explorer with the /e and /root options by entering **explorer /e,/root,c:\windows**.

6. Run Explorer with the /e, /root, and subobject options by entering **explorer /e,/root,c:\windows,system**.

7. Run Explorer with the /e, /root, /select and subobject options by entering **explorer /e,/root,c:\windows, /select,system**.

8. Exit by closing the various Explorer windows.

The exercise helps you understand the use of the various command-line switches with the Windows Explorer. You can expect at least one question about the Windows Explorer on the exam.

Exercise 3.11: Configuring the Mouse

Exercise 3.11 will help you configure the mouse under Windows 95. Your Mouse Properties sheet might vary, depending on the type of pointing device installed on your computer.

1. From the Start menu, choose Settings, Control Panel, and double-click on the Mouse icon to open the Mouse Properties sheet.

2. Alter the button configuration by switching the left mouse button from one side of the mouse to the other. Notice how the highlighted mouse changes to match the selection. The text that describes what each button does also changes to match the configuration. Set the mouse button configuration to match your preference.

3. Slide the double-click speed to match your style. Try it all the way to the fast end. The test area allows you to check the setting. This author could never activate jack-in-the-box using a double-click at the fast setting, can you? Adjust to match your preference.

4. From the Pointers tab, review the various bitmaps for the mouse pointer. Select a scheme that appeals to you. Keep in mind that animated cursors require more overhead to run.

5. Close the Mouse Properties sheet.

Exercise 3.12: Configuring a Properties Sheet

Exercise 3.12 will help you find and configure different properties sheets under Windows 95.

1. From the Start menu, choose Find, Files or Folders. The Find: All Files dialog box appears.

2. Enter the following file names. As each one is located, use the right mouse button to examine the properties sheet of each selected file.

continues

Exercise 3.12: Continued

a. Find "*.txt" (all text files) within the Windows 95 directory. Both faq.txt and tips.txt are good files for you to review. Open and examine their properties sheets.

b. Find "*.dll" (all dynamic link library files) within the boot drive, usually c:\. Open and examine several of the DLL files' properties sheets. The Version tab on the properties sheet contains useful information about the DLL file, including the file version. This information is useful when resolving DLL version problems.

c. Find "xcopy*.exe" (all xcopy executable files) in the Windows 95 directory. One, xcopy.exe, is an MS-DOS–based application, and the other, xcopy32.exe, is a Windows 95 application. Open and examine both of the properties sheets. You will see the differences between the properties sheets, depending on the type of application program.

d. Find the Windows folder in the boot drive, usually drive C. Open and examine the folder's properties sheet. This is a quick way to determine a folder's size. If the folder is shared on the network, the Sharing tab contains information on the shared folder's properties.

3. Exit by closing the Find: All Files dialog box and any open file properties sheets.

While this exercise did not have you make any changes in the properties sheet settings and parameters, you did examine several different kinds of properties sheets.

Exercise 3.13: Using the Windows 95 Interface

In Exercise 3.13, you accomplish some tasks in Windows 95 that might appear on the exam.

1. From your computer, find the Windows 95 SCANDISK.EXE program by using three different methods: (1) My Computer, (2) the Windows Explorer, and (3) the Find option on the Start menu.

2. Create a shortcut on the Desktop for the SCANDISK.EXE program and start the program from the shortcut.

3. Find all the TXT files in the Windows subdirectory.

4. Run Help from the Start menu, and examine each of the How To items in the Contents tab.

5. Open the System Tools folder by choosing Start, Programs, Accessories, System Tools. Check if the Windows 95 System Monitor is installed in the System Tools folder. If not, use the Add/Remove Programs option in Control Panel to install it. Run System Monitor.

6. Select multiple files and use the Send To option on the secondary mouse context-sensitive menu to send multiple files to a floppy disk.

7. Shut down and restart your computer.

Another set of exercises you might find useful can be found on the Microsoft TechNet CD-ROM, under Personal Systems, Windows 95, Training Materials, Labs 1 and 2.

Exercise 3.14:   Using WordPad

In an earlier exercise to configure the Start menu, WordPad (or your own favorite application) might have been added as an option to your Start menu. In Exercise 3.14, you use the WordPad application to create a document, print it, and save the file when you are done.

1. Open the WordPad application. If WordPad is not available, use Add/Remove Programs in Control Panel to install it.

2. Edit a new document, using the features of WordPad to change text font and color. Be creative; add a bitmap, change the text boldness and underline, and so on.

3. If a printer is installed, print the document. (See Chapter 7 for steps on how to configure a printer.)

4. Save the document to your My Documents folder.

5. Exit WordPad.

Exercise 3.15: Examining Your Registry

In Exercise 3.15, you explore your computer's Registry using a shortcut created in Exercise 3.9.

1. Start the Windows 95 Registry Editor program. The shortcut created on your Windows 95 Desktop uses the key combination of Ctrl+Alt+R. Either use the key combination or double-click on the shortcut.

2. Examine all six keys of the Windows 95 Registry. Do not make any changes to the information, just view the settings.

3. Exit the Windows 95 Registry Editor program.

Exercise 3.16: Modifying Your Registry

In Exercise 3.16, you make a very minor modification to the Windows 95 Registry. This modification changes the naming behavior so that unique, auto-generated, DOS 8.3 file names do not use tilde-type tails (refer to fig. 3.14). Remember to make a backup first. See the earlier section, "Determining Where the Registry Is Stored," for instructions on how to make a backup copy of your Registry.

1. If you have not backed up your Registry files on your computer already, please do so now.

2. Start the Windows 95 Registry Editor program. The shortcut created on your Windows 95 Desktop uses the key combination of Ctrl+Alt+R. Use the key combination or double-click on the shortcut itself.

3. Locate the following Windows 95 Registry entry:

   HKEY_LOCAL_MACHINE\System\CurrentControlSet\control\FileSystem

4. Add a binary value with the name NameNumericTail and value 00 by selecting Edit, New, Binary Value.

5. Exit from the Windows 95 Registry Editor.

Review Questions

The following questions will test your knowledge of the information in this chapter. For additional questions, see MCP Endeavor and the Microsoft Roadmap/Assessment Exam on the CD-ROM that accompanies this book.

1. With Windows 95, the Windows 95 Project Team tried to answer one basic question: "How can the user interface in Windows 3.1 be improved?" The end result was an operating system with a user interface that incorporates the following (choose the three best answers):

    A. Ease of use

    B. Better Windows 3.1 applications

    C. Speed and power

    D. Compatibility

    E. C2-level security

2. Windows 95 enables you to modify objects. An object has which of the following two characteristics, as defined under Windows 95?

    A. Behavior

    B. Polymorphism

    C. Form (icon)

    D. Inheritance

    E. Attributes (properties)

3. James is installing Windows 95 on a dozen computers in his company. Currently, the computers run a number of different operating systems and James has to make sure Windows 95 can dual-boot with the operating system already on a computer. Which one of the following operating systems cannot be dual-booted with Windows 95?

    A. MS-DOS 5.*x* or greater

    B. Novell (DR) DOS

C. IBM PC-DOS 5.*x* or greater

D. Windows NT

E. OS/2 2.*x* or greater

4. Nicole is migrating her existing version of Windows to Windows 95. She asks you to explain what will happen to her existing Windows installation. Which three of the following do you tell her?

   A. Dual-boot with your previous version of DOS is automatically set up.

   B. Your older versions of some DOS files are deleted—those that do not support long file names or conflict with Windows 95.

   C. Configuration settings in SYSTEM.INI, WIN.INI, and PROTOCOL.INI are used to configure Windows 95.

   D. The information in the Windows 3.*x* Registry, such as file associations and OLE, is added into the Windows 95 Registry.

   E. All your Windows applications have to be re-installed in order to work properly under Windows 95.

5. You are at the help desk when a caller tells you she tried to upgrade her existing operating system to Windows 95, but was not successful at it. She asks you why. You tell her that her operating system cannot be upgraded to Windows 95. Which one of the following operating systems did you tell her cannot be upgraded to Windows 95?

   A. MS-DOS 5.*x* or greater

   B. Novell (DR) DOS

   C. IBM PC-DOS 5.*x* or greater

   D. Windows NT

   E. OS/2 2.*x* or greater

6. Miles upgraded to Windows 95 and set it up to dual-boot with his previous version of DOS. He now cannot find his old DOS boot files. In a dual-boot setup with a previous version of DOS, the older DOS boot files have which of the following extensions when running Windows 95?

   A. SAV

   B. W40

   C. DOS

   D. OLD

   E. BAK

7. You set up Windows 95 to dual-boot with Windows NT, but you want Windows 95 to be the default operating system at boot times. This way Windows 95 boots (and not Windows NT) when you turn on your computer. You want to change the boot order in the Boot Loader program. The Windows NT Boot Loader program uses which of the following files to list the boot options?

   A. MSDOS.SYS

   B. CONFIG.SYS

   C. NTBOOT.INI

   D. BOOT.INI

   E. WIN.INI

8. Several users at your company ask you about which type of partition on which Windows 95 can be installed. Instead of waiting for the remaining 20 people in the office to ask you this same question, you send an e-mail to everyone announcing which one of the following statements? Pick the one that is true.

   A. Windows 95 can be installed into a FAT partition.

   B. Windows 95 can be installed into an NTFS partition.

   C. Windows 95 can be safely installed into the same directory as Windows NT.

D. Windows 95 can be installed into an HPFS partition.

E. Windows 95 can be installed into the same directory as OS/2.

9. Wesley is purchasing a new computer system for Windows 95 and wants to make sure his devices adhere to the Plug and Play specification. He asks your advice on which type of bus architecture to purchase so he knows it fully supports Plug and Play. You tell him one of the following. Which one?

A. ISA

B. EISA

C. MCA

D. SCSI

E. PC Card

10. Tammy drags and drops application programs onto the Start menu, but they do not appear where she expects them to. She calls you asking where they should appear. You tell her that application programs dragged and dropped onto the Start menu appear _____.

A. Under Programs

B. Under Settings

C. Under Run

D. In the Start menu itself

E. They cannot be placed in the Start menu

11. A system administrator installs Windows 95 on her assistant's new computer. When Windows 95 starts after it is completely installed, which of the following objects does not appear on the Windows 95 Desktop when first installed?

A. My Computer

B. Recycle Bin

C. Taskbar

    D. Control Panel

    E. Start menu

12. Rachel calls you late at night explaining to you she has to change her Windows 95 display settings to view a PowerPoint presentation. You help her out by telling her which of the following two answers? Choose the two best answers:

    A. Run the Display program.

    B. Right-click on the Windows 95 Desktop and select Properties.

    C. Open the Control Panel and select the Display icon.

    D. Reinstall Windows 95.

    E. Boot into safe mode.

13. As system administrator for your company, you are responsible for compiling a list of hardware needs for the next fiscal year. You want to make sure all new hardware devices adhere to the Windows 95 Plug and Play specification. Which three of the following are major components of the Plug and Play specification?

    A. Plug and Play connections

    B. Plug and Play hardware devices

    C. Plug and Play BIOS

    D. Plug and Play operating system

14. Bart has been using computers for several years, but has never installed new hardware devices. He wants to know how easy it is to set up Plug and Play devices under Windows 95. You tell him all but one of the following phrases. Which of the following is not a way to configure a Plug and Play hardware device?

    A. Windows 95 Setup program

    B. Add New Hardware icon in the Control Panel

    C. Flip a dip switch on the hardware device

D. During the normal boot process

E. During warm- or hot-docking situations

15. During a training session on Windows 95, the instructor calls upon you to describe the Windows 95 Taskbar. What are the three sections that comprise the Windows 95 Taskbar?

    A. Launch button

    B. Start menu

    C. Active program buttons

    D. Notification area

    E. Clock

16. To change the way the Taskbar looks and behaves, you display the Taskbar Properties sheet. Which of the following is not an option on the Taskbar Properties sheet?

    A. Always on Top

    B. Auto Hide

    C. Show Small Icons in Start Menu

    D. Show Date

    E. Show Clock

17. Abby uses the same application daily and grows tired of launching it from the Programs folder on the Start menu. You suggest that she create a shortcut on the Desktop to the application. To create a shortcut, you tell her to use which three of the following actions?

    A. Choose New, Shortcut using the right mouse button context-sensitive menu on an open spot of the Windows 95 Desktop.

    B. Choose Programs, Create Shortcut from the Start menu.

    C. Drag and drop an application from the Explorer to the Windows 95 Desktop.

    D. From an object itself, right-click to open the context-sensitive menu, create the shortcut.

    E. Copy a file from one folder on the C drive to another folder also on the C drive.

18. You upgrade to Windows 95 and use the Explorer to view the contents of a folder. Which of the following is not a view option when exploring a folder?

    A. Large Icons

    B. Small Icons

    C. List

    D. Group

    E. Details

19. Tori wants to know the settings and properties of an object on her Desktop. She can find the object's settings and properties where?

    A. Registry

    B. Control Panel

    C. INI file

    D. Properties sheet

    E. Readme file

20. You open the Registry Editor and examine its contents. What files comprise the Windows 95 Registry? Pick three answers.

    A. CONFIG.SYS

    B. SYSTEM.DAT

    C. WINSYS.DAT

    D. USER.DAT

    E. CONFIG.POL

21. Jake has a shortcut on the Desktop that is associated with the file named BUDGET.XLS. He uses the shortcut to launch Microsoft Excel with the BUDGET.XLS worksheet displayed. If he wants to move the file to a different folder on his system, what could happen to the shortcut to the file?

    A. It changes to a copy of the original file.

    B. It moves to the Network Neighborhood.

    C. It becomes an orphan shortcut.

    D. It displays a different long file name.

22. You receive a call at the help desk from a user asking you how a damaged Registry can be fixed. Which two files on the users' system must he specify at the DOS command line to restore his Registry?

    A. USER.DAT and SYSTEM.DAT

    B. CONFIG.SYS and WIN.INI

    C. CONFIG.POL and USER.DAT

    D. USER.DA0 and SYSTEM.DA0

23. During a Windows 95 seminar you attend, the speaker explains the differences between Windows 3.1 and Windows 95. Among these differences, he highlights a group of four. Pick one of the following groups that list all new features in Windows 95.

    A. Long File Names, Recycle Bin, File Manager, Program Manager

    B. Long File Names, Recycle Bin, Shortcuts, Print Manager

    C. Recycle Bin, Folders, Start menu, Taskbar

    D. Recycle Bin, Folders, Print Manager, Program Manager

24. You receive a call from a user who has been instructed by a software manufacturer to modify her Registry for a particular feature in the software to work properly. Before she edits the Registry, she calls you asking for advice. Which three of the following statements are valid responses to her query?

    A. She can edit the Registry using the Registry Editor.

    B. She should make a back up copy of the Registry using the Emergency Recovery Utility.

    C. She should always use the binary value 00 when creating a new entry.

    D. She can view six root keys of the Registry in the Registry Editor.

25. Sally installs a hardware device under Windows 95. She uses the Device Manager to view the resource allocations for devices on her computer. What two views are supported by Device Manager to enable her to view her devices?

    A. Connection

    B. IRQ settings

    C. Type

    D. Resources

Review Answers

1. A C D	8. A	15. B C D	22. D
2. C E	9. E	16. D	23. C
3. B	10. D	17. A C D	24. A B D
4. B C D	11. D	18. D	25. A C
5. D	12. B C	19. D	
6. C	13. B C D	20. B D E	
7. D	14. C	21. C	

Test Yourself

Stop! Before reading this chapter, test yourself to determine how much study time you will need to devote to this section.

1. As administrator you need to set up a training classroom so that all student computers running Windows 95 on a network have one default setting. Each time the computer is booted, you want this default setting to be invoked, regardless of any previous changes made by a user. Name two ways you can set up these computers to use a default setting at each boot-up.

2. You want to be able to administer Windows 95 computers on a network. You run a Windows NT network and have a Windows 95 computer from which you can administer these other Windows 95 computers. What service and its associated executable file do you need to install to remotely edit a user's Registry?

3. A user asks how she can modify her user profile. She's running a Windows 95 computer that is not connected to a network. What are the general steps for doing this?

4. Jill wants to create two user profiles for her computer, one named WORK and the other named GAMES. How does she enable user profiles on her computer?

5. What is the default name of the system policy file Windows 95 uses? Where is this file stored when a user is using share-level security? Where is this file stored when a user is using user-level security?

6. Stan asks you to define the System Policy Editor and why it is useful. Name two features of the System Policy Editor that help you administer Windows 95 workstations.

7. You want to view the connections to shared folders on the network. What is the name of the utility provided with Windows 95 that enables you to do this?

8. A user complains that his computer running Windows 95 is running low on memory. You ask him how many threads he has open. He doesn't know. How can you, from a networked Windows 95 computer, see the number of threads running on his system?

Answers

1. Set a default user profile that cannot be edited. Set a system policy that is downloaded to the computer each time the computer boots. Disable editing of the policy file. See "Modifying a User Workstation to Meet Specified Criteria."

2. The Microsoft Remote Registry service. You must install the REGSERV.EXE file (and related files). See "Granting Remote Administration Privileges on Your Computer."

3. Make sure the users can customize their Preferences and Desktop Settings option is enabled on the User Profiles tab of the Passwords Properties sheet. Next, advise the user to make any changes to the Desktop, Start menu, and program groups. Shut down and reboot the system. After logging in, the new changes will appear and will be part of the user profile for that user. See "Modifying User Profiles."

4. Choose Start, Settings, Control Panel, and double-click on the Passwords icon. Click on the User Profile tab and click on the Users Can Customize Their Preferences and Desktop Settings option. See "Setting Up User Profiles."

5. CONFIG.POL. Share-level security: usually C:\WINDOWS; user-level security: user's home directory on the Windows NT or the user's mail directory on a NetWare server. See "System Policy Editor."

6. Enables you to edit the Registry without using the Registry Editor. Enables you to set default settings on a user's or group of users' computers using a template file. See "User and System Policies."

7. Net Watcher. See "Using Net Watcher for Remote Administration."

8. Use System Monitor and connect to his computer. See "Remote Administration" and "Granting Remote Administration Privileges on Your Computer."

Chapter

Editing User and System Profiles

This chapter will help you prepare for the exam by covering the following objectives:

Test Objectives

- ▶ Modify a user workstation to meet specified criteria

- ▶ Set up user profiles

- ▶ Modify user profiles

- ▶ Define the System Policy Editor, and describe how it is used

- ▶ Set up computer policies

- ▶ Administer a remote computer

- ▶ Grant remote administration privileges on your computer

- ▶ Create, share, and monitor a remote resource

Windows 95 contains a number of features that can be used by an administrator to control computer-specific and user-specific settings on a Windows 95 computer. Some of these features include:

- ▶ The capability to modify a computer's settings through the Properties sheet, Control Panel, and Registry settings to modify many Windows 95 variables

- ▶ The use of hardware profiles

- ▶ The use of user profiles, which allow different user-specific settings on the same Windows 95 computer

- ▶ The capability to remotely administer another computer from the administrator's computer

- System and User policies, which enable the administrator to control various settings and restrict what a user can change

- The Net Watcher tool, which can be used to control and monitor shared folders remotely

In this chapter, the following Windows 95 administration topics are discussed:

- Using the Control Panel, Properties sheets, and the Registry to configure and administer a Windows 95 computer

- Using Hardware Profiles to maintain different hardware configurations for a Windows 95 computer

- Using User Profiles to maintain different software configurations for multiple users on a single Windows 95 computer

- Implementing User and System policies to enforce specific controls in a Windows 95 environment

- Using the Windows 95 Remote Administration tools

Administration

The configurable settings of the Windows 95 operating system, the computer hardware, and Windows 95–compatible applications are stored in a database known as the *Registry* on the Windows 95 computer. The Registry entries can be set automatically by Windows 95 or a compatible application, or they can be modified manually. To display or modify specific Registry entries, the following items can often be used:

- The Control Panel

- The Properties sheet of an object

- The Registry Editor

Many objects can be configured from any of these locations.

Control Panel

The Control Panel contains numerous applets for graphically configuring various components of the Windows 95 operating system. Exactly which configuration applets are present in a Windows 95 Control Panel depends on which Windows 95 components or compatible applications have been installed. For example, the Control Panel shown in figure 4.1 contains some standard Windows 95 Control Panel applets, in addition to the 32-bit ODBC configuration applet that was installed during a Microsoft Access 95 installation.

Figure 4.1

A typical Control Panel window.

Some of the Control Panel applets are described in table 4.1, although additional applets may be present. Online help is available for most of the Control Panel applets by choosing the question mark button in the upper-right corner of a dialog box and selecting a field.

Table 4.1

Some Common Control Panel Applets

Applet	Description
Accessibility Options	Options to make Windows 95 easier to use for individuals with disabilities
Add New Hardware	Used to configure new hardware

Applet	Description
Add/Remove Programs	Used to install or remove Windows components and other applications
Display	Used to change the display driver video monitor information, colors, screensavers, and the appearance of the Desktop
Fonts	Used to view installed fonts or to install new fonts
Keyboard	Used to change the type of keyboard used, the language of the keyboard, or such options as the rate of display of typed characters
Modems	Used to configure a modem
Mouse	Used to change mouse or pointer options
Multimedia	Used to change options and drivers for audio/video devices, such as MIDI devices, sound cards, or video boards
Printers	Used to add or configure printers
Password	Used to change the Windows password, enable remote administration, and enable user profiles
Sound	Used to modify sound schemes if a sound card or speaker driver is installed
System	Used to display and modify various settings related to the operating system and hardware properties

Properties Sheets

Many objects in Windows 95 have a Properties sheet that can be used to configure that object. The Properties sheets are often displayed by right-clicking on the object and selecting Properties from the context-sensitive menu that appears. For example, if you right-click on a blank space on the Desktop and select Properties, the Display Properties sheet appears enabling you to change such things as the wallpaper and screensaver used. Similarly, the

Properties sheet for a file in Explorer reveals the file properties (such as the time last modified) and attributes (such as Hidden or Read-Only).

Registry Editor

Information pertaining to a Windows 95 client's hardware devices, user settings, operating system settings, and application configurations is stored in the Windows 95 Registry on the local computer. Applications that are designed for Windows 95 can add additional information to the Registry and can query the Registry for existing information. To display a document as it would print, for example, word processing applications can query the Registry to find out what driver is currently set as the default printer.

As discussed in Chapter 3, "Customizing and Configuring Windows 95," the Registry information is stored in two files on the hard drive of the local computer:

- ▶ **SYSTEM.DAT.** Contains computer-specific information, such as the devices present and their configured settings.

- ▶ **USER.DAT.** Contains user-specific settings and preferences, such as the shortcuts displayed on the Desktop and the applications installed in the Start menu programs.

Windows 95 uses two files to build the Registry to separate the user-specific information from the system- (or computer-) specific information. By doing this, administrators can store user settings on the network server to enable user profiles or system policies to be enabled. You learn more about these topics in the "Profiles" and "User and System Policies" sections later in this chapter.

The hierarchical, tree-like structure of the Registry enables configuration information to be logically grouped together in branches of the tree called *keys*. Information about installed Microsoft applications, for example, may be found under the HKEY_LOCAL_MACHINE\SOFTWARE\Microsoft key.

The first level of the Registry hierarchy comprises the following root keys:

▶ **HKEY_CLASSES_ROOT.** Maintains Object Linking and Embedding (OLE) data with association mapping to support drag-and-drop operations. It also tracks aspects of the Windows 95 user interface, including shortcuts. Additionally, this subkey provides for the compatibility with Windows 3.1 registration database, REG.DAT.

▶ **HKEY_CURRENT_USER.** Maintains the current user's configuration and provides user preferences in much the same manner as did WIN.INI in Windows 3.*x*. It keeps information on the current user, such as application preferences, screen colors, security access permissions, and environment variables.

▶ **HKEY_LOCAL_MACHINE.** Stores specific computer and workstation configuration information. It enables you to track multiple Windows 95 configurations for the same computer.

▶ **HKEY_USERS.** Maintains information about default users and specific users who log onto the workstation. This subkey stores user settings and desktop configurations, and tracks matters including AppEvents, Control Panel, keyboard layouts, network, and most-recently used (MRU) applications.

▶ **HKEY_CURRENT_CONFIGURATION.** Maintains data about the current session's hardware configuration.

▶ **HKEY_DYN_DATA.** Stores dynamic status information for devices and provides support for Plug and Play features. This data is cached in workstation RAM for incidents in which Windows 95 needs fast modification and retrieval.

The Registry can be viewed and modified using the Registry Editor. To start the Registry Editor, enter **regedit** in the Run dialog box opened from the Start menu.

Any changes made to the Registry can prevent the operating system from functioning properly and can prevent the system from initializing. You should make a backup copy of the SYSTEM.DAT and USER.DAT files before using the Registry Editor in case you need to revert to the previous settings. Many settings in the Registry normally can be modified safely through the Control Panel or through the application involved. See Chapter 3 for more information on making backup copies of your Registry.

Modify a User Workstation to Meet Specified Criteria

One of the exam objectives you need to understand is how to modify a workstation based on specific criteria. Many users and system administrators are called upon to make changes to a workstation, such as modify desktop settings, install or uninstall applications, remove items from the desktop, change network settings, and so on. When you need to modify a workstation, you need to understand the best or quickest way to perform the task. As you've read in this section, there are three primary ways to modify a workstation in Windows 95: through the Control Panel, the Registry Editor, or the properties sheet of an object you are changing.

Suppose, for example, that you need to modify the resolution of a workstation's display. Depending on which tool you are most comfortable with, you might change the resolution by using the Control Panel or you might use the Display Properties sheet from the Windows desktop. The following steps show how to perform this modification using the Control Panel:

1. From the Start menu, choose Settings, Control Panel. The Control Panel appears.

2. Double-click on the Display icon in the Control Panel. The Display Properties sheet appears.

3. Click on the Settings tab.

4. In the Desktop Area group of the Settings tab, move the slider control to a new setting, such as to 800 by 600 pixels (if your setting is currently 800 × 600, change it to a different setting that your monitor supports).

5. Click on OK.

6. Click on OK in the Display Properties sheet.

7. Click on Yes in the Monitor Settings dialog box.

Now, to modify the screen resolution using the Display Properties sheet from the Windows desktop, use the following steps. These steps will return you to your previous screen resolution.

1. Right-click on the Windows 95 Desktop using the mouse.

2. From the context-sensitive menu, select Properties. The Display Properties sheet appears.

3. Click on the Settings tab.

4. In the Desktop Area group of the Settings tab, move the slider control to a new setting, such as 640 by 480 pixels (if your setting is currently 640×480, change it to a different setting that your monitor supports).

5. Click on OK.

6. Click on OK in the Display Properties sheet.

7. Click on Yes in the Monitor Settings dialog box.

You've now used two different methods in Windows 95 to achieve the same results. You also can use the Registry Editor to make the same modification to the workstation resolution. Before using the Registry Editor, you should make a backup of the SYSTEM.DAT and USER.DAT files, as well as attempt to make the modification using the Control Panel and property settings. Next, do the following:

1. Start the Registry Editor by entering **regedit** in the Run dialog box opened from the Start menu.

2. Locate the subkey HKEY_LOCAL_MACHINE\Config\ 0001\Display\Settings.

3. Double-click on the Resolution entry in the right pane of the Registry Editor.

4. In the Edit String dialog box, change the data in the Value Data field to another setting, such as **800,600**.

5. Click on OK.

6. Close the Registry Editor. The next time you restart Windows, the new settings take effect.

7. Shut down and restart Windows 95. The new display settings are used to display a different screen resolution.

As you've seen, Windows 95 enables you to modify a workstation to meet a specific criteria using different tools. Some tools, such as the Control Panel applications and Properties sheets, impose some limitations to what you can modify. These tools, however, generally protect you and other users from making changes to a workstation that are detrimental to it. On the other hand, the Registry Editor provides a way to modify almost everything on a workstation, but it is not easy to use nor does it include any protection against you or other users modifying or deleting a setting that is critical to the operation of Windows or applications running under Windows.

Profiles

Windows 95 uses profiles to customize the configurable settings for different circumstances. A profile enables the Registry to contain different configurations used for different scenarios. Completely different Desktop configurations, for example, may be maintained for different users who will access the Windows 95 computer. When one of the users logs on, Windows 95 can use the Registry settings specific to that user.

The following are the two types of profiles:

▶ Hardware profiles

▶ User profiles

Both of these profile types are described in the following sections.

Setting Up Hardware Profiles

For non-mobile configurations, Windows 95 usually uses a single hardware profile that contains all the computer-specific, hardware-related configuration information. Additional hardware profiles can be created, however, that use different configuration information. A mobile computer, for example, may have one hardware profile that is used when it is attached to a network and a different profile used when it is away from the network. The non-networked profile would not include a network adapter in the configuration settings, and therefore the computer would not waste time attempting to connect to the network at startup.

The hardware profiles affect the HKEY_LOCAL_MACHINE keys in the Registry, which are stored in the SYSTEM.DAT file. For more information on the use of hardware profiles, refer to Chapter 3 and to the section "Hardware Profiles" in Chapter 11, "Plug and Play."

Setting Up User Profiles

If multiple users use the same Windows 95 computer, each user can have his or her own user-specific configuration information stored in a different user profile. Some of the information that can be contained in a user profile includes:

▶ Shortcut icons on the Desktop

▶ Applications contained in the Start menu

▶ Customized Desktop settings, such as colors, backgrounds, fonts, and more

▶ Persistent network connections

▶ Recently used documents under the Start menu Documents list

By default, all users use the same profile. Also, Windows 95 does not have user profile support turned on; you must explicitly enable user profile support on a system before using it. To turn it on, use the following steps:

1. From the Start menu, choose Settings, Control Panel. The Control Panel opens.

2. Double-click on the Passwords icon. The Passwords Properties sheet appears.

3. Select the User Profiles tab. By default, the All Users of this PC Use the Same Preferences and Desktop Settings option is selected.

4. Select the Users Can Customize Their Preferences and Desktop Settings option. When you click this option, the following two options appear.

   Include Desktop Icons and Network Neighborhood Contents in User Settings. Displays shortcuts to files the user has established. Any user-defined links the user has created in Network Neighborhood are also included.

   Include Start Menu and Program Groups in User Settings. Includes the contents of the Start menu and Program groups in the user profile.

5. Choose OK. You are prompted to restart the computer.

6. Choose OK to restart the computer.

When Windows 95 boots, a log in window displays asking for the user name and password. You now are ready to set up a user profile for a specific user. The following steps lead you through setting up a user profile for a user named PROFILE-1. This user profile includes a shortcut to the Paint program on the Desktop and displays the Black Thatch wallpaper. Every time the

PROFILE-1 user logs into Windows, these items appear. When a different user logs in, a different set of shortcut(s) and wallpaper (if any) appears. Use the following steps to create the PROFILE-1 user profile:

1. Enter the name **PROFILE-1** in the Username field.

2. Enter a password in the Password field. For simplicity sake, enter **PASSWORD**. You'll be prompted to confirm the password. Do so.

3. Click on OK. A message appears asking if you want to save the settings for the user in a user profile.

If you are attached to a network using Windows Networking, you will be prompted that the user you just entered has not logged on to this network before. You also are asked if you want to set up this new user and have Windows save session settings in a profile. Click on Yes. You are then asked to confirm the password.

4. Click on Yes to save the sessions settings in a user profile. The default Windows 95 desktop appears.

5. Set up a shortcut on the Desktop to the Paint program. You can do this by right-clicking on the Desktop, selecting New and Shortcut, and then filling out the Create Shortcut Wizard.

6. After the shortcut is set up, select the wallpaper named Black Thatch and set it to tile on the screen. If that is not installed on your system, select another one. Just make sure it is different from the default wallpaper.

7. Shut down Windows 95. When the Shut Down Windows dialog box appears, select the Close All Programs and Log on as a Different User? option. Choose Yes.

8. When the Enter Windows Password logon screen appears, log on as a different user, such as **PROFILE-2**. The default Windows 95 desktop displays. Notice the settings you made

in steps 5 and 6 do not display. This is because you are logged on as a different user this time, using a different user profile.

9. Shut down Windows 95. When the Shut Down Windows dialog box appears, select the Close All Programs and Log on as a Different User? option. Choose Yes.

10. Log on as the PROFILE-1 user. The Paint shortcut and Black Thatch wallpaper appear when Windows 95 starts.

When a user profile is created, the user-specific information is stored in a subdirectory of the \\<*systemroot*>\\Profiles directory (where <*systemroot*> is WINDOWS, for example). The subdirectory has the same name as the user name and contains a USER.DAT file with the user-specific Registry entries. The user profiles are stored in the HKEY_USERS keys in the Registry. When a user is logged on, the USER.DAT file is accessed, and the entries for that user are copied to the HKEY_CURRENT_USER keys in the Registry. When a user logs off, the changes are saved to the USER.DAT file.

The following is an example of the way Windows 95 stores user profiles on a local workstation:

```
C:\
    \WINDOWS
        \PROFILES
            \PROFILE-1
                \DESKTOP
                \NETHOOD
                \RECENT
                \START MENU
```

User profiles also can be configured so that a network user can use the same user profile no matter which Windows 95 computer he or she logs on to. Thus, the user has the same settings, preferences, and shortcuts available on any Windows 95 computer. This is generally referred to as a *roving user*, because the user roams from computer to computer. To use the same profile on another Windows 95 computer attached to a network, that computer must have user profiles enabled. Next, a copy of the user's USER.DAT file should be copied to the user's home directory on a Windows NT server or the user's mail directory on a NetWare server. When the user logs on, his USER.DAT file is copied from the server to the Windows 95 computer. Those settings are then used for the session. When the user logs off, any further changes to the USER.DAT are copied back to the USER.DAT file on the server.

> For information on creating a home directory on a Windows NT or NetWare server, refer to the Windows NT or Novell NetWare documentation.

The following are some conditions that form the basis for use of user profiles on a network:

▶ Enable user profiles on the workstations.

▶ Synchronize the clocks on all computers attached to the network. You can use the NET TIME command from the command prompt to synchronize clocks.

▶ Install and use a Microsoft 32-bit protected mode network client on the workstation. This is either the Microsoft Client for NetWare or the Microsoft Client for Microsoft Networks.

▶ Establish long file name support on the NetWare server. This is required because Windows 95 folders, such as the Start menu or the Network Neighborhood, are actually seen as long file names. Windows NT Server already supports long file names.

▶ Make sure home directories exist for users on the Windows NT Server for the storage of the user profiles. On a NetWare server, the storage location is the *server*\MAIL*user_Id* directory that is created when a user is created.

▶ On each computer that will support profiles, make sure the directory for Windows 95 has the same directory names so the profiles subdirectory will be in the same named directory on each workstation. Note that C:\WINDOWS is not the same as D:\WINDOWS. Each Windows 95 workstation must have the same Windows directory structure and Windows subdirectory name to enable ease of downloading of user information during each logon time.

> When you store a user's profile on a NetWare server, the user is referred to by eight-digit bindery object identification—not by a logon name or other name. Check your NetWare documentation on how to determine this user id.

If a copy of a user's USER.DAT file exits on the workstation, it is found by Windows 95 and compared to the network server copy. Windows 95 uses the latest copy of the file and at logoff time updates both copies of the USER.DAT file (one on the server and one on the local workstation) so that they are identical. Date/Time stamp becomes important.

If you do not want to allow a user to customize her user profile settings, you can use a mandatory user profile. This is helpful if you have a setup for which you do not want changes saved, such as on a training room computer. Also, if you have a guest account available for a Windows 95 computer, for example, you might want all guests to use the same user profile settings, and thus not be able to save changes to the guest account user profile. To do this, copy the user's USER.DAT file to her home directory on the server. Next, rename the USER.DAT file to USER.MAN and change the file properties to Hidden and Read-Only. When the user logs on, the USER.MAN file is copied to the USER.DAT file on the local computer. When the user logs off, however, the changes are not copied to the server, so the original USER.MAN user profile settings are used the next time the user logs on.

Modifying User Profiles

Unless you specify a mandatory profile file for a user, any user can change his or her user profile. (To use a mandatory profile file, see the preceding paragraph.) A user can do this by logging into the computer with her username and password for the profile she wants to change. She then can make any changes to the environment, such as color changes, shortcut modifications, Start menu changes, and so on. The user then logs off the computer (she does not have to shut down Windows, just log off) and logs back on using the same profile. The modified user profile is used when Windows starts.

One thing to keep in mind about modifying user profiles is the way they are saved to a network server. If a user happens to be logged on to a network from two different Windows 95 computers at one time, the wrong profile settings may be saved for that user. The last settings saved to the profile overwrite all other profile settings; Windows does not merge the two setting changes.

For example, say a user logs onto the network from computer A, which is his main working computer, and his user profile downloads to his workstation. He makes some changes to the Desktop by adding two shortcuts to a shared document, but does not log out or shut down his computer. He then goes next door and logs onto the network using the same profile from computer B. He looks for his new shortcuts he made on computer A. They are not there (they have not been saved yet). He then manually creates the same shortcuts on computer B, but also decides to remove an older shortcut he no longer needs. He does his work and logs off computer B, saving his changes to his profile (two new shortcuts, one deleted shortcut). He returns to computer A, does his work, and logs off. When he logs back onto computer A (or computer B for that matter), the two new shortcuts are there, but so is the shortcut he deleted from computer B. This is because the last settings saved were from computer A, which overwrote the settings changed from computer B.

For even more control over what settings users can and cannot modify, you may define policies for the Windows 95 users and computers.

User and System Policies

Windows 95 policies enable an administrator to set various Registry entries and control whether a user can change such settings. Computer-specific (HKEY_LOCAL_COMPUTER) Registry entries can be enforced through a Computer policy. User-specific Registry entries can be enforced through User policies. In addition, Group policies can be created to enforce user-specific settings for groups of user accounts defined on a Windows NT or NetWare server.

System Policy Editor

Computer, User, and Group System policies are created using the System Policy Editor, POLEDIT.EXE. The System Policy Editor is located on the Windows 95 CD-ROM in the \ADMIN\APPTOOLS\ POLEDIT directory. The following steps show you how to install the System Policy Editor:

1. From the Start menu, choose Settings, Control Panel. The Control Panel opens.

2. Double-click on the Add/Remove Programs icon. The Add/ Remove Programs Properties sheet appears.

3. Select the Windows Setup tab and choose Have Disk. The Install from Disk dialog box appears.

4. Choose Browse and locate the \ADMIN\APPTOOLS\POLEDIT directory on the Windows 95 CD-ROM. The grouppol.inf and poledit.inf files are displayed.

5. Choose OK twice, select Group Policies and System Policy Editor, and choose Install. The files are copied to the hard drive, and the Start menu is updated.

6. From the Start menu, choose Programs, Accessories, System Tools, System Policy Editor. The System Policy Editor is displayed, and you are prompted for the template file to be used.

7. Select ADMIN.ADM as the template to use for creating policies. The System Policy Editor displays a blank window.

8. Close the System Policy Editor.

The System Policy Editor uses a template that defines which keys in the Registry can be affected by the System policy. The template ADMIN.ADM, which is included with the System Policy Editor, allows many standard policies to be enforced, such as the following:

▶ Restricting access to various Control Panel applets

▶ Disabling the Registry Editor

▶ Requiring a user to be validated by a Windows NT or NetWare server

▶ Specifying certain applications to run at startup

In addition to creating System policies, the System Policy Editor can be used to perform the following functions:

▶ Access the local Registry settings defined in the System policy template being used

▶ Access the Registry settings on a remote Windows 95 computer to change the settings defined in the template

note

Remote Administration must be enabled on a computer to allow another computer to access the Registry over a network. See the following section "Granting Remote Administration Privileges on Your Computer" to learn how to enable Remote Administration.

Policies created with the System Policy Editor are saved with the file-name extension POL. The System policy to be used should be given the name CONFIG.POL and must be placed in the default location. For computers using share-level security, CONFIG.POL should be placed in the *<systemroot>* directory (for example, C:\WINDOWS). For computers using user-level security, CONFIG.POL should be placed in the user's home directory on the

Windows NT server or in the user's mail directory on a NetWare server. The default location for the CONFIG.POL file can be changed later using a specific policy setting.

Registry information in the CONFIG.POL file can overwrite any existing information in the computer's Registry. The policy setting also can be configured so that it will not change the Registry setting if it already exists. Therefore, even if a Registry on a computer has a certain setting, that setting can be changed to the setting in the CONFIG.POL policy file.

Setup Computer Policies

In the following steps, you create a simple System policy and set up a system so the policy overwrites the previous Registry setting for the specified workstation.

1. Start the System Policy Editor. The System Policy Editor is displayed, and you are prompted for the name of the template file to be used.

2. Locate the \<*systemroot*>\INF\ADMIN.ADM file and choose OK. The ADMIN.ADM template is loaded, and a blank System Policy window is displayed, as shown in figure 4.2.

Figure 4.2

The System Policy Editor.

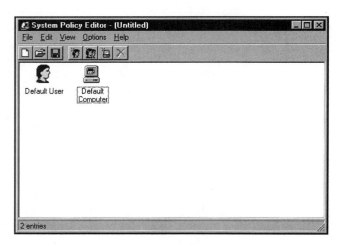

3. Choose File, New File. The Default User and Default Computer icons appear.

4. Double-click on the Default Computer icon. The Default Computer Properties sheet appears.

5. Click on the plus sign (+) next to Network. The Network policy subkeys are displayed, as shown in figure 4.3.

Figure 4.3

The System Policy Default Computer Properties sheet.

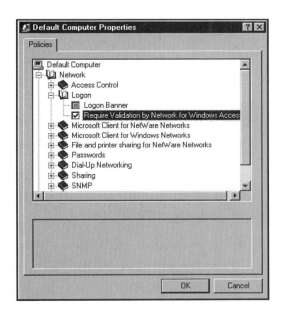

6. Click on the plus sign (+) next to Logon. The Network logon policy settings appear.

7. Click on the check box next to Logon Banner until a check mark appears in the box. The Caption and Text fields appear.

8. Type **System Policies Test** in the Caption field and **Welcome** in the Text field and choose OK. The Default User and Default Computer icons are again displayed.

9. Choose File, Save As and save the file name as CONFIG.POL in the *<systemroot>* directory.

10. If user-level security is used, move the CONFIG.POL file to the home directory for your user on the server.

11. Shut down and restart the computer. All applications will close.

12. Log on to the computer. The Logon Banner specified in CONFIG.POL is displayed during logon.

13. Delete the CONFIG.POL file to disable the policy.

The System policy check boxes will be in one of three states: cleared, checked, or gray. A clear or blank check box means the policy will not be implemented. A checked box means the policy will be implemented. A gray check box means the previous policy will be maintained if one previously existed. The gray check boxes are used when two or more policies will be enforced one after another, such as when Group policies are used.

A Group policy may be used to enforce a User policy for a group of users. The group must be defined on the Windows NT or NetWare server, and each computer in the group using the Group policy must have the GROUPPOL.DLL copied to their *<systemroot>*\system directory.

To create a Group policy, choose Edit, Add Group in the System Policy Editor and enter the name of the group.

A User policy is processed after a Group policy, and therefore overrides any policies set by the Group policy (that is, if a specific user policy file exists, group polices are not applied). If multiple Group policies are defined, and a user belongs to more than one group, the order in which the Group policies are processed can be defined in the Group Priorities option of the Options menu. Group policies with a higher precedence override the policies set by the lower precedence policies.

Other Registry keys can be set using System policies by using a different template. The template can be selected from the Options menu of the System Policy Editor. The templates are specially designed text files that define what policy options are available. For sample templates and information on creating a custom policy template, refer to the *Windows 95 Resource Kit*.

Granting Remote Administration Privileges on Your Computer

 Windows 95 includes several tools to enable you to administer Windows 95 computers from a remote location on the network. These Remote Administration tools include the following:

▶ Remote Registry Administration

▶ Net Watcher

▶ System Monitor

▶ Remote File System Administration

▶ System Policy Editor

These tools (except the System Policy Editor, which was discussed earlier) are described in the following sections.

Remote Registry Administration

If a Windows 95 computer has Remote Administration enabled, other computers that are granted permission to do so can remotely manipulate that computer's Registry. This service is available only if user-level security is being used. After permission has been granted to remotely administer a computer, the administrator can open the Registry of the remote client using either the Registry Editor or the System Policy Editor.

To enable the Remote Registry Editor feature, you perform the following two general steps:

1. Install the Microsoft Remote Registry Service (REGSERVE.EXE) file and associated files on all workstations, including the administrator's and all users' machines. This install code file is located on the Windows 95 CD-ROM in the \ADMIN\NETTOOLS\REMOTREG folder.

2. Connect to the remote Registry by choosing File, Connect Remote Registry while running the Registry Editor.

User-level security must be enabled on the workstation you want to administrate to allow the remote Registry editing feature to work. Enable this feature before attempting the following steps.

The following steps show how to install REGSERVE.EXE:

1. From the Start menu, choose Settings, Control Panel.

2. Double-click on the Network icon in the Control Panel.

3. Click on the Add button to open the Select Network Component Type dialog box.

4. Select Service and click on the Add button to open the Select Network Service dialog box.

5. Select Microsoft and click on the Have Disk button. The Install from Disk dialog box appears.

6. Click on the Browse button and select the path to the Windows 95 CD-ROM. Locate the \ADMIN\NETTOOLS\ REMOTREG folder.

7. Select the REGSRV.INF file and choose OK twice.

8. When the Select Network Service dialog box appears, make sure the Microsoft Remote Registry item is selected. Click on OK.

9. When the Network properties sheet appears, click on OK.

10. Follow the prompts for specific Windows disks.

11. After the Remote Registry Service installs, Windows 95 prompts you to restart Windows. Click on Yes to restart.

After Windows 95 reboots, use the following steps to connect to a remote Registry:

1. Start the Registry Editor from the administrator computer (this must be a Windows 95 machine).

2. Choose File, Connect Network Registry. The Connect Network Registry dialog box appears.

3. Enter the name of the computer that contains the Registry you want to edit remotely.

4. Choose OK. The Registry Editor displays the Registry settings from the other Windows 95 computer.

5. Close the Registry Editor when you finish making changes, if any. (Don't make any changes now.)

Using Net Watcher for Remote Administration

The *Net Watcher* is included in the Accessories group and can be used to view connections to the local computer or to remote computers if Remote Administration is enabled on the remote computer. Net Watcher is primarily used to display the status of connections to shared folders. The features of Net Watcher enable an administrator to remotely perform the following tasks:

▶ Create a new shared folder

▶ List the shared folders on a server

▶ Stop the sharing of a folder

▶ Show which users are connected to a shared folder

▶ Show how long a user has been connected to a shared folder and how long the user has been idle

▶ Disconnect users or close files opened by a user

Figure 4.4 shows an example of a Net Watcher display.

Net Watcher also can be accessed through the Network Neighborhood by right-clicking on a computer and selecting Properties from the context-sensitive menu. Choose Net Watcher from the Tools·tab to view the shared folders and the users accessing those folders on the selected computer.

Figure 4.4

A typical Net Watcher screen.

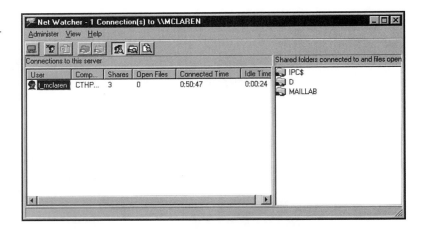

The following steps show how to monitor a remote computer using Net Watcher:

1. Start Net Watcher as previously described. You also can select the Start menu, and choose Programs, Accessories, System Tools, Net Watcher.

2. Choose Administer, Select Server. The Select Server dialog box appears.

3. Enter the name of the server (the remote computer) you want to view. Choose the Browse button to see a list of the computers you can connect to.

4. Click on OK. A view of the remote computer appears in Net Watcher.

5. Click on the Show Users button to see the users connected to the selected computer. On the left, you see the user name, computer name, number of shares, number of open files, time of connection, and idle time. On the right, you see the shared folders that are connected to and the files that are opened.

6. Click on the Show Shared Folders button to see the names of the shared folders on the selected computer. On the left, you see the shared folder, the name it is shared as, the access

type, and a comment associated with the folder. On the right, are the connections to the share and the files that are opened.

7. Click on the Show Files button to see files that are opened by other users. You see the name of the file, which share it is using, who is accessing it, and what the open mode is.

8. Press F5 to refresh the display.

9. Choose Administer, Exit to exit Net Watcher.

System Monitor

The *System Monitor* is a Windows 95 accessory used to display data on various performance counters in Windows 95. With System Monitor and Remote Administration enabled, you can connect to remote computers to view their system performance through the System Monitor as shown in figure 4.5.

Figure 4.5

A typical System Monitor screen.

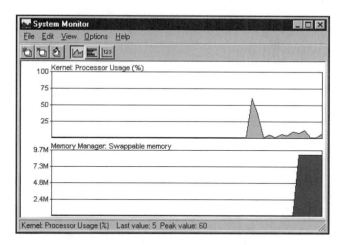

You also can quickly enable monitoring of a remote computer by right-clicking on that computer in Network Neighborhood and selecting Properties from the context-sensitive menu. Choose System Monitor to start the applet and connect to the selected computer. The Windows 95 System Monitor is discussed in further detail in Chapter 12, "Troubleshooting."

Remote File System Administration

Remote File System Administration enables an administrator to manipulate and control the sharing of files and printers on a remote system. This tool, along with Net Watcher and System Monitor, can be accessed through the Tools tab of the Properties sheet of a computer displayed in the Network Neighborhood.

Exercises

In Exercise 4.1, you change a value in the Network Control Panel Applet, the Network Neighborhood Properties sheet, and the Registry, and see how the change is reflected in the other locations. To perform this exercise, you must have a network adapter installed in the Network Control Panel Applet. If you do not already have one installed, install the Microsoft Dial-Up Adapter driver by opening the Network Control Panel Applet and adding Microsoft's Dial-Up Adapter driver from the list of adapters.

1. From the Start menu, choose Settings, Control Panel. The Control Panel opens.

2. Double-click on the Network icon. The Network dialog box appears.

3. Record the computer name on a piece of paper.

4. Select the Identification tab, type **CONTROLPANEL** for the computer name, and choose OK. The Network Control Panel Applet closes.

5. When you are prompted to restart the computer, choose No.

6. Right-click on the Network Neighborhood icon on the Desktop. The context-sensitive menu appears.

7. Select Properties. The Network dialog box again appears.

8. Select the Identification tab. The Computer Name now is listed as CONTROLPANEL, the name that was entered through the Network Control Panel Applet.

9. Change the computer name to **PROPERTIES** and choose OK. The Network Control Panel Applet closes.

10. If you are prompted to restart the computer, choose No.

11. Select Run from the Start menu. The Run dialog box opens.

12. Type **regedit** and choose OK. The Registry Editor appears.

continues

Exercise 4.1: Continued

13. Click on the plus sign (+) next to HKEY_LOCAL_MACHINE. The HKEY_LOCAL_MACHINE key expands.

14. Click on the plus sign next to System. The CurrentControlSet key appears.

15. Click on the plus sign next to CurrentControlSet and then expand the Control subkey to see the ComputerName subkey.

16. Click on the plus sign next to ComputerName to display the subkey that also is named ComputerName. Figure 4.6 shows an example of the ComputerName subkey.

Figure 4.6

Registry Editor subkeys.

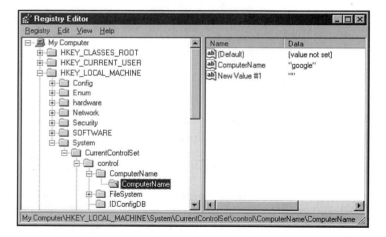

17. Select the ComputerName subkey. The Values named [Default] and ComputerName are displayed on the right of the Registry Editor.

   Notice that the ComputerName value is **PROPERTIES** as set from the Network Neighborhood Properties sheet.

18. Double-click on the ComputerName value to edit it. The Edit String dialog box appears.

19. In the Value Data field, enter the original computer name you recorded at the start of this exercise and choose OK.

The ComputerName value displays the original computer name.

20. Exit the Registry Editor.

Exercise 4.2:   Creating User Profiles

Exercise 4.2 demonstrates how to enable individual users to maintain user profiles.

1. From the Start menu, choose Settings, Control Panel. The Control Panel opens.

2. Double-click on the Passwords icon. The Passwords Properties dialog box appears.

3. Select the User Profiles tab. By default, the All Users of this PC Use the Same Preferences and Desktop Settings option is selected.

4. Select the following options:

   Users can customize their preferences and desktop settings.

   Include desktop icons and Network Neighborhood contents in user settings.

   Include Start Menu and Program groups in user settings.

   Choose OK. You are prompted to restart the computer.

5. Choose OK to restart the computer.

6. Log on with the user name TESTPROFILE and type **password** for the password. You will be prompted to verify the password by typing it again.

Do not press Enter after typing the user name without first typing a password. If you do, the password will be blank, and you will not see the user logon screen again when you next log on. If a blank password is used with a user name, that

continues

Exercise 4.2: Continued

user is automatically logged on, and a different user name cannot be used. To fix this situation, change the password to something other than blank using the Passwords Control Panel Applet.

7. Confirm the password by typing it again. A message appears asking if you want to save the settings for the user in a user profile.

8. Choose Yes to save the sessions settings in a user profile. The default Desktop is displayed.

9. Right-click on the Desktop and select Properties from the context-sensitive menu. The Display Properties sheet appears.

10. Select a different wallpaper for the Desktop and choose OK. The new wallpaper is displayed.

11. Select Shut Down from the Start menu. The Shut Down Windows dialog box opens.

12. Select Close All Programs and Log on as a Different User?, then choose Yes. All programs close, and the Enter Windows Password logon screen appears.

13. Log on with a different user name. The original default wallpaper or pattern appears on the Desktop.

14. Log off and log back on with the TESTPROFILE user name. The wallpaper that was selected for that profile appears on the Desktop.

15. Log off and then log on with your normal user name. The original settings are displayed.

16. Start the Explorer and open the Windows 95 folder and the Profiles subfolder. The Profiles folder contains a subfolder for each of the profiles that have been created on the computer.

17. Examine the contents of each folder in the Profiles folder. You will notice a user.dat file that was created for each profile. In addition, there may be Start Menu, NetHood, Desktop, and Recent folders for each profile, depending on which options were chosen in the User Profiles tab of the Passwords Control Panel Applet.

Exercise 4.3:   Installing the System Policy Editor

Exercise 4.3 demonstrates how to install the System Policy Editor.

1. From the Start menu, choose Settings, Control Panel. The Control Panel opens.

2. Double-click on the Add/Remove Programs icon. The Add/Remove Programs Properties dialog box appears.

3. Select the Windows Setup tab and choose Have Disk. The Install from Disk dialog box appears.

4. Choose Browse and locate the \ADMIN\APPTOOLS\POLEDIT directory on the Windows 95 CD-ROM. The grouppol.inf and poledit.inf files are displayed.

5. Choose OK twice, select Group Policies and System Policy Editor, and choose Install. The files are copied to the hard drive, and the Start menu is updated.

6. From the Start menu, choose Programs, Accessories, System Tools, System Policy Editor. The System Policy Editor appears, and you are prompted for the template file to be used.

7. Select ADMIN.ADM as the template to use for creating policies. The System Policy Editor displays a blank window.

8. Close the System Policy Editor.

Exercise 4.4:   Creating a System Policy

In Exercise 4.4, you create a simple System policy and set up a system so that the policy overwrites the previous Registry setting for the specified workstation.

continues

Exercise 4.4:   Coninued

1. Start the System Policy Editor. The System Policy Editor appears, and you are prompted for the name of the template file to be used.

2. Locate the \<*systemroot*>\INF\ADMIN.ADM file and choose OK. The ADMIN.ADM template is loaded, and a blank System Policy window appears (refer to fig. 4.2).

3. Choose File, New File. The Default User and Default Computer icons appear.

4. Double-click on the Default Computer icon. The Default Computer Properties sheet appears.

5. Click on the plus sign next to Network. The Network policy subkeys appear (refer to fig. 4.3).

6. Click on the plus sign next to Logon. The Network logon policy settings appear.

7. Click on the check box next to Logon Banner until a check mark appears in the box. The Caption and Text fields appear.

8. Type **System Policies Test** in the Caption field and **Welcome** in the Text field and choose OK. The Default User and Default Computer icons are again displayed.

9. Choose File, Save As and save the file name as CONFIG.POL in the <*systemroot*> directory.

10. If user-level security is used, move the CONFIG.POL file to the home directory for your user on the server.

11. Shut down and restart the computer. All applications close.

12. Log on to the computer. The Logon Banner specified in CONFIG.POL appears during logon.

13. Delete the CONFIG.POL file to disable the policy.

Exercise 4.5: Remote Administration Using the Registry Editor

Exercise 4.5 demonstrates how to remotely administer another computer using the Registry Editor.

1. From the Start menu, choose Settings, Control Panel. The Control Panel opens.

2. Double-click on the Passwords icon. The Passwords Properties dialog box appears.

3. Select the Remote Administration tab, and then select the Enable Remote Administration of this Server check box. The administrator accounts appear in the Administrators field as appropriate.

4. Add or remove administrator accounts to or from the Administrators field as required and choose OK. The dialog box closes.

5. From another Windows 95 computer, log on with one of the administrator's accounts from the previous step and enter **regedit** from a command prompt. The Registry Editor appears.

6. From the Registry menu, choose Connect Network Registry. The Connect Network Registry dialog box appears.

7. Type the computer name of the first Windows 95 computer and choose OK. The Registry settings from the other Windows 95 computer are displayed.

8. Close the Registry Editor.

Review Questions

The following questions will test your knowledge of the information in this chapter. For additional questions, see MCP Endeavor and the Microsoft Roadmap/Assessment Exam on the CD-ROM that accompanies this book.

1. You are manning the company help desk and receive a call from a system administrator who is new to Windows 95. He wants to know where he can view and configure settings for a computer running Windows 95. You tell him which three of the following are locations in which Windows 95 settings can be viewed and configured?

   A. The Control Panel

   B. The Properties sheet for the object

   C. The System Monitor

   D. The Windows 95 Registry

2. Phil wants to use the Registry Editor to modify his system. Before he does, he wants to exhaust all other avenues of changing settings in Windows 95. He knows several tools in Control Panel let him do this. Which three of the following are common Control Panel applets?

   A. System

   B. Display

   C. Accessibility Options

   D. Drivers

3. You need to edit the Registry on a Windows 95 workstation, but want to back up its constituent files first. You know there are two files. The Windows 95 Registry consists of which pair of files?

   A. USER.DAT and USER.REG

   B. USER.REG and SYSTEM.REG

   C. SYSTEM.DAT and CONFIG.POL

   D. USER.DAT and SYSTEM.DAT

4. For a PowerPoint presentation in front of the help desk staff, you create a slide with a bullet point describing the Windows 95 System policy feature. What would be the appropriate ending to the sentence: A Windows 95 System policy _____.

   A. assigns priorities to applications accessing memory

   B. assigns priorities to users

   C. enables an administrator to set various Windows 95 Registry entries

   D. is a summary of configuration details

5. On the same PowerPoint slide as in the previous question, you place another bullet point explaining what the primary purpose of a Windows 95 System policy is. From the following list, choose the correct answer for this statement: The primary purpose of a Windows 95 System policy is to _____.

   A. limit the ability of users to customize their environment

   B. increase the ability of users to customize their environment

   C. make the system run more efficiently

   D. make the system more adaptable

6. Tarkus is administering a Windows 95 computer from a remote location. She is using Windows 95. Which three of the following can be used as Windows 95 Remote Administration tools?

   A. Registry Editor

   B. Net Watcher

   C. Remote Access Manager

   D. System Monitor

7. Mickey cannot get his Windows 95 computer to connect to another Windows 95 computer to edit the Registry remotely. To edit a Windows 95 Registry from another computer on the same network, Mickey must enable Remote Administration from the _____ Control Panel Applet.

   A. System

   B. Passwords

   C. Modems

   D. Network

8. When you start the Windows 95 Registry, six root subkeys display. Pick three of the six subkeys from the following answers.

   A. HKEY_LOCAL_MACHINE

   B. HKEY_CONFIG_USER

   C. HKEY_DYN_DATA

   D. HKEY_USERS

9. Billie modifies her user profile so that each time she starts Windows 95, a shortcut to her finance spreadsheet displays on the Desktop. Which of the following cannot be done by setting user profiles?

   A. Display specific applications in the Start menu

   B. Customize desktop settings, such as colors and wallpaper

   C. Install an application only for a specific user

   D. Display recently used documents in the Start menu Documents folder

10. Michael administers a Windows NT network that has several Windows 95 workstations attached to the server. He stores user profiles for all workstations on the server to be downloaded during boot up time. The user profiles can be

updated by the users. To ensure that each profile is available from the server, where are they stored on the server?

A. User's home directory

B. User's C:\WINDOWS directory

C. Any directory on the server that the user has Read permission

D. None of the above

11. A user complains that the settings she made to her Desktop are not saved each time she logs into the network and starts Windows 95. You have her computer set up to download a user profile from the server and enable her to save changes to it. What might be one of the causes for her settings not to be saved properly?

A. Her version of Windows 95 needs to be updated

B. Her workstation's time is not synchronized with the server's time

C. She does not have the Remote Administration feature enabled

D. All of the above

12. In a training class you conduct for system administrators, you are asked why the Registry comprises two files. From the following list, what is the best answer to this question?

A. Makes editing configuration settings safer

B. Separates user and system information so system policies and user profiles can be created

C. Allows dynamic information from the hardware tree to be updated while user settings are idle

D. Enables a user to copy his USER.DAT from a floppy disk to a laptop and maintain the same look and feel as his desktop computer

13. Brenda uses Net Watcher to view connections to her local computer. She wants to see the users connected to her computer. Which toolbar button does she click to allow this?

    A. View Users

    B. Show Connected Users

    C. View Connected Users

    D. Show Users

14. As system administrator, you set up each user's computer so that a user cannot start an MS-DOS prompt from within Windows 95. How can this be done?

    A. Use the System Policy Editor, open the Default User Properties sheet, click on System, click on Restrictions, and select the Disable MS-DOS Prompt check box.

    B. Use the System Policy Editor, open the Default User Properties sheet, click on System, click on Restrictions, and deselect the Enable MS-DOS Prompt check box.

    C. Use the System Policy Editor, open the Default User Properties sheet, click on System, and select the MS-DOS Prompt check box.

    D. Use the System Policy Editor, open the Default User Properties sheet, click on System, click on Restrictions, and select the Disable Single-Mode MS-DOS Applications check box.

15. During a discussion you have with a fellow system administrator, you describe to her how to use the Registry Editor. She goes back to her workstation and cannot find the Registry Editor application on her system. Which command do you tell her to enter in the Run dialog box to start Registry Editor?

A. regedit32

B. regid

C. regedit

D. Any of the above

Review Answers

1. A B D	5. A	9. C	13. D
2. A B C	6. A B D	10. A	14. A
3. D	7. B	11. B	15. C
4. C	8. A C D	12. B	

Test Yourself

Stop! Before reading this chapter, test yourself to determine how much study time you will need to devote to this section.

1. Jenny wants to gain access to the Internet, but her company does not have a dedicated line to it. How can she, using Windows 95, connect to the Internet?

2. Steve is connecting his Windows 95 computer to a network running Novell NetWare. He wants to share files and a printer with other users. Can he do this? If so, what type of security must he use?

3. You configure a Windows 95 workstation to connect to a NetWare network. When installing Client for NetWare Networks, Windows 95 automatically installs a protocol. Which protocol is this? Can you change this to another protocol and still access the NetWare server?

4. Windows 95 is designed to run over a NetWare network, but there are some disadvantages to this. Name two.

5. Elizabeth sets up Windows 95 to connect to a Windows NT network. She wants to be able to share files and printers with other users on the network. What type of security must she install? Also, can she assign file-level rights?

6. As system administrator, you're bringing up the entire department on a single-server Windows NT network. For workstations, you're going to use the Windows 95 client. You also want to set up user-level security on the Windows 95 client. When you set up Windows NT, what should you remember to do to make sure user-level security will work?

7. You receive a call while stationed at the company help desk. The caller says she is trying to save her long file names to the NetWare server but the server does not support them. What do you have to do to enable NetWare to support long file names?

8. UNC is supported by Windows 95. What does UNC mean? What two items make up a UNC? Does UNC require a drive-letter assignment?

9. Chuck uses Network Neighborhood to view other computers on the network. What is the name of the list that stores the computers on a network?

10. As you configure the browse list on a NetWare network, you need to set up the option to have Windows 95 automatically determine whether the computer is needed as a browse server. What is the name of the property?

11. Name one advantage and one disadvantage of using user-level and share-level security.

12. Eugene creates a PowerPoint slide showing the Windows 95 networking architecture layers. He places a layer called the Network Providers in the slide. Is this the name of a layer in the architecture? If so, what two other layers are adjacent to the Network Providers layer?

13. When installing TCP/IP, it is recommended that a default gateway be configured for the Windows 95 client. What does a gateway do?

Answers

1. Use the Dial-Up Networking feature in Windows 95; configure the Dial-Up Adapter for an Internet service provider (ISP); use a modem to dial into the ISP. See "Connecting to the Internet."

2. Yes, he can do this, but he must install user-level security. See "File and Printer Sharing for NetWare Networks."

3. IPX/SPX. No you cannot change this. You can, however, use additional protocols with this. See "16-bit and 32-bit NetWare Clients."

4. Possible answers: long file names are not supported by NetWare by default; OS/2 Name Space must be added; users of Windows 95 can reassign print queue assignments; administrators may feel a lack of control over resources because Windows' 95 graphical user interface (GUI) makes it easy to change drive mappings. See "NetWare Networks."

5. User-level security. No, only directory-level rights can be set up under Windows 95. See "Configure Windows 95 to Use User-Level Security."

6. Set up a primary domain on the Windows NT server. See "Configure Windows 95 as a Windows NT Server Domain Client."

7. Load OS/2 Name Server Space (OS2.NAM) on the server. See "NetWare Networks."

8. Universal Naming Convention. Computer and share. No drive-letter assignment is needed. See "Universal Naming Convention (UNC)."

9. Browse list. See "Browsing."

10. The Enabled: May Be Master setting. See "Configure Browse Master for NetWare Networks.

11. Advantage: user-level requires user to authenticate access against an account list stored on a Windows NT or NetWare server. Disadvantage: user-level security can be set up only on an NT or NetWare server. Advantage: share-level security enables two Windows 95 workstations networked together to share resources using passwords. Disadvantage: share-level password can be used by anyone to gain access; that is, no authentication needed to access resource. See "Identify Advantages and Disadvantages for User-Level and Share-Level Security."

12. Yes, and it is adjacent to the Application Interface and the IFS Manager. See "Understanding the Windows 95 Networking Architecture."

13. Gateways help route TCP/IP messages to remote destinations. See "Gateway."

Chapter 5

Networking and Interoperability

This chapter will help you prepare for the exam by covering the following objectives:

Test Objectives

- ▶ Identify the limitations of a Windows 95 NetWare server

- ▶ Recognize how the UNC is used

- ▶ Identify elements of the Windows 95 operating system network architecture

- ▶ Identify advantages and disadvantages of user-level and share-level security

- ▶ Configure a Windows 95 computer as a client in a Windows NT Server domain

- ▶ Configure a Windows 95 computer to use Windows NT Server user-level security

- ▶ Configure a Windows 95 computer as a client or server in a NetWare network

- ▶ Configure a Windows 95 computer as a client in a NetWare network

- ▶ Configure a Windows 95 computer to use NetWare user-level security

- ▶ Install and configure TCP/IP for use with Windows 95

- ▶ Configure Browse Master for Microsoft networks

- ▶ Configure Browse Master for NetWare

- ▶ Configure a Windows 95 computer to access the Internet

Windows 95 includes many enhancements to the networking subsystem used in other Windows-based operating systems. This chapter explores the following Windows 95 networking topics:

- ▶ The new features of the Windows 95 networking subsystem

- ▶ The Windows 95 networking architecture

- ▶ How to share and manage files and printers over a network

- ▶ How to install and configure support for various network operating systems, including Microsoft and Novell NetWare networks

- ▶ The different Microsoft transport protocols available in Windows 95

- ▶ How to install and configure the Microsoft TCP/IP protocol with Windows 95

Windows 95 Networking Features

Windows 95 includes many new interesting networking features, including support for the following:

- ▶ File and printer sharing as a peer-to-peer server

- ▶ Windows 95 as a multi-protocol universal client

- ▶ Universal Naming Convention (UNC)

- ▶ Plug and Play network cards

- ▶ Unified logon and browsing

- ▶ Remote access

These features are discussed in the following sections.

Windows 95 as a Peer-to-Peer Server

A Windows 95 computer can act as a server for a peer-to-peer network, sharing its files and printers with other computers. In a *peer-to-peer network*, also known as a *workgroup*, there is no central user accounts database, unlike a Windows NT domain. Therefore, security in a workgroup is achieved by requiring passwords to connect to a peer server's directory and printer shares. This security model is known as *share-level security*.

> *Share* as a verb means to allow others to access a resource; as a noun it is a resource, such as a directory or print queue that others can access.

The other security model that a Windows 95 server can use is known as *user-level security*. With user-level security enabled, a Windows 95 server requires that peers accessing its resources be validated by a security provider, such as Windows NT Server, Windows NT Workstation, or NetWare bindery server. This process, known as *pass-through authentication*, is used when a client attempts to access a share on a Windows 95 server using user-level security.

> A Windows 95 server is simply any Windows 95 computer with the File and Printer Sharing Service enabled.

Windows 95 as a Universal Client

The networking functionality built into Windows 95 allows a Windows 95 computer to be a client on a wide variety of the most common networks. A Windows 95 client can run multiple network protocols, services, and clients at the same time and thus can be a client on many different networks at the same time.

Windows 95 includes software to support the following networks:

▶ Microsoft Windows NT

▶ Microsoft Windows 95

- ▶ Microsoft Windows for Workgroups 3.*x*

- ▶ Microsoft LAN Manager

- ▶ Novell NetWare version 3.11 and later

- ▶ Banyan VINES version 5.52 and later

- ▶ DEC Pathworks version 4.1 and later

- ▶ SunSoft PC—NFS version 5.0 and later

Windows 95 can have only one 16-bit network client installed at a time, but can run multiple 32-bit clients. The 32-bit clients that come with Windows 95 are the Microsoft Client for Windows Networks and Microsoft Client for NetWare Networks.

In addition, the modular architecture of Windows 95 allows Windows 95 components written by other network vendors to be installed.

The following sections look at some specific requirements for operating Windows 95 on a particular network.

Microsoft Networks

A Microsoft Network may include Windows NT, Windows 95, Windows for Workgroups, and LAN Manager Server computers. To communicate with another computer, both computers must run the same network protocol.

A *network protocol* is a set of rules and conventions used by computers to exchange messages on a network. It is analogous to a language by which two computers communicate. The terms *network protocol*, *transport protocol*, or *protocol* are often used interchangeably. For a more detailed description, refer to the section "Transport Protocols" later in this chapter.

Microsoft Network computers can communicate using any one or more of the following network protocols:

▶ Microsoft NetBEUI

▶ Microsoft TCP/IP

▶ Microsoft IPX/SPX-compatible (NWLINK)

For detailed information on each of these protocols, refer to the "Configuring Network Protocols" section later in this chapter.

For an exercise testing this information, see end of chapter.

For a Windows 95 computer to communicate with another computer on a network, both computers must have the same protocol installed. In addition, the appropriate client software and a network adapter card driver must be installed. In Exercise 5.1, at the end of the chapter, you learn how to install and configure a network protocol, Client for Microsoft Networks, and an adapter. To do this, you use the Network Properties sheet (see fig. 5.1).

Figure 5.1

A typical Network Control Panel Applet screen.

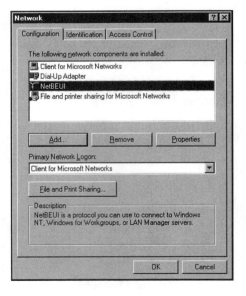

NetWare Networks

Windows 95 integrates well with NetWare networks running Novell NetWare version 3.11 or higher. Windows 95 includes the 32-bit Client for NetWare Networks; you can also use a 16-bit

NETX (NetWare 3.*x*) or VLM (NetWare 4.*x*) Novell NetWare client. For mixed NetWare 4.*x* (non-bindery mode) and Windows NT environments, Microsoft has a 32-bit Microsoft Service for NetWare Directory Services (NDS) available in Windows 95 Service Pack 1.

The advantages of using the 32-bit Microsoft Client for NetWare Networks include the following:

▶ It runs in protected-mode memory and thus does not use any conventional memory.

▶ The 32-bit architecture offers a 50–200 percent increase in network file I/O operations over the 16-bit versions running on Windows 3.*x*.

▶ It allows additional network clients to be used at the same time, such as the Microsoft Client for Microsoft Networks.

There are some disadvantages or limitations when running Windows 95 on a NetWare network:

▶ Long file names are not supported natively by NetWare. You must load the OS/2 Name Space (OS2.NAM) feature in NetWare for long file names to be supported on the network.

▶ If running the real-mode ODI and VLM or NETX real-mode shell, performance may suffer because it (the real-mode NetWare driver) uses RAM that MS-DOS applications could use.

▶ Administrators may feel a lack of control because users can use Windows' 95 Explorer and Network Neighborhood to access files and remap network drive letters.

▶ Users of Windows 95 can reassign print queue assignments.

continues

> ▶ Drive mappings and print queue assignments can be saved by the user as permanent and be reestablished every time the user logs onto the network and starts Windows 95.
>
> ▶ Users of Windows 95 can see whatever print queues the bindery or NDS provides them access to use.
>
> ▶ Although administrators can limit what Windows 95 users see through the Network Neighborhood and Explorer, users might still be able to access programs, files, and directories using the MS-DOS prompt or network mapping prompt if they know the Universal Naming Convention (UNC) of \\server\path.

The Client for NetWare Networks can be used to access NetWare servers running NetWare 2.15 and above and NetWare 4.x servers using bindery emulation. The Client for NetWare Networks runs only with the IPX/SPX-compatible protocol, which is installed by default when the client is installed.

Although the 16-bit Novell NetWare clients do not provide all of the advantages of the 32-bit client, a 16-bit NETX or VLM client is required if any of the following are used:

▶ NCP packet signature security (requires VLM)

▶ NetWare IP protocol (which does not use Microsoft's TCP/IP)

▶ Helper Terminate-and-Stay-Resident (TSR) applications loaded from DOS (such as 3270 emulators)

▶ Custom Virtual Loadable Modules (VLMs) with functionality not provided by the Windows 95 components, such as Personal NetWare (PNW.VLM)

▶ Novell utilities, such as NWADMIN or NETADMIN

▶ NetWare Directory Services (NDSes), although a separate Microsoft Service for NetWare Directory Services (NDS), is now available

- ▶ IPX ODI protocol

- ▶ Monolithic IPX (IPX.COM) or ARCnet protocols

Banyan VINES

Banyan VINES version 5.52 and above can be used with Windows 95. However, computers running only Banyan VINES cannot use the browser services. For example, Banyan VINES computers are not visible in the Network Neighborhood.

> Windows 95 Banyan VINES computers must use NDIS network card drivers rather than monolithic network drivers.

DEC Pathworks

Digital Equipment Corporation (DEC) Pathworks is a LAN Manager-compatible protocol. The Pathworks 4.1, 5.0, and higher protocols are included with Windows 95 for use with the Client for Microsoft Networks. Pathworks uses a STARTNET.BAT file called from AUTOEXEC.BAT to load the Pathworks drivers.

Windows 95 Pathworks computers can use the Microsoft Net-BEUI, Microsoft TCP/IP, or DEC DECnet protocols. DECnet is not included with Windows 95.

PC-NFS

The SunSoft PC-NFS client and protocol support is included with Windows 95 for use on PC-NFS networks running version 5.0 or later. Computers running only PC-NFS cannot use the browser service, nor are they visible when browsed from other computers.

Universal Naming Convention (UNC)

The *Universal Naming Convention* (UNC) is a standardized nomenclature for specifying a share name on a particular computer. The computer name is limited to 15 characters, and the share name is usually limited to 15 characters, depending on the network. Share names can be given to a print queue or a directory of files; WINAPPS or HP4, for example.

The UNC uniquely specifies the path to the share name on a network. The UNC path takes the form of *computername**sharename* [*optional path*]. For example, the UNC path of the printer share LPS20 created on the server ALPHA would be \\ALPHA\LPS20.

A UNC name does not require a drive-letter assignment. Windows 95 takes full advantage of network connectivity using UNC names so you can connect to a remote directory or printer share without having to map a drive letter to it. However, for MS-DOS–based applications that require a drive letter or port to be used, you can map a drive letter to a shared directory or a port to a shared printer.

The UNC also can specify the full path to a file in a subdirectory of a file share. For example, to share the entire C drive on the computer BIGBEN, the share name CDRIVE could be created for the root directory c:\. To specify the directory c:\windows\system using a UNC path with these share names, use \\BIGBEN\ CDRIVE\windows\system.

Add a dollar sign ($) to the end of the share name to prevent a share name from being visible to another computer through a browser, such as Network Neighborhood. The share name TOPSECRET$, for example, would not be visible to other computers browsing the computer.

All Windows 95 functions support using a UNC name, including the Run option on the Start menu and the command prompt. NetWare servers, like Windows NT servers, can be accessed through a UNC name. Instead of share name, substitute volume name to access a NetWare server.

Share names in Windows 95 can be as long as the involved protocols and user interfaces will allow. However, NetBIOS names can be only 15 characters long and cannot contain embedded blanks. Therefore, when establishing share names on your servers, keep them short, do not use spaces within the name, and use 15 or fewer total characters so Windows 95 can view them from within Network Neighborhood when browsing for network resources. Some network printers might even require 14 or fewer characters total.

The actual folder name under Windows NT and Windows 95 can still be a long file name (LFN) of up to 260 characters— only the share name needs to follow the preceding guidelines. For example, your TOPSECRET$ share can be on a folder named "My Top Secret Projects."

Plug and Play Network Cards

If a network interface card is Plug and Play compliant, it can be automatically detected and configured with Windows 95. Simply plug the network card into the appropriate expansion slot and start Windows 95. The model of the card will be detected, and the appropriate Windows 95 driver will be installed. Windows 95 then assigns an available interrupt request (IRQ) line and memory address range to the network card as appropriate and configures the card to use these settings. The administrator needs only to install the client and protocol software to be used with the network card.

For more information on Plug and Play hardware, refer to Chapter 11, "Plug and Play."

Unified Logon and Browsing

As mentioned previously, a Windows 95 computer can have more than one network client installed at a time. A single network wire may have multiple network protocols running on it. For example, if a network contains both Windows NT and Novell NetWare servers, the Windows 95 computer can run both the Client for Microsoft Networks and the Client for NetWare Networks. If the passwords are the same for the two networks, the unified logon feature of Windows 95 requires that the password be entered only once for both networks. Similarly, if the Windows password is the same as the network password, the password needs to be entered only once. If the passwords are not the same, they need to be entered individually.

Windows 95 also features *unified browsing*—all computers that can be browsed by Windows 95 are displayed together in the Network Neighborhood. For example, NetWare servers appear along with Windows-based computers in the Network Neighborhood if both the Client for Microsoft Networks and Client for NetWare Networks are installed.

Remote Access

Windows 95 enables network connections to be made via a modem or null-modem cable, as Dialup Networking connections. For more information on remote access, refer to Chapter 9, "Mobile Services."

Understanding the Windows 95 Networking Architecture

Windows 95 has a modular, layered architecture. Each layer needs to communicate directly only with the layers immediately above and below it. Therefore a component of the architecture, such as a network adapter driver, needs to be compatible only with the layer adjacent to it, which is the device driver interface in this case. Thus, only one version of the network adapter driver needs to be created because the driver will work with any of the Windows 95–compatible transport protocols.

The modularity of the Windows 95 networking architecture means that components can be interchanged and new components easily added, as long because the component can communicate properly with the adjacent layers. The interoperability is made easier by the use of programming interfaces that are written by Microsoft and contain a standardized set of commands and procedures that the adjacent layers can use to intercommunicate.

The layers of the Windows 95 networking architecture, starting from the top-most layer, are as follows:

1. Application Interface

2. Network Providers

3. Installable File System (IFS) Manager

4. Redirectors and Services

5. Transport Programming Interface

6. Transport Driver Protocols

7. Device Driver Interface

Application Interface

The Application Interface layer contains two interfaces that allow an application to access the Windows 95 networking services. The application interfaces contain a standardized set of commands and procedures that an application can use to communicate with the network provider. This allows a developer to create an application that works with any Windows 95 network protocol, because the application only needs to be able to communicate directly to the application interfaces.

The two interfaces functioning at this layer are the Win32 Print Applicator Programming Interface (API) and the Win32 WinNet Interface.

The Win32 Print API handles network printing-related functions. For more information on the Print API, see the "Architecture" section of Chapter 7, "Managing Printers."

The Win32 WinNet Interface handles all other networking functions not performed by the Win32 Print API. In addition, it provides a high-level set of browsing APIs used to access resources, such as directories, printers, and other network resources.

Network Providers

The network providers provide a more network-specific programming interface for access to networking services. Windows 95 ships with three network providers, but other third-party network providers written for Windows 95 can be incorporated into a third-party network protocol.

The network providers allow access to shared files and printers and provide browsing services. The network providers included with Windows 95 are as follows:

▶ Windows Network Provider/Print Provider

▶ NetWare Network Provider/Print Provider

▶ WinNet16

The Windows Network Provider/Print Provider is a 32-bit provider that supports networking products that use the Server Message Block (SMB) file-sharing protocol. It can be used by both WIN16 and WIN32 applications.

The NetWare Provider/Print Provider is a 32-bit provider for use with NetWare networks that use the NetWare Core Protocol (NCP) file sharing service. The NetWare Provider/Print Provider can be accessed by both 16-bit and 32-bit applications on a NetWare network.

The WinNet16 network provider can be used for backward-compatibility with older network applications that require it.

Installable File System (IFS) Manager

Installable File Systems (IFSes) can be dynamically loaded into memory to handle files in Windows 95. Examples of Installable File Systems are the Compact Disk File System (CDFS) and the virtual file allocation table (VFAT).

The IFS Manager handles the communication between the various IFSes, the Network Provider, and the network redirectors and services.

Redirectors and Services

At this layer, information passing between the application and transport protocol layers is processed and converted to the proper data format for the next layer. The redirectors and services residing at this layer each perform a specific function on the information.

Redirectors

The redirector maps network names used by an application to network device names to which the transport can send the information.

Windows 95 includes the following two redirectors:

▶ Microsoft Networking Redirector used with SMB-based networks

▶ NetWare Networking Redirector used with NCP-based networks

Services

Networking services are individual dynamic-link libraries (DLLs) or virtual device drivers (VxDs) that can be loaded into memory to provide certain networking services. The networking services are installed using the Add button from the Network Control Panel Applet (NCPA).

Table 5.1 shows the networking services included with Windows 95. Additional services not included with Windows 95 can also be added through the NCPA, for example, the Microsoft Service for NetWare Directory Services (NDS).

Table 5.1

Networking Services Included with Windows 95	
Service	Description
Arcadia Backup Exec Agent	Network file backup service
Cheyenne ARCserve Agent	Network file backup service
Hewlett-Packard (HP) JetAdmin	Remote Administration for HP JetDirect Network Interface Printers
HP JetAdmin for NetWare	Remote Administration for HP JetDirect Network Interface Printers on NetWare networks
Microsoft File and Printer Sharing for Microsoft Networks	Printer and file sharing on a Microsoft network
Microsoft File and Printer Sharing for NetWare Networks	Printer and file sharing on a NetWare network
Microsoft Network Monitor	Reports information to a Remote Network Agent Monitoring Utility, such as System Management Server (SMS)
Microsoft Remote Registry Agent	Allows the Registry to be administered by another computer
Simple Network Management (SNMP) Protocol Agent	Reports information to a third-party SNMP Manager

> Only one file and print sharing service can be installed on a computer at a time. The Network Monitor Agent, Remote Registry Service, and SNMP Agent are found on the Windows 95 CD-ROM in the \admin\nettools directory.

Transport Programming Interface

The Transport Programming Interface provides a standardized set of commands to allow the network redirector and services to send information to the underlying transport protocols.

The Transport Programming Interface allows the services of the upper layers of the networking architecture to communicate with any of the Windows 95–compatible transport protocols, such as NetBEUI, TCP/IP, or IPX/SPX.

Windows 95 has two Transport Programming Interfaces:

▶ **NetBIOS Interface.** The Network Basic Input/Output System (NetBIOS) interface allows NetBIOS names and commands to be passed to the transport protocol layer. Examples of NetBIOS names are computer names, share names, and workgroup names. Thus, when a Windows 95 computer connects to a computer named SERVER01 using the NetBEUI protocol, the NetBIOS interface passes instructions from the redirector to the NetBEUI protocol to start a connection with the NetBIOS computer named SERVER01.

▶ **Windows Sockets Interface.** The Windows Sockets Interface allows sockets-based applications to pass instructions back and forth to the transport protocols. Sockets are two-way communication paths between two computers. Sockets have traditionally been used with TCP/IP applications, such as File Transfer Protocol (FTP), but can be used with any Windows 95 protocol.

Transport Protocols

The transport protocol is responsible for putting the information in the correct format so it can be understood by the network device to which the message is being sent.

A transport protocol essentially is a language that network devices use to communicate. For one network device, such as a computer, to communicate with another, both devices need to use the same transport protocol. In other words, they both need to "speak the same language."

The following protocols are included with Windows 95:

▶ Microsoft NetBEUI

▶ Microsoft TCP/IP

▶ Microsoft IPX/SPX-compatible (NWLINK)

▶ Microsoft DLC

In addition, several protocols written by third-party vendors are included with Windows 95:

▶ Banyan VINES

▶ DEC Pathworks versions 4.1 and 5.0

▶ IBM DLC

▶ Novell IPX ODI

▶ SunSoft PC-NFS

These protocols and additional Windows 95–compatible transport protocols can be installed using the Network Control Panel Applet.

For more information on choosing the protocol to use on a network, refer to the "Configuring Network Protocols" section later in this chapter.

Device Driver Interface

The Device Driver Interface handles communication between the transport protocol and the network card driver. This interface contains a standardized set of commands and procedures that the protocol and network card driver can use to communicate with each other. Because the protocol directly communicates with only the Device Driver Interface, it doesn't matter which network card driver is used as long as it can understand the Device Driver Interface specifications. Therefore, a hardware vendor needs to develop only a single device driver that can be used with any Windows 95–compatible protocol.

The transport protocol and the device driver must be written to one of the three specifications supported by Windows 95:

- ▶ **NDIS 3.1.** A specification that supports NDIS 3.*x* protected-mode drivers in addition to Plug and Play. Protected-mode drivers do not use conventional memory. An NDIS 3.*x* driver usually has a VXD extension.

- ▶ **NDIS 2.** A specification for real-mode drivers, which use conventional memory. The NDIS 2 drivers usually have a SYS or DOS extension.

- ▶ **Open Datalink Interface (ODI).** Designed by Novell, ODI is similar to the NDIS 2 specification.

If your network adapter only comes with an NDIS 3.0 driver, contact the manufacturer for an updated driver. NDIS 3.*x* is a portable network driver architecture designed to run on either Windows 95 or Windows NT computers.

Identify Advantages and Disadvantages of User-Level and Share-Level Security

If a Windows 95 computer has the file and print sharing service enabled, the print queues and directory on that computer can be shared with others on the network.

To ensure a computer can share its printers and directories, select both check boxes of the File and Printer Sharing option in the Network Control Panel Applet. These check boxes are I Want to Be Able to Give Others Access to My Files and I Want to Be Able to Allow Others to Print to My Printer(s).

After file or print sharing has been enabled, a user must share the file or printer with others and decide whether, and how, they will prevent unauthorized access to these resources.

Windows 95 enables you to leverage security access to users either in the bindery (the database of network objects) from a NetWare server or the user security list from a Windows NT server in a number of situations without delving deeply into the security system. Users can see the servers and directories and files for which they have access. These facts have caused some NetWare administrators to change queue access rights from the default group EVERYONE. Others have attempted to remove the file scan rights from the application directory.

Most specifically, you can establish a NetWare or Windows NT server as a validating source for a user wanting to use a workstation. This function means that you can require a Windows 95 user to be a recognized and valid user on a specified server to be able to log on to the Windows 95 workstation.

If you establish a workstation to use file and printer sharing for NetWare or Microsoft networks, a NetWare or Windows NT server must provide the access list. This access list provides the list of users and groups that you can use to create the user-based security for shared resources for that Windows 95 workstation. Regardless of whether you use a NetWare or NT server to store the list, one particular server must be the reference point, even if users do not specifically log on to that server or have any rights on that server.

Windows 95 has two security models for determining who can access a share Windows 95 resource; these security models are share-level and user-level. The user must decide which of these two security models to implement on the Windows 95 computer.

Configuring Share-Level Security

Share-level security is used by default when File and Printer Sharing for Microsoft Networks is installed.

File and Printer Sharing for NetWare Networks must use user-level security. The share-level security option is unavailable if File and Printer Sharing for NetWare Networks is installed. If you are concerned about extra SAP and RIP network traffic, using File and Printer Sharing for NetWare Networks makes your Windows 95 computer appear "like" a NetWare server, and is generally not recommended.

With share-level security, passwords are assigned to permit access to a directory or printer share. To access the share, a user must supply the correct password.

To set share-level options, you open the Properties sheet for the shared object (see fig. 5.2). You can access this sheet by right-clicking on the object (such as a directory) and selecting Properties from the context-sensitive menu.

Figure 5.2

The Properties sheet for a shared directory using share-level security.

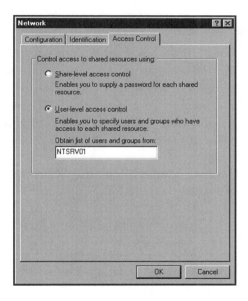

When creating a shared directory using share-level security, one of three types of access can be granted:

▶ **Read-only.** If the correct password is entered, a remote user can access a directory, its subdirectories, and its files, but the user cannot delete files or write files to that directory.

> ▶ **Full.** A remote user who supplies the correct password has read and write privileges to that directory and all its files and subdirectories.

> ▶ **Depends on password.** Two different passwords can be created—one allowing read-only access, and one allowing full access. The type of access granted to a user depends on the password the user supplies.

> If no password is used, any user will have full or read-only access to the directory, depending on which option was specified when the shared directory was created.

For an exercise testing this information, see end of chapter.

In Exercise 5.3 at the end of the chapter, you create a directory share using share-level security.

Print queues also can be shared with other network users using share-level security. If a password is specified for the share, a network user has to enter that password to access the print queue and connect to that printer. If a printer is shared with a blank password, any user can connect to and print to that printer. For more information on sharing a printer, see Chapter 7.

Because share-level security relies on access passwords, this form of security has the following disadvantages:

> ▶ To access different shares, a network user has to know numerous passwords.

> ▶ Passwords can easily be forgotten. Windows 95 can cache passwords so that a user must enter them each time. However, if the creator of the share forgets the password, the password has to be changed to allow another user to access the share.

> ▶ Nothing prevents a user from disclosing the password to an unauthorized user.

Configuring User-Level Security

User-level security can be used to overcome the shortcomings of share-level security. With user-level security, specific user accounts or group accounts can be granted access to a shared directory or printer. Instead of relying on a password that could be used by anyone, the user account accessing a shared resource must be authenticated to ensure that the account has been granted access.

Windows 95 does not manage user accounts by itself. User-level security enables you to create a list of users who have access to a particular resource; you can store that list on a server (called the *central server*). Before a user can gain access to a resource, he or she must be on this list of users. When a user logs on to the server, he or she must use pass-through authentication to have a Windows NT or NetWare server authenticate the user who is trying to access the resource.

The pass-through authentication process involves the following four steps:

1. Client requests access to a Windows 95 server user-level security share.

2. User-level security share requests security provider (where access list is stored) to verify the ID and password of client.

3. Security checks ID and password against user list and reports back to Windows 95 server that the client is valid.

4. Windows 95 user-level security server grants client access to resource if client is on list as user or belongs to a group that has access privileges.

You can use user-level security to provide security for a variety of services beyond network access. The following is a list of services you can control using user-level security:

▶ File and print sharing

▶ Backup agent

▶ Network management

▶ Dial-up networking

▶ Create groups of users, such as Managers

To use user-level security, the Windows 95 computer must obtain a copy of the accounts list from one of the following sources:

▶ Windows NT Server 3.5 (or later) computer

▶ Windows NT Workstation 3.5 (or later) computer

▶ NetWare 3.x server running SYSCON

▶ NetWare 4.x server running NETADMIN and bindery emulation

With user-level security, when a directory is shared, the users or groups that have access to the share are assigned privileges. Each user or group can be given one of the following privileges:

▶ **Read-only.** Users can access files and subdirectories in a directory, but cannot delete or save files to that share.

▶ **Full access.** Users can read, write, and delete files in the directory.

▶ **Custom.** Any number of the following privileges can be granted. Access privileges are for all files in a folder, not a single file:

Read Files

Write to Files

Create Files

List Files

Delete Files

Change File Attributes

Change Permissions

When sharing a printer, users or groups can be added to a list of users with access to that printer. For more information on sharing printers, see Chapter 7.

Although you can change from user-level to share-level security, or from share-level to user-level security, you probably should not. The two security environments do not share any features. When you switch from one to the other, you lose all of the current security settings. You must recreate all security settings from the ground up, such as invoke directory or printer sharing for a specific object. You should develop a plan before setting up either security model to help avoid the possibility of switching from one to the other.

For an exercise testing this information, see end of chapter.

In Exercise 5.4 at the end of the chapter, you learn how to give a network user access to a directory share.

Networking Configuration

The flexible networking architecture of Windows 95 allows many interchangeable networking components to be installed and configured to meet the requirements of a network. The configurable networking components of Windows 95 include the following:

- ▶ Client software

- ▶ Adapter drivers

- ▶ Transport protocols

- ▶ Network services

Most of these components are interchangeable, allowing a Windows 95 computer to be configured to support many network environments. For example, multiple 32-bit clients, network adapters, protocols, and services can be installed to allow a Windows 95 computer to perform many different tasks in a heterogeneous networking environment.

> Only one 16-bit client may be installed at a time. Similarly, only one file and print sharing service may be installed on a Windows 95 computer.

The following sections look at how to install and configure the various Windows 95 networking components.

Configuring Network Clients

The Windows 95 networking clients provide a user interface for the networking software. Each type of network requires the proper client to be used to interact with the rest of network. The following client software is included with Windows 95:

▶ The 32-bit Client for Microsoft Networks

▶ The 32-bit Client for NetWare Networks

▶ Various 16-bit clients for other networks

Microsoft Networks

The 32-bit Client for Microsoft Networks is recommended for all SMB-based networks. The configuration of the Client for Microsoft Networks is different depending on whether the Windows 95 computer is part of a Windows NT domain or part of a peer-to-peer workgroup without a domain controller or centralized accounts database.

Configure Windows 95 as a Windows NT Server Domain Client

A Windows NT domain contains at least one Windows NT Server that acts as the domain controller and maintains a user accounts database. When a Windows 95 computer participates in a domain, it can use user-level security to share and access resources on a per user account basis. Furthermore, Windows 95 can process Windows NT logon scripts during logon.

There are many other benefits to participating in a Windows NT domain; they're discussed in the Windows NT documentation.

For an exercise testing this information, see end of chapter.

In Exercise 5.5 at the end of the chapter, you learn how to configure a Windows 95 computer to participate in a Windows NT domain.

Peer Workgroup

A peer workgroup consists of Windows-based computers that are not part of a Windows NT domain. Workgroups must use share-level security because the clients do not access a central Windows NT or NetWare accounts database.

To configure a Windows 95 computer to participate in a peer-to-peer workgroup you need to specify only the computer name and workgroup name in the Identification tab of the Network Control Panel Applet.

File and Printer Sharing for Microsoft Networks

To allow other computers on a Microsoft Network to access a Windows 95 computer's print queues or files, you need to configure the following:

▶ Enable the appropriate sharing option(s) in the File and Print Sharing dialog box of the Network Control Panel Applet.

▶ If user-level security is to be used, configure that option in the Access Control tab of the Network Control Panel Applet.

▶ The specific directory or printer queue must be shared and the appropriate access permissions must be granted.

Configure Windows 95 to Use Windows NT User-Level Security

In the section, "Configuring User-Level Security," earlier in the chapter, you learned about Windows' 95 user-level security feature. You can enable user-level security when you connect a Windows 95 client to a Windows NT server.

For an exercise testing this information, see end of chapter.

To set up Windows 95 to use Windows NT user-level security, you must have Windows 95 running on a Windows NT server, such as a Windows NT Server domain or a Windows NT Workstation server. You also need to have Client for Microsoft Networks enabled (see Exercise 5.5 to learn how to set up this client). Next, perform the following steps:

1. Choose Add in the Network Properties sheet to display the Select Network Component Type dialog box.

2. Select Service and click on Add. The Select Network Service dialog box appears.

3. Select File and Printer Sharing for Microsoft Networks and click on OK. The service is added to the Network properties sheet.

4. Click on the Access Control tab of the Network Properties sheet.

5. Choose the User-Level Access Control option.

6. In the Obtain List of Users and Group From field, enter the name of the Windows NT server that contains the access account list for the user. This is the list that authenticates the user when he or she wants access to a resource.

7. Click on OK. Insert the Windows 95 Setup CD-ROM or any disks Windows asks for.

8. After the files for File and Printer Sharing for Microsoft Networks are installed, Windows prompts you to shut down and restart Windows. Click on Yes to do so. After Windows reboots, the client is set up to use the new service on a Windows NT network.

You now can set up folders and printers to be shared on the Windows 95 client computers. You can share a folder, for example, by opening Explorer in Windows 95, locating the folder you want to share, and right-clicking. Select Sharing from the context-sensitive menu and set up access rights as explained in the previous section, "Configuring User-Level Security."

Configure Windows 95 as a NetWare Network Client or Server

 Windows 95 clients can easily join existing Novell NetWare networks and share many of the benefits of other NetWare clients. For interoperability with NetWare networks, Windows 95 includes the following components and features:

▶ The 32-bit Client for NetWare Networks (using the NWREDIR.VXD driver)

▶ Support for 16-bit Novell NetWare clients, either NETX or VLMs

▶ A NetWare login script processor

▶ The IPX/SPX-compatible protocol

▶ The IPX ODI protocol for compatibility with older NetWare networks

▶ The File and Printer Sharing for NetWare Networks service

The last item in the preceding list is used when you want to set up Windows 95 to act like a NetWare file and printer server to NetWare clients. You can do this by using the peer-to-peer capabilities of Windows 95. One of the advantages of doing this is to provide the Windows 95 user interface to networks that have dissimilar user interfaces. Some of the server-type commands you can use on a Windows 95 "server" is ATTACH, SLIST, and VOLINFO.

One reason for running Windows 95 as a server is to share expensive printers that you might have attached to Windows 95 workstations with less fortunate NetWare workstations on the same network. This feature also can prove useful if you phase out a

NetWare network and phase in a Windows 95 network. Both a Windows 95 server and a NetWare server can be set up on the same network. Because both servers can share information, Windows 95–based workstations can replace older NetWare workstations one at a time, thus distributing the expense and shock of converting all the computers at once.

The services that Windows 95 offers to enable it to act as a NetWare server are 32-bit protected mode drivers that (like other network components) have no conventional memory footprint and prevent memory problems associated with real-mode drivers. You learn more about setting up File and Printer Sharing for NetWare Networks so Windows can act like a NetWare server in the section, "File and Printer Sharing for NetWare Networks," later in this chapter.

16-Bit and 32-Bit NetWare Clients

Where possible, the 32-bit Client for NetWare Networks is recommended for interoperability with NetWare networks. The 32-bit client does not use any conventional memory and provides other benefits, such as unified logon and unified browsing services, which have been discussed previously.

When you install the Client for NetWare Networks, the IPX/SPX-compatible protocol automatically installs as well. This protocol must be used with the Client for NetWare Networks, although additional protocols also can be installed.

For an exercise testing this information, see end of chapter.

In Exercise 5.6 at the end of this chapter, you learn how to install and configure the Client for NetWare Networks. You must have a network adapter driver already installed in the Network Control Panel Applet for exercise to work.

File and Printer Sharing for NetWare Networks

To enable directories and print queues to be shared with other NetWare users, add the File and Printer Sharing for NetWare Networks service in the Network Control Panel Applet. If the File and Printer Sharing for Microsoft Networks service is already installed, remove that service first.

After File and Printer Sharing for NetWare Networks is installed, enable sharing by choosing the appropriate File and Printer Sharing options from the Network Control Panel Applet.

> File and Printer Sharing for NetWare Networks must use the user-level security model. See the next section, "Configure Windows 95 to Use NetWare User-Level Security," for more information on this model.

The computer name of the NetWare server that maintains the list of user accounts must be specified in the Access Control tab of the Network Control Panel Applet.

Configure Windows 95 to Use NetWare User-Level Security

You can use user-level security when running Windows 95 on a NetWare network and want to have peer services enabled for the Windows 95 clients. The user-level security available with NetWare networks is similar to user-level security with Microsoft networks. When using user-level security with NetWare networks, security authentication requests are handled using the pass-through security method. This type of security method passes the authentication requests to a NetWare server for authentication.

User-level security on NetWare is used to protect shared network resources by storing a list of users and groups who have access to a network resource. To gain access to a resource, a user must be on the access account list stored on the NetWare server bindery and then have the proper access rights for that resource. Administrators can set up access rights on a per user or per group basis. The rights that can be assigned to a user for a specific resource includes read, write, create, delete, change attribute, directory search, and access control.

An example of setting up user-level security on a NetWare network is when setting up the File and Printer Sharing for NetWare Networks service (see the previous section for an introduction to this service). You can use this service to control access to a client computer's file and attached printer. File and Printer Sharing for NetWare Networks is supported by NWSERVER.VXD, which requires NWREDIR.VXD to be installed and functioning.

> Remember that File and Printer Sharing for NetWare Networks cannot run on the same machine you have File and Printer Sharing for Microsoft Networks installed. You must remove the latter before installing the former.

The File and Printer Sharing for NetWare Networks service is established in the protected mode with the NWSERVER.VXD, which is supported by the NWSP.VXD, the virtual device driver that handles the security for the Windows 95 client computer that shares its files and printers. Because File and Printer Sharing for NetWare Networks depends on the bindery security from the NetWare server, an additional function is necessary to read the NetWare server's bindery. This function is provided through the NWAB32.DLL file, which is responsible for reading the access account list from the NetWare server bindery.

For an exercise testing this information, see end of chapter.

Before you install the File and Printer Sharing for NetWare Network service, you should have the Client for NetWare Networks client installed. You can read how to do this in the previous section, "16-Bit and 32-Bit NetWare Clients," and by following Exercise 5.6 at the end of the chapter. You then open the Network Properties sheet again by double-clicking on the Network icon from Control Panel. Next, use the following steps:

1. Click on Add in the Network Properties sheet to open the Select Network Component Type dialog box.

2. Select Service and click on Add. The Select Network Service dialog box appears.

3. Select File and Printer Sharing for NetWare Networks and click OK. The service is added to the Network Properties sheet.

4. Click on the Access Control tab of the Network Properties sheet.

5. Choose the User-Level Access Control option.

6. In the Obtain List of Users and Group From field, enter the name of the NetWare server that contains the access account list for the user. This is the list that authenticates the user when he or she wants access to a resource.

7. Click on OK. Insert the Windows 95 Setup CD-ROM or any disks Windows asks for.

8. After the files for File and Printer Sharing for NetWare Networks are installed, Windows prompts you to shut down and restart Windows. Click on Yes to do so. After Windows reboots, the client is set up to use the new service on a NetWare network.

Specifying the folders and printers to be shared on a client computer is accomplished at a user level. To set up a folder as a shared resource, for example, a user opens Explorer, locates the folder to share, and right-clicks on it. From the context-sensitive menu, the Sharing command is selected and the Sharing tab is filled out. You can learn more about sharing a folder in the previous section, "Configuring User-Level Security." To set up a printer as a shared resource, see Chapter 7.

Enabling the peer services of user-level security is not used by all network administrators. For administrators who like to maintain security and access through one source using such a utility as NetWare's SYSCON, user-level security is handy. This is because administrators can set up groups and users to their needs. An administrator might, for example, set up one group that has only read-only users, and set up a group that has full-access rights users. To see who is in each group, the administrator only needs to use SYSCON.

On the other hand, large installations that have networks connecting many users together may not want to set up user-level security or offer peer services to their end users. This way all resource sharing is controlled at the NetWare server level, and not at the workstation level. This provides the administrator with much more control over the shared resources.

Other Networks

To install network clients for other networks, refer to the documentation provided by the third-party network vendor.

> Windows 95 computers can be configured to use dial-up access to access a network over a modem line. This allows users to connect to a remote network, including the Internet, from any location with a telephone connection. For more information on remote network access, see Chapter 9. For information on using remote network access to connect to the Internet, see the "Connecting to the Internet" section later in this chapter.

Configuring Network Adapter Drivers

Windows 95 includes drivers for many of the most popular network adapter drivers. Additional network adapter drivers may be supplied by the network adapter vendor for use with Windows 95. Before you can install any other Windows 95 networking components, you must first install a network adapter driver through the Network Control Panel Applet. If you do not have an actual network card in the computer, you can use the Microsoft Dial-Up Adapter driver along with a compatible modem for network connectivity.

Network adapter card drivers are configured by selecting the adapter in the Network Control Panel Applet and choosing Properties. If the network card supports the Plug and Play standard, Windows 95 can automatically configure the driver according to information the card provides to the Windows 95 operating system. Otherwise, the card should be configured according to the manufacturer's documentation.

Configuring Network Protocols

A network transport protocol is similar to a language that the network computers use to communicate among themselves. For two computers to communicate, they both must speak the same language—they must both use the same network transport protocol. The following transport protocols are included with Windows 95:

▶ Microsoft NetBEUI

▶ Microsoft IPX/SPX-compatible (NWLINK)

▶ Microsoft TCP/IP

▶ Microsoft DLC

▶ Other third-party vendor transport protocols

The NetBEUI and IPX/SPX-compatible protocols are installed by default when a network adapter driver is installed.

If the Windows 95 computer needs to communicate with other computers, it must have the same protocol installed as the other computers. For example, if the other computers on the network are running DEC Pathworks 4.1, install that protocol on the Windows 95 computer. If a common protocol on the network has not yet been established, refer to the following sections for information on each of the protocols.

Unless you are required to use a third-party protocol to communicate with other computers, use one of the Microsoft protocols to take full advantage of the Windows 95 networking features. Furthermore, the third-party protocols provided often require extra components, licenses, and configuration.

NetBEUI

The NetBIOS Extended User Interface (NetBEUI) protocol is relatively easy to implement because it does not require the configuration of additional network addresses for each computer other than the computer name and domain or workgroup name.

The advantages of the NetBEUI protocol include the following:

▶ Communication is fast.

▶ Performance is dynamically self-tuned.

▶ The only configuration required is a NetBIOS computer name and workgroup or domain name.

IPX/SPX

The IPX/SPX protocol is a routable protocol that is commonly used with NetWare networks. IPX/SPX must be installed if the Client for NetWare Networks is used, although other protocols can be installed as well.

TCP/IP

Windows 95 comes with the Microsoft 32-bit TCP/IP protocol, related connectivity utilities, and an SNMP client.

To install the TCP/IP protocol on a Windows 95 computer, follow these steps:

1. From the Start menu, choose Settings, Control Panel.

2. Double-click on the Network icon and select the Configuration tab.

3. Choose Add to open the Select Network Component Type dialog box.

4. Select Protocol and choose Add to open the Select Network Protocol dialog box.

5. Select Microsoft from the Manufacturers list and TCP/IP from the Network Protocols list.

6. Choose OK to return to the Network dialog box.

After installing TCP/IP on a Windows 95 computer, the tabbed TCP/IP Properties dialog box appears from which you configure the appropriate values. To reconfigure TCP/IP, choose the Network icon from the Control Panel to open the Network dialog box again.

To configure TCP/IP for Windows 95, follow these steps:

1. From the Network dialog box Configuration tab, select TCP/IP and choose Properties.

2. From the TCP/IP Properties sheet, select the IP Address tab (see fig. 5.3). Select Obtain an IP address automatically if there is a Dynamic Host Configuration Protocol (DHCP) server on the network configured to supply this machine with an IP address. Otherwise, type the IP address and subnet mask in the spaces provided.

Figure 5.3

The IP Address tab of the TCP/IP Properties sheet.

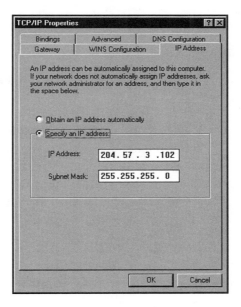

An incorrect IP address or subnet mask can cause communication problems with other TCP/IP nodes on the network. If an IP address is the same as another already on the network, it also can cause either machine to hang. DHCP can help prevent duplicate addresses by automatically configuring TCP/IP on the client using parameters set on the DHCP server. The DHCP server will keep track of IP addresses it has assigned to clients, and will not assign the same IP address to two different DHCP clients.

3. Each of the other tabs in the TCP/IP Properties sheet contain optional configuration information. For each of these tabs, enter the appropriate values as required. Choose OK when done to restart the computer and initialize TCP/IP.

The other tabs of the TCP/IP Properties sheet, discussed in the following sections, contain optional TCP/IP configuration parameters.

It is highly recommended that a default gateway be configured for the Windows 95 client using the Gateway tab. The default gateway can help route TCP/IP messages to remote destinations.

Gateway

When the route needed for an IP message to reach a destination is not known, the message is forwarded to the default gateway. The default gateway is a router connected to other TCP/IP network segments to which messages are initially sent when the destination segment is unknown. The Gateway tab contains the IP addresses of default gateways that can be used in the order they appear on the list.

Only one gateway is used to route messages. If a gateway is unavailable (due to hardware problems, for example), then the next gateway on the list is used. If that gateway does not respond, the next gateway is used. A second gateway never is used if the first one is available, even if the destination computer is unavailable, or the message is undeliverable.

WINS Configuration

A Windows Internet Name Service (WINS) server can be used to register and resolve NetBIOS names to IP addresses. For example, if the Windows 95 computer wants to map a drive to the computer named SERVER3 on a remote TCP/IP network, it can query the WINS server to find out the IP address of SERVER3.

Communication using TCP/IP must always use IP addresses; therefore a WINS server or some other form of NetBIOS name-to-IP-address-resolution must be used if communication using NetBIOS names is required. The alternatives to using a WINS server include using a static LMHOSTS file in the <systemroot> directory, which contains NetBIOS name-to-IP-address mappings. However, a WINS server is preferred because NetBIOS names can be automatically and dynamically registered with the WINS server, which is much more flexible and accurate than an LMHOSTS file or other method.

The three choices of WINS configuration for a Windows 95 TCP/IP client are as follows:

▶ **Enable WINS Resolution.** If WINS resolution is enabled, you must enter the IP address of one or two WINS servers in the appropriate fields. If the primary WINS server is unavailable for some reason, TCP/IP accesses the secondary WINS server if one is configured.

▶ **Disable WINS Resolution.** If WINS is disabled, an alternate form of NetBIOS name resolution is required to resolve NetBIOS names to computer names for destinations on remote networks.

▶ **Use DHCP for WINS Resolution.** If DHCP has been enabled in the IP address tab, you can select the Use DHCP for WINS Resolution option to use the WINS servers specified by the DHCP Server options.

This last option does not mean that a DHCP server provides name resolution. The option is used when a DHCP server has been configured to advise the DHCP clients of the IP address(es) of the WINS server(s).

DNS Configuration

The Domain Name Service (DNS) provides address resolution for DNS host and domain names. Host names are used with Windows Sockets applications. The host name for a Windows-based computer is often the same as the computer name, but the domain name is usually something like domain.company.com. World Wide Web addresses often consist of DNS host names appended to the DNS domain name to form a Fully Qualified Domain Name, such as www.microsoft.com, where www is the host (computer) name, and microsoft.com is the domain name.

To access a computer using a DNS name over TCP/IP, the DNS name must be resolved to an IP address. This can be done using a static HOSTS file in the *<systemroot>* directory, or by accessing a DNS server. The DNS server contains a database that is distributed over an internetwork. If a DNS server cannot fully resolve a domain name to an IP address, it can pass the request on to another DNS server until the name is found and resolved.

The DNS Server Search Order list in the TCP/IP Properties sheet, shown in figure 5.4, lists the order in which DNS servers will be queried for DNS name resolution. The Domain Suffix Search Order list lists the order in which domain names can be appended to a host name to try to resolve the resulting Fully Qualified Domain Name. For example, if the Domain Suffix Search Order list contains microsoft.com, and if the host name fred cannot be resolved, DNS then attempts to resolve the name fred.microsoft.com.

Figure 5.4

The DNS Configuration tab of the TCP/IP Properties sheet.

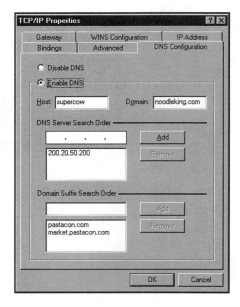

When DNS is enabled on a Windows 95 computer, it will set some internal Registry flags. However, if WINS is also providing DNS information, then DNS is often disabled on the DNS Configuration tab. A trick to getting DNS to work correctly through WINS is to first enable DNS with a valid host name and domain name, reboot, then disable DNS.

Bindings

The Bindings tab shows network components that can use the TCP/IP protocol. If a component has a check mark next to it, it will bind to TCP/IP and can then use the TCP/IP protocol for communication. To improve performance, remove the check marks from any components that do not require TCP/IP.

Advanced

Use the Advanced tab to specify whether you want the TCP/IP protocol to be the default or preferred protocol. By default, the NetBEUI protocol is the default protocol if it is installed.

Microsoft DLC (Data Link Control)

The other Microsoft-written network protocol included with Windows 95 is Microsoft DLC. However, this protocol is used only for communicating with certain network interface printers and mainframe systems. DLC is not used for peer-to-peer networking of Windows 95 computers.

Other Protocols

Other third-party vendor protocols may be installed to support preexisting third-party networks. For information on each, refer to the vendor documentation.

Configuring Network Services

The network services included with Windows 95 include third-party network backup software, Hewlett-Packard network printing software, and the Microsoft File and Printer Sharing services. For information on the network backup software, contact the appropriate vendor. The Hewlett-Packard network printer support services are discussed in Chapter 7. The File and Printer Sharing services are discussed throughout this chapter and in the following section.

Browsing

When users access the Network Neighborhood, they are viewing a list of computers on the network known as a *browse list.*

Microsoft and NetWare networks can use NetBIOS to distribute browse lists throughout a domain. The browse list contains all NetBIOS computers and shared resources in the domain; it is compiled by the master browser of the domain.

When the master browser has compiled the browse list, it distributes the list to the backup browsers. When a client requires access to the browse list, it obtains it from a backup browser so the master browser does not become overloaded with requests from all the computers.

The decision of which computers are master and backup browsers is determined through browse elections. If a primary domain controller is present, that controller will always be the master browser. Each type of operating system in the network has a different potential to be a browser. Windows NT computers are more favored to be browsers than Windows 95 computers. If a computer is a preferred browser, it can be elected to be a browser depending on the operating system it is running and whether it has been manually configured to be a preferred browser.

When a network client needs to consult a browse list to browse the network, it contacts one of the backup browsers for a copy of the current browse list. The backup browsers periodically receive updated browse lists from the master browser to make sure the browse lists remain current.

Normally, the browse lists are maintained and exchanged using local broadcasts. If the domain spans routers, however, extra steps are required to ensure the browse lists are passed across the routers. Refer to your network protocol documentation if this is the case.

A Windows 95 computer can be configured to maintain or to not maintain browse lists by configuring the File and Printer Sharing service with one of the following options:

- ▶ Automatically decide if the Windows 95 computer is needed to be a browser by participating in the browser elections

- ▶ Disable browse list maintenance so that the Windows 95 computer does not compile browse lists

- ▶ Be a preferred browser for the browser elections

Normally, you let the browser elections automatically determine which computers are the browsers. However, if you do not want the potential performance load on the Windows 95 computer that can result from browsing, you can configure the computer to never be a browser. In addition, you can set a particular computer, on which an extra network load would have little effect, to be a preferred browser.

The browser configuration is performed using the properties for the File and Printer Sharing for Microsoft Networks service or the File and Printer Sharing for NetWare Networks service.

Windows 95 computers actually make lousy browse masters, simply because they do not share browse lists properly. You will achieve better browsing capability by placing NT class computers on your networks to provide service as browse masters and domain browse masters. If your Windows 95 workgroup name also happens to be the same as a Windows NT domain name, you will be able to receive even better, or what has been called "enhanced," browsing from the domain master browser.

Configure Browse Master for Microsoft Networks

To access the browser configuration options for a computer running File and Printer Sharing for Microsoft Networks, perform the following steps:

1. Start the Network Control Panel Applet and select the File and Printer Sharing for Microsoft Networks service.

2. Choose Properties and select the Browse Master property (see fig. 5.5).

Figure 5.5

Configuring browse list maintenance for Microsoft Networks.

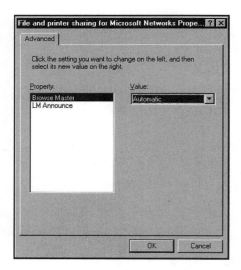

3. Choose one of the following options from the Value drop-down list:

   ▶ Select Automatic as the value to have Windows 95 automatically determine whether the computer is needed as a browse server.

   ▶ Select Disabled as the value to prevent the computer from maintaining browse lists for the network.

note

> Selecting the Disabled option does not prevent the computer from browsing the network resources. It prevents the computer from maintaining a browse list for itself and other computers. As long as at least one computer on the network is a browser, other computers can use the browsing service.

> ▶ To give the computer a higher weighting for the browse elections, select Enable for the value. This computer then will be preferred over other Windows 95 computers that have Automatic set for the Browse Master value for the browse elections.

4. Choose OK twice and restart the computer.

Configure Browse Master for NetWare Networks

To access the browser configuration options for a computer running File and Printer Sharing for NetWare Networks, perform the following steps:

1. Start the Network Control Panel Applet and select the File and Printer Sharing for NetWare Networks service.

2. Choose Properties and select the Workgroup Advertising property (see fig. 5.6).

3. Choose one of the following options from the drop-down list:

   ▶ To have Windows 95 automatically determine if the computer is needed as a browse server, select Enabled: May Be Master for the value.

   ▶ To prevent the computer from maintaining browse lists for the network, select Enabled: May Not Be Master for the value.

Figure 5.6

Configuring browse list maintenance for NetWare Networks.

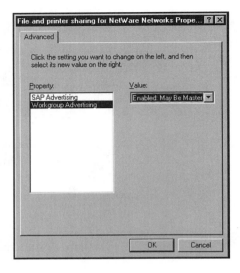

 note ✐

The Enabled: May Not Be Master option does not prevent the computer from browsing the network resources; it prevents the computer from maintaining a browse list for itself and other computers. Select the Disabled option to prevent the computer from using the browse service.

▶ To give the computer a higher weighting for the browse elections, select Enabled: Preferred Master for the value. This computer will then be preferred over other Windows 95 computers that have automatic set for the Browse Master value for the browse elections.

▶ To prevent the computer from using the browser service to browse network resources, select Disabled for the value.

▶ To allow the computer to send SAP broadcasts announcing its presence to real-mode NetWare clients, select the SAP Advertising property and change the value to Enabled.

4. Choose OK twice and restart the computer.

Connecting to the Internet

Windows 95 supports connecting to the Internet in two ways: you can connect through a permanent connection or through a dial-up connection. A *permanent connection* usually means you will be leasing a dedicated phone line from a local communication provider. This line will connect you with your local Internet service provider (ISP). In most cases, you will install a router between your network and the dedicated line to route traffic to the Internet. You use Windows' 95 TCP/IP networking protocol to connect the Internet.

Routers are devices that interconnect networks to route data toward its destination.

Unless you are connected to the Internet through a permanent connection at a company or organization, you probably will gain access through a commercial provider via a dial-up connection using a modem and regular telephone line. Windows 95 includes the Dial-Up Adapter, which you can set up to connect to an ISP. You then bind this adapter to the TCP/IP protocol, dial into your ISP (using the Dial-Up Networking (DUN) feature), and communicate over the Internet.

Setting Up Dial-Up Networking

The following steps show you how to set up Windows 95 to access the Internet through a dial-up connection. Before you begin, you need to make sure the following requirements are met:

▶ A modem is installed and works properly with Windows 95.

▶ You have an Internet account set up with an ISP. You need a user name, IP information (see the "TCP/IP" section earlier in the chapter), telephone number of the ISP, password, e-mail address, and DNS Server name. Your ISP can provide you with this information.

> ▶ Internet software is installed on your computer. The software can vary, but users usually have a WWW browser (such as Microsoft Internet Explorer), an e-mail application, and a newsgroup reader.

After these requirements are met, follow these steps:

1. From the Start menu, choose Settings, Open Control Panel. In the Control Panel, double-click on the Network icon.

2. On the Configuration tab of the Network Properties sheet, click on the Add button. The Select Network Component Type dialog box appears.

3. Select Adapter and click on the Add button. The Select Network Adapters dialog box appears.

4. Scroll down the Manufacturers list and click on Microsoft. This displays Dial-Up Adapter in the Network Adapters list.

5. Click on OK. The Dial-Up Adapter component and a network protocol are added to the list of components shown on the Configuration tab. The default protocol added is Net-BEUI. If you do not have the TCP/IP protocol installed yet, you'll need to add it as the protocol for Dial-Up Networking, as shown in the next steps.

6. Click on the Add button on the Configuration tab of the Network Properties sheet and select Protocol from the Select Network Component Type dialog box.

7. Click on Add again. The Select Network Protocol dialog box appears.

8. Select Microsoft in the Manufacturers list and click on the TCP/IP item in the Network Protocols list. Click on OK. You return to the Configuration tab.

9. Select the TCP/IP Dial-Up Adapter component and click on the Properties button. The TCP/IP Properties sheet appears.

10. On the IP Address tab, specify how your IP address is set up. If you have a dynamic IP address, choose the Obtain an IP

Address Automatically option. If your ISP assigned a permanent IP to you, choose the Specify an IP Address option and fill in the IP Address field. If your ISP also assigned you a subnet mask, which is used with your IP address to further identify which network your computer is on, fill in the Subnet Mask field with that number.

See the previous section, "TCP/IP," for more information about TCP/IP.

11. Click on the DNS Configuration tab to set the Domain Name Service information. Choose the Enable DNS option and fill in the following options:

   ▶ **Host.** Specifies the name of your computer on the Internet. The host name is combined with the domain name (see the next item) to make up your Internet address.

   ▶ **Domain.** Specifies the domain to which your computer belongs.

   ▶ **DNS Server Search Order.** Specifies the DNS server on which information about your specific computer (host) is stored. Enter the DNS server number in the DNS Server Search Order field and click on the Add button. This adds the number to the box below the field. If you have more than one number, continue adding them.

   ▶ **Domain Suffix Search Order.** Specifies multiple domain names if your ISP has them.

The other tabs on the TCP/IP Properties sheet usually do not need to be filled out for most ISPs or networks. However, if your network uses the Windows Internet Naming Service (WINS) for the NetBIOS protocol, you need to obtain the primary and secondary (optional) WINS server address, scope ID, and whether the server uses DHCP (Dynamic Host Configuration Protocol) for WINS resolution. This information needs to be entered on the WINS Configuration tab.

This information must be obtained from your ISP network administrator.

12. Click on OK to save your settings and to return to the Network property page. Click on OK.

13. When prompted to restart Windows 95, click on Yes to shut down and restart Windows 95.

Setting Up a Dial-Up Networking Connection

After Windows 95 restarts, you now need to configure a Dial-Up Networking connection for the client computer. This is so you can actually dial out from your computer and connect to another computer that is attached to the Internet (this other computer is your ISP's computer). After you make a dial-up connection to the other computer, you become attached to the Internet and can communicate and navigate on it. Do this by using the following steps:

1. Double-click on the My Computer icon on the client computer.

2. Double-click on the Dial-Up Networking icon to display the Dial-Up Networking folder.

3. Double-click on the Make New Connection icon to start the Make New Connection Wizard. Enter a name for the connection in the Type a Name for the Computer You Are Dialing field, such as the name of your ISP.

4. In the Select a Modem drop-down list, pick the modem you want to use to dial out using the new Dial-Up Networking connection. Click on the Next button.

5. In the next Make New Connection screen, enter the area code and telephone number for the host computer. Click on the Next button.

6. Click on Finish to create a new Dial-Up Networking connection. A new icon for that connection is added in the Dial-Up Networking folder.

After you install DUN, you can dial into your ISP, establish an Internet connection, and start using Internet resources. For more information on what the Internet offers, see *Inside the World Wide Web*, published by New Riders.

Installing SLIP and Working with SLIP Scripts

With most ISPs today, you can use the Point-to-Point Protocol (PPP) to enable you to use TCP/IP over a dial-up connection. By default, Windows 95 installs PPP when you install Dial-Up Networking, as you did in the previous two sections. You learn more about PPP in Chapter 9.

If your ISP does not support PPP, it probably supports *SerialLine Interface Protocol*, commonly known as SLIP. At one time, SLIP was the only protocol used to transport TCP/IP over a dial-up connection, but it is now losing ground to the newer PPP protocol. You learn more about SLIP in Chapter 9.

If your ISP requires you to install and use SLIP over DUN, you need to perform the following steps to get SLIP working properly:

1. Open the Control Panel and double-click on the Add/Remove Programs icon. The Add/Remove Programs Properties sheet appears.

2. Click on the Windows Setup tab and choose the Have Disk button.

3. In the Install From Disk dialog box, specify the location for the SLIP files as the \ADMIN\APPTOOLS\DSCRIPT folder on the Windows 95 CD-ROM. Specify the RNAPLUS.INF file in the File name field.

4. Click on OK twice until the Have Disk dialog box appears.

5. Click on the SLIP and Scripting for Dial-Up Networking option. Click on Install to install the SLIP files.

6. After the files install, click on OK in the Add/Remove Programs Properties sheet to close it.

7. Open the My Computer folder and open the Dial-Up Networking folder.

8. Right-click on the icon that is set up as your Dial-Up Networking connection (see the preceding section on setting up this item).

9. Select Properties from the context-sensitive menu to display the General tab of the Dial-Up Networking connection icon.

10. Click on the Server Type button to open the Server Types dialog box.

11. From the Type of Dial-Up Server drop-down list, select SLIP: UNIX Connection. Make sure the TCP/IP option in the Allowed Network Protocols area is selected.

12. Click on OK to close the Server Types dialog box.

13. Click on OK in the Dial-Up Networking Connection Properties sheet.

You now can dial into your ISP and use SLIP to transport TCP/IP over the phone line.

In some cases, you may want to use the Windows 95 SLIP scripting tool to help automate connection tasks. To start this tool, use the following steps:

1. Create the SLIP script using Windows Notepad (see the list of commands following these steps for information on which commands are available).

2. From the Start menu, choose Programs, Accessories, Dial-Up Scripting Tool. The Dial-Up Scripting Tool appears.

3. From the Connections list, select the DUN connection with which you want to associate the script.

4. In the File Name field, enter the path and file name of the scripting file you created in step 1.

5. Click on the Apply button to associate the script with the DUN connection.

Now when you launch the DUN connection, the SLIP script you created will launch and run your script.

When you create a script, you can use the commands shown in the following list. Windows 95 uses script commands compliant with the SLIP standard.

- ▶ **proc *name*.** Starts the script procedure. You must have a main procedure, which is named using the command proc main.

- ▶ **endproc.** Ends the script procedure.

- ▶ **delay *numseconds*.** Pauses the script for the number of seconds specified by the *numseconds* variable.

- ▶ **waitfor "*string*."** Pauses until the case-sensitive "*string*" is received from the remote computer.

- ▶ **transmit "*string*"|$USERID|$PASSWORD.** Transmits the designated "*string*," user ID, or password to the remote computer. $USERID and $PASSWORD are automatically set to the values for the selected remote service.

- ▶ **set port databits *number*.** Sets the databits for the communications port to a number between 5 and 8.

- ▶ **set post stopbits *number*.** Sets the stopbits for the communications port to either 1 or 3.

- ▶ **set port parity none|odd|even|mark|space.** Sets parity for the communications port to the value specified.

- ▶ **set ipaddr.** Sets the IP address.

- ▶ **set screen keyboard on|off.** Turns keyboard input to the screen on or off.

- ▶ **getip *optional_index_number*.** Returns the IP address from the remote computer. Can be used with set ipaddr to set the local IP address to that of the remote computer. If more than one address is returned, you can select which one to use by including the *optional_index_number* parameter.

▶ **halt.** Stops the script.

▶ **;.** Begins a comment.

The following list describes the characters you can use in a SLIP script:

▶ **Any character enclosed in double quotes.** Indicates a character in a string.

▶ **.** Indicates a control character, as in M, which indicates a carriage return.

▶ **<cr>.** Indicates a carriage return.

▶ **<lf>.** Indicates a line feed.

▶ **\".** Indicates a double-quote in a string.

▶ **\.** Indicates a carat in a string.

▶ **\<.** Indicates a left angle bracket in a string.

▶ **\\.** Indicates a backslash in a string.

As you create a script, you should place each command on a separate line. Also, you should use the extension SCP on script files to help distinguish them as script files.

Exercises

Exercise 5.1: Configuring Windows 95 for a Microsoft Network

Exercise 5.1 demonstrates the installation of three networking components by installing the NetBEUI protocol, Client for Microsoft Networks, and an appropriate network adapter card driver.

1. From the Start menu, choose Settings, Control Panel. The Control Panel appears.

2. Double-click on the Network icon. The Network dialog box appears (refer to fig. 5.1).

3. Before removing all components, except the network adapter, write down the name of each component and any additional configuration information from the properties sheet(s) for each component. Double-click on an item to display its properties sheet.

4. Remove all components except the adapter card by selecting the item and choosing Remove. The adapter is displayed.

5. Choose Add, select Client, and choose Add. The manufacturers list is displayed.

6. Select Microsoft and Client for Microsoft Networks and choose OK. The Client for Microsoft Networks is added, along with the NetBEUI and IPX/SPX-compatible protocols.

7. Select IPX/SPX-compatible protocol and choose Remove. The client, adapter, and NetBEUI protocol remains.

8. Choose OK and restart the computer.

Exercise 5.2: Using UNC Names

Exercise 5.2 illustrates the use of a UNC name. For this exercise, you must be connected to a network and be able to browse file shares on other computers on the network.

1. Open Network Neighborhood from the Desktop. The other computers in your workgroup or domain are displayed.

continues

Exercise 5.2:   Continued

2. Double-click on another computer that contains a share to which you have access. The shares on that computer are displayed.

3. Note the computer name and share name on a piece of paper.

4. From the Start menu, choose Programs, MS-DOS Prompt. A command prompt window opens.

5. Enter **DIR** *computername\sharename*, using the computer name and share name you recorded. The directory listing from the remote network share is displayed.

Exercise 5.3:   Sharing a Directory Using Share-Level Security

In Exercise 5.3, you create a directory share using share-level security.

1. From the Start menu, choose Settings, Control Panel. The Control Panel appears.

2. Double-click on the Network icon. The Network dialog box appears.

3. Select the Access Control tab and select Share-Level Access Control.

4. Select the Configuration tab and choose File and Print Sharing. The File and Print Sharing dialog box appears.

5. Select both the I Want to Be Able to Give Others Access to My Files and the I Want to Be Able to Allow Others to Print to My Printer(s) check boxes to allow others to access your printers and files and choose OK. File and Printer Sharing for Microsoft Networks is automatically installed.

6. Choose OK and restart the computer.

7. Start Explorer and select a directory on your hard drive.

8. Right-click on the selected directory and choose Sharing from the context-sensitive menu. The Sharing dialog box opens.

9. Type **TEST** for the share name and select Access Type: Read-Only. Enter a password for read-only access and choose OK. The sharing hand symbol replaces the folder symbol for the shared directory.

10. If you have another computer on the network, browse the first computer in Network Neighborhood to display the share name. The share name TEST is displayed under the appropriate computer name.

11. Double-click on the share name TEST. You are prompted for the password.

12. Enter the password and choose OK. The directory contents are displayed.

13. Try to copy a file to the local hard drive. The file read will be successful.

14. Try to delete a file in the shared directory. The file delete will not be allowed.

Exercise 5.4: Sharing a Directory Using User-Level Security

In Exercise 5.4, you are shown how to give a network user access to a directory share. For this exercise, you must be part of a domain that contains a server with a user accounts database. If the user accounts are on a NetWare server, you should install the Client for NetWare Networks, the IPX/SPX-compatible protocol, and File and Printer Sharing for NetWare Networks.

1. From the Start menu, choose Settings, Control Panel. The Control Panel appears.

2. Double-click on the Network icon. The Network dialog box appears.

3. Select the Access Control tab and select User-Level Access Control (see fig. 5.7).

continues

Exercise 5.4: Continued

Figure 5.7

Enabling user-level security.

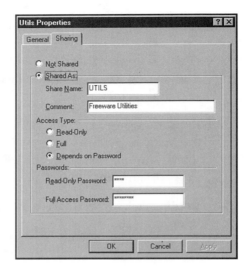

4. Type the name of the server with the user accounts database on it. Windows 95 attempts to access the Windows NT or NetWare server to obtain the users list.

5. Select the Configuration tab and choose File and Print Sharing. The File and Print Sharing dialog box appears.

6. Select both the I Want to Be Able to Give Others Access to My Files and the I Want to Be Able to Allow Others to Print to My Printer(s) check boxes to allow others to access your printers and files and choose OK. File and Printer Sharing for Microsoft Networks is automatically installed.

7. Choose OK and restart the computer.

8. Start Explorer and select another directory on your hard drive. The new directory is highlighted in Explorer, but the directory from the previous exercise is no longer shared due to the changed security model.

9. Right-click on the selected directory and choose Sharing from the context-sensitive menu. The Sharing tab of the Properties sheet appears (see fig. 5.8).

Figure 5.8

The Properties sheet for a shared directory using user-level security.

10. Type **TEST2** for the share name and give a user full access privileges by selecting the user and choosing Full Access. Choose OK. The folder symbol for the shared directory is replaced with a folder being held by a hand.

11. Log on to another computer on the network using the user name to which you gave full access permissions. Locate the share name TEST2 in the Explorer by browsing the entire network. The share name TEST2 is displayed under the appropriate computer name.

12. Double-click on the share name TEST2. The directory contents appear.

13. Try to copy a file to the shared directory. The file write is allowed.

Exercise 5.5: Configuring Windows 95 for Use in a Windows NT Domain

In Exercise 5.5, you configure a Windows 95 computer to participate in a Windows NT domain. If the Client for Microsoft Networks is not already installed, perform Exercise 5.1 before proceeding.

1. From the Start menu, choose Settings, Control Panel. The Control Panel appears.

continues

Exercise 5.5: Continued

2. Double-click on the Network icon. The Network dialog box appears.

3. Select Client for Microsoft Networks and choose Properties. The Client for Microsoft Networks Properties sheet appears.

4. Select Log on to Windows NT domain, enter the Windows NT domain name, and choose OK. The Client for Microsoft Networks Properties sheet again appears.

5. Select the Identification tab and type the Windows NT domain name in the Workgroup field.

6. Enter a computer name and optional description in the other fields and choose OK. You are prompted to restart the computer.

7. Restart the computer and log on to Windows 95 using your Windows NT domain account. If your domain password is the same as your Windows password, enter the password once.

Exercise 5.6: Configuring the Client for NetWare Networks

In Exercise 5.6, you install and configure the Client for NetWare Networks. You must have a network adapter driver already installed in the Network Control Panel Applet.

1. From the Start menu, choose Settings, Control Panel. The Control Panel appears.

2. Double-click on the Network icon. The Network dialog box appears.

3. Choose Add, select Client, and choose Add. The Manufacturers list is displayed.

4. Select Microsoft and Client for NetWare Networks and choose OK. The Client for NetWare Networks and the IPX/SPX-compatible protocols are installed.

5. Select the Client for NetWare Networks and choose Properties. The Client for NetWare Networks Properties sheet appears.

6. Select the General tab and enter the name of the NetWare server that should process the logon in the Preferred Server field.

7. In the First Network Drive field, select the first drive letter to be available to be mapped by a NetWare login script and choose OK twice. You are prompted to restart the computer.

8. Restart the computer and enter your NetWare user name at the unified logon screen. If your NetWare password is the same as your Windows password, you have to enter the password only once.

   If your NetWare password is different from your Windows password, change your NetWare password to your Windows password by entering the SETPASS command from the SYS/ PUBLIC directory on the NetWare server.

Review Questions

The following questions test your knowledge of the information in this chapter. For additional questions, see MCP Endeavor and the Microsoft Roadmap/Assessment Exam on the CD-ROM that accompanies this book.

1. You are responsible for connecting Windows 95 to a heterogeneous network. You're running a number of different network operating systems on this large network and want to be sure Windows 95 is compatible with them. Windows 95 includes software to support which three of the following networks?

    A. Banyan VINES

    B. DEC Pathworks

    C. Novell NetWare

    D. Apple AppleShare

2. Jason installs a network adapter card on a computer running Windows 95. When he does this, Windows 95 automatically installs two protocols for this card. Which two protocols are installed by default when the first network adapter driver is installed?

    A. AppleTalk

    B. NetBEUI

    C. TCP/IP

    D. IPX/SPX-compatible

3. You want to install Windows 95 on a Novell NetWare network. Which two of the following are advantages of Microsoft Client for NetWare Networks as opposed to Novell's NETX workstation software?

    A. Microsoft Client for NetWare Networks allows you to use TSR applications loaded from DOS.

   B. Microsoft Client for NetWare Networks runs in protected mode and thus does not use any conventional memory.

   C. Microsoft Client for NetWare Networks allows additional network clients to be used at the same time.

   D. Microsoft Client for NetWare Networks supports the ArcNet protocols.

4. In a training class you are teaching, you explain to end users how to use UNC to access resources on the network. You provide this example to the class: What is the full UNC path for a file named test.bat in a directory named BATCH located in a share named PUBLIC on a server named FREDSPC? Select the correct answer.

   A. \\PUBLIC\BATCH\test.bat

   B. \\FREDSPC\BATCH\test.bat

   C. \\FREDSPC\PUBLIC\BATCH\test.bat

   D. None of the above

5. In your office you have a single network with multiple network protocols running on it. Because users may need to log on to several networks at boot time, you want to use the Unified Logon feature in Windows 95. To use Unified Logon, the _____ for all networks must be the same.

   A. network operating systems

   B. topologies

   C. network protocols

   D. passwords

6. Windows 95 has a modular, layered architecture. Which two of the following are interfaces functioning at the Windows 95 Application Interface layer?

   A. Win32 WinNet Interface

   B. WinNet 16

    C. HP JetAdmin

    D. Win32 Print Applicator Programming Interface

7. Susan prepares for a presentation describing the Windows 95 network architecture. One of the bullet points is this: a _____ maps network names used by an application to a physical network device name. Pick the appropriate answer to fill in the blank.

    A. device driver

    B. redirector

    C. requestor

    D. transport interface

8. Which three of the following are layers in the Windows 95 networking architecture?

    A. Transport Programming Interface

    B. Internal File System Manager

    C. Device Driver Interface

    D. Network Providers

9. Isabel is configuring her Windows 95 computer with the TCP/IP protocol. As she fills out the properties for the protocol, she comes across a blank for the DNS entry. What does DNS stand for?

    A. Downloadable Network Share

    B. DOS-Node Server

    C. Domain Name Service

    D. Domain Network Server

10. You run a network with the NetBIOS protocol. The _____ registers and resolves NetBIOS names to IP addresses.

    A. DNS Server

    B. IFS Manager

C. Network Adapter Card

D. WINS Server

11. Chuck is setting up a network to use user-level security. From the following list, pick the two places where the user list can be stored?

A. Windows NT domain

B. Window 95 home directory

C. NetWare bindery server

D. Banyan VINES server

12. To access the Internet, you need to use Windows' 95 Dial-Up Adapter and associated software. Pick three items from the following list that you must have before setting up Windows 95 to access the Internet via a dial-up mode.

A. ISP account

B. modem

C. gateway

D. DNS information

13. While stationed at the company help desk, you receive a call from a user accessing the Internet. He asks what a fully qualified domain name is. From the following list, pick the one that would not meet this criteria.

A. www.microsoft.com

B. www3.iquest.net

C. www.microsoft_com

D. www.mcp.com\newriders

14. Name the protocol supported by Windows 95 that is used only for communicating with certain network interface printers and mainframe systems. It also is not used for peer-to-peer networking of Windows 95 computers.

    A. TCP/IP

    B. DLC

    C. IPX/SPX

    D. NetBIOS

15. You have Windows 95 installed on a computer connected to a network running only one network operating system (NOS). A user calls and says she cannot browse network resources using Network Neighborhood. Which NOS could you be running that does not support browser services?

    A. Novell NetWare 3.12

    B. Banyan VINES

    C. Windows NT

    D. None of the above

16. Stuart is attaching his Windows 95 computer to another Windows 95 computer using the Microsoft Network. He wants to provide access from one computer to the other so each computer has access to files and printers on either machine. What must he do to enable this in Windows 95?

    A. Set up user-level security

    B. Disable File and Printer Sharing for Microsoft Networks

    C. Set up share-level security

    D. All of the above

17. You are asked to connect 10 Windows 95 computers to a Novell NetWare network. From the following list, pick the two components or features that Windows 95 has for NetWare networks.

    A. Capability to run File and Printer Sharing for NetWare with File and Printer Sharing with Microsoft Networks

    B. Share-level support of File and Printer Sharing for NetWare

C. IPX/SPX-compatible protocol

D. 32-bit Client for NetWare Networks

18. As you instruct a user on how to configure a peer-to-peer network with five Windows 95 computers connected together, you use the term "Windows 95 server" several times. After you finish, he asks you what a Windows 95 server is. What do you tell him?

A. A computer that is the Primary Domain Controller (PDC) on the LAN.

B. A computer running Windows 95 that has the Enable Windows 95 Server Registry option turned on.

C. A Windows 95 computer that has the File and Printer Sharing Service enabled.

D. A computer running Windows 95 that performs as an application and database server for the LAN.

19. Windows' 95 modular architecture includes the Installable File Service (IFS) Manager. The IFS Manager manages communication between three of the following answers. Pick the three best answers.

A. The Miniport Driver

B. The various Installable File Systems

C. The Network Provider

D. The network redirectors and services

20. Martina has been told that she can run multiple network clients under Windows 95, but is having problems getting this feature to work on her system. She calls you and asks you to help her. From the following list, what would be the best question to ask her to start diagnosing her problem?

A. Does she have protocols for IPX/SPX set up?

B. Is Windows 95 set up to handle user profiles?

C. Is there a Primary Domain Controller (PDC) established on a Windows 95 Server?

D. Are all the network clients 32-bit clients?

Review Answers

1. A B C	6. A D	11. A C	16. C
2. B D	7. B	12. A B C	17. C D
3. B C	8. A C D	13. C	18. C
4. C	9. C	14. B	19. B C D
5. D	10. D	15. B	20. D

Test Yourself

Stop! Before reading this chapter, test yourself to determine how much study time you will need to devote to this section.

1. Cindy calls you from marketing and tells you she just created a file in Microsoft Excel 95 and saved it as a long file name called Marketing Budget.XLS. She copies the file to her laptop, which also runs Windows 95, but the version of Excel on the laptop was released prior to Windows 95. She says she can't find the Marketing Budget.XLS file. What is one possible short file name you tell her to look for?

2. You migrate to Windows 95 on a system that has a 1 GB hard drive. You want to compress part of the drive, but not all of it, to conserve space. What is the maximum size of a compressed volume using Windows' 95 DriveSpace program?

3. You take a call at a help desk from a user who has two disk-management issues he wants to correct. First, he wants to correct cross-linked files and lost clusters; then he wants to recover deleted files. Name the two utilities included with Windows 95 that the caller can use to correct these problems.

4. Explain how a fragmented disk depreciates the performance of Windows 95. Also, what utility included with Windows 95 can you use to defragment a hard drive?

5. In a training class, a student asks you when she should run ScanDisk under Windows 95. She also asks you to explain lost clusters. What are your answers?

6. Jason is setting up a backup schedule to back up several of his machines. What are three storage media types Windows 95 supports? Also, what is the name of the utility included with Windows 95 that Jason can use to backup his data?

Answers

1. MARKET~1.XLS. See "Long File Name (LFN) Support."
2. 512 MB. See "Further Notes on Windows 95 Disk Compression."
3. ScanDisk and Recycle Bin. See "Choosing a Disk Management Tool."
4. Fragmented files are saved to the hard drive in non-contiguous areas on the hard drive. This forces Windows 95 to take longer to read the whole file from one location when you request it. Use Disk Defragmenter. See "Disk Defragmenter."
5. You should use ScanDisk regularly, such as once a week or at least twice a month. When files are saved to disk in non-contiguous areas, they use pointers to the next cluster of the file. Sometimes the pointer for one of these clusters becomes corrupted (this is called a *lost cluster*). See "ScanDisk."
6. Jason can back up to a tape drive, a floppy disk(s), or a network location. He can use Backup. See "Backup."

Managing Disk
Resources and Utilities

6

This chapter will help you prepare for the exam by covering the
following objectives:

**Test
Objectives**

▶ Manage long and short file names in a mixed environment

▶ Troubleshoot problems and perform disk compression

▶ Select the appropriate disk-management tool for a given
situation

▶ Use Disk Defragmenter to optimize for speed

▶ Use ScanDisk in appropriate situations

▶ Back up in appropriate situations

One of the key functions of any operating system is its capability
to manage the storage and retrieval of information. The software
processes and drivers that enable writing to storage devices and
reading from them are known collectively as the *file system*. Prior
to Windows 95, MS-DOS–based computers used a *FAT-based* file
system. FAT stands for *File Allocation Table*, which is the storage
area on any hard disk or floppy disk that tracks the used/unused
space on that medium. Windows 95 also implements a FAT-based
file system, but the Windows 95 FAT-based file system includes
numerous enhancements intended to maximize performance and
usability.

In addition to providing an enhanced file system, Windows 95
includes utilities that enable users to perform various maintenance tasks, as well as safeguard their data against corruption or
destruction.

This chapter examines the structure and features of the Windows 95 file system and disk utilities. The major topics of discussion include the following:

- ▶ Installable file system architecture
- ▶ File system caching
- ▶ Long file name support
- ▶ Troubleshooting the file system
- ▶ Disk utilities

Installable File System Architecture

A key feature of Windows 95 that allows it to adapt to developing technologies is its modular design. With Windows' 95 modular design, generic features of Windows 95 subsystems, such as networking, printing, and communications, are implemented into a universal component (for example, the Universal Printer Driver). Functions specific to a type or brand of hardware/software are implemented in a type-specific driver (for example, the printer mini-driver for a Hewlett-Packard LaserJet). In this way, if a generic printing function is called by the operating system, it is handled by the Universal Printer Driver, and functions specific to an HP LaserJet are handled by the mini-driver.

Microsoft uses a modular architecture for the Windows 95 file systems; all I/O requests are first handled by a universal file system manager. Thus, instead of reengineering the operating system to implement compatibility with other existing or future file system structures, all that is needed to accommodate a new type of file system is to develop a file system driver that can communicate with the universal file system driver and that handles the unique functions of that file system. Figure 6.1 illustrates the file system architecture of Windows 95.

Figure 6.1

File system components.

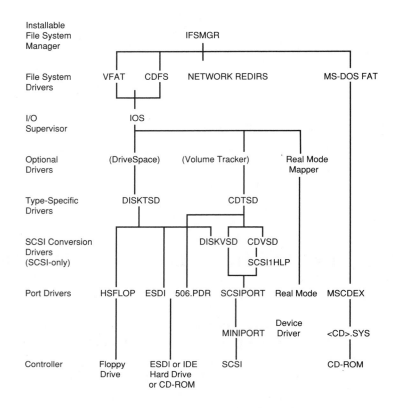

The Windows 95 file systems are known as *installable* file systems because they can be loaded into and removed from the system memory as needed; another indication of the modularity of the Windows 95 file system components.

File operations are handled by the Installable File System (IFS) components of Windows 95. These components include the following:

▶ IFS Manager

▶ File System Drivers

▶ I/O Supervisor

▶ Volume Tracker

- ▶ Type Specific Drivers

- ▶ Port Drivers

IFS Manager

The *IFS Manager* is responsible for analyzing incoming I/O requests from applications and other processes and determining which file system driver can fulfill requests most effectively. When you install a new file system driver, it registers itself with the IFS Manager, notifying the IFS Manager of what types of I/O requests it is able to process. The important thing to note is that the file system driver does not need to know how to communicate with applications or other processes directly; it only needs to know how to communicate with the IFS Manager.

File System Drivers

The file system drivers enable I/O requests to be sent to and from the installed file systems. Windows 95 includes support for the following file systems (although you can add others using third-party drivers):

- ▶ 32-bit Virtual-FAT (VFAT)

- ▶ 32-bit CD-ROM file system (CDFS)

- ▶ 32-bit network redirectors

- ▶ 16-bit FAT

VFAT File System Driver

The VFAT *file system driver* (FSD) is the primary FSD for the system and cannot be disabled. It is responsible for all local hard disk I/O requests (including SCSI). This FSD gives Windows 95 a fully 32-bit virtualized MS-DOS FAT file system. Like all FSDs, VFAT supports long file names (which are discussed in more detail in the section "Long File Name (LFN) Support" later in this chapter).

> VFAT is used only for hard drives that have the 32-bit disk access components installed. If a drive is accessed through real-mode drivers (for example, an Ontrack Disk Manager driver in the CONFIG.SYS), the drive is accessed through MS-DOS Compatibility Mode and will not take advantage of the 32-bit VFAT.

In the case of SCSI drives, after the TSD for hard drives determines that a given I/O request is intended for a SCSI drive, a number of sublayers come into play. The TSD passes the request to one of two SCSI translators: for hard drives or for CD-ROM drives. The translator is responsible for translating generic I/O commands into commands the SCSI bus can understand—these are known as *SCSI Command Descriptor Blocks*.

The SCSI Manager then takes control and acts as the intermediary between the SCSI Translator and the lowest layer—the miniport drivers, which are responsible for communicating with specific brands of SCSI adapters. For example, there might be a specific miniport driver for all Adaptec SCSI controllers or for one particular product line.

CDFS File System Driver

Because data on a CD-ROM is stored and accessed in a different way than data on a hard drive, a separate FSD for CD-ROM file access is required. CDFS passes on the CD-ROM I/O request to a specific device driver based on one of four possible CD-ROM configurations:

▶ **IDE CD-ROM.** With this configuration, the CD-ROM typically is attached to the IDE hard drive controller of the computer and the I/O request is passed on to the ESDI_506.PDR port driver, which is the same driver used to communicate with IDE hard drives.

▶ **SCSI CD-ROM.** This type of CD-ROM is connected on the SCSI bus of the computer, along with any SCSI hard drives or other SCSI devices. It is supported through the various SCSI driver layers mentioned earlier (see the section "VFAT File System Driver").

▶ **Proprietary CD-ROM controller.** This type of CD-ROM controller is often integrated on a sound card. Currently, Windows 95 ships with protected-mode drivers for proprietary controllers from Sony, Panasonic, and Mitsumi. Any other type of proprietary CD-ROM controller must be supported through protected-mode drivers from the OEM or through real-mode CD-ROM drivers until protected-mode drivers become available.

▶ **Real-mode CD-ROM drivers specified in CONFIG.SYS or AUTOEXEC.BAT.** All CD-ROM drives that do not fall in the preceding categories are supported using MS-DOS–based drivers specified in CONFIG.SYS or AUTOEXEC.BAT. The CD-ROM drive is said to be operating in MS-DOS compatibility mode.

Any hard drive or CD-ROM drive running in MS-DOS compatibility mode cannot take advantage of protected-mode caching. Smartdrive must be used instead.

Network Redirector File System Drivers

If the IFS Manager determines that an I/O request cannot be satisfied locally and is likely intended for a remote device, it attempts to pass the request to one of the 32-bit network FSDs (if any Windows 95 networking components have been installed). Chapter 5, "Networking and Interoperability," examines the network redirectors in more detail.

16-bit FAT

Windows 95 includes support of the 16-bit FAT file system, which was used in MS-DOS and Windows 3.1. These operating systems used 16-bit, real-mode code to manage the 16-bit FAT, as well as to read and write from the disk. Under Windows 95, protected mode drivers can be used to access the 16-bit FAT. MS-DOS file I/O access performance is actually increased under Windows 95 because the disk file system can be accessed from protected mode without dropping into real mode.

I/O Supervisor

The *I/O Supervisor* is responsible for overseeing all local I/O requests (as opposed to network-based requests). When the IFS Manager has determined that a given I/O request can be fulfilled on the local computer, it passes on the request to the I/O Supervisor. The I/O Supervisor's other duties include registering port and mini-drivers when a new device is installed, and sending dynamic messages to drivers as needed (for example, in the case of a Plug and Play event).

Volume Tracker

The *Volume Tracker* component is responsible for identifying and monitoring removable media, such as CD-ROMs, floppies, and removable hard drives. It must ensure that the correct type of media is present and that the media is not removed or inserted at the wrong time. For example, the Volume Tracker enables CD-ROMs to auto-execute when inserted by polling the CD-ROM drive constantly for new insertions. When the Volume Tracker detects such an event, it scans the CD-ROM for a file called AUTORUN.INF. If it finds this file, it executes the commands in the file. The Volume Tracker also identifies disk geometry, noting, for example, when a 1.44 MB floppy is removed, and a 720 KB floppy is inserted.

Type Specific Drivers

Type Specific Drivers (TSDs) are drivers intermediate to the I/O Supervisor and the physical device drivers (port drivers) that actually communicate with the hardware. TSDs are responsible for all functions associated with a particular type of hardware, such as CD-ROMs, floppy drives, or hard disks. Thus, a TSD for CD-ROM drives handles functions specific to CD-ROMs, but not those specific to SCSI CD-ROMs.

Port Drivers

Port drivers, the last in the chain of command, are responsible for translating logical I/O requests (for example, "put this data on the CD-ROM") into physical requests (for example, "put these bytes on track 9, section 5 of the CD-ROM").

File System Caching

One of the main performance issues associated with hard drive or CD-ROM access is repetitive requests for information. A cache enables your computer to store recently used (or frequently used) information in RAM so you can access it quickly when you need it again. Because hard disk access speeds are much slower than memory access speeds (milliseconds versus nanoseconds), it's much faster to read the discarded data from the cache than to access it from the hard disk. This process is known as *read-ahead caching* and is implemented for hard drives using VCACHE, and for CD-ROM drives using CDFS caching.

VCACHE Hard Drive Caching

VCACHE is the Windows 95 successor to Windows 3.1 Smartdrive. It is a 32-bit, protected-mode cache subsystem used by all FSDs except CDFS. Two types of caching are implemented by VCACHE: read-ahead caching (described in the preceding paragraph) for read operations, and lazy-write or write-behind caching for write operations.

Because the number of requests to write data to a hard disk tends to fluctuate a great deal from moment to moment, another way to increase the efficiency of the file system is to stagger those requests by a matter of seconds to create a more constant level of activity and to prevent bottlenecks. These staggered writes are termed "lazy" writes because they do not happen immediately when requested.

CDFS Caching

The CDFS maintains its own cache separate from the VCACHE because the nature of CD-ROM data and the way it is accessed is fundamentally different from that of hard drive data.

First, the CDFS cache uses only read-ahead caching, because you cannot write to a conventional CD-ROM drive.

Furthermore, CD-ROMs typically contain large amounts of multimedia information, such as video clips or sound recordings. Data of this type usually does not benefit from an MRU (most recently used) approach to keeping data in a cache. For example, if you have just finished playing a video clip, under the standard read-ahead cache system, the cache currently holds data pertaining to the end of the video clip. If you want to replay the video clip, there are no performance benefits to having the last part of it cached because you will likely want faster access to the beginning of the clip.

In addition, due to the sheer volume of data that can be accessed from a CD-ROM, sharing a cache with the rest of the operating system quickly results in the cache being overrun with multimedia data that likely will not be reused.

A unique feature of the CDFS cache is that it is swappable, which means it can be written to disk if the operating system needs to maximize available memory. Because CD-ROM drives are much slower than hard drives, it remains more efficient to read the data from the hard drive than reread it from the CD-ROM drive.

Long File Name (LFN) Support

Windows 95 has built-in support for descriptive file names up to 255 characters, including blank spaces. The path for a file may have up to a total of 260 characters. However, if both the path and the file name are specified, the total is still only 260 characters. To remain backward-compatible with Windows 3.1 and DOS applications, however, Windows 95 also automatically generates an 8.3 format short file name (known as the *alias*) for each LFN. The algorithm for the auto-generation of this short file name is as follows:

1. Remove any characters illegal in an MS-DOS file name, such as spaces and so on.

2. For the eight-character name, take the first six remaining characters of the LFN and add a tilde character (~) and an incremental number beginning with 1.

The number is added to ensure unique short file names. It is possible, for example, that two files named "November Sales Forecast" and "November Marketing Report" would both auto-generate the character name "Novemb~". To differentiate them, one would be named "Novemb~1", and the other named "Novemb~2". If more than nine similar files exist, the first five characters are used, plus a tilde (~) and a two-digit number.

3. To create the three-character extension, take the first three remaining characters after the last period. If the long file name contains no period, the extension is omitted.

Long file names preserve the case of characters, but are not case-sensitive. When you copy long file names to floppy disks, they are preserved. Also, 8.3 file names are not case-sensitive and they do not preserve the case of characters (see table 6.1 for examples).

In table 6.1, you can see how sample long file names convert to short file names. Each of the files shown in the table are assumed to be saved to the same folder and created in the order shown.

Table 6.1

Converted Long File Names to Short File Names	
Long File Name	Converted Short File Name
Fiscal Report Quarter 1.XLS	FISCAL~1.XLS
Fiscal Report Quarter 2.XLS	FISCAL~2.XLS
Fiscal Report Quarter 4.XLS	FISCAL~3.XLS
Employee Benefits 1997.DOC	EMPLOY~1.DOC
Employee Benefits 1998.DOC	EMPLOY~2.DOC
Taxes.Mdb	TAXES.MDB

Rules for the Construction of Long and Short File Names

The following rules are applied when creating a long file name and when generating a short file name alias:

▶ The symbols \ / : * ? " < > | are illegal in both long and short file names.

▶ The symbols + , ; = [ ] are permitted in a long file name, but not in a short file name alias.

▶ Lowercase characters in a long file name are converted to uppercase in a short file name alias.

Long File Name Data Structure

In a standard FAT-based operating system, the root directory of a hard disk can contain a maximum of 512 directory entries. Under MS-DOS, each file or subdirectory typically takes up an entry. In the case of long file names, however, each requires a minimum of two directory entries: one for the alias and one for every 13 characters of the long file name. Thus, a long file name that consists of 79 characters would require seven entries (78÷13=6, plus 1 for the alias).

This requirement for additional directory entries is especially important to remember when dealing with LFNs in the root directory because the MS-DOS limit of 512 entries in the root directory still applies. Those entries are used up much more quickly with LFNs.

Issues with Long File Names

When working in an environment where both long and short file names may be in use, you should be aware of a number of issues. These issues include the following:

▶ LFNs are active only when Windows 95 is running. Because they are integrated with the 32-bit file system native to Windows 95, LFNs are not visible, for example, when Command Prompt Only is selected from the Boot Menu when the system is booted (however, LFNs are visible from a DOS prompt inside Windows 95).

▶ When specifying LFNs with embedded spaces, it is necessary to enclose the name in double quotes, such as "MARKETING BUDGET WORKSHEET".

▶ Even if you do not add an extension to a file when you create it, the application you are using may automatically add an extension to the file (for example, WordPad would, by default, add the extension DOC to any saved file). File names enclosed with double quotes will not usually have the extension added.

▶ Using file utilities that are not long file name-aware (such as those in MS-DOS 6.x and earlier) to copy or rename a long file name destroys the long file name, leaving only the alias.

▶ If you are using a Windows 3.1 application and choose Save As (effectively renaming the file), the long file name is lost, but if you choose Save, the long file name is preserved because the existing name is reused.

▶ Using a disk-repair utility that is not long file name-aware, such as MS-DOS 6.*x* ScanDisk or Norton Disk Doctor, on a volume that contains LFNs might destroy the LFNs. The utility interprets the new long file name data structure as errors in the file system that must be corrected.

▶ Windows 95 can read LFNs from an NTFS volume, but only at a remote location (across a network). For security reasons pertaining to Windows NT, Windows 95 does not read local NTFS volumes at all.

▶ Windows 95 can read LFNs from a NetWare server, but only at a remote location (across a network). The NetWare server needs to be running OS/2 Name Space to store LFNs using HPFS rules (not Windows rules) for the naming of the 8.3 alias.

▶ If you perform a search on a group of files, Windows 95 searches both the long file name and the alias for occurrences of the given search criteria.

▶ It is possible to disable long file name support by altering the Registry, as shown in figure 6.2.

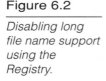

Figure 6.2

Disabling long file name support using the Registry.

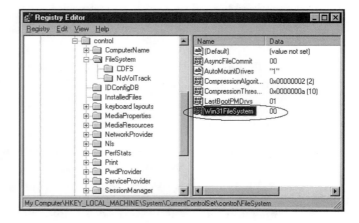

If you need to remove long file names from a disk, such as to run hard disk utilities released prior to Windows 95, run the LFNBK.EXE utility. (The DriveSpace utility included with Windows 95 is compatible with long file names, so you can use it to manage compressed disks that have been created with older versions of DriveSpace or DoubleSpace.) This utility is located on the Windows 95 CD-ROM in the \ADMIN\ APPTOOLS\LFNBACK folder, or can be downloaded from the Microsoft World Wide Web site at http://www.microsoft.com/ windows/common/aa2724.htm. When the LFNBK utility runs at the command prompt, it renames each file with an alias. After running LFNBK and restarting Windows, the Start menu appears with its default settings, not with your custom Start menu. You can restore your custom Start menu by restoring long file names by running the LFNBK utility with the /r switch.

Before running LFNBK, read the LFNBK.TXT file in the \ADMIN\APPTOOLS\LFNBACK folder on the CD-ROM. This text file explains how to use LFNBK, as well as the switches and other options you can use.

Adding Long File Name Support for Novell NetWare

When you run Windows 95 on a Novel NetWare volume, you must install a module called 0S2.NAM (the OS/2 Name Space feature) to activate long file names. NetWare does not support long file names by itself. To install the OS/2 Name Space feature, type the following at the file server console:

```
LOAD OS/2
ADD NAME SPACE OS/2 TO VOLUME volume_name
```

In the preceding command, the *volume_name* parameter should be replaced by the name of the volume on which you want Name Space to be added. You also need to add the following to the STARTUP.NCF configuration file:

```
LOAD OS/2
```

After you make these changes, shut down the server and bring it back up to make the OS/2 Name Space feature functional at the server. In general, the Name Space feature places additional memory burdens on your server, so you also will probably want to add more server RAM.

Troubleshooting the File System

If you encounter difficulty with any applications and you suspect the file system might be involved, you can disable a number of file system features using the Performance tab of the My Computer Properties sheet to isolate the problem. The features that can be disabled include the following:

▶ **File sharing.** File sharing can be disabled for applications that are incompatible with the way Windows 95 typically implements file sharing (SHARE.EXE can be used until the application is updated to support Windows 95 file sharing).

▶ **Long file name preservation for old programs.** If an application requires the directory space used by LFNs in Windows 95, you might have to disable this support for older applications.

▶ **Protected-mode hard disk interrupt handling.** The Disable Protected-Mode Hard Disk Interrupt Handling option disables Windows' 95 normal practice of intercepting all MS-DOS–level disk I/O requests and handling them with a 32-bit protected-mode driver. Disk performance is degraded, but compatibility with older applications is enhanced.

▶ **32-bit protected-mode disk drivers.** If a hard drive is experiencing problems reading or writing information while Windows 95 is running, you can disable all 32-bit disk drivers to enhance compatibility with older applications. Once again, disk performance is degraded.

▶ **Write-behind caching.** The Disable Write-Behind Caching for All Drives option is useful when data integrity is crucial and you cannot risk losing data due to it being in the write-behind cache when a power failure occurs. When write-behind is disabled, all write operations are performed immediately. Yet again, performance likely will be degraded.

Disk Compression

For an exercise testing this information, see end of chapter.

Windows 95 implements a form of disk compression known as *on-the-fly compression*. On-the-fly compression is so named because the compression/decompression process occurs automatically in the background and is transparent to the user. On-the-fly compression is the process of intercepting normal MS-DOS read/write calls and compressing the data before writing it to the hard disk, thus allowing the data to consume less space. Similarly, when the data is read back, it is automatically uncompressed before being transferred to the application or process that requested it.

Disk compression, as implemented in Windows 95 (and in the versions released with MS-DOS 6.*x*), consists of two processes. The first, called *token conversion*, replaces with a token, which takes up less space, repetitive patterns that occur in a given piece of data.

The second, called *sector allocation granularity*, involves changing the way data is stored on a hard drive by circumventing the often large amounts of wasted space created under a normal FAT file system. Any FAT file system operates based on a cluster being the smallest traceable unit of measure. Therefore, if the cluster size is 4 KB, for example, and a 2 KB file is stored in that cluster, 2 KB can be wasted. If 1,000 such files exist on a hard drive, 1,000×2 KB would be wasted. With disk compression in place, the smallest allocation unit shrinks to one sector, or 512 bytes, which can greatly reduce the amount of wasted space on a drive.

DoubleSpace and DriveSpace Structure

Disk compression (called *DoubleSpace*) was first introduced in version 6.0 of MS-DOS. It was later re-released as *DriveSpace* in version 6.2, with some changes to the compression routines and with a new feature: the capability to uncompress a drive. The compression structure has remained fairly consistent.

As shown in figure 6.3, after disk compression is installed and the files initially compressed, the files are stored in the *Compressed Volume File* (CVF), which is actually a large hidden file that sits on the physical drive C. When the system boots up, however, the CVF is assigned the drive letter C. The physical C drive, which now contains only a few files because everything else is in a compressed state inside the CVF, is assigned a higher drive letter, typically H. The process of switching the drive letters and making the CVF available for viewing in MS-DOS and Windows is called *mounting*. From this point on, any file operation is handled through the disk compression routines, which are responsible for compressing and uncompressing files as disk I/O requests are made by the operating system.

Figure 6.3

Compression structure under MS-DOS and Windows 95.

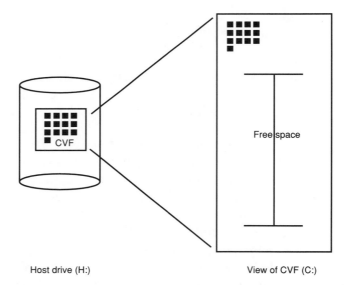

Host drive (H:)   View of CVF (C:)

Advantages of Windows 95 Disk Compression

Windows 95 disk compression contains many features that have been specifically optimized. The main advantages to using Windows 95 disk compression are as follows:

▶ Disk compression is implemented with 32-bit code for better performance.

▶ It does not use any conventional memory.

▶ It is integrated with the operating system for ease of use and better performance.

For an exercise testing this information, see end of chapter.

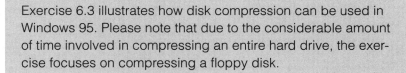

Exercise 6.3 illustrates how disk compression can be used in Windows 95. Please note that due to the considerable amount of time involved in compressing an entire hard drive, the exercise focuses on compressing a floppy disk.

When a floppy is compressed, the DriveSpace drivers load only when the floppy is in the drive. In general, the DriveSpace drivers load only when compressed media (hard drive or floppy) is detected.

Further Notes on Windows 95 Disk Compression

The following information should be noted whenever a user is considering Windows 95 disk compression:

▶ Windows 95 is compatible with third-party compression software such as Stacker versions 2.*x*, 3.*x*, and 4.*x*, and with all versions of SuperStor, but these use real-mode compression and thus take up conventional memory and are usually slower.

▶ The maximum size of a compressed volume is 512 MB when using DriveSpace 2.0, which comes with Windows 95. If you use Microsoft Plus!, which includes DriveSpace 3.0, the maximum size of a compressed volume is 2 GB.

▶ The best compression ratio of a compressed volume is 2:1 (using DriveSpace 2.0, which comes with Windows 95). If you use Microsoft Plus!, which includes DriveSpace 3.0, this improves to approximately 2.4:1.

Choosing a Disk Management Tool

There are five key disk-management utilities included with Windows 95. Each is intended to address particular file system issues or problems. Table 6.2 provides a summary of the disk-management utilities and the issues they address.

Table 6.2

Windows 95 Utilities for Various File System Issues

Utility	Issue
Disk Defragmenter	Preventing file system performance degradation due to inefficient hard disk access
ScanDisk	Correction of cross-linked files, lost clusters, and other hard disk errors
Backup	Prevention of data loss due to power failures, corruption, hard disk failures
Disk Compression	Maximizing available hard disk space
Recycle Bin	Recovery of deleted files

Disk Defragmenter

One of the most common performance issues related to the FAT file system, which is native to both MS-DOS and Windows 95, is disk fragmentation. When a hard drive is new and contains no information, it is possible for the file system to write all the data for a new file to a contiguous area of the hard drive. As the hard drive fills up and files are deleted and copied numerous times, the space available to new files no longer is contiguous. The file system is forced to put part of the new file in one location, part at another location, and so on. When a request is made to read the file, the hard disk must access all these different locations to reconstitute the file. This takes longer than reading the whole file from one location on the hard disk.

Windows 95 includes a utility called *Disk Defragmenter* that is designed to address this issue. It does so by rewriting all the files on the hard drive to contiguous locations, thus enhancing file system performance for that drive. This procedure can be time-consuming because, as the drive becomes full, there is less room to temporarily store the various parts of a file before it is rewritten to a new location.

Although the Disk Defragmenter existed in MS-DOS 6.2 and is still a 16-bit application, the Windows 95 Disk Defragmenter utility has the following enhancements:

- ▶ It is much faster at optimizing DoubleSpaced and DriveSpaced drives from MS-DOS 6.*x*.

- ▶ The utility no longer requires any INI files because all settings are stored in the Registry.

- ▶ The utility now has a Windows 95 GUI interface.

- ▶ The Windows 95 Disk Defragmenter is capable of running as a background application, freeing the user to perform other tasks.

It is important to remember that, although the Disk Defragmenter can run in the background while you work in other applications, if another application is writing to disk (and consequently changing the locations of files), the Disk Defragmenter may be forced to restart the defragmentation process from the beginning. If the process reaches 50 percent, and disk writes occur, the process will restart at 50 percent rather than zero. In the long run, you may be better off running Disk Defragmenter while your system is not currently being used.

Certain types of files are not handled by Disk Defragmenter in the normal fashion:

- ▶ Files with both Hidden and System attributes are not moved.

- ▶ Files with either Hidden or System attributes are moved.

- ▶ Mounted DriveSpace or DoubleSpace volumes are not moved.

The following points should also be noted when using the Disk Defragmenter:

▶ If Disk Defragmenter reports errors (usually at the beginning of the process), you should run ScanDisk (including a surface scan).

▶ This utility should not be run on Stacker drives, because the compression scheme on such drives is different from that of DriveSpace and DoubleSpace.

For instructions on running Disk Defragmenter, see Exercise 6.4 at the end of the chapter.

ScanDisk

Another file system issue that pertains to both performance and data integrity is the issue of cross-linked files and lost clusters. If either of these problems is suspected or if the user wants to ensure they do not impact the integrity or performance of the computer's drives, ScanDisk should be used regularly.

ScanDisk is a utility provided with Windows 95 that analyzes your hard disk for errors and repairs any found. When you run the Windows 95 Setup program to install Windows 95, ScanDisk runs automatically. To run ScanDisk after installation, you must start it manually, or place it in your Startup folder to launch each time Windows 95 starts. The following are areas on which ScanDisk checks and fixes errors:

▶ File system structure, including lost clusters and cross-linked files

▶ Long file names

▶ File allocation table

▶ Physical surface of the drive

▶ Directory tree structure

▶ DriveSpace or DoubleSpace volumes

Under a FAT file system, such as that of MS-DOS and Windows 95, data is stored on a hard drive in such a way that the clusters (an allocation) containing data pertaining to a certain file are not necessarily stored contiguously on the drive. Often, the clusters for a specific file are scattered throughout the drive. Each cluster for a file contains both data and a pointer to the location of the next cluster in the chain. When a file is requested, the file system looks up the name of the file in the directory tree (which tells where the first cluster for the file is located) and begins to read through the various clusters, collecting the file's data.

Problems can occur when the pointer to the next cluster becomes corrupted. If, for example, file A has a cluster with some data and a pointer to cluster 12, and file B has a cluster that also points to cluster 12, these files are said to be *cross-linked*. The data at cluster 12 cannot belong to both files; therefore, there is a logical inconsistency in the file structure of the drive. ScanDisk is able to detect such inconsistencies, but it is unable to determine to which file the cluster truly belongs. ScanDisk defaults to making a copy of the cluster so that each file can make use of the information in the cluster. This increases the chance that at least one of the two files in question can be salvaged.

Another associated problem is that the clusters that should have been in the chain after the corrupted cluster are now not referenced by any file, and are thus "orphaned" or lost. These clusters may still contain valid data, but they no longer are part of any file on the drive. ScanDisk is able to find these clusters and either save them as files to be examined later, or mark the clusters as available to the file system, thus freeing up space on the drive.

Operation Modes

ScanDisk can perform two levels of testing on hard drives: standard and thorough. Standard mode is best used on a daily basis, whereas thorough mode is best used when you suspect a problem with the hard drive.

In *standard* mode, ScanDisk performs logical tests against the File Allocation Table (FAT) of the file system, checking for the logical inconsistencies outlined earlier. In addition, the standard scan checks for various other potential problems, such as invalid file names and invalid date and time stamps.

In *thorough* mode, ScanDisk performs all the tests included in standard mode, but also performs a surface scan. Each cluster on the drive is checked for physical defects that would make the cluster in question unsafe for data storage. A surface scan is performed by reading the information from the cluster and rewriting it back to the same cluster. If the information matches what ScanDisk read the first time, the cluster is likely to be safe. If the data is different, a media problem might exist, in which case ScanDisk marks the cluster as bad.

ScanDisk does not test clusters that have been marked as bad in the FAT by other programs. You must fix those clusters using other programs.

Other Features of ScanDisk

ScanDisk contains a number of additional features, such as the following:

For an exercise testing this information, see end of chapter.

▶ ScanDisk can be run from the command line (SCANDSKW.EXE), with parameters to specify how it will run, or from the Windows 95 graphical interface.

An MS-DOS version of ScanDisk also is included with Windows 95 (SCANDISK.EXE). It also is found on any Windows 95 Startup disk you may create (see Chapter 1, "Planning and Installation").

▶ ScanDisk can fix problems on hard drives, floppy disk drives, RAM drives, and removable media (such as PCMCIA hard cards and Bernoulli drives).

> ScanDisk can detect and repair errors in LFNs (the MS-DOS version can only detect them).

> ScanDisk can be used to test and maintain the integrity of DoubleSpace and DriveSpace volumes (if the volumes are mounted; if not, the volumes can be tested from the command-line version of ScanDisk).

> It is possible to have ScanDisk log activities (the results of the scan are stored in the file SCANDISK.LOG in the root of the drive that has been examined).

Further Notes on ScanDisk

Additional information that the user should note when using the ScanDisk utility includes the following:

> ScanDisk cannot fix errors on CD-ROMs, network drives, drives created by the DOS command INTERLNK, or drives referenced via MS-DOS commands (such as ASSIGN, JOIN, or SUBST).

> As with the Disk Defragmenter, it is possible to multitask with ScanDisk, but if any disk write activity occurs, ScanDisk may be forced to restart the testing process.

Backup

To ensure that data on the system is not lost due to power failures or other forms of corruption, Windows 95 includes a Backup utility that enables users to make a copy of the data on their hard drives and store it on alternate media. There are several decisions you need to make regarding backup procedures; these are discussed in the following sections.

Backup Destinations

When making a backup copy of important data, a number of media types can be used to store the copy. The Windows 95 Backup program supports backup to three storage media types:

- ▶ Backup to a tape drive

- ▶ Backup to floppies

- ▶ Backup to a network location

Backup to Tape

The capability to back up to a tape drive is new to the Windows 95 version of Backup (previous MS-DOS versions supported only floppy backups). The type of tape media that is supported is called *Quarter-Inch Cartridge* (QIC) and it comes in various specifications. The supported tape drive specifications are as follows:

- ▶ QIC 40, QIC 80, and QIC 3010 tape drives connected through the primary floppy disk controller (various manufacturers)

- ▶ QIC 40, QIC 80, and QIC 3010 tape drives connected to a parallel port (Colorado Memory Systems only)

SCSI tape backup units are not supported by Windows 95 Backup.

Windows 95 should be able to detect any supported tape drives automatically. If it cannot detect the tape drive, a message to that effect appears upon starting Backup, and a number of troubleshooting suggestions are listed.

Backup to Floppies

Floppies are the standard backup destination for both the MS-DOS and Windows 3.1 versions of Backup. Files are transferred from the local hard drive to a number of floppies.

Backup to a Network Location

This backup destination enables the user to back up files to a remote location on the network. Backing up to a remote network location can be useful if, for example, a network administrator wants all users to back up their files to one central location on the network to simplify the administrator's management tasks.

Backup Types

Files can be backed up in two ways: by a full backup and by an incremental backup. In a full backup scenario, all selected files are backed up. An incremental backup copies only those files that have changed since the last full backup. Such files are determined by the time/date stamp on the file. Typically, incremental backups are used to maintain archives without unnecessarily backing up files that have not changed since the last full backup, thus conserving disk space at the backup destination.

Backup Sets and File Sets

For an exercise testing this information, see end of chapter.

A *backup set* is a collection of files that have been backed up. A backup set is created during each backup procedure and contains not only the actual files, but also the parameters that were set for the backup (for example, which file types to include in the backup). A *file set* is a list of files you want to backup. You can save file sets so you don't have to reselect the files for backup every time you perform the backup.

Exercise 6.6 demonstrates the use of the Windows 95 Backup utility. Please ensure that you have at least 6 MB of free space on drive C to complete this exercise.

Other Features of Windows 95 Backup

Windows 95 contains a number of additional features, including the following:

▶ It is possible to perform a compare between a backup set and the directories from which it was backed up to determine any differences between the two.

▶ LFNs are fully supported.

▶ It is possible to drag and drop backup sets onto a Backup icon to restore the set.

▶ During a full system backup, Windows 95 also backs up the Registry by copying it to a temporary file. When the backup set is restored, the Registry files are merged back into the existing Registry.

▶ Backup allows the filtering of file types for inclusion or exclusion from a file set.

> MS-DOS 6.2 and Windows 3.1 backup sets cannot be restored using the Windows 95 Backup utility due to incompatibility issues with LFNs in MS-DOS 6.2 and earlier.

Recycle Bin

Another Windows 95 disk management tool you can use to minimize the consequences associated with the accidental deletion of files is the Windows 95 utility known as the *Recycle Bin*. The Recycle Bin reduces the chance of losing deleted data by storing the data for a time before it is actually deleted. When a file is deleted using the Explorer, for example, rather than being erased from the hard drive, it is copied to a hidden directory on the drive called \RECYCLED. The file is kept in \RECYCLED until the maximum amount of space allocated to the \RECYCLED directory is reached (expressed as a percentage of total space on the drive—the default is 10 percent). At this point, the file is actually deleted to make room for more recently deleted files. Thus, on a 100 MB drive, 10 MB is allocated by default for recycled items.

At any point before the file is actually deleted, the user can open the Recycle Bin on the desktop (which is a specialized view of the \RECYCLED directory) and restore the file to its original location.

Exercises

Exercise 6.1: Creating and Using Long File Names

Exercise 6.1 illustrates the creation and use of LFNs in Windows 95.

1. Choose Start, Programs, and MS-DOS Prompt. A DOS window appears.

2. Type **MD\LFNTEMP** and press Enter. A directory called LFNTEMP is created.

3. Type **CD\LFNTEMP** and press Enter. The current directory changes to LFNTEMP.

4. Type **DIR > "Directory Listing"** and press Enter to save the directory listing to a file. You are returned to a command prompt (note the quotations around the file name).

5. Type **DIR** and press Enter. Note that the alias for the file that was created is listed on the left, whereas the LFN is on the right.

6. Type **DIR > "Directory Listing 2"** and press Enter. You are returned to a command prompt.

7. Type **DIR** and press Enter. Note how the alias has been auto-numbered sequentially, and yet the full name is preserved on the right.

8. Type **DIR >*DIRLIST** and press Enter. You receive a `File creation error` error message because the * is illegal.

9. Shut down Windows 95. You are in MS-DOS mode (no LFN support).

10. Type **CD\LFNTEMP** and press Enter. The current directory changes to LFNTEMP.

11. Type **DIR** and press Enter. Note that LFNs no longer are displayed in the directory.

continues

Exercise 6.1: Continued

12. Type **COPY DIRECT~1 C:** and press Enter. The file that was created earlier is copied to the root of C.

13. Restart Windows 95 by typing **EXIT** and pressing Enter.

14. When Windows 95 is open, open a DOS window and type **CD** and press Enter, then type **DIR** and press Enter. Note that the file that was copied to the root no longer has an LFN associated with it (only the alias remains).

Exercise 6.2: Using File System Troubleshooting Switches

Exercise 6.2 illustrates how to access the troubleshooting switches for the file system.

1. Right-click on the My Computer icon and choose Properties. The System Properties sheet appears.

2. Choose the Performance tab. Various statistics regarding the performance status of the operating system are displayed.

3. Click on the File System button at the bottom of the window. The File System Properties sheet appears.

4. Click on the Troubleshooting tab. The list of troubleshooting switches appears.

5. Select the Disable All 32 Bit Protect-Mode Disk Drivers check box and choose OK to close the File System Properties sheet and the System Properties sheet. You are prompted to restart your system.

6. Choose Yes to restart.

7. When Windows 95 has rebooted, go back to System Properties, choose Performance, and note that all drives are listed as being in MS-DOS compatibility mode. Notice that the system performance has been degraded.

8. Choose File System Properties again from the System Properties Performance tab and select the Troubleshooting tab.

9. Deselect the Disable All 32 Bit Protect-Mode Disk Drivers check box, and choose OK twice to close the File System Properties sheet and the System Properties sheet. You are prompted to restart your system.

10. Choose Yes to restart. The system restarts, and the 32-bit drivers are loaded once again.

Exercise 6.3: Using Windows 95 Disk Compression

Exercise 6.3 illustrates how disk compression can be used in Windows 95. Please note that due to the considerable amount of time involved in compressing an entire hard drive, the exercise focuses on compressing a floppy disk. The exercise requires a formatted floppy with at least 512 KB of free space.

1. Choose Start, Programs, Accessories, System Tools, and then click on DriveSpace. The DriveSpace menu appears.

2. Select the A drive and choose Drive, Compress. A window appears, showing the free/used space before and after compression (estimated).

3. Choose the Start button. The drive is checked for errors, and a status bar shows the progress of the compression procedure.

4. When the procedure is complete, choose Close. You are returned to the main DriveSpace window. (Note that drive A now shows as compressed, and there is now a host drive H for drive A.)

Exercise 6.4: Using the Disk Defragmenter

Exercise 6.4 demonstrates how to initiate the defragmentation process.

1. Right-click on the My Computer icon and choose Explore. The Exploring window appears.

2. From the list of drives, right click on C: and choose Properties. The Properties sheet for drive C appears.

continues

Exercise 6.4:   Continued

3. Select the Tools tab. From this tab, you can run ScanDisk, Backup, or the Disk Defragmenter.

4. Click on the Defragment Now button. A Disk Defragmenter window appears, telling you what percentage of drive C is fragmented.

5. Choose the Advanced button, make certain that the Full Defragmentation and Check Drive for Errors check boxes are selected, and choose OK. You are returned to the previous screen.

> The Full Defragmentation option places all files in contiguous order and at the start of the hard drive's allocable space, whereas Defragment Files Only places the files in contiguous order, but does not move them to the start of the hard drive. The Consolidate Free Space option simply moves files to the start of the hard disk.

6. Choose the Start button and then the Show Details button. You are presented with a screen showing all the clusters on drive C as they are reorganized.

7. Choose the Legend button. You are shown a list of the different color codes for clusters and what each color code signifies.

8. At this point, you can allow the defragmentation to complete (which might take some time), or you can choose Stop and then Exit to halt the procedure. If you choose to stop, you are returned to the hard drive Properties sheet. If you choose to follow through, you are notified when the procedure is complete.

Exercise 6.5:   Using ScanDisk to Correct Drive Problems

Exercise 6.5 demonstrates how you can use ScanDisk to correct various drive problems.

1. Right-click on the My Computer icon and choose Explore. The Exploring window appears.

2. From the list of drives, right-click on C: and choose Properties. The Properties sheet for drive C appears.

3. Click on the Tools tab. From this tab, you can run ScanDisk, Backup, or the Disk Defragmenter.

4. Click on Check Now to start ScanDisk. The ScanDisk window appears.

5. Choose the Advanced button, verify that Make Copies is selected under Cross-Linked Files and that Convert to Files is selected under Lost File Fragments; then choose OK. You are returned to the main ScanDisk window.

6. Verify that Standard Testing is selected and choose the Start button. The status bar shows the progress of the tests.

7. When the tests are complete, choose Close to clear the Scan-Disk Results window. You are returned to the main ScanDisk window.

8. Optionally, you may run the Thorough test, although it is very time-consuming.

Exercise 6.6:   Using the Windows 95 Backup Utility

Exercise 6.6 demonstrates the use of the Windows 95 Backup utility. Please ensure that you have at least 6 MB of free space on drive C to complete this exercise.

1. Right-click on the My Computer icon and choose Explore. The Exploring window appears.

2. From the list of drives, right-click on C: and choose Properties. The Properties sheet for drive C appears.

3. Click the Tools tab. From this tab, you can run ScanDisk, Backup, or the Disk Defragmenter.

4. Click on the Backup Now button. The Microsoft Backup screen appears.

continues

Exercise 6.6: Continued

5. Click on the plus sign (+) next to the C drive. The tree expands to show the subdirectories of C.

6. Click on the + next to the Windows subdirectory. The tree expands to show the subdirectories of Windows.

7. Click on the + next to the Media subdirectory. The tree expands to show the files in the Media subdirectory.

8. Click on the check box next to Media. Note that all the files in the Media subdirectory now are marked for backup.

9. Having selected the files for backup, choose the Next Step button. You are prompted for a backup destination.

10. Click on the A drive icon. This selects the root of A as the destination directory.

11. Click on the Start Backup button. You are prompted for a backup set name.

12. Type **TEST** and press Enter. A status screen appears, showing the progress of the backup.

13. Choose OK when the backup is complete. You are returned to the main Backup window.

14. Click on the Restore tab. You are prompted to select a backup set to restore.

15. Click on the icon for the A drive. The TEST backup set is displayed in the root of A.

16. Double-click on the TEST backup set. You are prompted to select the files you want to restore.

17. Click three times in the check box next to TEST to select all files in the backup set.

18. Choose Settings, Options. The Settings - Options dialog box appears.

19. Click on the Restore tab, verify that Overwrite Files is selected under Advanced Options, and choose OK. You are returned to the main Backup window.

20. Click on the Start Restore button. A status screen shows the progress of the restore procedure.

21. When the restore is complete, choose OK twice to return to the main Backup window.

Exercise 6.7:   Restoring Files from the Recycle Bin

Exercise 6.7 illustrates how to restore files from the Recycle Bin.

1. Right-click on the My Computer icon and select Explore. The Exploring window appears.

2. Click on the plus sign (+) next to the C drive. Subdirectories of the C drive are displayed.

3. Click on the + next to the Windows subdirectory. The tree expands to show the subdirectories of Windows.

4. Click on the Command folder. The files in the Command folder are displayed on the right side of the Explorer window.

5. Click on the Attrib file on the right side of the Explorer window and press Delete. You are prompted to verify whether you want to move this item to the Recycle Bin.

6. Choose Yes. The item is removed from the directory.

7. From the Desktop, right-click on the Recycle Bin icon and choose Open. The Recycle Bin window appears, showing the ATTRIB file.

8. Right-click on the ATTRIB file and choose File, Restore. The file is restored to its original location.

Review Questions

The following questions will test your knowledge of the information in this chapter. For additional questions, see MCP Endeavor and the Microsoft Roadmap/Assessment Exam on the CD-ROM that accompanies this book.

1. Third-party developers can create file systems that extend Windows 95 capabilities. A key feature of Windows 95 that will allow this and will let Windows 95 adapt easily to future technological developments is its _____.

   A. preemptive multitasking

   B. VCACHE cache subsystem

   C. modular design

   D. peer-to-peer networking support

2. You are responsible for training users on Windows 95 Installable File System (IFS). You create a diagram to display the different components of it. Which three of the following are components of the IFS?

   A. I/O Supervisor

   B. VFAT file system driver

   C. TSD Supervisor

   D. CDFS file system driver

3. On a diagram showing the IFS, you point out the role for each of the components. One of these components is responsible for the insertion and removal of media. Which one?

   A. Drive Controller

   B. IFS Manager

   C. System Driver Supervisor

   D. Volume Tracker

4. Stephanie is using an older version of Windows and wants to know if she can use an older CD-ROM drive with Windows 95. You tell her yes. However, you tell her that a drive that is accessed through _____ cannot take advantage of the 32-bit VFAT.

   A. protected-mode drivers

   B. real-mode drivers

   C. virtual device drivers

   D. network redirector file system drivers

5. VCACHE is an upgrade to Smartdrive and is used for read-ahead and lazy-write (or write-behind) caching. VCACHE is used by all Windows 95 file system drivers except _____ file system drivers.

   A. CDFS

   B. VFAT

   C. network redirector

   D. SCSI

6. Brenda saves her files under Windows 95 in long file name format. She asks you to explain how Windows 95 will save the file as a short file name. You tell her, for example, that the auto-generated alias for the long file name The Departmental Budget.wks is _____.

   A. THEDEPAR.~1

   B. THEDEP~1.WKS

   C. THEDEP~1

   D. BUDGET~1.WKS

7. A user receives an error message saying that a file cannot be opened due to lost clusters, and asks you to explain what's wrong. You tell him that using a disk utility can help solve the problem. What Windows 95 disk utility should he use to locate and free lost clusters?

A. DoubleSpace

B. DriveSpace

C. Disk Defragmenter

D. ScanDisk

8. A client asks how he can fit more data on his existing hard drive without adding another hard drive or storing files on a network. What Windows 95 disk utility should he use to compress the data on his hard drive?

A. DoubleSpace

B. DriveSpace

C. Disk Defragmenter

D. ScanDisk

9. ScanDisk is used to help clean up cluster problems under Windows 95. One cluster problem is when clusters from two files have pointers to the same cluster. If this happens, the two files are said to be _____.

A. cluster-crossed

B. cross-referenced

C. linked

D. cross-linked

10. Jennifer asks you how Disk Defragmenter under Windows 95 works. You tell her that it rewrites files to contiguous locations. However, you let her know that Disk Defragmenter will not move files that have both of which two of the following attributes?

A. System

B. Read-only

C. Hidden

D. Archived

11. You suspect that the integrity or performance of a computer running Windows 95 is suffering. You decide to run Scan-Disk on the system. ScanDisk, however, cannot fix problems on _____.

    A. compressed hard drives

    B. defragmented hard drives

    C. high-density floppy disks

    D. CD-ROMs

12. As system administrator, you draft a purchase order to acquire tape backup devices. Windows 95 supports QIC tape systems, but not universally. Which of the following tape backup systems is not supported by Windows 95?

    A. QIC 3010 through parallel port

    B. QIC 3010 through floppy disk controller

    C. QIC 3010 through SCSI port

    D. QIC 80 through floppy disk controller

13. When John runs Disk Compression under Windows 95, he calls asking you how files are compressed. You tell him which two of the following are ways in which disk compression maximizes disk space.

    A. Cluster conversion

    B. Token conversion

    C. ASCII collapse

    D. Sector allocation conversion

14. Your company runs Windows 95 with a NetWare server, but you experience problems with the long file name support. A help desk administrator tells you to install a specific feature under NetWare to enable long file name support. What is this feature?

A. Install OS/2 on the server

B. Run an NLM released by Microsoft

C. Install OS/2 Name Space

D. NetWare cannot support Windows 95 long file names

15. Vanessa creates a file named Budget For Department. She wants to rename the file to Budget For Marketing Team. Which of the following commands can she use at the command prompt and retain the long file name?

A. Type **RENAME Budget For Department TO Budget For Marketing Team**

B. Type **RENAME Budget For Department Budget For Marketing Team**

C. Type **REN Budget For Department Budget For Marketing Team**

D. Type **RENAME "Budget For Department" "Budget For Marketing Team"**

16. You are assigned a new department to administer. This department has a mixture of computers, including many MS-DOS and Windows 3.1 computers and some Windows 95 computers. Because this department shares files a great deal and the file naming conventions must remain consistent, you instruct your Windows 95 users to use short file names at all times. To guarantee that these users do not create LFNs, you disable this feature using which Registry change? You make this change in the HKEY_LOCAL_MACHINE\System\CurrentControlSet\control\FileSystem.

A. Set the Registry value **LongFileNames=** to **00**.

B. Set the Registry value **Win31FileSystem=** to **00.**

C. Set the Registry value **Win31FileSystem=** to **Yes**

D. Set the Registry value **ShortFileNames=** to **Yes**.

17. You receive a help desk call from a user who thinks the file system may be at fault for some problems he's experiencing. He wants to know which file system features can be disabled in Windows 95. Which two of the following features do you tell him he can disable using the Performance tab of the My Computer Properties sheet?

    A. File sharing

    B. Long file name support

    C. Clustering

    D. Write-behind caching

18. Many of your users run Disk Defragmenter in the background while running other applications. Some grow aggravated, however, when Disk Defragmenter restarts the defragmentation process during this time. At what times does Defragmenter restart?

    A. When an application is inactive for 30 minutes

    B. After an application opens a document

    C. When Defragmenter finds lost clusters

    D. When an application is writing to disk

19. Wendy migrates to Windows 95. The CD-ROM installed on her hardware is a legacy device and requires protected-mode drivers. Which of the three proprietary controllers does Windows 95 ship with?

    A. Sony

    B. NEC

    C. Mitsumi

    D. Panasonic

20. Charles restores deleted files from the Recycle Bin often. He wants to know which folder stores a file when it is deleted. Pick the correct hidden folder name.

A. \Windows\Recycle

B. \Recyled

C. \Recycle Bin

D. \Windows\Recycled

Review Answers

1. C	6. B	11. D	16. B
2. A B D	7. D	12. C	17. A D
3. D	8. B	13. B D	18. D
4. B	9. D	14. C	19. A C D
5. A	10. A C	15. D	20. B

Test Yourself

Stop! Before reading this chapter, test yourself to determine how much study time you will need to devote to this section.

1. When a Plug and Play printer is detected by Windows 95 during boot up, the device is set up automatically. This setup process also includes setting up the correct printer driver, if already installed on your system. If Windows 95 cannot determine the correct driver, what is the name of the wizard you use to install the driver?

2. Nikki prints from two different computers running Windows 95. What are the two types of printer spooling Windows 95 supports? Name an advantage to using each one.

3. Shannon sets up Point and Print printing for her Windows 95 computers on a network. Name three operating and networking systems that support Point and Print.

4. You are migrating your users on a NetWare network to use Windows 95. What is the name of the service available with Windows 95 that enables you to despool print jobs from a NetWare or Windows 95 print queue?

5. Name three settings you can make for a print queue from Windows 95.

6. Roy downloads an updated printer driver for the printer attached to his Windows 95 stand-alone computer. What is the name of the tab on the Properties sheet that Roy uses to change the printer driver?

7. On a network you administer, you have several clients and servers running. You need to set up print servers that support Windows 95 on the network. Name the four print servers that ship with Windows 95.

Answers

1. Add Printer Wizard. See "Installing a Plug and Play Printer."

2. EMF and RAW. EMF renders the print job as a background process and turns control back to the application sooner. RAW does not consume as many resources as EMF. See "Enhanced Metafile (EMF) Spooling."

3. Windows 95, Windows NT Server, and Novell NetWare. See "Point and Print Setup."

4. Microsoft Printer Server for NetWare utility (PSERVER). See "Microsoft Print Agent for NetWare Networks."

5. Specify a separator page; set the printer as the default printer; and set the printer off-line so jobs queue but do not print until you specify. See "Managing a Print Queue."

6. Details. See "Adding and Removing Printer Drivers in Windows 95."

7. Microsoft Print Server; Microsoft Print Agent for NetWare Networks; HP JetAdmin Print Server; and Digital (DEC) PrintServer. See "Print Servers."

C h a p t e r

Managing Printers

7

This chapter will help you prepare for the exam by covering the following objectives:

Test Objectives

- ▶ Implement printers for Windows 95

- ▶ Identify situations in which metafile spooling is appropriate

- ▶ Set up Point and Print printing

- ▶ Access a printer through a NetWare network

- ▶ Create, reorder, and delete a Windows 95 print queue

- ▶ Set up and remove printer drivers in Windows 95

- ▶ Use Windows 95 to share a printer on the network

Windows 95 includes many improvements to the printing process for both local and network printers. This chapter looks at the following aspects of printing under Windows 95:

- ▶ The new features of the Windows 95 printing subsystem

- ▶ How Windows 95 handles print jobs using different printer driver models

- ▶ How to install a local printer and create a printer queue

- ▶ Configurable settings for a print queue

- ▶ The Windows 95 network printing architecture

- ▶ Creating a shared network print queue on various types of operating systems

- ▶ How Windows 95 can ease the configuration process for connecting to shared network print queues

- ▶ The Registry keys associated with network printing support

- ▶ How to manage documents in a print queue

- ▶ How to configure third-party network printing providers

Windows 95 Printing Features

Windows 95 includes many new printing features, including support for the following:

- ▶ Plug and Play (PnP) Printers

- ▶ Extended Capabilities Ports (ECPs)

- ▶ Image Color Matching (ICM)

- ▶ A unidriver/minidriver Printer Driver model

- ▶ Point and Print Setup

- ▶ Drag and Drop Printing

- ▶ Enhanced Metafile (EMF) Spooling

- ▶ Improved Conflict Resolution

- ▶ Deferred Printing

Plug and Play (PnP) Printers

Windows 95 can take full advantage of the automatic configuration features of Plug and Play (PnP) printers. Devices complying with the PnP standards are automatically detected and configured by Windows 95 each time the operating system is initialized. Thus, when a PnP-compliant printer is plugged into a port on the computer, and Windows 95 is started, the operating system can detect the model of the printer and set up the printer in the Printers folder.

The PnP setup uses bidirectional communication through the printer cable to obtain information on the printer, including the following:

▶ Manufacturer and model

▶ Memory installed

▶ Font cartridges installed

The printer model is reported as a device ID defined in the IEEE1284 PnP standards. If Windows 95 has a printer driver for that specific device ID, then it installs the driver and creates a print queue for that printer in the Printers folder.

If Windows 95 does not have the exact driver for that device ID, a dialog box appears, giving the following options:

▶ The user can insert a floppy disk with a Windows 95 driver for the printer.

▶ The user can select a driver for a printer that Windows 95 has determined to be compatible.

▶ The user can choose not to install the printer.

The bidirectional printer communication capability of Windows 95 also enables printers to send unsolicited messages to the operating system, such as being out of paper, low on toner, or other messages that the printer can report.

To enable the bidirectional printing features of Windows 95 including PnP configuration, you must have the following:

▶ A printer that supports bidirectional communication

▶ A printer with a PnP BIOS (if PnP is to be used)

▶ An IEEE 1284-compliant printer cable (this has "1284" stamped on the cable)

▶ A port configured for two-way communication in the Windows 95 Device Manager. For example, if the port is in AT-compatible mode, it should be changed to PS/2-compatible mode.

For more information on the PnP features of Windows 95, see Chapter 11, "Plug and Play."

Extended Capabilities Port (ECP)

An *Extended Capabilities Port* (ECP) allows Windows 95 to use data compression to speed the data transfer to an attached printer. The improvements in printing speed are even faster if the printer is also ECP-compliant.

By default, the ECP features are not enabled, even though the ECP port may have been detected by Windows 95. To enable ECP support, you must follow these steps:

You must have an ECP printer port installed to perform the following steps.

1. Determine the IRQ and DMA settings required for the ports according to the documentation for the computer or ECP card.

2. Double-click on the System icon in Control Panel and select the Device Manager tab.

3. Click on the plus sign (+) next to Ports to display the installed ports. Select the ECP port and choose Properties.

4. Select the Resources tab to display the I/O address range that has been automatically detected for the ECP.

5. Select Basic Configuration 2 in the Settings Based On field.

6. In the Resource settings list box, select Interrupt Request and choose Change Setting.

7. Type the IRQ value you noted in Step 1 in the Edit Interrupt Request dialog box and choose OK. The Conflict information field should report "No devices are conflicting." If it

does not report this, you must change the IRQ setting for the conflicting device.

8. In the Resource settings list box, select Direct Memory Access and choose Change Setting.

9. Type the DMA value you noted in step 1 in the Edit Direct Memory Access dialog box and choose OK. The Conflict information field should report "No devices are conflicting." If not, you must change the DMA setting for the conflicting device.

10. Shut down and restart the computer so the changes can take effect. After restarting, you can take advantage of fast I/O capabilities offered by the ECP.

Image Color Matching (ICM)

A problem that has always been associated with color printing is that you can never be too sure what a color will look like when it is printed, or how closely it will match what you see on-screen. A traditional solution was to use hard copy color samples, printed on the color printer so you could see exactly what shade the red would be, or how blue the blue really was. Unfortunately, this required a hard copy for each printer to be used, which could be cumbersome, especially if you were working with 64 million colors.

To solve this problem, a group of industry hardware vendors (chiefly Kodak, Microsoft, Apple Computer, Sun Microsystems, and Silicon Graphics) created a color matching specification (known as InterColor 3.0). Windows 95 implements Kodak's Image Color Matching (ICM) technology, which conforms to the InterColor 3.0 specification to ensure that the colors displayed on a monitor closely match colors printed from any ICM supporting printer.

Each color monitor, printer, and scanner supporting ICM has a color-matching profile stored in the *<systemroot>*\SYSTEM\COLOR directory (where *<systemroot>* is WINDOWS, for example). The profile takes into account how closely the device matches various colors to the international (CIE) color reference standards. The Windows 95 operating system then takes these color-matching capabilities into account and makes any modifications necessary when displaying that color on the monitor, so what you see is as close as possible to the color printed out.

For example, if printer A generally prints a darker red than printer B, the ICM profile for printer A tells Windows 95 to display a darker red on the screen when the driver for printer A is selected. In addition, if that document is open at another computer whose monitor displays the colors slightly differently, the ICM profile for the monitor causes Windows 95 to adjust the on-screen colors so they look the same as in the original document.

In summary, the benefits of ICM are as follows:

▶ The color on-screen closely matches the color of the printout if ICM devices and applications are used.

▶ The colors used are consistent on any ICM-compliant devices, ensuring colors that match the international standards regardless of which ICM device they are printed to or displayed on.

Printer Drivers

The Windows 95 printer driver architecture is similar to that used with Windows NT. Printing is controlled through a Microsoft-written universal driver along with a small machine-specific minidriver supplied by the printer manufacturer. Thus, a printer manufacturer needs to write only a small amount of code to customize the driver to the particular requirements and features of that printer.

Unidrivers

Windows 95 uses two universal drivers: one for PostScript printers and one for non-PostScript printers.

Non-PostScript

The non-PostScript universal driver (unidriver) has built-in support for almost all the existing printer control languages, such as the following:

- ▶ HP PCL

- ▶ Epson ESC P/2

- ▶ Canon CaPSL

- ▶ Lexmark PPDS

- ▶ Monochrome HP-GL/2

- ▶ Most dot-matrix technologies

The non-PostScript driver also supports device-resident Intellifont and TrueType scalable fonts, as well as downloading TrueType fonts for rasterizing by the processor of a PCL printer.

PostScript Universal Driver

Unlike the Windows 3.*x* PostScript driver, the Windows 95 PostScript universal driver supports PostScript Level 2 commands for advanced PostScript printing support. In addition, Adobe PostScript Printer Description (PPD) files are supported for version 4.2 and older PPDs. Another new feature of the Windows 95 PostScript universal driver is the off-loading of ICM processing to the printer's PostScript processor. This reduces the processor load on the computer, which improves system performance.

Minidrivers

Windows 95 includes a large number of minidrivers for the most common printers. In addition, because of the Windows 95 driver architecture, a manufacturer can create a minidriver for its printer much more quickly and easily. Furthermore, because most of the driver code is in the universal driver, the possibility of the minidrivers needing to be updated to fix programming bugs is decreased.

Point and Print Setup

A network printer serving as a Windows 95, Windows NT, or NetWare print server can be configured as a Point and Print printer. When a Windows 95 client on the network first attempts to print to the network printer, or "points" to the printer by opening the print queue in Network Neighborhood, the printer driver files can be automatically copied to and installed on the Windows 95 client. In addition, if the print queue is on a Windows 95 server, such settings as printer memory, paper size, and so on can be automatically configured on the client. The Windows 95 INF files define the files required for a particular printer.

> You must have the File and Printer Sharing for Microsoft Network or the File and Printer Sharing for NetWare feature enabled for Point and Print to work.

With a print queue configured for Point and Print setup, a Windows 95 user can have the printer drivers automatically installed on the Windows 95 client, without having to worry about what the printer model is, what driver to use, and so on. The information obtained from a printer when you enable Point and Print can include the following:

▶ Printer driver name and file information

▶ Model information about the printer

▶ Which printer driver to retrieve from the Windows folder on a local or network computer. Printer driver files are located in the \WINDOWS\SYSTEM folder.

▶ Server name on which the printer files are stored

The \WINDOWS\SYSTEM folder is automatically set up as a read-only share when you share a printer under Windows 95. It uses the share name PRINTER$ and has no password. It is part of the UNC share name of the computer that shares the printer. So, if a computer named \\PEART is sharing a printer, Windows 95 automatically creates a share named \\PEART\PRINTER$. You cannot see this share in Explorer because it is a hidden share. You can, however, map to the hidden share using the NET USE command. This hidden PRINTER$ share is needed for Point and Print support so the printer driver files can be available across the network.

When a print server supports Point and Print and UNC (Universal Naming Convention) names, the remote printer does not have to be associated with any the local computer's printer ports. On the other hand, if the server does not support UNC names, you can set up one of the local printer ports with the network printer. In fact, the printer port can be a virtual port—that is, a port that is not physically part of the computer. This means, for example, you can associate LPT3 up to LPT9 to a remote printer.

For information on how to configure and use a printer for Point and Print setup, refer to the section "Connecting to a Network Printer Using Point and Print Setup" later in this chapter.

Drag and Drop Printing

Do you have a document that you want to quickly send to a printer without having to manually open the document in an application? Simply click on the document, keep the mouse button held down, and drag the document until it is over the printer icon. When you release the mouse button, the application associated with the document opens, the document is sent to the print queue, and the application then automatically closes.

Most applications support this feature. If an application does not support this feature, you have to open the file in the application and then print the file.

If you right-click on a document and select Print from the context-sensitive menu, the same process occurs, except the document is sent to the default printer. If you want to print to a different print queue, you can use the drag and drop method if the application supports printing to a non-default printer.

Enhanced Metafile (EMF) Spooling

For non-PostScript printing, Windows 95 generates an *Enhanced Metafile* (EMF) instead of sending the raw data directly to the printer. Spooling to an EMF allows control to be returned to an application approximately two times faster than if the data is sent directly to the printer. Thus, the printing process time that makes your computer inaccessible is much shorter in Windows 95 than Windows 3.1.

With Windows 3.1, raw printer data (such as HPPCL commands or escape codes) is sent directly to the printer driver for rendering and submission to the Print Manager queue. The application is busy until all the data has been rendered and sent to the Print Manager queue. During this time, the user is unable to do anything else in that application, such as work on another document.

With Windows 95, the *Graphical Device Interface* (GDI) generates an EMF using the document information generated by the application. The EMF is a collection of Windows 95 commands for creating an image, such as commands to draw a rectangle and put some text underneath it. The EMF print API has a command to draw a rectangle and instructions on placing the text underneath it. The EMF can be created in about half the time it would take to send the raw data directly to the printer. After the EMF is created, the application no longer is busy, and the user can continue to work in it.

The GDI in Windows 95 is the key to understanding EMF. The GDI handles most graphical I/O tasks in Windows 95. These include painting the screen, sending output to printers, and rendering graphical objects and text. The EMF file that is created when you send a print job to a printer set up for EMF contains GDI commands, a color palette, and additional data used to render the image defined by the GDI commands.

The EMF is then interpreted in the background by the 32-bit printing subsystem, which translates the EMF into raw printer data that can be sent to the printer (called *rasterizing*). EMF spooling adds an intermediate step in the print process, but returns control to an application much more quickly.

PostScript printers handle the rasterizing process itself, so EMF is not necessary when you print to a PostScript printer. Instead of using EMF, PostScript uses page description language commands to rasterize the print job, so you may need to disable the EMF spooling on these Postscript printers.

Figure 7.1 illustrates the differences between the Windows 3.*x* and Windows 95 print processes.

Figure 7.1

The Windows 3.x and Windows 95 print processes.

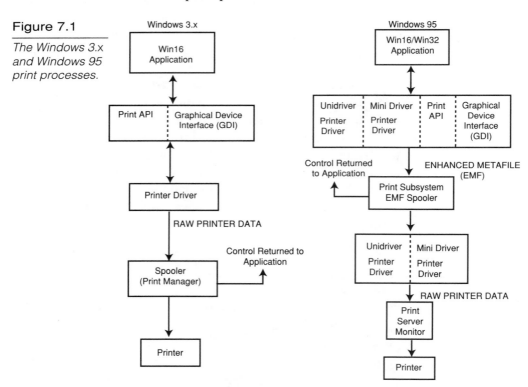

To set the spooler settings for a printer, open the Printers folder (from My Computer or Control Panel), right-click on the printer you want to examine, and choose Properties from the context-sensitive menu. The Properties page for that printer displays. Click on the Spool Settings button to display the Spool Settings dialog box (see fig. 7.2).

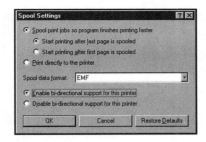

From this dialog box, you can turn the spooler on or off, and control when the system begins printing. The following options control when printing starts:

▶ Start printing after last page is spooled

▶ Start printing after first page is spooled

Some options in the Spool Settings dialog box may be disabled depending on the printer driver installed.

EMF spooling works with most Windows applications; some applications, however, may be capable of printing to a driver using only raw printer data. For these applications, you might need to bypass the EMF spooling. The following steps show how to disable EMF spooling:

1. Right-click on the Printer icon and select Properties. The Properties sheet for the printer appears.

2. Select the Details tab and choose Spool Settings. The Spool Settings dialog box appears.

3. In the Spool Data Format list box of the Spool Settings dialog box, select RAW and choose OK. Data sent to this printer no longer will be spooled to an EMF file.

For most situations, using EMF is a good idea if your system can handle the background printing. If your computer suffers in performance due to background tasks like this, you may want to follow the preceding steps to disable EMF. Also, you're going to see a slight decrease in free hard disk space when you send a print job to a printer using EMF. This is because the EMF file consumes disk space until the print job finishes. If you encounter a problem with EMF, run ScanDisk to check for disk integrity and free disk space. If you still experience problems after running ScanDisk, switch to RAW printing.

The following list describes instances in which EMF rendering is processed when sending a print job from Windows 95 to a network or local printer:

▶ Printing to a local printer. Rendering occurs on the local computer.

▶ Printing to a Windows 95 Server across a peer-to-peer network. Rendering occurs on the server instead of on the client computer that sends the print job.

▶ Printing to a Windows NT or Novell NetWare print server. Rendering occurs on the client computer that sends the print job.

DOS applications do not benefit from EMF spooling. However, as you read in the next section, "Conflict Resolution," DOS applications can use Windows' 95 spooling feature so as not to encounter conflicts with other applications when sending print jobs to the printer.

Conflict Resolution

The Windows 95 printing subsystem handles conflicts between different MS-DOS and Windows applications trying to print to a printer port simultaneously. This functionality is an improvement over the Windows 3.1 printing subsystem.

In Window 3.1, conflicts usually occur when attempting to print from an MS-DOS–based application and Windows-based application simultaneously because the DOS application could not use the Windows 3.1 Print Manager. The Print Manager sets up a spooler to spool all print jobs. Because a DOS application cannot use the Print Manager, the DOS print job goes straight to the printer, conflicting with other jobs.

Under Windows 95, however, printer spooling is automatically set up (that is, the user does not need to manually configure this support) for DOS applications. When sending a print job from a DOS application now, it goes to the spooler first, then to the printer. This spooling action also has the benefit of turning control back to the DOS application sooner under Windows 95 than when printing under Windows 3.1.

Deferred Printing

The spooling capabilities of Windows 95 allow a job to be spooled to a print queue, even if the printer is currently unavailable. For a remote user, Windows 95 automatically detects that the laptop is not connected to a local or network printer and sets the print queue to Work Offline mode. The job still is sent to the print queue but does not print until a connection to that printer is detected. For example, when the user returns to the office, attaches to the printer or the network, and starts Windows 95, the jobs can be sent to the printer as a background process.

You also can manually set a print queue to hold print jobs by right-clicking on the Printer icon and selecting Pause Printing. This may be useful if you want to hold the jobs until later in the day, for example. To resume sending jobs to the printer, right-click on the printer icon and deselect Pause Printing.

Windows 95 Printing Process

The printing model for Windows 95 is made up of modular components, which enable a great deal of flexibility because individual components can be substituted. For example, if a PostScript printer driver is used, the EMF component of the printing model is not used.

To illustrate the Windows 95 printing model, the following list contains the three different printing processes that can occur:

▶ Printing from a non-Windows application

▶ Printing from a Windows application to a non-PostScript printer

▶ Printing from a Windows application to a PostScript printer

Regardless of which print process is used, the print job eventually is formatted into raw printer data that is sent to the local print spooler on the Windows 95 computer.

Print Spooler

A *print spooler* essentially is an internal print queue where the print job data is written while the print job is being processed. Any printing done in Windows 95 uses the local print spooler on the Windows 95 client. In addition, if a Windows application prints Ito a non-PostScript printer, an additional spooler known as the *EMF print spooler* may be used. If the network printer is used, the local print spooler passes the print job to the spooler on the network print server.

As the print jobs are spooled, they are written to a temporary file on the hard disk. For Windows 95 computers, the print jobs are queued in *<systemroot>*\SPOOL\PRINTERS; for example, C:\WINDOWS\SPOOL\PRINTERS.

When a job begins to spool, it is the responsibility of the Print Monitor to decide when to send the information to the printer. Using the default settings, and assuming that the printer is available to accept a new print job, the Print Monitor starts sending the job to the printer after the first page has spooled. To change this, choose Spool Settings from the Details tab of the Properties sheet for the printer. The Print Monitor writes the spooled data either to a port (if the printer is locally connected) or to a print spooler on a network print server.

After the job has printed, the Print Monitor can display a pop-up message informing the user that the job has printed.

Printing from a Non-Windows Application

For non-Windows (that is, DOS) applications, the application sends information to the printer driver, which converts the information into raw printer data using a printer control language that the printer understands. For example, to print a circle, an HP LaserJet driver would send an HPPCL command to the printer specifying the size of the circle and the location on the page. The raw data is then sent to the print spooler, and control is returned to the application after all the raw data has been submitted to the print spooler.

Printing from a Windows 95 Application to a Non-PostScript Printer

When you select a network printer in a Windows application, Windows 95 can copy the printer driver to the local directory *<systemroot>*\SYSTEM (for example, C:\WINDOWS\SYSTEM). If the file has already been copied, then the print server driver is not copied to the local computer unless the local driver is an older version than the driver on the print server. Similarly, if a local printer is selected, then the driver already is on the local computer.

When the client has the correct printer driver on the hard drive, the driver is loaded into RAM. The Windows application can then query the printer driver for the current print settings (such as page orientation) to produce a What-You-See-Is-What-You-Get (WYSIWYG) image on the screen.

To print the document, the Windows 95 GDI (which is responsible for displaying how the screen looks—for example, drawing the text in a certain font) sends a series of commands to the Windows 95 graphics engine. The Windows 95 graphics engine then translates the GDI commands into an EMF, using the EMF spooler.

After the EMF has been created, control is returned to the application. The EMF spooler then processes the EMF information in the background using the printer minidriver. The minidriver converts the EMF to raw printer data, which is then spooled to the print spooler.

Printing from a Windows Application to a PostScript Printer

This process is the same as for non-PostScript printers, except the GDI does not generate commands for an EMF file. Instead, to print a document, the PostScript driver generates a series of raw printer commands to tell the printer how to print the specified pages. The raw printer data (in the PostScript language) is then sent to the print spooler.

Installing a Local Printer in Windows 95

A local printer can be installed in Windows 95 using either PnP hardware detection or the Add Printer Wizard, if the printer is not PnP-compliant.

Installing a Plug and Play Printer

If a PnP-compliant printer is connected to the Windows 95 computer at startup, the printer is detected, and the appropriate printer driver is automatically installed. If Windows 95 cannot determine the proper driver to be used, it prompts the user to specify the correct driver.

Installing a Printer Using the Add Printer Wizard

The Add Printer Wizard is used to install a printer driver in Windows 95. The Add Printer Wizard can be accessed from the Printers folder. To access the Printers folder, select it from the Start menu Settings option or open it after opening My Computer.

The Printers folder can be used to perform the following functions:

- ▶ Install a printer

- ▶ Share a printer on a network

- ▶ Set permissions for accessing a printer

- ▶ Connect to a network printer

- ▶ Manage printers

- ▶ Change printer properties, such as page size

The following steps show you how to use the Add Printer Wizard to install a locally attached printer.

If you do not have an actual printer attached to your computer, you can still perform the following steps and select FILE: as the port to print to. When you print to FILE:, you are prompted for a file name and path to which to save the output. Printing to FILE: is usually used with the Generic / Text Only printer driver to create text output in a file.

For an exercise testing this information, see end of chapter.

1. Open the Printers folder.

2. Double-click on the Add Printer Wizard and choose Next. You are asked whether the printer is attached directly to the computer or is accessed from the network.

3. Select Local Printer and choose Next.

4. Select the printer manufacturer from the Manufacturers list.

5. Select the printer model from the Printers list. If you do not have an actual local printer, you may select the Generic / Text Only driver after selecting Generic as the manufacturer.

6. From the list of Available ports, select the port to which the printer is connected. For example, for a parallel port, you may need to select LPT1:. If you do not have a local printer attached, select FILE:.

7. Choose Next and assign the printer a printer name. You can accept the default name, or you can use a more descriptive name, such as LaserJet II in Room 312.

8. If you want print jobs to be sent to this printer by default, choose Yes and then choose Next. Otherwise, choose No and then Next.

9. The Add Printer Wizard then asks you whether you want to print a test page, and then copies the files from the Windows 95 distribution media. If Windows 95 cannot find these files, you are prompted for the path.

10. An icon for the printer is created in the Printers folder. To configure the printer, see the following section.

Configuring a Printer in Windows 95

The settings on a printer are controlled through the Properties sheet for that printer. To access the Properties sheet, right-click on the printer icon and select Properties.

The Properties sheet contains the following tabs:

- ▶ General
- ▶ Details
- ▶ Paper
- ▶ Graphics
- ▶ Fonts
- ▶ Device Options
- ▶ PostScript

These tabs are described in the following sections.

General

The General tab specifies the printer name and any additional descriptive comments that the user enters. In addition, if the user wants to print a separator page between print jobs, this instruction can be specified here.

Details

The Details tab specifies the printer driver to be used, as well as various port settings. For example, the Transmission Retry setting specifies the number of seconds Windows 95 will wait before reporting a timeout error if the printer is not responding. In addition, the Spool Settings dialog box is accessed from the Details tab.

Paper

The type of information in this tab varies depending on the printer driver used. The Paper tab may contain configuration settings for some of the following items:

- ▶ Default paper size

- ▶ Default orientation (for example, landscape or portrait)

- ▶ Paper source (for example, tractor feed or upper paper tray)

- ▶ The number of copies to print for each print job

Graphics

The configurable information in this tab varies depending on the printer driver used. It may contain settings such as the following:

- ▶ **Resolution.** Specifies the number of dots per inch (dpi) used for printing graphics or scaleable fonts.

- ▶ **Dithering.** Specifies how the colors are blended together for a color printer.

▶ **Intensity.** Specifies the degree of lightness or darkness of the print job.

Figure 7.3 shows an example of a typical Graphics tab from the Properties sheet of a printer.

Figure 7.3

A typical Graphics tab from a printer Properties sheet.

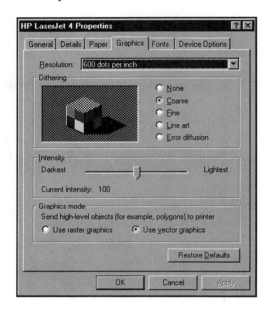

Fonts

The Fonts tab is usually available for laser printers. If cartridges are installed on the printer, they can be specified here. In addition, you can specify whether to use TrueType fonts or built-in printer fonts. In general, the fonts built into the printer can be rendered more quickly. For PostScript printers, a font substitution table can be configured to substitute TrueType fonts with PostScript fonts.

Device Options

If this tab is available, it can be used to configure information specific to the printer. For example, the printer manufacturer may include options to specify the amount of memory installed or other printer-specific features. Figure 7.4 shows an example of the Device Options tab.

Figure 7.4

*A typical printer
Properties Device
Options tab.*

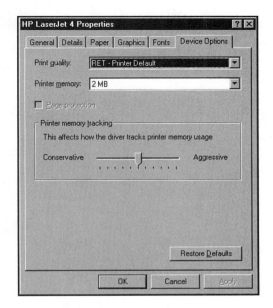

PostScript

This tab is available on PostScript printers and can be used to
configure the PostScript options, such as the following:

- ▶ **Output Format.** Used for file compatibility.

- ▶ **Header.** By default, a PostScript header is sent with each
  print job containing printer-specific configuration information. If the printer is accessed only locally, you may want to
  change this setting so that a header need not be sent with
  each print job.

- ▶ **Error Information.** Allows error messages to be printed out
  by the printer.

- ▶ **Advanced.** Additional information, such as the PostScript
  language level and data format, can be specified. Windows
  95 supports PostScript Levels 1 and 2.

Figure 7.5 shows an example of the PostScript tab for a PostScript
printer.

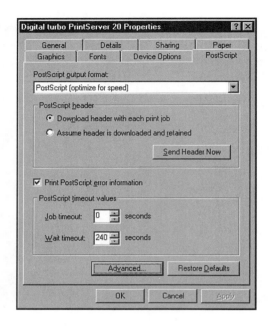

Figure 7.5

The PostScript tab for a PostScript printer.

Windows 95 Network Printing

Windows 95 network printing support includes a number of new features:

▶ A modular architecture, which allows for different print providers for different types of networks

▶ Point and Print installation, which allows printer drivers to be automatically installed over the network

▶ The capability to assign network permissions to print queues, which can prevent unauthorized changes to the print queues or print jobs

▶ Support for different network print servers, including HP JetDirect printers and DEC PrintServer printers

Architecture

The modular format of the Windows 95 printing subsystem uses a layered model. The four layers are the following:

> ▶ Print Application Programming Interfaces (APIs)

> ▶ Print Router

> ▶ Print Provider Interface

> ▶ Print Providers

Print Application Programming Interfaces (APIs)

The *Print Application Programming Interfaces* (APIs) are used to pass information to and from the Windows application and the print router. Windows 95 includes the 16-bit Win16 API for use with WIN16 applications, as well as the 32-bit Win32 API for use with WIN32 applications. The Print APIs provide such functions as opening, writing, and closing print jobs. The Print APIs also are used for print queue management.

Print Router and Print Provider Interface

The *Print Router* passes printing requests from the Print APIs to the proper Print Provider Interface (PPI). The PPI in turn passes on this information to the correct print provider. For example, if the printing request is for a local printer, the Print Router sends the information through the PPI to the Windows 95 Local Printing Print Provider.

Print Providers

A *Print Provider* is a 32-bit dynamic-link library (DLL) that contains code for printing and network support, as appropriate. The print providers translate requests from the PPI to the appropriate network or local printer requests.

The following print providers are included with Windows 95:

> ▶ Local Printing Print Provider

> ▶ Microsoft 32-bit Network Print Provider

> ▶ Microsoft 16-bit Network Print Provider

> ▶ NetWare Network Print Provider

In addition, third-party network vendors can supply their own print providers, which can be designed to fit in with the modular Windows 95 printing subsystem.

Local Printing Print Provider

The Local Printing Print Provider is found in the SPOOLSS.DLL file along with the Print Router. This print provider handles the local print queue and manages print jobs that are sent to local printers (a printer directly connected to a port on the Windows 95 client).

Microsoft Network Print Provider

Two print providers for Microsoft Network printing support exist. The 32-bit print provider, known as WinNet32 Network Print Provider, is contained in the file MSPP32.DLL. The 16-bit print provider, WinNet16 Network Print Provider, is actually a part of MSPP32.DLL, which translates PPI requests into 16-bit WinNet16 requests for backward compatibility with 16-bit Microsoft Network drivers.

When a print job is submitted to a Microsoft Network printer, the PPI interacts with the Microsoft Network Print Provider (MSPP32.DLL) and the Microsoft Network support library (MSNET32.DLL if a 32-bit network client is used; MSNET16.DLL if a 16-bit network client is used) and sends the print job to the network printer using the Installable File System (IFS) Manager (IFSMGR.VXD). The IFS Manager then interacts with the network redirector (VREDIR.VXD) to send the job over the network.

For print queue management (for example, viewing a print queue), the print provider and network support library send requests directly to the network redirector.

The Registry subkey that contains information about the print provider for the Microsoft Network is as follows:

```
HKEY_LOCAL_MACINE\System\CurrentControlSet\Control\Print\
Providers\Microsoft Networks Print Provider
```

Microsoft provides the Microsoft Remote Procedure Call (RPC) Print Provider on the Windows 95 CD-ROM. You can find the RPC in the \ADMIN\NETTOOLS\RPCPP folder on the Windows 95 CD-ROM; you can set it up from the Network icon in Control Panel. This provider improves network printing and remote administration of printers by providing Win32 APIs for Windows 95 clients to be able to administer print queues on Windows NT servers. When you install this RPC, you can use a Windows 95 client to obtain print job status information and accounting information from a Windows NT server.

NetWare Network Print Provider

Similar to the Microsoft Network Print Provider, the NetWare Network Print Provider (the NWPP32.DLL file) uses the IFS Manager (the IFSMGR file) to submit jobs to the network redirector. NWPP32.DLL also interacts with the NWNET32.DLL file, which is the NetWare Network Support library. For a NetWare network, the network redirector is NWREDIR.VXD.

Windows 95 currently supports bindery-based NetWare print queues, but not NetWare Directory Services (NDS)-based print queues common with NetWare 4.x servers.

As well, the NetWare Network Print Provider can translate print requests into 16-bit calls if a real-mode (16-bit) NetWare client is used. When a 32-bit network DLL, such as NWPP32.DLL or NWNET32.DLL, accesses a NetWare service, the file NW16.DLL provides the translation and thunking necessary for real-mode NetWare clients. It (NW16.DLL) then sends the call to NETX or VLM via VNETWARE.386.

You can use the Microsoft Printer Server for NetWare utility (PSERVER) with Windows 95 to despool print jobs from NetWare queues to Windows 95 printers. You can connect a Windows 95 printer directly to a NetWare print queue using the

continues

NetWare queue configuration. After you share the printer on the Windows 95 network, any NetWare print queue can use it. See "Microsoft Print Agent for NetWare Networks" later in this chapter.

The Registry subkey that contains information about the print provider for NetWare is as follows:

```
HKEY_LOCAL_MACINE\System\CurrentControlSet\Control\Print\
Providers\Microsoft Print Provider for NetWare
```

Third-Party Network Print Providers

Third-party network vendors can write their own print provider and print provider interface that communicates with their own network redirector software. A third-party network print provider can be installed using the Control Panel Network applet.

Printing to a Network Printer

To connect to a network printer, you must first install, configure, and share the printer on the network server. For information on installing and configuring the driver on the network server, refer to the preceding sections on local printer installation and configuration.

After the Windows 95 printer driver has been configured on the network print server attached to the printer, the printer must be shared to allow other users to access it. To share a printer in Windows 95, the network print server must be running a 32-bit, protected-mode client, and a file and printer sharing service must be enabled. (Refer to Chapter 5, "Networking and Interoperability," for information on enabling file and printer sharing.) The following steps demonstrate how to share a network printer:

1. Right-click on the Printer icon and select Properties to open the Properties sheet.

2. Select the Sharing tab to display the Sharing configuration settings, as shown in figure 7.6.

Figure 7.6

*The printer
Sharing tab.*

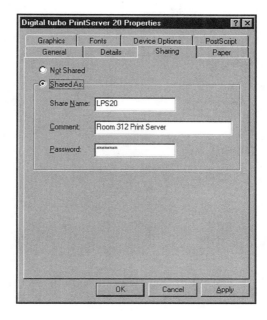

3. Select Shared As and enter a share name and an optional descriptive comment for the printer. Windows 95 does not allow a share name to contain invalid characters, including spaces. The share name also must not exceed 12 characters.

4. You also must grant permissions to access this printer. If share-level permissions are used, you must assign a password to the printer. To access the print queue, users must supply the correct password. If user-level permissions are used, you must add the users who will be granted access to this print queue. For example, to allow everyone to print to the print queue, you would add the Everyone group and give it the print access right.

5. Choose OK to share the printer. The printer icon now appears as a hand holding or sharing the printer with others. Remote users with the correct permissions can now access the print queue after setting up the correct printer driver on their computers.

When the printer has been configured and shared on the network print server, a Windows 95 client can be configured to connect to the print server and print to the printer over the network.

This configuration can be done either manually with the Add Printer Wizard or by configuring the network printer for Point and Print setup.

Connecting to a Network Printer Using the Add Printer Wizard

For an exercise testing this information, see end of chapter.

To manually configure a Windows 95 client to print to the network printer using the Add Printer Wizard, perform the following steps:

1. Start the Add Printer Wizard from the Printers folder.

2. In the Printer Type field, select Network Printer and choose Next.

3. Enter the Universal Naming Convention (UNC) path of the network printer; for example, \\SARAH\HP4.

4. If you will not be using MS-DOS applications to print to this printer, you can select No under Do You Print from MS-DOS–Based Programs?. To have the printer associated with a printer port, such as LPT1:, you should select Yes for this option. Choose Next.

5. If you have specified that you will print to this printer using MS-DOS–based applications, you are prompted to select the desired port from the Capture Printer Port dialog box. Choose OK to continue.

6. Choose Next and select the printer manufacturer and model from the Manufacturers and Printers lists.

7. Enter a name for the printer; for example, HP4 in Room 11.

8. If you want to test that you can print properly to the network printer, select Send Test Page. Choose Finish to have Windows 95 begin copying the printer driver files to the hard drive if the latest drivers are not already on the hard drive. If Windows 95 cannot find the files, you are prompted to enter the path to the Windows 95 distribution files.

9. An icon for the network printer is created in the Printers folder. If desired, you can drag a copy of this icon to the Desktop to create a shortcut.

Connecting to a Network Printer Using Point and Print Setup

To connect to a network printer that is *not* configured for Point and Print setup, a client must know the correct printer driver to be used. In addition, the client must know other information, such as the share name and network server name. However, after a network printer has been configured to enable Point and Print setup, the printer driver installation on the client is greatly simplified. The Point and Print printer supplies the client with information such as the UNC path, the printer driver to be used, and other information.

To install the printer drivers for the Point and Print printer on a Windows 95 client, locate the icon for the printer in the Network Neighborhood. Next, drag the printer icon onto the Desktop. Alternatively, you can right-click on the network Printer icon and select Install.

In Network Neighborhood, if you double-click on the name of a network printer not set up on your computer, Windows 95 displays a Printers message asking if you want to set up the printer now. Click Yes to start the Add Printer Wizard and walk through the wizard to set up the printer.

In addition, if you try to drag and drop a document onto the network printer icon, the printer driver will be installed on the Windows 95 client, if it has not already been installed. If the driver version on the network printer is more recent than the version on the client, the later printer driver version will be copied to the client.

A Point and Print printer can be configured on any of the following servers:

▶ Windows 95 server

▶ Windows NT server (including both Windows NT Server and Windows NT Workstation servers)

▶ NetWare bindery-based server

Windows 95 Server

A Windows 95 server is simply a computer running Windows 95 that has a file and printer Sharing service enabled. Any printers directly connected to the Windows 95 server are automatically enabled for Point and Print setup. No further configuration is required.

When you use Point and Print over a Windows 95 server, printer information is communicated between the client (the computer sending the print job) and the server (the computer to which the printer is attached) using VREDIR and VSERVER drivers. VREDIR initiates a request for Point and Print printer setup. VSERVER replies to VREDIR with the friendly name of the printer. Then the following events take place:

1. The Windows 95 client displays the friendly name to the user.

2. VSERVER receives a message from VREDIR asking which files are needed on the client machine and where those files are located.

3. In response VSERVER tells VREDIR the name of the files and that they are in the *server_computername*\PRINTER$ folder.

4. VREDIR connects to the *server_computername*\PRINTER$ folder and makes copies of the necessary printer files. If the client machine already has a printer driver or other software that matches the files in the *server_computername*\PRINTER$, Windows 95 asks the user if she wants to keep the existing files. The user should respond Yes to make sure the latest files are copied to the client computer.

5. VREDIR terminates the connection to the *server_computername*\PRINTER$ folder.

6. A new icon pointing to the network printer displays in the Printers folder on the client computer.

Any settings that have been configured for the server printer (such as memory) also are copied to the Windows 95 client.

Windows NT Server

Point and Print setup is also automatically enabled for a printer queue on a Windows NT server running Windows NT (Server or Workstation) version 3.1 or greater. Because Windows 95 uses a slightly different printer driver than that on the Windows NT server, however, the driver is not actually copied to the Windows 95 client. Instead, Windows 95 attempts to install a printer driver with the same name from the Windows 95 distribution files. If no Windows 95 printer driver bears the same name as the Windows NT printer driver, the user is prompted to select the proper driver to be installed.

Because the Windows NT printer driver is not copied to the client, any settings required for this driver must be manually configured on the Windows 95 client. Only Windows 95 servers have the capability to pass on their configuration settings to the Windows 95 client.

Point and Print from a Windows NT client to a Windows 95 server is not supported. You can only use Point and Print from a Windows 95 client to a Windows NT server.

NetWare Bindery-Based Server

Because the NetWare server software does not know about Windows 95 Point and Print setup, some Point and Print configuration information must be written to the NetWare server's bindery to provide Point and Print services. To write this information, you must log onto the NetWare server with Supervisor or equivalent privileges from a Windows 95 client.

To enable Point and Print setup for a NetWare bindery-based print server, perform the following steps:

1. Log onto the NetWare server from a Windows 95 client using an account with Supervisor or equivalent privileges. For more information on performing this step, refer to Chapter 5.

2. Select a NetWare print queue from the Network Neighborhood and click the right mouse button to display the context-sensitive menu. Select Point and Print Setup from the menu to display the Set Printer Model and Set Driver Path options.

3. Select Set Printer Model and select the printer model from the list. Choose OK to continue.

4. Select Set Driver Path and enter the UNC path where the printer driver files for this printer are located. For example, enter **\\NW312\SYS\PUBLIC**.

5. Copy the required Windows 95 printer drivers from the Windows 95 distribution files to the directory specified in the preceding step.

6. To use Point and Print setup, a user must have at least Read and File Scan privileges to the directory specified in step 4. If the SYS\PUBLIC directory is used, all users have these privileges by default.

7. The printer queue, driver, and privileges information is written to the NetWare bindery. Users then can automatically install the printer driver on the Windows 95 client after dragging the printer icon from the Network Neighborhood onto the Desktop. The printer driver also is installed on the Windows 95 client if a document is dragged and dropped onto the NetWare printer icon.

Registry Keys

Windows 95 stores configuration information in the Registry. Printers that have been set up in the Printers folder have entries found under the HKEY_LOCAL_MACHINE\System\ CurrentControlSet\Control\Print key. To view the subkeys, open the Registry by running the REGEDIT application from a command prompt.

Any changes made to the Registry can severely affect the operating system. You should make a backup copy of the Registry files to prevent accidental changes. See the section "Registry Editor" in Chapter 4, "Editing User and System Profiles," for more information.

Managing a Print Queue

Double-clicking on a printer icon displays the print queue for that printer. The print queue shows the status of any jobs that are printing or waiting to print on that printer. The print jobs are sent to the printer in the order in which they appear.

Settings for the print queue can be changed from the Printer menu when the print queue is displayed or from the context-sensitive menu displayed after right-clicking on the printer icon. These settings include the following:

▶ Using a separator page between print jobs—this can be set in the General tab of the printer's Properties sheet

▶ Setting the printer to be the default printer for the Windows 95 client

▶ Setting the printer offline so jobs will queue but not be printed until otherwise specified

In addition to being used to change print queue settings, a Windows 95 print queue window also can be used to manage print jobs.

Managing Print Jobs

Any user can display a print queue that he or she has permission to access. Users also can manage the print queue if the printer is attached locally. If the print queue is on a network printer, users can manage the print queue if they have the proper permissions, and if user-level security is used. If a user does not have permission to manage the print queue, that user can still manage print jobs that he or she has submitted. The following functions can be performed on a print job:

▶ Canceling a print job

▶ Pausing a print job

▶ Resuming a print job

▶ Changing the order of print jobs

Figure 7.7 shows an example of a Windows 95 print queue. In this example, the first job sent to the queue has been paused, the second job is being deleted, and therefore the third job will be printed next.

Figure 7.7

A Windows 95 print queue.

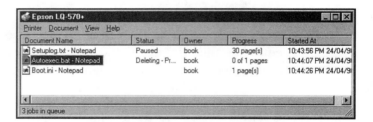

Canceling a Print Job

If a print job has not already started printing, you can delete it from the print queue by selecting the print job from the print queue and pressing the Delete key. Alternatively, you can choose Document, Cancel Printing in the print queue after selecting the print job.

For a network print queue, users can delete only their own print jobs. For a local printer, users can delete any print jobs in the print queue.

If a document is already printing, then you cannot cancel the print job. If for some reason the job hangs in the print queue, you might have to manually delete the spooled file from the print spool directory. For a Windows 95 print queue, this usually is C:\WINDOWS\SPOOL\PRINTERS.

Pausing a Print Job

If a print job has not yet started printing, you can pause the job, which allows other print jobs to print ahead of it. To pause a print job, select the print job and choose Document, Pause Printing from the print queue. The print job remains in the queue until the user selects the paused print job and deselects Pause Printing from the Document menu.

For a network print queue, users usually can pause only their own print jobs. A user with administrator privileges may be able to pause any print jobs, if the network software supports that action.

> Any user with access to a local print queue can pause any or all of the print jobs.

You also can pause the entire print queue by selecting Pause Printing from the context-sensitive menu or from the Printer menu of the print queue. You also can pause a network print queue if you have the proper permissions.

Resuming a Print Job

To allow a print job to be sent to the printer, select the paused job and deselect Pause Printing from the Document menu of the print queue. To resume a paused print queue, deselect Pause Printing on the Printer menu or from the context-sensitive menu. Again, you must have the proper permissions to resume printing on a network print queue.

Changing the Order of Print Jobs

If more than one print job is waiting in the print queue, you can change the order in which these jobs print by dragging one of the documents and placing it in front of another. For a network print queue, user-level security must be used, you must have administrator permissions, and the network software must support this operation.

Print Servers

 A benefit of the modular architecture of the Windows 95 printing subsystem is that several different types of print servers can be used depending on the network requirements. The print servers that ship with Windows 95 include the following:

▶ Microsoft Network Print Server

▶ Microsoft Print Agent for NetWare Networks

▶ HP JetAdmin Print Server

▶ Digital (DEC) PrintServer

Microsoft Network

The Microsoft Network Print Server is the default print server used for Windows 95 printing. This print server is used even if File and Printer Sharing for NetWare Networks is installed. No additional configuration is required beyond installing the appropriate printer and network drivers.

Microsoft Print Agent for NetWare Networks

The Microsoft Print Agent for NetWare Networks (MSPSERV) service can be used to despool print jobs from a NetWare or a Windows 95 print queue. If the computer running the Microsoft Print Agent for NetWare Networks service is attached to a printer, jobs originating from Windows 95 or NetWare print queues can be printed.

Whereas a NetWare PSERVER print server must be running on a dedicated MS-DOS computer, a Windows 95 print server running Microsoft Print Agent for NetWare Networks also can run numerous other applications at the same time.

> The Microsoft Print Agent for NetWare Networks service uses the queue management services (QMS) API for queue services. For single printers connected to a local Windows 95 client, the QMS service works with only one queue.
>
> Also, Microsoft Print Agent for NetWare Networks service is located on the Windows 95 setup CD-ROM in the \ADMIN\NETTOOLS\PRTAGENT directory.

When you start the Microsoft Print Agent for NetWare Networks, the service logs on to the NetWare print server and obtains information on how to configure the print jobs. For example, the NetWare print server may specify the banner to be used preceding each print job. The Microsoft Print Agent for NetWare Networks then can obtain jobs from the NetWare print queue, print them, and send a message to the NetWare print queue saying the job has been printed. The NetWare print queue then removes the job and informs the user that the job has been printed.

The Microsoft Print Agent for NetWare Networks service must be installed on a Windows 95 computer running the Microsoft Client for NetWare Networks. The Windows 95 computer need not be running File and Printer Sharing for NetWare Networks, however.

Because MSPSERV runs in the workstation's background, it (MSPSERV) uses no resources except when it periodically polls for data packets at a designated interval. As mentioned in the preceding Note, MSPSERVE uses QMS to attach to a print queue. Receiving an identity handle from that print queue allows MSPSERV to poll the NetWare print server periodically to print jobs. The default polling period is set to 30 seconds.

The polling process timer is adjustable for different workstation and network traffic considerations. For those workstations that will be serving multiple applications and have a high load on them, you might want to use a long period of time between polling—three minutes or longer. This lengthy interval between polling also might be required for busy network segments. If the workstation is not heavily used or if you want to make network print jobs available as quickly as possible, polling can be set for as often as every 15 seconds.

When notified of a job coming in, MSPSERV will receive print job information in the form of a header. These instructions include any print banner text or number of copy information. The data is then sent to the workstation from the print server and MSPSERV receives the print job and uses WIN32 calls to deliver the job to the local printer port and printer. Upon completion of the job, MSPSERV notifies the NetWare print server that the job is complete.

For an exercise testing this information, see end of chapter.

Exercise 7.4 at the end of the chapter demonstrates how to install and enable Microsoft Print Agent for NetWare Networks.

HP JetAdmin

The HP JetAdmin Print Server is used to send and administer print jobs to a Hewlett-Packard printer connected directly to the network using an HP JetDirect network interface card. The HP JetAdmin utility can be used to perform the following functions:

▶ Configure an HP JetDirect network interface card

▶ Configure printer settings

▶ Filter and sort HP JetDirect network printers in the list

▶ Add or remove print queues

▶ Select printer drivers to install

▶ Select the printer operating mode

▶ Set a description for the printer

To install the HP JetAdmin utility, follow these steps:

1. From the Start menu, choose Settings, Control Panel, and then double-click on the Network icon. The Network Control Panel Applet appears.

2. Choose Add and select Service from the Select Network Component Type dialog box.

3. Choose Add and select HP JetAdmin from the list of Network Services.

4. Choose OK to install the HP JetAdmin utility.

5. If you will be using HP JetAdmin with NetWare, you must supply the following files:

   ▶ NWCALLS.DLL

   ▶ NWIPXSPX.DLL

   ▶ NWLOCALE.DLL

   ▶ NWNET.DLL

   ▶ NWPSRV.DLL

The preceding files are provided with the Novell NetWare VLM client and by Microsoft with Windows 3.11.

6. After all the files have been copied, restart Windows 95 for the changes to take effect.

   The HP JetAdmin icon is then to be added to the Control Panel.

Digital Equipment Corporation (DEC) PrintServer

Like HP JetDirect printers, Digital Equipment Corporation (DEC) PrintServer printers can be connected directly to a network using a network interface card. For any network interface printer, the benefit of a direct connection is that computer resources are not needed to spool the print jobs. The results are a much quicker printing completion time and less network traffic. In addition, multiple print spool files are not required for printers connected directly to the network.

To install the DEC PrintServer and DEC Print Monitor, the network must be running TCP/IP. In addition, the printer must be configured as a DEC PrintServer.

To install the DEC PrintServer on a Windows 95 client, perform the following steps:

1. Ensure that both the DEC PrintServer printer and the Windows 95 computer are properly configured to use TCP/IP.

2. From the Printers folder, start the Add Printer Wizard, choose Next, and select Local Printer.

3. Choose Next and select Digital from the list of printer manufacturers. Select the specific model of PrintServer from the list and choose Next. The printer files are copied from the Windows 95 distribution media.

The driver used should have "/Net" at the end of the driver name. This will allow you to add a port during installation and assign it a network address. Alternatively, you can install any printer driver, choose Add Port from the Details tab of the Properties sheet, select Other, and then select Digital Network Port.

4. Choose Add Port to open the Digital Network Port dialog box (see fig. 7.8).

5. Select TCP/IP and type the host name and IP address of the printer's network interface card in the Name and Address fields, respectively.

6. Type a name to use to refer to the port in the Port Name field and choose OK.

7. Enter a name for the printer, choose Next, and then choose Finish. You can now print to the Digital PrintServer printer located at the specified IP address.

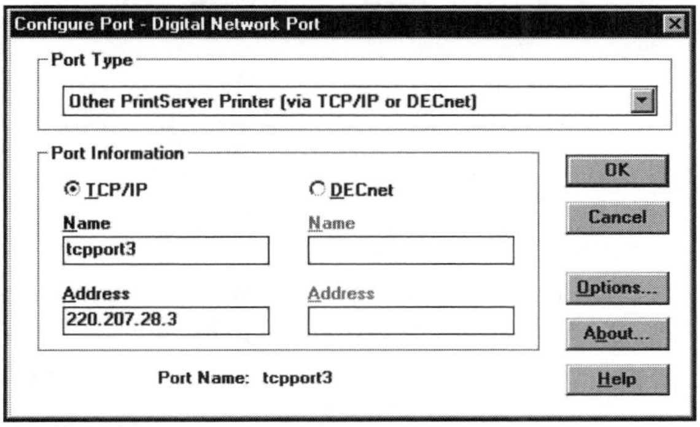

Figure 7.8

Configuring a DEC network printer port.

Adding and Removing Printer Drivers in Windows 95

At times you may need to add or remove printer drivers in Windows 95. You might, for example, acquire or download an updated driver from a printer manufacturer or Microsoft that supersedes the driver you currently use. A driver may need to be removed if it is replaced by a newer one and remains on your system. Or, you may want to remove a driver to troubleshoot a problem you think is being caused by the driver.

You use a printer's Detail tab on the Properties sheet to install a new driver. To display the Detail tab, use the following steps:

1. Open the Printer folder (from Control Panel or My Computer).

2. Right-click on the printer you want to modify.

3. Choose Properties from the context-sensitive menu.

4. Click on the Details tab.

5. On the Details tab, click on the New Driver button. A message displays a warning you that you are about to change the driver for a printer you already have set up.

6. Choose Yes to open the Select Device dialog box.

7. Locate the manufacturer and model for the printer. Or, click on Have Disk if the driver is on a disk or another part of your hard drive (such as a download folder).

8. Click on OK and follow the other screens to install the driver. From this point on, the steps are the same as when you use the Add Printer Wizard.

You remove a printer driver from your Printers folder by clicking on the printer you want to remove and pressing Delete. You also can right-click on the printer and select Delete from the context-sensitive menu. A Printers message box asks if you are sure you want to delete the printer. Choose Yes.

Exercises

Exercise 7.1:   Disabling EMF Spooling

Exercise 7.1 illustrates how to disable EMF spooling.

1. Right-click on the Printer icon and select Properties. The Properties sheet for the printer appears.

2. Select the Details tab and choose Spool Settings. The Spool Settings dialog box appears.

3. In the Spool Data Format list box of the Spool Settings dialog box, select RAW and choose OK. Data sent to this printer no longer will be spooled to an EMF file.

Exercise 7.2:   Adding a Local Printer with the Add Printer Wizard

Exercise 7.2 demonstrates how to use the Add Printer Wizard to install a locally attached printer.

If you do not have an actual printer attached to your computer, you can still perform this exercise and select FILE: as the port to print to. When you print to FILE:, you are prompted for a file name and path to which to save the output. Printing to FILE: is usually used with the Generic / Text Only printer driver to create text output in a file.

1. Open the Printers folder.

2. Double-click on the Add Printer Wizard and choose Next. You are asked whether the printer is attached directly to the computer or is accessed from the network.

3. Select Local Printer and choose Next.

4. Select the printer manufacturer from the Manufacturers list.

5. Select the printer model from the Printers list. If you do not have an actual local printer, you can select the Generic / Text Only driver after selecting Generic as the manufacturer.

continues

Exercise 7.2: Continued

6. From the list of Available ports, select the port to which the printer is connected. For example, for a parallel port, you may need to select LPT1:. If you do not have a local printer attached, select FILE:.

7. Choose Next and assign the printer a printer name. You can accept the default name, or you can use a more descriptive name, such as LaserJet II in Room 312.

8. If you want print jobs to be sent to this printer by default, choose Yes and then choose Next. Otherwise, choose No and then Next.

9. The Add Printer Wizard asks whether you want to print a test page, and then copies the files from the Windows 95 distribution media. If Windows 95 cannot find these files, you are prompted for the path.

10. An icon for the printer is created in the Printers folder. To configure the printer, see the following exercise.

Exercise 7.3: Using the Add Printer Wizard to Connect to a Network Printer

Exercise 7.3 shows how to manually configure a Windows 95 client to print to a network printer.

1. Start the Add Printer Wizard from the Printers folder.

2. In the Printer Type field, select Network Printer and choose Next.

3. Enter the Universal Naming Convention (UNC) path of the network printer; for example, \\SARAH\HP4.

4. If you will not be using MS-DOS applications to print to this printer, you can select No under Do you print from MS-DOS–based programs?. To have the printer associated with a printer port such as LPT1:, you should select Yes for this option. Choose Next.

5. If you have specified that you will print to this printer using MS-DOS–based applications, you are prompted to select the desired port from the Capture Printer Port dialog box. Choose OK to continue.

6. Choose Next and select the printer manufacturer and model from the Manufacturers and Printers lists.

7. Enter a name for the printer; for example, HP4 in Room 11.

8. If you want to test that you can print properly to the network printer, select Send Test Page. Choose Finish to have Windows 95 begin copying the printer driver files to the hard drive if the latest drivers are not already on the hard drive. If Windows 95 cannot find the files, you are prompted to enter the path to the Windows 95 distribution files.

9. An icon for the network printer is created in the Printers folder. If desired, you may drag a copy of this icon to the desktop to create a shortcut.

Exercise 7.4:   Installing and Enabling Print Services for NetWare

For this exercise, the Windows 95 computer must be able to access a NetWare print server and an MS-DOS computer running the PSERVER utility. Furthermore, the Microsoft Client for NetWare Networks must be installed prior to starting this exercise. Attempting to install both the client and the service at the same time will cause the installation to fail.

Exercise 7.4 demonstrates how to install and enable Microsoft Print Agent for NetWare Networks.

1. From the Start menu, choose Settings, Control Panel, and then double-click on the Network icon. The Network Control Panel Applet appears.

2. Choose Add and select Service from the Select Network Component Type dialog box.

continues

Exercise 7.4: Continued

3. Choose Add and then choose Have Disk.

4. Type the path to the \ADMIN\NETTOOLS\PRTAGENT directory and choose OK.

5. Select Microsoft Print Agent for NetWare Networks and choose OK.

6. Ensure that the NetWare print server and the MS-DOS computer running PSERVER are functioning correctly.

7. From the Printers folder, select the printer on the Windows 95 client to which you will direct the NetWare print queue jobs.

8. Right-click on the Printer icon and select Properties from the context-sensitive menu to display the Properties sheet for the printer.

9. From the Print Server tab, select Enable Microsoft Print Server for NetWare.

10. From the NetWare Servers drop-down list, select the NetWare Server that contains the NetWare print queue.

> You must be logged onto the NetWare server with an account that has access to the NetWare print queue for the previous step to succeed.

11. After a NetWare server is selected, the available print servers appear in the Print Server list. Select the MS-DOS PSERVER from this list.

12. Under Polling, specify the time interval between attempts to obtain print jobs from the NetWare print queue. The default is 30 seconds.

13. Choose OK to start the Microsoft Print Agent for NetWare Networks service.

Review Questions

The following questions will test your knowledge of the information in this chapter. For additional questions, see MCP Endeavor and the Microsoft Roadmap/Assessment Exam on the CD-ROM that accompanies this book.

1. Windows' 95 print subsystem supports ICM. What does ICM stand for?

    A. Integrated Circuit Mesh

    B. Image Color Monitor

    C. Image Color Matching

    D. Independent Color Matching

2. You use Windows NT and know that its printer driver architecture is similar to that of Windows 95. The Windows 95 printer driver architecture calls for a _____ (supplied by Microsoft) that interfaces with machine-specific software.

    A. minidriver

    B. unidriver

    C. Print Manager

    D. Print Spooler

3. For non-PostScript printing, Windows 95 can create an EMF file. An end-user asks why he should keep EMF turned on. You tell him that the major benefit of Enhanced Metafile Spooling is _____.

    A. faster return-to-application time

    B. better control of print queues

    C. better support for color printing

    D. shorter time in the print queue

4. _____ allows a job to be spooled to the print queue even if the printer is currently unavailable.

    A. Print pending

    B. Print holding

    C. Print waiting

    D. Deferred printing

5. You create a help desk document to aid users in understanding how the Windows 95 print subsystem works. In it, you discuss print queues. The _____ is essentially an internal print queue where the print job data is written while the print job is being processed.

    A. Print Manager

    B. Print Monitor

    C. Print Spooler

    D. Print Cache

6. In the same help desk document described in question 5, you draw a diagram of the Windows 95 print subsystem. Which three of the following are Windows 95 print subsystem layers?

    A. Print Transport Interface

    B. Print Router

    C. Print Provider Interface

    D. Print Providers

7. Which of the following procedures can be used to enable a Windows 95 client to submit print jobs to a network printer? Assume the proper permissions have been granted.

    A. Use the Add Printer Wizard to connect to a shared printer on a Windows NT Workstation. The printer share name is NT351WS_2.

    B. Use the Add Printer Wizard to connect to a shared printer on a NetWare print server running the PSERVER utility.

    C. Use Network Neighborhood to view a printer attached to another Windows 95 computer and drag the printer icon to the Windows 95 Desktop.

    D. Select Install from the context-sensitive menu for a printer configured for Point and Print Setup.

8. You run Windows 95 on a network and have printer support enabled so you can print from Windows 95 across the LAN. Windows 95 currently supports _____.

    A. bindery-based NetWare print queues

    B. NDS-based NetWare print queues

    C. both bindery-based and NDS-based NetWare print queues

    D. only Microsoft Network print queues

9. Jamie does not have a printer attached to her computer, but she wants to set up a printer anyway. This way she can print offline. What is one way she can set up a printer under Windows 95 without actually having one installed?

    A. Use the Add Printer Wizard and specify NONE as the printer type.

    B. Install the Generic / Text Only printer driver under the Microsoft choice from the Add Printer Wizard.

    C. Set up to print to FILE: as the port.

    D. None of the above.

10. Wendy is migrating to Windows 95. She asks you what the Printers folder does. You tell her it can perform which of the following three tasks?

A. Install a printer

B. Manage printers

C. Display number of pages printed

D. Set permissions for accessing a printer

11. Windows' 95 EMF feature is used for non-PostScript printing. Why doesn't PostScript printing need EMF? From the following list, select the best answer.

A. Page description language is not supported by Windows 95

B. Page description language rasterizes files for PostScript

C. Windows 95 has internal PostScript drivers at architectural level

D. PostScript printers read only RAW printer data without the need of special commands

12. You send a print job to the printer and you have EMF enabled. At what stage does Windows 95 return control to the application that issued the print job?

A. After the EMF file is created

B. As soon as the GDI receives the print job

C. When the printer receives the print job

D. None of the above

13. Joe has a document that is saved to his hard drive from a network user and he needs to print each time the file is updated. Joe doesn't want to have to open the application associated with the document each time he prints the file. What is one way he can print the file in Windows 95 to meet his criteria?

A. Click on the file and press F12

B. Double-click on the document while holding down the Shift key

C. Use Drag and Drop printing

D. All of the above

14. From Windows 95, you set up a printer on a NetWare network using Point and Print. After you log onto the NetWare server, you can't get Point and Print to work. What could be one of the problems?

A. NetWare does not support Point and Print

B. You are not logged into the NetWare server with Supervisory rights

C. Windows 95 does not have share-level security enabled

D. You are not using NetWare 4.x

15. Judy opens the Registry Editor to examine her printer configuration information. What subkey should she look under for this information?

A. HKEY_LOCAL_MACHINE\System\CurrentControlSet\Control\Print

B. HKEY_CURRENT_USER\System\CurrentControlSet\Control\Print

C. HKEY_USERS\System\CurrentControlSet\Control\Print

D. All of the above

16. The HP JetAdmin Print Server is used to send and administer print jobs to an HP printer. The printer must be connected using an HP JetDirect network interface card. Name two functions from the following list that the HP JetAdmin utility can do.

A. Forward fax documents to mail boxes

B. Filter and sort HP JetDirect network printers on the list

C. Set a description for the printer

D. Route print jobs from the Internet

17. Stephanie sends a print job from her Windows 95 computer to another Windows 95 computer and it doesn't print. The two computers are connected as a peer-to-peer network and have File and Print Sharing for Microsoft Networks enabled. She has share rights to the other printer. What are three possible reasons why she can't print to the shared printer?

    A. The remote computer does not have share-level security enabled

    B. The print job is paused on the remote computer

    C. The printer is off-line

    D. The remote computer is out of disk space

18. You want to use the bidirectional printer communication feature of Windows 95 with a PnP printer device. Choose two items from the following list that you must have to use this feature.

    A. An IEEE 1284-compliant printer cable

    B. A PostScript compatible printer

    C. A printer with a PnP BIOS

    D. An ICM-compliant device

19. You are manning the company help desk phone when you receive a call from a user running Windows 95. He wants to know where his print jobs are spooled on his computer when he sends a print job. Which one of the following is correct?

    A. C:\WINDOWS\PRINTERS\SPOOL

    B. C:\SPOOL\PRINTERS

    C. C:\WINDOWS\SYSTEM\SPOOL\PRINTERS

    D. C:\WINDOWS\SPOOL\PRINTERS

20. Vanessa is configuring a printer under Windows 95. On the Properties sheet for the printer, she clicks on the Graphics tab. She isn't sure what the Dithering option is used for. You tell her which of the following?

A. It specifies the DPI of the printer

B. It's used to specify the lightness or darkness of the print job

C. It specifies how the colors blend together for a color printer

D. All of the above

Review Answers

1. C	6. B C D	11. B	16. B C
2. B	7. A C D	12. B	17. B C D
3. A	8. A	13. C	18. A C
4. D	9. C	14. B	19. D
5. C	10. A B D	15. A	20. C

Test Yourself

Stop! Before reading this chapter, test yourself to determine how much study time you will need to devote to this section.

1. Jennifer runs an MS-DOS–based application under Windows 95. She wants to take advantage of Windows' 95 32-bit protected-mode driver support, preemptive multitasking, and increased conventional memory. Which mode should Jennifer try to run her DOS application in to use these features?

2. You are working at a help desk when you receive a call from a user. He says he is having difficulty running an MS-DOS application in a DOS virtual machine (VM). You can't give him specific reasons for why his application isn't running, but you can give him some general reasons why a DOS application may not run properly under Windows 95. What are two reasons why a DOS application cannot run in a VM?

3. You're conducting a training session teaching other users how to run applications under Windows 95. You're asked to describe the way Windows 95 runs MS-DOS applications. What are the three ways MS-DOS applications can run under Windows 95?

4. Blake is migrating from Windows 3.1 to Windows 95. He wants to run MS-DOS applications in DOS Mode under Windows 95. What are two disadvantages to running applications in DOS Mode?

5. Taylor receives a General Protection Fault (GPF) when running a 32-bit application under Windows 95. She thought Windows 95 was exempt from having these. You explain to her that 32-bit applications do have GPFs, but they differ from 16-bit and DOS-based applications because they do not offend other programs when you terminate them. Why is this?

6. A user says that a 16-bit application she is running under Windows 95 hangs. She doesn't know what to do to remedy the situation. What are the steps she needs to take to return the system to normal operations?

Answers

1. MS-DOS virtual machine mode. See "MS-DOS Virtual Machine."

2. Possible answers include the following: the application requires direct access to the hardware; the application has incompatible memory requirements; the application's installation program checks to see if Windows is running and will not continue if Windows is detected; and the application has video problems. See "Predict Potential Problems When Configuring 16-bit Windows Applications."

3. In an MS-DOS VM, in MS-DOS mode after shutting down the Windows 95 GUI, and in MS-DOS mode outside of Windows 95 using parameters that are customized for the application. See "MS-DOS Applications."

4. Possible answers include the following: Windows 95 unloads itself and the computer runs in a single-tasking MS-DOS environment; all protected-mode support and drivers are removed; and you may need to customize AUTOEXEC.BAT and CONFIG.SYS for each application. See "Determine When to Run Applications in MS-DOS Mode."

5. 32-bit applications reside in their own separate address space and each has a separate message queue. See "General Protection Faults."

6. Perform a local reboot by pressing Ctrl+Alt+Delete once. In the Close Program dialog box, select the offending process, and click on the End Task button. See "What to Do When Application Stops Responding to the System."

C h a p t e r

Running Applications

8

This chapter will help you prepare for the exam by covering the following objectives:

Test Objectives

▶ Configure Windows 95 to run MS-DOS–based applications

▶ Predict potential problems when configuring 16-bit Windows-based applications

▶ Distinguish between MS-DOS Mode and the standard method for running MS-DOS–based applications

▶ Determine when an application should be run in MS-DOS Mode

▶ Resolve General Protection Faults (GPFs)

▶ Determine the appropriate course of action when the application stops responding to the system

The key function of any operating system is to provide the framework within which applications can be run to perform specific tasks. The measure of an operating system is the speed and efficiency with which it performs the tasks that are required of it by an application. Windows 95 provides significant increases in performance over Windows 3.*x* for most application types, due to the 32-bit Windows 95 architecture and the use of preemptive multitasking.

This chapter discusses the issues relating to the use of applications under Windows 95. The topics include the following:

- ► Windows 95 application support architecture

- ► 16-bit Windows applications

- ► MS-DOS applications

- ► 32-bit Windows applications

- ► Application properties and interaction

- ► Troubleshooting problems with applications

Windows 95 Application Support Architecture

Windows 95 is capable of running three types of applications:

- ► MS-DOS 16-bit applications

- ► Windows 3.1 16-bit applications (also known as WIN16 applications)

- ► 32-bit Windows applications (also known as WIN32 applications; includes most Windows NT software)

Windows 95 can run these varying applications because of a number of architectural design factors, the most important being the idea of virtual machines. In a single-tasking, single-threaded environment like MS-DOS, in which only one application at a time is requesting the operating system's resources, managing those resources is much easier. In an environment such as Windows 95, which is intended to manage multiple applications that might be operating simultaneously, a much greater need for careful management of the system's resources exists, because the computer remains primarily a single-task machine (one processor equals one task at a time, no matter how fast it performs those tasks). In this single-task environment, two processes requesting the use of a device at the exact same moment would be very problematic. Clearly, a procedure in place to arbitrate such requests is necessary.

Windows 95 implements this procedure through virtual machines (VMs). A *virtual machine* is designed so that every application executed in the Windows 95 environment is executed from within a specialized container created specifically for that application (or type of application). This container is intended as much as possible to keep applications separate from each other, thus minimizing the chance that they might not work together. Because some applications (MS-DOS applications) were not designed to function in a multitasking environment, the operating system must deceive them into thinking that they are the only process running on the computer (or they would fail to operate properly).

This deception requires the operating system to simulate all devices and resources that would be present if the system were running under MS-DOS only. This process is called the *virtualization of hardware devices*. Thus, what looks to an MS-DOS application like exclusive access to the computer's devices is in fact hardware access that is being shared with all other running processes of the operating system—but in a way that a legacy application can understand. To varying degrees, this is done for all types of applications.

A number of components in Windows 95 are responsible for managing the elements needed to create virtual machines. They include the following:

▶ Memory

▶ Processor modes

▶ Multitasking

▶ Multithreading

▶ Hardware virtualization

▶ Internal messaging

Chapters 2, "Architecture and Memory," and 3, "Customizing and Configuring Windows 95," introduced you to some of these elements. The following sections describe how Windows 95 uses these elements to run DOS and Windows applications.

Memory

One of the key elements to successfully creating VMs lies in creating virtualized memory areas where given applications can function as they expect to under their own environment (if Windows 95 is not their native environment). A space within the total memory available to Windows 95 (which includes both RAM and the paging file) is created and reserved for the operations of that application. One of the main challenges to operating in such a way is ensuring that other applications do not attempt to write or read data from another application's memory space inappropriately, because this can cause serious integrity problems, which are detailed in the "Troubleshooting Problems with Applications" section of this chapter.

Processor Modes

Beginning with the Intel 386 processor, processors have been designed with a number of features to meet the needs of multitasking environments. The most important of these is the capability to switch between real mode (the mode in which MS-DOS operates) and protected mode. Protected mode has the capability to regulate the behavior of multitasking processes in two ways: through memory address protection and through graduated levels of processor privilege.

Memory address protection allows the processor to track which memory areas have been allocated to which processes. If an application attempts to access memory other than that allocated to it, the processor interprets this as an error and traps it (see the section "General Protection Faults" later in this chapter).

The second protection scheme consists of having four different levels of privilege or rings at which applications can operate. Each ring, numbered from 3 to 0, has a higher level of privilege with the operating system and so can access a broader set of processor functions. Ring 0 privilege allows complete control of the processor. To simplify operation, Windows 95 uses only Ring 3 and Ring 0. Typically, applications run at Ring 3, and operating system components run at Ring 0. This is done to limit the damage a misbehaving application can do to the operating system (and other applications) because, at Ring 3, applications have very little access to critical system functions.

Multitasking

Another important aspect of creating VMs is the creation of virtualized access to the processor. Because the processor can process only one request at a time, no matter how fast it is, in a multi-application environment the processor must switch back and forth between requests from different processes. If this switching is done quickly enough, it creates the illusion that these processes are occurring simultaneously. The operating system queues all requests from running processes and issues them a priority, which can be reevaluated as time passes and other events occur in the computer. The processor always takes the highest-priority request first.

Two types of multitasking are used in Windows 95, depending on the type of application involved: preemptive multitasking and cooperative multitasking. *Preemptive multitasking* involves dividing the processor's capacity into time slices that are allocated equally among processes requiring them. Thus, one application processes for *x* number of milliseconds; then it is suspended, and another application processes for the same amount of time, and so on.

Cooperative multitasking is different in that it allows a given process to engage the processor until it voluntarily cedes its control to another process. The disadvantage of this type of multitasking is that a misbehaving application can monopolize the processor's time and effectively stop other processes from executing.

Multithreading

Windows 95 is an operating system. That is, an application designed to take advantage of multithreading is able to submit multiple independent requests to the processor simultaneously. Thus the application can have two separate execution processes multitasked by the processor, creating the impression that the application is itself performing two tasks simultaneously. For example, Word can repaginate a document and allow the user to type at the same time. All multitasking is done at a thread level, with applications submitting either single or multiple threads, depending on the application type.

Hardware Virtualization

Another important component in the creation of VMs is hardware virtualization. Especially in the case of legacy MS-DOS and (to a lesser extent) Windows 3.1 applications, simulating the hardware environment in which the application is accustomed to running is necessary. It must seem that all devices are available when needed. This is implemented through software drivers called *Virtual Device Drivers* (VxDs), which are responsible for arbitrating requests (often simultaneous) from running processes and queuing them so they do not conflict with each other or cause the device in question to fail because it is trying to do two things at once.

Internal Messaging

A message is generated each time a key is pressed or the mouse is clicked, effectively asking an application to do something. In a single-tasking environment, there is no question which application the keyboard or mouse input is intended for. In a multitasking environment, a more complex system of determination and delivery is required. Because you can have multiple applications on-screen simultaneously, where the mouse is clicked or what window is active when a key is pressed determines which application the message is intended for. After the intended application is targeted, the message is placed in the appropriate message queue to be processed.

16-Bit Windows Applications

16-bit Windows applications generally are those created for Windows 3.1. You need to remember the following when dealing with WIN16 applications:

▶ Windows applications (including WIN32 applications) exist in the System Virtual Machine, which is a special VM designed to provide one hardware virtualization layer for all Windows software.

▶ Within this VM, WIN16 applications share a common address space (this is necessary to maintain backward compatibility with the way Windows 3.1 applications are designed to interact).

▶ WIN16 applications operate on a cooperative multitasking basis (this also is due to the way applications were designed for Windows 3.1, which did not support preemptive multitasking).

▶ A single message queue is used for all WIN16 applications.

▶ All WIN16 applications are single-threaded, because Windows 3.1 does not support multithreading.

▶ WIN16 applications generally load themselves into the virtualized space between 3 GB and 4 GB, and some use a space between 0 and 4 MB to be able to share data with other WIN16 applications.

▶ WIN16 applications do not access the Registry because they are designed to use INI files for their stored settings. However, Windows 95 can migrate certain settings from the INI files into the Registry. The WIN16 applications can still continue to access and modify the INI files, and these modifications can then be migrated to the Registry.

▶ WIN16 applications are not designed to recognize or use LFNs because LFNs are not implemented in Windows 3.1.

▶ Whereas under Windows 3.1 system resource stacks are 64 KB, these have been converted to 32-bit stacks in Windows 95, dramatically decreasing the likelihood of running out of system resources.

Configuring 16-Bit Windows Applications

When Windows 95 is installed, it automatically migrates the settings for existing WIN16 applications from their native INI files into the Registry. In the event that an application subsequently modifies the INI file again (because a Windows 3.1 application does not know how to write the Registry directly), Windows 95 scans these files at every boot and migrates changes into the Registry as well. In the case of proprietary INI files, these files generally are left untouched, because Windows 95 likely will not recognize the settings they contain.

Predict Potential Problems When Configuring 16-Bit Windows Applications

As you work with Windows 95, you need to aware of some of the problems inherent with running WIN16 applications under Windows 95 and be able to predict when problems may arise. The majority of problems you run into are associated with the way WIN16 applications are written to run on the 16-bit Windows operating system (such as Window 3.11 for Workgroups), which does not support multithreading or the Registry. Typically, WIN16 applications will run under Windows 95 without any modification. Certain software, however, is known to need specific configuration parameters to run under Windows 95. These software packages (and the correct parameters) are listed in the APPS.INF file in the \WINDOWS\INF directory (which is hidden by default).

The following are some things to keep in mind to predict potential problems when configuring and using WIN16 applications under Windows 95:

> ▶ Poorly written WIN16 applications may interfere with other WIN16 applications you are running. This can cause the applications (or just one application) to hang, or cause Windows 95 to suspend. There's not much you can do to avert this problem except upgrade your applications to 32-bit versions of the applications (if they exist), or run the offending application by itself under Windows 95.

▶ Because WIN16 applications share the same address space in the System VM, other WIN16 applications may have difficulty in protecting themselves from a misbehaving WIN16 application. One application, for example, may attempt to write over data that does not belong to it. When this happens, the Windows 95 system traps the failure to try to prevent the program from damaging the other programs. This results in a GPF and requires you to terminate the offending application.

▶ Having a single message queue can become an issue if one application stops responding and thus is not checking the message queue. Because all applications cede control voluntarily in a cooperative multitasking scenario, an application that has stopped responding will not relinquish control and therefore will not allow other WIN16 applications to check the message queue and respond to those messages. All WIN16 applications then appear to be hung.

▶ WIN16 applications do not support long file names. Because of this, you may experience some confusion between files when sharing files between WIN16 and WIN32 applications. This is a result of WIN16 applications truncating the file names to 8.3 file names. One way around this is to standardize on short file names (8.3 file names) until all your applications are WIN32 applications.

▶ If you run two or more WIN16 applications at the same time, you may notice a decline in available resources until you close all WIN16 applications. This is because some WIN16 applications may use resources in Windows 95 that the system (Windows 95) may not be aware of, including resources shared by other WIN16 applications. What this results in is resources (such as RAM and GDI memory) not being released by the 16-bit application until all 16-bit applications are closed.

You may notice that even after closing all WIN16 and WIN32 applications, not all your resources are returned. This is due to Windows' 95 caching of frequently shared resources. Some of these shared resources do become available if resources become critically low. However, you often need to shut down and restart Windows 95 to recapture all cached resources.

MS-DOS Applications

MS-DOS applications are 16-bit applications designed to work with MS-DOS version 6.*x* or earlier. As stated previously, because these applications have no understanding of multitasking environments, simulating an MS-DOS environment is necessary for them to function properly. Windows 95 includes a number of improvements in handling MS-DOS applications:

▶ The capability to run in a window in most cases

▶ Better access to system resources due to the new 32-bit structure of the system resource stacks

▶ Improved support for sound devices

▶ Improved memory protection schemes that allow you to isolate the MS-DOS system area to prevent its corruption by misbehaving MS-DOS programs

▶ Support for scaleable True Type fonts in MS-DOS windows

▶ The capability to customize individual MS-DOS VMs with environment variables run from a batch file

The following additional information should be noted when using MS-DOS applications in Windows 95:

▶ Each MS-DOS application that is executed is assigned its own VM, with separate virtualized device access and addressable memory space.

▶ The memory space created for an MS-DOS application mirrors that of a stand-alone DOS environment, with 640 KB of conventional memory, 384 KB of upper memory, and whatever extended or expanded memory is specified in the configuration settings of the MS-DOS session.

▶ Each MS-DOS application run under Windows 95 can execute only one thread at a time because MS-DOS does not support multithreading.

> MS-DOS applications cannot actually create threads of execution themselves. They generate MS-DOS hardware interrupts, which are intercepted by Windows 95 and translated into logical requests for executing a particular function.

▶ Each MS-DOS application has its own separate message queue to receive keyboard and mouse input.

▶ The APPS.INF file also contains configuration parameters for MS-DOS applications that are known to require them.

MS-DOS applications can be run in one of three modes:

▶ In an MS-DOS VM

▶ In MS-DOS mode after shutting down the Windows 95 GUI

▶ In MS-DOS mode outside of Windows 95 using parameters that have been customized for the application

By default, if Windows 95 detects that the application should be run in MS-DOS Mode, it shuts down the Windows 95 GUI and runs the application in an environment similar to that if Command Prompt Only were selected from the Boot Menu. However, the options on the shortcut Properties sheet for the MS-DOS application can be set to force the application to always run in MS-DOS Mode or in a customized MS-DOS Mode, if required.

If the application does not require or is not configured to use MS-DOS Mode, then it will run in an MS-DOS VM.

There are several parameters that can be configured to determine how an application runs in each of the preceding modes. These parameters are set through the Properties sheet of the shortcut for the application and are described in the following sections.

MS-DOS Virtual Machine

 MS-DOS VM mode should be used whenever possible because the application can then take advantage of 32-bit protected-mode driver support, preemptive multitasking, increased conventional memory, and other Windows 95 enhancements. By default, all MS-DOS applications are set to run in an MS-DOS VM, whether they are executed by double-clicking on the application from the Explorer or by typing the name of the file from a DOS prompt within Windows 95. However, if Windows 95 detects that the application must have exclusive use of the system resources and must run in MS-DOS mode, you are prompted to have Windows 95 automatically shut down the system and run the application in MS-DOS mode. Most applications should be able to function without incident in a VM. If an application functions, but not as well as it should, you can alter the configuration of the MS-DOS environment for that application.

Numerous settings can be modified to facilitate the operation of MS-DOS programs. These settings are grouped into the following tabs on the Properties sheet for the MS-DOS application:

- ▶ Program tab

- ▶ Font tab

- ▶ Memory tab

- ▶ Screen tab

- ▶ Misc tab

Program Tab

The Program tab includes settings defining the location of files used to run the application as well as some other settings. The Advanced button of the Program tab is used to force the application to run in MS-DOS mode, as is explained in the later section "MS-DOS Mode."

Figure 8.1 displays the various parameters of the Program tab.

Figure 8.1

The Program tab of the MS-DOS Properties sheet.

The following list describes the parameters of the Program tab:

- ▶ **Cmd Line.** The path and file name of the MS-DOS program in question. Including command-line parameters is permitted.

- ▶ **Working.** Indicates where data files should be stored if they are not in the directory in which the program resides.

- ▶ **Batch File.** The name of a batch file that runs and loads any TSRs or specific environment variables that the program needs. For example, you can specify DOSKEY to run before opening up a command prompt.

- ▶ **Shortcut Key.** The key combination that can be used to run the program.

Verify that the key combination you select is not in use by any other application, because that application will no longer be able to respond to that combination of keys after it is specified.

- ▶ **Run.** Indicates whether to run the program in a normal window, minimized, or maximized.

- ▶ **Close on Exit.** If checked, the DOS VM window closes automatically when the application finishes processing.

Font Tab

The parameters on this tab enable you to specify whether you want to use True Type fonts, bitmap fonts, or both to display characters in the MS-DOS session. You also can select from various font sizes and preview them before making a final selection. Figure 8.2 shows an example of the Font tab.

Figure 8.2

The Font tab of the MS-DOS Properties sheet.

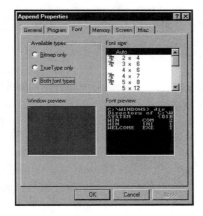

Memory Tab

You can use the Memory tab to specify what type and quantity of memory the program needs access to in order to function. The four supported types are as follows:

- ▶ Conventional

- ▶ Expanded (EMS)

- ▶ Extended (XMS)

- ▶ DOS protected mode (DPMI)

By default, Windows 95 automatically allocates the memory the application needs when the application first requests it during operation, but some applications function better if a fixed amount is allocated to them from the beginning.

The Initial Environment setting is used to specify additional environment memory for variables and other MS-DOS settings.

When you have many named variables being set within the AUTOEXEC.BAT file, the default environment memory can be used up rapidly. The lack of sufficient environment memory can prevent MS-DOS applications from running properly. In a real-world example, this lack of sufficient environment memory prevented the Microsoft System Management Server RUNSMS.BAT file from executing. Using the Memory tab settings of the MS-DOS Properties sheet can help correct these problems.

As previously stated, you can use the Protected check box to provide a higher level of security for the MS-DOS memory of this program by preventing it from being paged to disk.

Using the Protected check box to provide greater security can have a detrimental effect on overall system performance. However, if you include a statement in the CONFIG.SYS file that loads EMM386.EXE with the noems parameter, DOS-protected mode memory cannot be provided. Use the ram parameter when loading EMM386.EXE in CONFIG.SYS or use the x=mmmm-nnnn statement to allocate enough space in the upper memory area for Windows 95 to create an EMS page frame. See the *Windows 95 Resource Kit* for more details.

Figure 8.3 shows an example of the Memory tab for an MS-DOS application.

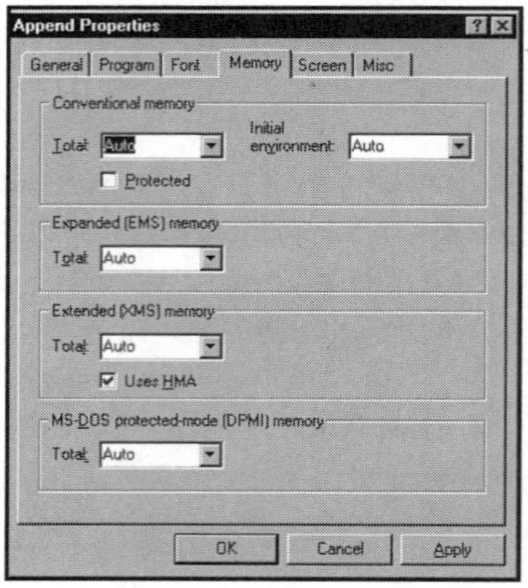

Figure 8.3

The Memory tab of the MS-DOS Properties sheet.

Screen Tab

The Screen tab contains settings to control how the application is displayed and how it uses video memory. Figure 8.4 shows an example of the Screen tab.

Figure 8.4

The Screen tab of the MS-DOS Properties sheet.

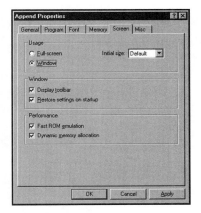

The settings of the Screen tab include the following:

▶ **Usage.** Specifies in which video mode the program initially appears. The choices are Full-Screen (equivalent to what the program would look like in MS-DOS) or Window (a graphical mode simulation), which coexists with other windowed applications. The initial width and height (in characters) also can be specified using the Initial Size field.

▶ **Display Toolbar.** Used to specify whether Windows 95 will display a toolbar at the top of a windowed MS-DOS session. The toolbar contains Cut, Paste, and Full-Screen buttons, among others.

▶ **Restore Settings on Startup.** When selected, restores all window settings (such as size, position, and so on) to what they were when the MS-DOS program was exited after the last time it was run. If this check box is not selected, the window uses the default MS-DOS window positioning settings.

▶ **Fast ROM Emulation.** Allows screen updates to be accelerated by simulating video ROM drivers in protected mode. If display problems occur, this option should be disabled.

▶ **Dynamic Memory Allocation.** Involves reserving video memory for the application when it switches between video and text mode, in order to speed up this operation.

Misc Tab

The Misc tab contains other miscellaneous uncategorized settings for the application. Figure 8.5 shows a sample Misc tab for an MS-DOS application shortcut.

Figure 8.5

The Misc tab of the MS-DOS Properties sheet.

The following list describes the parameters of the Misc tab:

▶ **Allow Screen Saver Box.** If selected, prevents any system screen saver from executing while the application is in the foreground. This is useful for applications that are easily disrupted or have a known problem with screen saver activity.

▶ **Always Suspend.** If selected, the application ceases execution when not in the foreground.

▶ **Idle Sensitivity.** This slide bar allows control of the amount of time the operating system waits before declaring the program to be inactive and suspending it.

▶ **Quick Edit.** If selected, enables the user to highlight text in an MS-DOS window with the mouse. This feature should be disabled for applications that have their own DOS-based mouse support.

- ▶ **Exclusive Mode.** If selected, contains the mouse within the borders of the MS-DOS window, to enforce compatibility with programs that cannot track the mouse properly when the mouse leaves the MS-DOS window.

- ▶ **Warn If Still Active.** If selected, warns users of potential data loss when they attempt to close an MS-DOS window without exiting the application.

- ▶ **Fast Pasting.** Should be disabled if the application in question does not handle pasting from the Windows 95 Clipboard.

- ▶ **Windows Shortcut Keys.** Each check box allows or disallows use of a Windows shortcut key combination within an application. This is useful if an application has a number of shortcut keys that overlap with those of Windows 95.

Determine When to Run Applications in MS-DOS Mode

Some MS-DOS applications are unable to run in an MS-DOS VM for one of several reasons:

- ▶ The application requires direct access to the hardware, which is not permitted in a multitasking environment because of potential device conflicts (this is the most common reason).

- ▶ The application has incompatible memory requirements.

- ▶ The application's install program, for compatibility reasons, checks to see whether Windows is running and will not continue if Windows is detected.

- ▶ The application has video problems (usually with MS-DOS games).

If any of these situations applies to the application in question, you may have to run the application in MS-DOS mode.

In MS-DOS mode, Windows 95 unloads itself from memory, leaving the computer in a single-tasking MS-DOS type of environment. All protected-mode support and drivers are removed, permitting the application to use only the CONFIG.SYS and AUTOEXEC.BAT parameters that were in effect at boot time before Windows 95 loaded. If the application needs a more particular configuration than that provided by default in the normal CONFIG.SYS and AUTOEXEC.BAT, you can create a customized MS-DOS environment for each application.

Customized MS-DOS Mode

If the application in question requires specific configuration parameters that differ significantly from those needed by most MS-DOS applications, you can create a customized CONFIG.SYS and AUTOEXEC.BAT that will be swapped with the standard versions of these files when you double-click on the application. For the settings in these customized files to take effect, Windows 95 must reboot the computer.

When Windows 95 restarts the computer, it uses the customized configuration files and inserts a special command into the CONFIG.SYS. The command reads DOS=SINGLE and indicates that this CONFIG.SYS and AUTOEXEC.BAT are to be used only once and that the system should return to the normal versions of these files when this application terminates.

You need to remember that for Windows 95 to remove this parameter from the CONFIG.SYS and to allow Windows 95 to reboot properly, the application must be exited in the normal fashion. If the application hangs, or the computer is turned off without exiting, the parameter will not be removed, and the system will boot back into the MS-DOS application directly. To remedy this problem, restart the application and exit properly, or press F8 during the boot process and choose to go to a command prompt only, and then manually edit the CONFIG.SYS to remove the DOS=SINGLE parameter.

32-Bit Windows Applications

Windows 95 is designed to support and best interact with 32-bit applications specifically designed for Windows 95 or for Windows NT. These applications are best suited to take advantage of the new architectural design features of Windows 95. These design features include the following:

▶ The capability to take advantage of Windows' 95 flat 32-bit, 4-GB memory address space (WIN32 applications typically load into the 4-MB to 2-GB range of memory)

▶ The capability to pass more information in a single 32-bit programming call than is possible with a single 16-bit programming call, thus increasing processing performance

▶ The capability to submit multiple simultaneous threads for processing, allowing greater user productivity within the 32-bit application because the user does not need to wait for one task to finish to start another

▶ The capability to take advantage of Windows' 95 preemptive multitasking, which is more efficient and runs more smoothly than Windows' 3.1 cooperative multitasking

▶ More comprehensive protection from other applications because each WIN32 application is assigned its own separate address space that is not visible to other applications

▶ A separate message queue for each thread in a WIN32 application, which prevents other applications from interfering with the receipt or processing of system messages

▶ The capability to use the Registry to store all application settings on a generic or per-user basis

▶ The capability of the application to uninstall itself more easily than previous application types, because all changes to the Registry can be tracked and rolled back in the case of uninstallation

WIN32 API Set in Windows 95 versus Windows NT

An *Application Programming Interface* (API) is a library of preprogrammed functions upon which application developers can call when they require an operation to be performed and do not want to develop the programming code for the operation from scratch (for example, drawing a box on the screen with a message in it). To speed up development and to enhance the consistency of the Windows 95 look and feel by having developers use the same programming routines to do the same things, Microsoft provides various API sets. Many of the 32-bit functions that are used both internally by the Windows 95 operating system and by third-party developers are contained in an API set called the WIN32 API.

Although a form of this WIN32 API set is available for Windows 3.1 (called WIN32s), the version standard to Windows 95 has these additional features:

- ▶ Multithreading

- ▶ The capability to create Bézier curves mathematically

- ▶ The use of paths to create outlines, shapes, and filled areas

- ▶ The capability to generate Enhanced Metafiles, a new page description format used primarily for printing

Windows NT also uses a WIN32 API set, but one that is slightly different from that of Windows 95 in that it supports NT-specific features, such as the following:

- ▶ Security functions

- ▶ Logging system events

- ▶ Unicode (multilanguage support)

- ▶ Functions specific to the Windows NT Registry

Finally, some features are new to Windows 95 and thus are supported in the Windows 95 WIN32 API but not in that of Windows NT (although they are expected to be implemented in the next release of Windows NT). These features are discussed elsewhere in this book. Briefly, they are as follows:

- ▶ Image Color Matching support

- ▶ Enhanced modem support features (primarily TAPI)

- ▶ User interface-related functions (right-clicking, the Taskbar, and so on)

- ▶ Plug and Play support

- ▶ Advanced Power Management

- ▶ Video for Windows support

Configuring 32-Bit Applications

Almost any configuration that needs to be done on 32-bit applications can be done from within the application or from its Properties sheet. As previously stated, all settings for WIN32 applications are stored in the Registry, usually under the key HKEY_LOCAL_MACHINE\SOFTWARE.

In rare instances, these settings can become corrupted due to the following circumstances:

- ▶ Corruption of the actual Registry file SYSTEM.DAT

- ▶ Aborted application installations, which only partially create the requisite Registry entries

- ▶ Repeated installation/uninstallation

In these instances, editing the settings manually in the Registry may be necessary.

Attempt to edit the Registry only if you know exactly which setting to modify in the SOFTWARE subkey. Improper modification of parameters in the Registry can seriously damage the operating system.

Application Properties and Interaction

For an exercise testing this information, see end of chapter.

The following steps show how the properties of different types of applications are reflected in the operating system's behavior. Verify that the System Monitor component is installed for the purposes of the exercise. As well, make certain no applications other than the System Monitor are running, unless otherwise directed during the steps. Results during these steps may vary based on timing, especially where threads are concerned.

These same steps appear as Exercise 8.2, "Configuring Application Properties," later in this chapter.

1. From the Start menu, choose Programs, Accessories, System Tools, System Monitor. The System Monitor window appears, typically showing Processor Usage by default.

2. Choose View, Numeric Charts. The display changes from graphical to numeric.

3. Choose Edit, Remove Item. A list of all currently tracked system items appears.

4. Select all items in the list and choose OK to remove them. The items are removed, and you are returned to a blank System Monitor window.

5. Choose Edit, Add Item. The Add Item dialog box appears.

6. From the Kernel category, hold down the Ctrl key and select Threads and Virtual Machines as the items to be tracked. Choose OK. You return to the System Monitor window, showing the number of currently active threads and VMs (note these numbers—they include threads and VMs run by the operating system itself).

7. From the Start menu, choose Run and open the 16-bit Notepad.exe program. A Notepad window appears (the number of threads should increase by 1, and the number of VMs should stay constant).

8. Minimize Notepad and, from the Start menu, open an Explorer window (a 32-bit program). An Explorer window appears (note that the number of threads jumps by 2 or 3, and the number of VMs again remains the same).

9. From the Start menu, choose Programs, MS-DOS Prompt. An MS-DOS window appears (note that the number of threads jumps by 2, and the number of VMs jumps by 1).

10. Minimize the MS-DOS window and open another MS-DOS Prompt. A second MS-DOS window appears (note that the number of threads again jumps by 2, and the number of VMs jumps by 1).

11. Close all applications except System Monitor. Eventually, the number of threads and VMs should return to their original values.

The important points to note about the preceding steps are the following:

▶ All WIN16 and WIN32 applications reside in the System VM, which is always active from the time Windows 95 boots (that is why the VM count started at 1), but each MS-DOS session requires its own VM (thus, as you opened MS-DOS sessions, the VM count increased).

▶ When a WIN16 application (Notepad) is started, it creates a single thread, whereas a WIN32 application (Explorer in this example) can create several threads.

▶ MS-DOS sessions generate only one thread.

Although these steps show that opening an MS-DOS session actually creates two threads, remember that the application itself uses only one, whereas the other thread is used by associated processes.

Thunking

Windows 95 is divided into two types of core components: those implemented with 16-bit code, and those implemented with 32-bit code. The decision of how to implement each core component was based on issues of performance and compatibility. In other words, if the component's main function was to support backward compatibility with WIN16 applications (the user interface, for example), the component was implemented with 16-bit code. If the main function or objective of the component was to enhance performance (the file system), the component was implemented in 32-bit code.

This creates the problem of communication between the different components, however, because 16-bit applications understand only 16-bit code, and 32-bit applications understand only 32-bit code. To facilitate communication between 16-bit applications that need access to 32-bit components and vice versa, thunking was developed. *Thunking* is the process of translating a 16-bit API call into a 32-bit API call (called *thunking up*) or vice versa (called *thunking down*).

Troubleshooting Problems with Applications

Although applications should normally run without interruption, situations do arise where, due to either programming errors or incompatibilities, applications cease to function properly. The two main problems that occur with applications are GPFs and application hangs.

General Protection Faults

 A *General Protection Fault* (GPF) typically is caused by an application that attempts to violate system integrity in one of a number of ways:

▶ By making a request to read or write to a memory address space owned by another application

▶ By attempting to access the system hardware directly

▶ By attempting to interact with a failing hardware driver (drivers operate at Ring 0 and so can seriously impact the operating system)

The GPF is generated when the operating system shuts down an offending application to prevent a system integrity violation. How the offending application is specifically handled is dependent on its application type.

Because MS-DOS applications reside in their own VM and have their own message queue, if they cause a GPF, a message is displayed, and the application is simply terminated without impacting the rest of the operating system.

In the case of WIN16 applications, the procedure is somewhat more complex. Because WIN16 applications share both a common address space and a common message queue, when one application creates a GPF, all others are suspended until the offending application is terminated. After this is done, the remaining applications resume processing.

Finally, with 32-bit applications, the procedure is quite straightforward. Because 32-bit applications exist in their own separate address space, and each has a separate message queue, a GPF in one 32-bit application in no way impacts any other 16- or 32-bit programs. The offending program is simply terminated.

What to Do When an Application Stops Responding to the System

An application is said to be "hung" when it is running but is not responding to messages from the operating system. Much improved support exists in Windows 95 for a local reboot of the application in question, which permits the application to be terminated without impacting other currently running processes. A local reboot is performed by pressing Ctrl+Alt+Delete once, which brings up a Close Program dialog box. Listed in this dialog box are all currently running tasks (including system processes not otherwise listed on the Taskbar). You must then select a process (next to the process name, "Not Responding" usually is indicated in brackets) and click on the End Task button. The operating system then attempts to terminate the process (which might take several seconds). Depending on the reason that the application is hung, you also might be presented with the option to wait a few seconds for the application to respond, and then to terminate the application if no response is received.

The following sections describe some considerations you should make when an application hangs, based on the application type:

▶ MS-DOS

▶ Windows 16-bit Subsystem (WIN16)

▶ Windows 32-bit Subsystem (WIN32)

MS-DOS Application

A normal local reboot as described previously should work on an MS-DOS session because the MS-DOS application exists in its own VM and has its own message queue—a hung MS-DOS session does not impact the operation of any other process.

> An MS-DOS session also can be terminated from the Properties sheet of the session if the session is in a window.

16-Bit Windows Application

As stated earlier, because WIN16 applications share a common memory address space and a common message queue, if a WIN16 process hangs while in the foreground, all other WIN16 processes cease to receive messages from the operating system and also appear hung.

This is due to a flag that is set for WIN16 processes, known as the *WIN16 mutex* (Mutually Exclusive). Because 16-bit code is considered non-reentrant (it cannot be used by more than one process at a time), a system must be in place to ensure that no two processes attempt to use the same piece of 16-bit code simultaneously. Under Windows 95, this is done by enforcing the rule that only the process that currently owns the rights to the WIN16 mutex is able to make requests to 16-bit API functions. When the given process is finished using the 16-bit code, it hands the WIN16 mutex to the next process.

If an application hangs while it owns the WIN16 mutex, no other application can access 16-bit API functions. Thus, all 16-bit applications appear to be hung. In addition, any 32-bit application that requires the use, through thunking, of a 16-bit API function (such as writing to the screen) also appears to be hung. The application is still running but cannot make any updates to the screen, and thus appears to be inactive or unresponsive.

To remedy this situation, the 16-bit application that currently holds the WIN16 mutex must be locally rebooted through the means described previously. After this is done, the WIN16 mutex should be reset and available for use by other processes.

32-Bit Windows Application

Just testing to see whether you have been paying attention! A 32-bit application will not hang the system, because it will be preemptively multitasked. In other words, control will be taken away from a misbehaving WIN32 application even if does not want to relinquish control.

Running Windows 95 Applications: Notepad and WordPad

Two readily available applications you can run under Windows 95 are Notepad and WordPad. These applications are included with Windows 95 and are installed when you install Windows 95. Both of these applications are easy to use and come in handy at times. The following sections discuss Notepad and WordPad.

Using Notepad

Notepad is a text editor and is an upgrade to the Notepad application bundled with previous versions of Windows. One of Notepad's strengths is its capability to read and create ASCII text files.

This is important when you must generate files in plain ASCII without formatting included, such as when creating or modifying a DOS batch file or other system file. You can, for example, open and modify CONFIG.SYS and AUTOEXEC.BAT in Notepad as long as you use the original names and extensions when you save them. When you use Notepad to do these edits, you are assured that a character or set of characters is not added to the file that the system cannot understand, such as a piece of text that has boldface characterization applied to it.

Another reason to use Notepad is that it saves files in text format (TXT), which most applications can read; most word processors, spreadsheet programs, databases, and other applications can read text files. As a way to extend the Windows 95 Clipboard feature, you can use Notepad to store text you want to transfer from one application to another.

You also can use Notepad to view (but not edit) the Windows 95 Registry file. This is handy when you want to search for a text string in the Registry and the Registry Find command cannot locate the specific string. Just open the Registry as a text file, open the file in Notepad, and run a search (by choosing Search, Find) for the specific information. When you locate the string in the text file, switch to the Registry Editor and search for the Registry subkey under which the string is listed.

The following is an overview of Notepad's editing features:

▶ You can turn on the wrap text feature by choosing Edit, Word Wrap. You must activate this feature each time you open a text file if you want the text to wrap.

▶ You can modify the size of the margins by choosing File, Page Setup. In the Page Setup dialog box, set the new margins in the Margins box. You can set the left, right, top, and bottom margins.

▶ You can add a header and footer to the document by choosing File, Page Setup. Next modify the Header and Footer fields to create your header and footer for the document.

▶ You can change the orientation of the paper by choosing File, Page Setup and changing the Orientation box values. The default is Portrait.

▶ You can insert a time and date stamp at the end of the document each time you open the file using Notepad. This is handy when you want to create a log file that stores information over a period of time and you need to know the time and date when the action occurred. To use this feature, enter **.LOG** at the top of the document. You must enter this command exactly, including the period and in uppercase.

▶ You can manually insert a time and date by clicking on F5 or by choosing Edit, Time/Date.

A downside to using Notepad is it is limited to handling files that are smaller than 50 KB. To get around this limitation, many users open large text files in WordPad, which is discussed in the following section. Also, if you attempt to open a file in Notepad that exceeds the 50 KB limitation, Windows 95 automatically asks if you want to open the file in WordPad. Upon confirmation, the file opens in WordPad.

You also cannot open multiple documents in Notepad, called *multiple document interface* (MDI). When you attempt to open a document when another document is currently displayed, Notepad closes the first document you have open and opens the new one you specified. If the first document is new or includes changes to it since the last time you saved it, Notepad prompts you to save the changes before closing the document. A way to get around the MDI limitation is to open multiple occurrences of Notepad on your desktop, each with a different document displaying.

Using WordPad

WordPad is a word processing program that comes free with Windows. It is an upgrade to the Write application that came bundled with previous versions of Windows. One of the strongest features of WordPad is its capability to handle Microsoft Word formatted files (DOC files). This makes it convenient for users who do not have a copy of Word for Windows installed on their system; they can read documents created in Word in WordPad.

WordPad also supports text files (TXT) and rich-text formatted (RTF) documents. Text files include plain ASCII documents (those that do not any formatting), as well as DOS batch files and other system files. RTF files are documents that include rich-text, such as varying font types, tabs, character-formatting (including italics, boldface, and underlining), and font colors. Because Word-Pad does not have the same 50 KB restriction that Notepad has, you can open any size text file in WordPad.

WordPad also can be used to display OLE objects. You can, for example, use WordPad to create a document that includes a bit-map picture. Then, to edit the picture, you can double-click on the image to edit the image in WordPad. WordPad's menu and toolbar are replaced by Windows' Paint menu and toolbars. (Paint is another application bundled with Windows 95.) After you make changes to the image, click outside the object (the picture in this case) to return to the normal WordPad interface.

The following are some additional WordPad features:

▶ WordPad supports *MAPI* (Mail Application Programming Interface) so you can send e-mail and faxes from within WordPad.

▶ WordPad enables you to create scraps on the Desktop. *Scraps* are selections of documents from a WordPad (or other OLE2-compliant application that supports creating scraps) dragged to the Windows 95 Desktop.

▶ WordPad enables you to open binary files, such as word processing, graphics, or other files. Although you cannot edit these files (all you'll see in most cases is hexadecimal or similar coding), you might be able to read header information at the beginning of the file. This may help you troubleshoot problems with that particular file, or view version information about what kind of application will open the file you are viewing.

Exercises

Exercise 8.1: Configuring MS-DOS Applications

Exercise 8.1 demonstrates how to configure the various MS-DOS modes for a given application.

1. Right-click on the My Computer icon and choose Explore. The Exploring window appears.

2. Click on the plus sign (+) next to the C drive. Subdirectories of the C drive appear.

3. Click on the plus sign next to the Windows subdirectory. The tree expands to show the subdirectories of Windows.

4. Right-click on the COMMAND file in the right panel and choose Properties. The COMMAND.COM Properties sheet appears.

5. Click on the Memory tab. The list of configurable memory settings appears.

6. Set the XMS memory parameter to 4096 and choose OK. You return to the Explorer window.

7. Double-click on the COMMAND file. An MS-DOS window appears.

8. Type **MEM** and press Enter from the command prompt. Note that the free XMS reads as 4096 KB.

9. Type **EXIT** and press Enter. You return to the Explorer window.

10. Go back to the Properties sheet of the COMMAND file and change the XMS memory parameter to 16384 KB, choose OK, and double-click on the COMMAND file again. An MS-DOS window appears.

11. Type **MEM** and press Enter. Note that the free XMS memory now reads 16384 KB.

continues

Exercise 8.1: Continued

> Even if the amount of memory you assign exceeds the physi-
> cal RAM of the computer, the parameter will be accepted. The
> additional memory comes from the paging file system.

12. Type **EXIT** and press Enter. You return to the Explorer
    window.

13. Reset the XMS memory parameter to its original setting of
    Auto and choose OK. You return to the Explorer window.

14. Click on the Command folder. The files in the Command
    folder appear in the right panel of the Explorer window.

15. Right-click on the EDIT file and choose Properties. The
    Properties sheet for the EDIT file appears.

16. Click on the Program tab and then click on the Advanced
    button. The Advanced Program Settings window appears.

17. Select the MS-DOS Mode check box to enable use of stan-
    dard MS-DOS mode support for this program. Some of the
    options below MS-DOS mode parameter become available.

18. Verify that Use Current MS-DOS Configuration is selected
    and choose OK. You return to the Properties sheet, and all
    other settings are disabled, because this file will now inherit
    all default MS-DOS settings.

19. Double-click on the EDIT file and click on Yes to continue.
    Windows 95 is unloaded, and the EDIT file is executed.

20. Choose File, Open (or press Alt+F, O) to open a file for edit-
    ing, type **CONFIG.SYS** as the file name, and press Enter.
    The CONFIG.SYS file appears.

21. Note the contents of the file and press Alt+F, X to exit the
    program. Windows 95 restarts automatically.

22. When Windows 95 has restarted, go back to the Advanced Settings tab and choose to specify a new MS-DOS configuration. The CONFIG.SYS and AUTOEXEC.BAT for MS-DOS mode are now available and have default settings already in place.

23. Click on the Configuration button. A Wizard appears that helps you select which options you want to be active in your MS-DOS environment.

24. Verify that Expanded Memory is deselected and that Disk Cache is selected; choose OK three times to close all Properties sheets. You return to the Explorer window.

25. Double-click on the EDIT file again and choose Yes to continue. The system restarts, and the EDIT program is executed.

26. Choose File, Open to open a file for editing, type **\CONFIG.SYS** as the file name, and press Enter. The CONFIG.SYS file appears for editing (note that DOS=SINGLE has been added to the file).

27. Choose File, Open to open a file for editing, type **\AUTOEXEC.BAT** as the file name, and press Enter. The AUTOEXEC.BAT file appears for editing (note that a Smart-Drive command has been added).

28. Choose File, Exit (or press Alt+F, X) to exit the program and then press any key. The system restarts, and Windows 95 loads normally.

29. Go back to the Properties sheet of the EDIT file and disable MS-DOS mode.

Exercise 8.2: Configuring Application Properties

Exercise 8.2 shows how the properties of different types of applications are reflected in the operating system's behavior. Verify that the System Monitor component is installed for the purposes of the exercise. As well, make certain no applications other than the System Monitor are running, unless otherwise directed during the

continues

exercise. Results during this exercise may vary based on timing, especially where threads are concerned.

1. From the Start menu, choose Programs, Accessories, System Tools, System Monitor. The System Monitor window appears, typically showing Processor Usage by default.

2. Choose View, Numeric Charts. The display changes from graphical to numeric.

3. Choose Edit, Remove Item. A list of all currently tracked system items appears.

4. Select all items in the list and choose OK to remove them. The items are removed, and you return to a blank System Monitor window.

5. Choose Edit, Add Item. The Add Item dialog box appears.

6. In the Kernel category, hold down the Ctrl key and select Threads and Virtual Machines as the items to be tracked. Choose OK. You return to the System Monitor window, showing the number of currently active threads and VMs (note these numbers—they include threads and VMs run by the operating system itself).

7. From the Start menu, choose Run and open the 16-bit Notepad.exe program. A Notepad window appears (the number of threads should increase by 1, and the number of VMs should stay constant).

8. Minimize Notepad and, from the Start menu, open an Explorer window (a 32-bit program). An Explorer window appears (note that the number of threads jumps by 2 or 3, and the number of VMs again remains the same).

9. From the Start menu, choose Programs, MS-DOS Prompt. An MS-DOS window appears (note that the number of threads jumps by 2, and the number of VMs jumps by 1).

10. Minimize the MS-DOS window and open another MS-DOS Prompt. A second MS-DOS window appears (note that the number of threads again jumps by 2, and the number of VMs jumps by 1).

11. Close all applications except System Monitor. Eventually, the number of threads and VMs should return to their original values.

Exercise 8.3: Creating a Time Log File in Notepad

Exercise 8.3 shows you how to create a time log file in Notepad. Each time you open this document, Notepad places a time/date stamp at the end of the document. You can use this file to record tasks, journal entries, and so on.

1. From the Start menu, choose Programs, Accessories, Notepad. Notepad opens with a blank document displaying.

2. On the first line of the new document, enter **.LOG**.

3. Save the document and close Notepad. As an alternative, you can keep Notepad open and open another document in Notepad to close your new document.

4. Reopen Notepad with your new document displaying. Notice how the current time and date display at the end of the document.

Exercise 8.4: Creating a Scrap Using WordPad

Exercise 8.4 shows you how to create a scrap on your Desktop using part of a document you create in WordPad.

1. From the Start menu, choose Programs, Accessories, WordPad. WordPad opens with a blank document displaying.

2. Enter a string of text in the document, such as **Ten quick tips for passing exam 70-63**.

3. Highlight the text or a section of the text.

continues

Exercise 8.4: Continued

4. Hold down the left mouse button on the selection and drag the selection to the Windows 95 Desktop. You may need to resize or move the WordPad window to see the Desktop.

5. Release the mouse button. Windows displays a Desktop icon with a few words from the scrap selection. This file is saved in the Desktop folder automatically, even if your original document is not saved. You can rename the scrap file if you want.

6. To read the file, double-click on it to open it in WordPad.

Review Questions

The following questions will test your knowledge of the information in this chapter. For additional questions, see MCP Endeavor and the Microsoft Roadmap/Assessment Exam on the CD-ROM that accompanies this book.

1. You are migrating to Windows 95 and will be upgrading many of your applications to 32-bit applications designed to run under Windows 95. You know that Windows 95 runs 32-bit applications differently than Windows 3.1 applications (16-bit applications). Every Windows 95 application is executed from within a specialized container called _____.

    A. an application box

    B. a virtual partition

    C. a task space

    D. a virtual machine

2. Jim is upgrading to Windows 95 and wants to be sure his existing computer can run Windows 95. Windows' 95 multitasking feature requires an Intel processor to perform in two types of modes. Which two of the following are operating modes for Intel processors?

    A. Enhanced mode

    B. Protected mode

    C. Fault mode

    D. Real mode

3. Windows' 95 protected mode feature has the capability to regulate the behavior of multitasking process in two ways. One way is through graduated levels of processor privilege, commonly called Rings. In the Intel ring protection scheme, Ring _____ allows complete control of the processor.

    A. 1

    B. 0

C. 3

D. 4

4. Typically applications running under Windows 95 do so at a specific Ring level. The operating system runs at a specific Ring level as well. This way applications do not have access to critical system functions. Which of the following is true about Rings?

   A. Most Windows 95 applications run in Ring 3.

   B. Most operating system components run in Ring 3.

   C. Windows 95 uses all Intel rings.

   D. Windows 95 uses only Rings 1, 2, and 3.

5. Linda is considering upgrading from Windows 3.*x* to Windows 95. She is not sure how to justify the upgrade based on application support, because Windows 3.*x*, like Windows 95, supports multitasking. However, you explain the differences between how 16-bit applications and 32-bit applications support multitasking. You tell her that WIN16 applications use _____ multitasking.

   A. fault-tolerant

   B. preemptive

   C. cooperative

   D. real-mode

6. It's important for your users to understand how 16-bit applications are handled by Windows 95. Which of the following is true?

   A. WIN16 applications do not access the Registry.

   B. WIN16 applications do not use the System VM.

   C. WIN16 applications support multithreading.

   D. Each WIN16 application has its own message queue.

7. Leslie has several MS-DOS applications she runs under Windows 95. She wants to optimize the way they run under Windows 95, as well as run 32-bit applications simultaneously with her DOS applications. If possible, you advise her it is best to run MS-DOS applications in _____.

   A. MS-DOS mode

   B. customized MS-DOS mode

   C. a WIN16 VM

   D. an MS-DOS VM

8. A user calls you while you are manning a help desk. He asks how his MS-DOS program and Windows 95 will work together in MS-DOS mode. You tell him that in MS-DOS mode Windows 95 _____.

   A. unloads itself from memory

   B. remains in memory

   C. runs the application in protected mode

   D. can multithread multiple DOS sessions

9. You are a systems administrator in a company that migrated to Windows 95. Many users still use MS-DOS applications and must run them under Windows. Because of some compatibility problems with the older DOS applications, you customize the DOS-mode applications. What command is added to the CONFIG.SYS when you run a customized MS-DOS–mode application?

   A. DOS=Custom

   B. MODE=DOSCUST

   C. DOS=CMODE

   D. DOS=SINGLE

10. The Registry is a centralized database that stores Windows 95 and applications settings. You are instructed by a software manufacturer's technical support operator to locate a Registry setting for a 32-bit application you have installed under

Windows 95. Settings for WIN32 applications are stored primarily in the Registry under the key _____.

    A. HKEY_CURRENT_CONFIG\SOFTWARE

    B. HKEY_LOCAL_MACHINE\SOFTWARE

    C. HKEY_LOCAL_MACHINE\APPLICATIONS\WIN32

    D. HKEY_CLASSES_ROOT\WIN32

11. Windows 95 is divided into two types of core components: those implemented with 16-bit code and those implemented with 32-bit code. Because Windows 95 supports both 16-bit and 32-bit code, a translation must take place for Windows 95 to understand both types of codes. The process of translating a 16-bit API call to a 32-bit API call is called _____.

    A. bumping

    B. trans-interfacing

    C. retooling

    D. thunking up

12. Dan migrated to Windows 95 primarily in hopes that Windows 95 would eliminate the GPFs he experienced running applications under Windows 3.1. He has noticed, however, that under Windows 95 he still receives GPFs at times. Which three of the following are common causes for General Protection Faults?

    A. An attempt to access system hardware directly

    B. Failure of a hardware driver

    C. A request to read or write to a memory address space owned by another application

    D. An attempt to access an unTimized protection ring

13. You receive a call from a user on your network asking if she can use Ctrl+Alt+Delete under Windows 95 the same way she did under Windows 3.1. You explain to her how Windows 95

handles this command sequence. In Windows 95, pressing Ctrl+Alt+Delete once produces _____.

    A. a reboot of the system

    B. nothing

    C. a system shutdown

    D. a Close Program dialog box that lets you close the current application

Review Answers

1. D   6. A   11. D

2. B D   7. D   12. A B C

3. B   8. A   13. D

4. A   9. D

5. C   10. B

Test Yourself

Stop! Before reading this chapter, test yourself to determine how much study time you will need to devote to this section.

1. In your company, you set up a Dial-Up Networking Server so users can access resources remotely. You enable these users to access files on a Windows NT server. What should you do to provide the highest level of protection from unauthorized access to these files?

2. You are the system administrator for a company and have set up Dial-Up Networking for your sales staff to access remote services. What are two applications these users can use over Dial-Up Networking?

3. Gerald sets up Windows 95 with Dial-Up Networking as a client. What are two general requirements for doing this?

4. Windows 95 can be configured as a Dial-Up Networking server to enable other callers to connect to and access resources from the server machine. What, if any, other software do you need to configure this feature?

5. You set up a modem to work with Windows 95. After using the modem several times, you want to disable the modem speaker. How can you do this from within Windows 95?

6. Matt carries a laptop to and from work. He uses a modem to dial into different remote services. When he dials from work, but not from home, he must enter a 9 to receive an outside line. From home, however, he must enter a company calling card number so all his calls are paid for by the company account. What should Matt do to ease the transition of calling from work to home and vice versa?

7. Sometimes on weekends you modify a database at home that you use every day at the office during the week. When you get to work and copy the revised database to your system, you're not sure of the changes that have been made. Can Briefcase give you a summary of these changes? Why?

Answers

1. At least set up user-level security. See "Security Considerations."
2. Various answers can work here, including World Wide Web browsers, e-mail applications, and Microsoft Exchange. See "Using Applications with a Dial-up Networking Connection."
3. A modem must be installed and 2 MB of free disk space is needed. See "Configuring a Dial-Up Networking Client."
4. Microsoft Plus! Pack for Windows 95. See "Using the Microsoft Plus Pack Dial-Up Networking Server."
5. Set the Speaker Volume control on the Modem Properties sheet to Off. See "Installing and Configuring Modems Under Windows 95."
6. Create two dialing locations, one for work and one for home. Use the appropriate one for each location. See "Implementing Telephony Options for Windows 95."
7. No. Briefcase is designed only to synchronize files based on revision dates and times, not content changes or updates. See "Using the Briefcase."

Chapter

Mobile Services

9

This chapter will help you prepare for the exam by covering the following objectives:

Test Objectives

- ▶ Configure a modem to meet a specific set of user requirements

- ▶ Implement the various telephony options to meet a specific set of user requirements

- ▶ Configure Dial-Up Networking to be a client

- ▶ Choose applications that would be appropriate to run over Dial-Up Networking

- ▶ Configure Dial-Up Networking on a server

- ▶ Implement the appropriate level of security for use with Dial-Up Networking

- ▶ Use Briefcase to transfer and synchronize data between two computers

Windows 95 Mobile Services are a collection of services designed to enhance the connectivity and productivity of remote users. A remote user can be a traveler with a laptop or a desktop user who needs to access a network from a remote location.

In this chapter, the following components of the Windows 95 Mobile Services are discussed:

- ▶ Dial-Up Networking architecture

- ▶ Configuring a Dial-Up Networking client

- ▶ Configuring a modem

- ▶ Using applications with a Dial-Up Networking connection

- ▶ Using the Microsoft Plus! Pack Dial-Up Networking Server

- ▶ Optimizing Dial-Up Networking performance

- ▶ Using the Briefcase

With the exception of the Briefcase, you access most of the Windows 95 Mobile Services features through the Dial-Up Networking tools. Dial-Up Networking typically is used to connect to an Internet service provider (ISP) or to connect a corporate network from a remote location. For example, Dial-Up Networking can be used to access an Internet e-mail account, or to dial into the company network from home.

Windows 95 offers numerous enhancements to the remote connectivity features of Windows for Workgroups 3.11, as shown in table 9.1. Windows 3.1 does not include any integrated remote networking features, and therefore is not listed.

Table 9.1

Mobile Services Features of Windows 95 and Windows for Workgroups	
Windows for Workgroups	Windows 95
As a client, can use only Remote Access Service (RAS)	Can be a RAS, SLIP, PPP, or Novell NetWare Connect client
With a Windows for Workgroups RAS server, a RAS client cannot access the rest of the network	Can function as a RAS or PPP server and act as a gateway to the rest of the network
One phone book for all users using the client computer	Allows user-specific connection settings and phone books
Log file for troubleshooting is MODEMLOG.TXT, which logs only modem commands	MODEMLOG.TXT and PPPLOG.TXT can be used to log connection-specific information and PPP information
Direct cable connections are difficult to establish and are supported only over serial links	Direct cable connections are wizard-driven supported over serial and parallel links

Additional features of Dial-Up Networking with Windows 95 include the following:

▶ The capability to configure a Windows 95 computer as a remote access server for clients running Windows 95, Windows for Workgroups, or Windows 3.1 using Dial-Up Server capabilities from Microsoft Plus! For Windows 95

▶ Support for most LAN topologies, such as Ethernet, FDDI (fiber optic), Token Ring, and ARCnet

▶ The capability to connect to Windows NT, LAN Manager, Windows for Workgroups, IBM LAN Server, Shiva LAN Rover, and other remote access systems using any number of supported protocols

▶ Advanced security features, such as password encryption

▶ Support for all modems recognized by Windows 95

▶ The capability to use link compression to increase data throughput

Dial-Up Networking Architecture

Figure 9.1 shows the architectural reference model for Dial-Up Networking. *Dial-Up Networking* is a networking feature in Windows 95 that enables users to connect to remote servers via dial-up connection and access resources from that network. In some situations (depending on the server type and a user's access privileges), the client may become part of the network (such as connecting to an Internet server), or just have access to server resources (such as accessing files from a file server). Data from an application passes down through the layers, across the phone line, and up through the layers to the receiving application. In this respect, the Dial-Up Networking architecture is similar to the OSI Reference Model for networks. The top layer of the Dial-Up Networking reference model represents the network-aware applications, whereas the bottom layer represents the modem and phone line over which the network protocol frames are sent. The intermediate layers translate and package the application requests into a particular network protocol (TCP/IP, NetBEUI, or IPX/SPX-compatible), and then into a particular line protocol (SLIP, PPP, or RAS). When the data is in a line protocol format, it can be sent over the line (phone, serial cable, or other) to be received by another computer on the other end of the line.

Figure 9.1

The Dial-Up Networking architecture model.

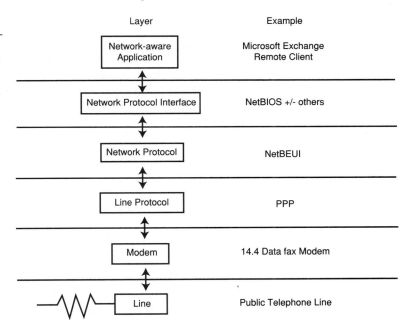

Dial-Up Networking Architecture Model

Network Interfaces

Dial-Up Networking supports any of the following network interface standards:

▶ NetBIOS

▶ Mailslots

▶ Named pipes

▶ Remote Procedure Calls (RPCs)

▶ LAN Manager function calls

▶ TCP/IP utilities

▶ Windows sockets

Network Protocols

Dial-Up Networking supports the following network protocols:

▶ **NetBEUI.** Protocol primarily used by Microsoft network LANs and other NetBIOS-compatible networks. NetBEUI stands for *NetBIOS Extended User Interface.* It is relatively easy to implement because it does not require additional network addresses be configured for each computer other than the computer name and domain or workgroup name. By default, Windows 95 installs the NetBEUI and IPX/SPX when you install an adapter, including the Dial-Up Adapter.

▶ **IPX/SPX-compatible.** Protocol primarily used by Novell NetWare. IPX stands for *Internetwork Packet Exchange Protocol.* It is a network-layer protocol that provides connectionless (datagram) service. As a network-layer protocol, IPX is responsible for internetwork routing and maintaining network logical addresses. Routing uses the RIP (Router Information Protocol) protocol to make route selections. SPX stands for *Sequence Packet Exchange.* It is a transport-layer protocol that extends IPX to provide connection-oriented service with reliable delivery. Reliable delivery is ensured by retransmitting packets in the event of an error.

▶ **TCP/IP.** Protocol used by UNIX hosts, the Internet, and most large networks. TCP/IP stands for *Transmission Control Protocol/Internet Protocol.* TCP is an internetwork protocol that provides full-duplex, connection-oriented transport. TCP corresponds to SPX in the NetWare environment. TCP maintains a logical connection between the sending and receiving computer systems. In this way, the integrity of the transmission is maintained. TCP detects any problems in the transmission quickly and takes action to correct the problem. TCP also provides message fragmentation and reassembly. TCP fragments message streams into segments that can be handled by IP.

These listed networking protocols are supported only in their 32-bit protected-mode implementations as provided with Windows 95. You cannot use Dial-Up Networking with a real-mode IPX protocol, such as that provided by Novell and installed through the AUTOEXEC.BAT, for example.

A networking protocol bound to a Dial-Up Adapter is shown with an arrow pointing to the adapter in the Network Properties sheet. You can open the Network Properties sheet by double-clicking on the Network icon in Control Panel.

Line Protocols

Line protocols (also called *communications protocols* or *connection protocols*) are the means by which network protocols are transported over communication media types for which they were not originally intended. In this way, for example, TCP/IP can be supported over a phone line even if it was actually designed to be transported over network cable. Windows 95 supports four line protocols:

▶ Point-to-Point Protocol (PPP)

▶ Serial Line Interface Protocol (SLIP)

▶ Remote Access Service (RAS)

▶ NetWare Remote Networking (NRN)

Point-to-Point Protocol (PPP)

The Point-to-Point Protocol is the default when you install Dial-Up Networking. It was originally developed for the TCP/IP environment but has replaced the less flexible RAS as the line protocol of choice.

PPP was designed for the capacity to transport a wide variety of networking protocols across serial links. It has the following additional features:

- ▶ Allows multiplexing of sessions across a single serial link, enabling multiple network applications to appear to communicate simultaneously

- ▶ Allows multiple network protocols to be transported simultaneously over a single link

- ▶ Supports software compression to increase throughput

- ▶ Supports automatic negotiation of addressing, thus allowing a dynamic IP address to be assigned to the dial-up client

To use software compression over PPP, software compression must be supported by both the client and the server portion of the link. Typically only Microsoft applications support both client and server software compression over PPP, so you likely are required to connect to a Microsoft-based server product (such as Windows 95 or Windows NT) to take advantage of compression.

- ▶ Supports error detection

The following network protocols are supported for use over a PPP line connection:

- ▶ TCP/IP

- ▶ IPX/SPX-compatible

- ▶ NetBEUI

Because PPP supports multiple network protocols, you can connect to many different types of remote systems, including these:

- ▶ Windows 95 Dial-Up Networking servers

- ▶ Windows NT 3.5 RAS servers

- ▶ Shiva LANRover

- ▶ Internet dial-up service providers

The resources that can be accessed after you are connected to any of these systems depends entirely on how the remote system is configured (what protocols are being supported, whether the system is connected to a network and acting as a gateway, and so on).

Windows 95 Dial-Up Networking Servers

Connecting to a Windows 95 Dial-Up Networking server gives a PPP client potential access to the following:

- ▶ NetWare servers, if the server is attached to a Novell network and is using IPX/SPX as one if its protocols

- ▶ Microsoft-based servers, such as Windows NT, Windows 95, Windows for Workgroups, and LAN Manager, if the Windows 95 Dial-Up Networking server has NetBEUI installed (or another protocol common to all connected systems) and is connected to a network

The Dial-Up Networking Server is *not* included with Windows 95. You must purchase the Microsoft Plus! for Windows 95 software to acquire this dial-up server product. In the "Using the Microsoft Plus! Pack Dial-Up Networking Server" section later in this chapter, you learn how to install and configure the Dial-Up Networking Server.

Windows NT 3.5 RAS Servers

If you dial in to a Windows NT 3.5 server, you can access the following:

- ▶ NetWare servers, if the server is attached to a Novell network and is using IPX/SPX as one if its protocols

- ▶ Microsoft-based servers, such as Windows NT, Windows 95, Windows for Workgroups, and LAN Manager, if the Windows NT server Dial-Up Networking server has NetBEUI installed (or another protocol common to all connected systems) and is connected to a network

▶ The Internet, if the Windows NT server is set to act as an Internet gateway and is connected to the Internet

Shiva LANRover

Windows 95 Dial-Up Networking clients can access a Shiva LANRover remote access server to connect to NetWare servers. For information on configuring the Shiva LANRover remote access server, refer to documentation for that product.

Internet Dial-Up Service Providers

By dialing into an ISP and using TCP/IP, you can access resources connected to the Internet. For example, many ISPs include Internet mail services that you can connect to using PPP.

Serial Line Interface Protocol (SLIP)

SLIP is an older line protocol specification that was popular before the development of PPP. Although SLIP, like PPP, was developed primarily for the TCP/IP environment, it has the following limitations:

▶ It does not support addressing information, thus both client and server must have pre-configured IP addresses or the user is prompted at logon for the client IP address.

▶ It does not support multiple protocols, therefore only a single protocol can be transported over the line.

▶ It has no error detection or correction.

▶ It has no data compression support (although you can compress the IP header information).

TCP/IP is the only supported network protocol for use with a SLIP line connection.

SLIP can be used to connect to resources such as the following:

▶ The Internet

▶ Private TCP/IP networks

By default, Windows 95 does not install SLIP software on your system. You must install it from the \ADMIN\APPTOOLS\ DSCRIP folder on the Windows 95 CD-ROM by running the Add/Remove Programs Wizard from Control Panel. You can read a text file associated with this software in the \ADMIN\ APPTOOLS\SLIP folder on the same CD-ROM.

Microsoft does not provide any products capable of being a SLIP server. The dial-in SLIP server must be an ISP or other third-party server product.

Remote Access Service (RAS)

Originally introduced in Microsoft LAN Manager 2.1, RAS (AsyBEUI or Asynchronous BEUI connection protocol as it is sometimes called) is a proprietary protocol developed by Microsoft. Although it is a relatively fast and efficient line protocol, it does not support the transmission of multiple network protocols. It should be used strictly for backward compatibility with older Microsoft products.

The network protocol that RAS supports is NetBEUI. Using RAS, Windows 95 can connect to the following:

▶ Windows 95 Dial-Up Networking servers

▶ Windows NT 3.1 and above

▶ Windows for Workgroups 3.11

▶ LAN Manager 2.1 and above

The resources that are available when you are connected depend on the configuration of the dial-up server. Generally, the following conditions hold true:

▶ If connected to Windows for Workgroups 3.11, only the shared resources of the dial-up server are available.

▶ If connected to a Windows 95 Dial-Up Networking server or any Windows NT server, all NetBIOS-compatible resources on the local network are available.

▶ If connected to a LAN Manager server, all shared NetBEUI resources on the local network are available.

NetWare Remote Networking (NRN)

The NRN line protocol is used exclusively to connect to Novell NetWare Connect servers using the IPX/SPX-compatible network protocol. When you are connected, all NetWare servers that share the network with the NetWare Connect server should be accessible.

NetWare Connect servers also provide the capability to create modem-sharing pools and to remotely control other workstations. These capabilities are not supported using Dial-Up Networking.

Whereas Windows 95 Dial-Up Networking clients can dial into NetWare Connect servers, native Novell workstations cannot dial into Windows 95 Dial-Up Networking servers because they do not support the Microsoft NetBIOS-compatible implementation of the Microsoft IPX/SPX-compatible protocol; that is, Windows 95 can act only as a client for connecting to a NetWare Connect server, not a server.

When you set up Dial-Up Networking to connect to a NetWare Connect server, the following must also be set up:

▶ Microsoft Client for NetWare Networks

▶ IPX/SPX-compatible protocol

▶ IPX/SPX must be bound to the Microsoft Dial-Up Adapter

▶ Type of dial-up server must be set to NRN: NetWare Connect

> When you use Windows' 95 Dial-Up Networking feature to access a NetWare Connect server, you cannot control a remote computer. You can only access data. If you want to control a computer remotely using Windows 95 and NetWare Connect, you must use software provided by Novell.

Wide Area Network (WAN) Support

In addition to traditional modem-based Dial-Up Networking support, Windows 95 also supports the following communication media:

- ► **X.25.** A networking communication standard that uses a packet-switching protocol to carry data over a worldwide network, often using public carriers (for example, Datapac). Locally, the Windows 95 computer would use a device called a Packet Assembler/Disassembler (PAD) in place of a modem.

- ► **Integrated Services Digital Network (ISDN).** A relatively new standard for digital telephone communication. This standard offers much higher and more reliable transfer rates than analog phone lines (usually 64 Kbps to 128 Kbps) but requires a proprietary ISDN modem type.

> Although modems are treated as analog communication media, X.25 and ISDN hardware are treated as network cards, and provide a direct data feed across the wide area network.

- ► **Public Switched Telephone Networks (PSTN).** The normal telephone service networks for most of the world. Windows' 95 Dial-Up Networking works over these phone lines to send and receive data via modem.

Using Log Files to Diagnose Connection Problems

To diagnose connection problems when using Dial-Up Networking, Windows 95 provides two log files:

▶ PPPLOG.TXT

▶ MODEMLOG.TXT

PPPLOG.TXT

The PPPLOG.TXT file contains information on how the software layers of PPP have processed a Dial-Up Networking call. This logging feature is disabled by default. To enable PPP logging, select the Dial-Up Adapter in the Network Control Panel Applet, select the Advanced tab of the Properties sheet, and change the value for "Record a log file" to Yes.

The following is a sample PPPLOG.TXT file:

```
04-29-1996 22:19:40.52 - Remote access driver log opened.
04-29-1996 22:19:40.52 - Installable CP VxD SPAP     is loaded
04-29-1996 22:19:40.52 - Server type is  PPP (Point to Point
➡_Protocol).
04-29-1996 22:19:40.52 - FSA : Adding Control Protocol 80fd (CCP)
➡_to control protocol chain.
04-29-1996 22:19:40.52 - FSA : Adding Control Protocol 803f
➡_(NBFCP) to control protocol chain.
04-29-1996 22:19:40.52 - FSA : Protocol not bound - skipping
➡_control protocol 8021 (IPCP).
04-29-1996 22:19:40.53 - FSA : Protocol not bound - skipping
➡_control protocol 802b (IPXCP).
04-29-1996 22:19:40.53 - FSA : Adding Control Protocol c029
➡_(CallbackCP) to control protocol chain.
04-29-1996 22:19:40.53 - FSA : Adding Control Protocol c027 (no
➡_description) to control protocol chain.
04-29-1996 22:19:40.53 - FSA : Adding Control Protocol c023 (PAP)
➡_to control protocol chain.
04-29-1996 22:19:40.53 - FSA : Adding Control Protocol c223
➡_(CHAP) to control protocol chain.
04-29-1996 22:19:40.53 - FSA : Adding Control Protocol c021 (LCP)
➡_to control protocol chain.
```

```
04-29-1996 22:19:40.53 - LCP : Callback negotiation enabled.
04-29-1996 22:19:40.54 - LCP : Layer started.
04-29-1996 22:19:51.38 - Remote access driver is shutting down.
04-29-1996 22:19:51.38 - CRC Errors              0
04-29-1996 22:19:51.38 - Timeout Errors          0
04-29-1996 22:19:51.38 - Alignment Errors        0
04-29-1996 22:19:51.38 - Overrun Errors          0
04-29-1996 22:19:51.38 - Framing Errors          0
04-29-1996 22:19:51.38 - Buffer Overrun Errors   0
04-29-1996 22:19:51.38 - Incomplete Packets      0
04-29-1996 22:19:51.38 - Bytes Received          1
04-29-1996 22:19:51.38 - Bytes Transmitted       213
04-29-1996 22:19:51.38 - Frames Received         0
04-29-1996 22:19:51.38 - Frames Transmitted      4
04-29-1996 22:19:51.38 - Remote access driver log closed.
```

The PPP log file shows the date and time for each entry to the log file as well as a description of the entry. In the preceding log file, the PPP protocols were successfully bound to the Remote Access driver, except that the IPX and IP protocols were not bound, because they were not installed on the client. The log file then shows only a brief callback negotiation period, followed by the Remote Access driver shutting down. This is probably because the client was unable to make a successful connection to the dial-up server. The latter part of the log file shows the transmission and error statistics.

MODEMLOG.TXT

Although the MODEMLOG.TXT log file is not specific to Dial-Up Networking, it is nonetheless very useful in troubleshooting connection difficulties. It records all AT-type commands sent to the modem, and logs responses from the modem. This logging feature is disabled by default.

> Modem command logging is available only when you use Windows 95 TAPI-compliant communication software. Because Windows 3.1 communication software does not use the same software layers to communicate with the modem, Windows 95 cannot trap the AT commands that these applications send to the modem.

To enable modem command logging, select the modem in the Modems Control Panel Applet, select the Connection tab of the Properties sheet, choose Advanced, and then choose Record a log file.

The following is a sample MODEMLOG.TXT file:

```
04-29-1996 22:14:14.75 - 14.4 Data FAX Modem in use.
04-29-1996 22:14:14.78 - Modem type: 14.4 Data FAX Modem
04-29-1996 22:14:14.78 - Modem inf path: MDMCPI.INF
04-29-1996 22:14:14.78 - Modem inf section: Modem20
04-29-1996 22:14:15.05 - 57600,N,8,1
04-29-1996 22:14:15.36 - 57600,N,8,1
04-29-1996 22:14:15.38 - Initializing modem.
04-29-1996 22:14:15.38 - Send: AT
04-29-1996 22:14:15.38 - Recv: AT
04-29-1996 22:14:15.52 - Recv: <lf>OK<lf>
04-29-1996 22:14:15.52 - Interpreted response: Ok
04-29-1996 22:14:15.52 - Send: AT &F E0 V1 &D2 &C1 S95=47 W1
➥ S0=0
04-29-1996 22:14:15.54 - Recv: AT &F E0 V1 &D2 &C1 S95=47 W1
➥ S0=0
04-29-1996 22:14:15.67 - Recv: <lf>OK<lf>
04-29-1996 22:14:15.67 - Interpreted response: Ok
04-29-1996 22:14:15.67 - Send: ATS7=60S30=0L1M1&K3B0N1X4
04-29-1996 22:14:15.82 - Recv: <lf>OK<lf>
04-29-1996 22:14:15.82 - Interpreted response: Ok
04-29-1996 22:14:15.82 - Dialing.
04-29-1996 22:14:15.82 - Send: ATDT;
04-29-1996 22:14:17.09 - Recv: <lf>OK<lf>
04-29-1996 22:14:17.09 - Interpreted response: Ok
04-29-1996 22:14:17.09 - Dialing.
04-29-1996 22:14:17.09 - Send: ATDT#######
04-29-1996 22:14:43.63 - Recv:
04-29-1996 22:14:43.63 - Interpreted response: Informative
04-29-1996 22:14:43.63 - Recv: <lf>
04-29-1996 22:14:43.63 - Interpreted response: Informative
04-29-1996 22:14:43.63 - Recv: CARRIER 2400
04-29-1996 22:14:43.63 - Interpreted response: Informative
04-29-1996 22:14:43.63 - Recv:
04-29-1996 22:14:43.63 - Interpreted response: Informative
04-29-1996 22:14:43.63 - Recv: <lf>
04-29-1996 22:14:43.63 - Interpreted response: Informative
04-29-1996 22:14:43.63 - Recv:
```

```
04-29-1996 22:14:43.63 - Interpreted response: Informative
04-29-1996 22:14:43.63 - Recv: <lf>
04-29-1996 22:14:43.63 - Interpreted response: Informative
04-29-1996 22:14:43.63 - Recv: PROTOCOL: NONE
04-29-1996 22:14:43.63 - Interpreted response: Informative
04-29-1996 22:14:43.64 - Recv:
04-29-1996 22:14:43.64 - Interpreted response: Informative
04-29-1996 22:14:43.64 - Recv: <lf>
04-29-1996 22:14:43.64 - Interpreted response: Informative
04-29-1996 22:14:43.64 - Recv:
04-29-1996 22:14:43.64 - Interpreted response: Informative
04-29-1996 22:14:43.64 - Recv: <lf>
04-29-1996 22:14:43.64 - Interpreted response: Informative
04-29-1996 22:14:43.64 - Recv: CONNECT 2400
04-29-1996 22:14:43.64 - Interpreted response: Connect
04-29-1996 22:14:43.64 - Connection established at 2400bps.
04-29-1996 22:14:43.64 - Error-control off or unknown.
04-29-1996 22:14:43.64 - Data compression off or unknown.
04-29-1996 22:14:43.64 - Recv:
04-29-1996 22:14:44.04 - 57600,N,8,1
04-29-1996 22:14:57.18 - Remote modem hung up.
04-29-1996 22:14:59.20 - Recv: <no response>
04-29-1996 22:14:59.20 - WARNING: Unrecognized response.
➥_Retrying...
04-29-1996 22:15:00.46 - Session Statistics:
04-29-1996 22:15:00.46 -                   Reads : 344 bytes
04-29-1996 22:15:00.46 -                   Writes: 98 bytes
04-29-1996 22:15:00.46 - 14.4 Data FAX Modem closed.
```

In the preceding log file, the following information might be useful for troubleshooting:

```
57600,N,8,1
```

The preceding line shows the maximum transmission rate, parity, data-bits, and stop-bits that have been configured.

```
Send: ATS7=60S30=0L1M1&K3B0N1X4 ... Interpreted response: Ok
```

The preceding line shows a successful modem initialization string.

```
Connection established at 2400bps
```

The preceding line might explain why the connection was so slow. The server modem was likely 2400 bps.

```
Remote modem hung up.
```

The preceding line may result either due to the client having logged off, or to the server having terminated the connection.

Understanding Modems and Data Communications

Before you begin using the remote access features of Windows 95, you need an understanding of the key piece of hardware used to connect your local computer to a remote system—the modem. A *modem* is a special piece of computer hardware that converts the data coming from your computer to a signal that can be transmitted through normal telephone lines. This process is called *modulation*. The modem also converts signals from the phone line into data that your computer can understand through a process called *demodulation*. From these two processes (MOdulate/DEModulate) comes the term modem.

Most computers now come with modems already installed. If your computer does not already have a modem, however, you can purchase one separately. There are many brands and varieties of modems available today, though most fall into one of a few main categories: internal, external, PCMCIA format (for notebook computers), and portable.

Modems also have a variety of attributes and features, such as error correction, compression, and flow control. Perhaps the most important attribute, however, is the speed with which the modem can transfer data over the telephone line. This speed is measured in bytes per second (Bps, or commonly referred to as baud). As might be expected, faster transfer rates are generally better. As recently as five years ago, 1200 Bps was considered standard and 2400 Bps was fast. Currently, however, 28800 Bps and 33600 Bps are standard, with 56000 Bps right around the corner.

Windows' 95 Dial-Up Networking supports modems supported by the miniport driver. This includes modems that use the standardized set of modem commands, called the AT command set. Some of the advanced modem features that Dial-Up Networking supports include MNP/5 and v.42bis compression and error controls, as well as RTX/CTS and XON/XOFF software follow control.

To find out if a modem you have or intend to purchase is supported by Windows 95, read the Windows 95 Hardware Compatibility List. You can locate this on the Windows 95 CD-ROM in the \DRIVERS folder. The file name is HCL95.HLP; it is a Windows Help file. You can display it by double-clicking on the file in Windows Explorer. Obtain the most recent version of the Windows 95 Hardware Compatibility List, HCL95.EXE, and the most recent versions of the Windows 95 Driver Library drivers, from the following site: `ftp://ftp.microsoft.com/kb/softlib`.

As mentioned in the preceding paragraph, Windows 95 supports v.42bis and MNP/5 compression and v.42 error correction. Flow control, which regulates data traffic between communication devices, is a key component to implementing data compression and error correction in modem devices.

In Windows for Workgroups 3.11, Windows NT clients, and Windows NT Server, flow control is supported. However, MS-DOS RAS client software does not support flow control or software compression.

Installing and Configuring Modems Under Windows 95

Windows 95 makes installing and configuring your modem a simple process. If you have a modem installed in your computer, for example, the Windows 95 Setup program will attempt to detect the modem brand and the modem speed, then install the proper driver files.

If you want to change your modem or install a new modem after you already are running Windows 95, you can install and configure the modem yourself from the Windows 95 Control Panel. You also can reconfigure an existing modem. To display the Modem Properties sheet, which you use to add, remove, or modify a modem, use the following steps:

1. From the Start menu, choose Settings, Control Panel.

2. Double-click on the Modems icon to display a general Modems Properties sheet (see fig. 9.2).

Figure 9.2

The Modems Properties sheet.

To reconfigure an existing modem from this sheet, click on the Properties button to display the Properties sheet for the selected modem (see fig. 9.3). To change the connection settings for a modem, click on the Connection tab on this Properties sheet. Some of the connection settings you can change include stop bits, parity, and data bits.

To install a new modem, click on the Add button on the Modems Properties sheet (refer to fig. 9.2). A Windows 95 wizard guides you through the process of installing the new modem, including specifying the manufacturer and name of the modem (which installs the proper modem drivers), port number, and other information). After installing the new modem, you can, if necessary, change its properties using the information in the preceding paragraph.

Figure 9.3

A specific modem's properties sheet.

Examining COM Ports

Modems are configured to transfer data to and from your computer through connections called *COM ports* (communication ports). COM ports are connected (either physically or electronically) to your computer's main motherboard and allow communications devices to pass data into and out of the computer.

The Windows 95 Setup program automatically detects your COM ports and attempts to configure any devices (such as modems) attached to those ports. Alternatively, you can select a specific COM port for your modem from the Connections tab of a modem's properties sheet. Windows 95 attempts to communicate with the COM port and creates the computer files and connections necessary to allow data to flow from the computer to the device.

To manually configure a COM port (without a modem attached), open the Control Panel and double-click on the System icon. Next, select the tab for Device Manager and a list of all of the computer devices in your computer displays.

Double-click on the COM port you want to configure and a Communications Port Properties sheet with several tabs appear, as shown in figure 9.4.

Figure 9.4

The Communications Port Properties sheet.

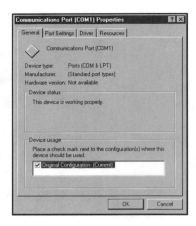

From this properties sheet, you can configure the port to any necessary specifications you need. These settings include port settings, device driver setup, and resource allocation information.

You can run the Modem Diagnostics tool in Windows 95 to identify and solve modem problems. Open the Modems Properties sheet and click on the Diagnostics tab. Next, click on the modem you want to troubleshoot and choose More Info. Windows displays a message letting you know that this process may take a few minutes. After the Modem Diagnostics tool runs, you see a window with information about your modem, including the port it uses, resources, highest speed, and command set configured for it. Note, however, you cannot run this utility while you are using the modem.

Implementing Telephony Options for Windows 95

Windows 95 supports the Windows Telephone Application Programming Interface (TAPI). TAPI acts as a device driver for a telephone network and allows telephony applications to be written to a standard programming environment.

The Dialing Properties sheet is an example of TAPI settings in Windows 95. After you install and configure a modem, you must specify certain properties. Each modem running under Windows

95, for example, has an associated Dialing Properties sheet. These properties control the manner in which the modem dials the various numbers used to connect to other services, such as remote computers using Dial-Up Networking.

There are several ways to specify the dialing properties. Most applications, for example, enable you to specify properties from within the application. You also can specify dialing parameters from the Modems icon in the Control Panel. To change the dialing properties in this manner, click on the name of the modem in the Modems Properties sheet you want to change, then click on the Dialing Properties button to open the Dialing Properties sheet (see fig. 9.5).

Figure 9.5

The Dialing Properties sheet.

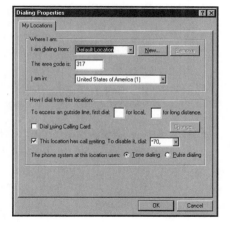

On this sheet, you can specify a dialing location, such as Home, Office, Remote, or other descriptive name, or you can leave the name as Default Location. Windows 95 enables you to create several locations for each modem. This way you can quickly select a new location depending on where (or when) you use a modem. The settings for the modem, then, change to the settings for the location you have set up. This is convenient for users who have a laptop computer and make calls from several different places, such as from the office, from home, or from a hotel room. You can set up a location for each of these places that has different settings, such as calling card numbers (for calling from hotels, for example), disabling call waiting (from home), or using a prefix to reach an outside line (from work).

The settings on the Dialing Properties sheet are largely self-explanatory and include the following:

▶ **I Am Dialing From.** Includes the location name you can select from a drop-down list. Click on the New button to create a new location. Click on the Remove button to remove a dialing location.

▶ **The Area Code Is.** Includes the area code from where you are calling.

▶ **I Am In.** Specifies the country of the location from which you are calling. This selection (along with the area code) helps Windows 95 determine when special codes and prefixes are needed to dial long distance.

▶ **For Local.** Specifies the special access number, if any, that you must dial at this location to get an outside, local line. In many telephone systems, for example, you must dial a 9 to get an outside line. In some hotels, you also must dial a special number or set of numbers to get a local line.

▶ **For Long Distance.** Specifies any special access number you may need to dial for a long distance connection. Note that this number is in addition to the "1" used to dial toll calls. Windows 95 automatically adds the "1" for long distance.

▶ **Dial Using Calling Card.** Specifies that Windows 95 should use a calling card when dialing this number. When you select this check box, the Change Calling Card dialog box appears (see fig. 9.6). In this dialog box, you fill out your calling card information. This includes card name (such as AT&T Direct Dial) and calling card number. Click on the Advanced button to fill in Dialing Rules for the card. This includes such rules as country codes, pause for a fixed time, and other commands. Click on OK when you finish filling out the Change Calling Card dialog box.

Figure 9.6

The Change Calling Card dialog box.

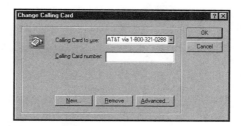

After you save the calling card number, Windows TAPI scrambles the card number and does not display it again. By doing this, you are ensured that someone else cannot steal your calling card number simply by reading your calling card profile in Windows 95.

▶ **This Location Has Call Waiting.** Specifies when a phone from which you are calling has call waiting. You can disable call waiting temporarily each time you use a modem by inserting a special code here (such as *70). You may need to contact your phone company and ask them how to turn off call waiting. If you don't turn off call waiting and someone calls while you are online (that is, when your modem is connected to another modem), the call waiting signal will disconnect your modem. (This is aggravating when you are downloading data or communicating with someone via your modem.) Windows 95 automatically re-enables call waiting when your modem disconnects.

▶ **Tone Dialing and Pulse Dialing.** Specifies the correct dialing method for your telephone system. Most modern phone systems in the United States use tone dialing.

Choose OK on the Dialing Properties sheet to save your new location information and to return to the Modems Properties sheet. Choose OK to exit that sheet.

After you have installed and properly configured your modem, you can use Windows 95 (or another communications program) to remotely access a variety of systems.

A *telephony SERVICE PROVIDER* is a Windows telephony driver that enables a telephony application to control your telephony hardware via the Windows TAPI. Usually, the telephony driver is included as part of the setup procedure when you install the application to work with your hardware.

Phone Dialer is an example of a telephony application (see fig. 9.7). Phone Dialer is bundled with Windows 95 and usually is located in your Accessories folder under the Programs folder on the Start menu. Phone Dialer enables you to use your modem to dial a regular phone number, then, after you're connected, you can pick up the handset of your phone and begin conversing with the person on the other end. You can set dialing properties as you were shown in the preceding list, such as create multiple dialing locations, set calling card information, and more. You also can store up to eight frequently called numbers as well as keep a log file of your calls. The log file comes in handy when you want to keep track of who you called, when you called them, and how long you were connected to them. This is a handy way to create a phone log for expense reimbursements or reconciling phone calls with your phone bill at the end of each month. In Exercise 9.2 at the end of the chapter, you learn how to save a number in Phone Dialer and how to make a call using it.

Figure 9.7

The Phone Dialer main window.

Configuring a Dial-Up Networking Client

 To install Dial-Up Networking (client or server components), the following requirements must be met:

▶ One or more modems must be installed and configured.

▶ 2 MB of free disk space for client and server software must be available.

▶ Optionally, hardware for X.25 or ISDN connections must be installed.

The following steps demonstrate the configuration of Dial-Up Networking for the Internet. These steps assume you have not yet configured a modem for Windows 95, but that one is physically installed in your computer and has a port associated with it in the Device Manager (for example, an internal modem configured to use COM3 should show up in Device Manager as a COM3 port). If not, you may have to use the Add New Hardware icon to allow Windows 95 to detect the port before proceeding with these steps.

The Dial-Up Networking components should already have been installed through Add/Remove Programs in the Control Panel. The TCP/IP protocol also should have been installed through the Network option in Control Panel. Finally, because this is an Internet-related process, if you do not have Internet access, you can substitute another connection type, but your results might vary with those in this process.

1. From the Start menu, choose Settings, Control Panel. Control Panel icons appear.

2. Double-click on the Modems icon. The Install New Modem Wizard appears.

3. Choose the Next button. Windows 95 searches existing modem ports to find an attached modem, and should return with the correct modem type(see fig. 9.8).

Figure 9.8

Detecting a modem.

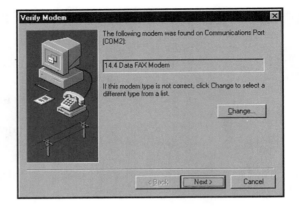

If your modem is not auto-detected, you may need to manually specify it, based on the supported modem types with which it is compatible. Contact your modem manufacturer or consult your documentation for this information.

4. Choose the Next button. Windows 95 installs the modem driver.

5. Choose the Finish button. The Modems Properties sheet appears.

6. Choose Dialing Properties to open the Dialing Properties sheet.

7. Select your country, area code, and dialing method, and choose OK twice to close the Modems Properties sheet.

8. From the Control Panel, double-click on the Add/Remove Programs icon and select the Windows Setup tab to display the optional Windows 95 components.

9. Double-click on Communications and select Dial-Up Networking. Choose OK twice to close the Add/Remove Programs applet and start the copying of files from the distribution media.

10. When prompted, restart the computer to initialize the Dial-Up Networking components.

11. From the Start menu, choose Programs, Accessories, Dial-Up Networking. The Dial-Up Networking folder appears, and the Make New Connection Wizard is launched. Choose Next.

12. Select the modem to be used and type a name to use for the connection settings. Choose Next.

13. Type the phone number and country for the connection you want to make (you may need to get this information from your ISP). Choose Next.

14. Choose Finish to exit. The Dial-Up Networking folder will now show the new connection settings you created as an icon.

15. To verify the network-related settings for the new connection, right-click on the icon you created and choose Properties. The main properties sheet for the new connection appears.

16. Choose Server Type to view the network settings. The Server Types Properties sheet appears (see fig. 9.9).

Figure 9.9

Configuring a dial-up connection.

By default, Dial-Up Networking is configured for a PPP connection using the TCP/IP, IPX/SPX-compatible, and NetBEUI protocols. You should deselect a protocol if it is not needed for better performance.

17. Deselect the NetBEUI and IPX/SPX Compatible protocols and click on the TCP/IP Settings button. The current settings for TCP/IP appear.

18. Enter the appropriate settings for your ISP (you need to obtain these from your provider) and click on OK three times until all properties sheets are closed. You return to the Dial-Up Networking folder.

19. Double-click on the connection icon you created. You are prompted for a user name and password.

20. Type your user name and password for your Internet account, and choose the Connect button. A connection is attempted. If successful, the connection window displays the connection baud rate and active protocols (if Details is selected). You now can use your Internet tools to access Internet resources.

If the logon process for your ISP requires more information than just the user name and password, you might have to use the Dial-Up Scripting tool to provide this information at logon time. Consult your documentation for details. Also, see Chapter 5, "Networking and Interoperability," for details on setting up a connection to the Internet.

Using Applications with a Dial-Up Networking Connection

You should note that, when you consider applications for use over a dial-up connection, focusing on applications already installed at the server-side is best, because having to download and run the application at the client-side greatly reduces performance over the link. Ideal candidates for dial-up networking applications would be, for example, client/server products, which send only high-level commands over the link, reducing network traffic.

The following is a brief list of applications you can use when you have a remote access connection via Dial-Up Networking:

▶ World Wide Web (WWW) browser to navigate the WWW and Internet

▶ Internet e-mail applications to send and receive e-mail

▶ Windows 95 Explorer to access shared folders on remote computers

▶ Microsoft Exchange for e-mail and messaging applications

When you connect to a Windows 95 computer remote access host (server) and use Network Neighborhood on the client to access shared resources, you won't see the resources. This is because the browse feature on the server computer is turned off by default. To see these resources, you can set the Browse Master setting for the server computer to Enable. The browse feature is then enabled for all sessions after that.

If you want to enable browsing each time you connect (this provides some security on the server), you can do so from the client. From the Start menu, select Run. In the Run command line, enter the name of the server computer followed by the name of the shared resource. You must use UNC naming for this to work. For a server named LIFESON with a shared resource name of LEE, for example, you would enter \\LIFESON\LEE. Click on OK. Depending on whether the shared resource is password-protected, you may need to enter a password to access the resource.

Examining Implicit Connections

Dial-Up Networking includes a feature called implicit connections. The *implicit connections* feature enables Dial-Up Networking to remember network connections in the event that you try to access a resource from a network when you are not connected.

When this happens, Dial-Up Networking prompts you to select a Remote Connector to start a remote access session. After you connect to the remote access source, Windows 95 completes the task.

A simple example of this is if you usually use Dial-Up Networking to access a WWW page on the Internet. If you click on a hyperlink in a document that is linked to a WWW page and you are not currently connected to the Internet via Dial-Up Networking, Windows displays the Connect To dialog box to enable you to connect to the remote source. After you're connected to the Internet, your WWW browser application attempts to link to the selected WWW page.

Using the Microsoft Plus! Pack Dial-Up Server

Besides functioning as a client, Windows 95 is capable of acting as a dial-up server to other clients. The Windows 95 Dial-Up Server is included with the Microsoft Plus! Pack, which must be purchased separately from the Windows 95 operating system software.

In addition to providing remote users with access to the resources of the dial-up server itself, the Windows 95 Dial-Up Server also can provide remote clients with access to the NetBEUI or IPX/SPX-based resources of any network to which it is connected, effectively acting as a gateway to those resources.

Unlike Windows NT, Windows 95 cannot act as a gateway to TCP/IP resources or the Internet. It also cannot act as a gateway to a SLIP or IPX network.

The Windows 95 Dial-Up Server can be configured as a PPP server or as a RAS server. RAS must be used by the older Microsoft operating systems because they do not support PPP. The clients that the Windows 95 Dial-Up Server supports are as follows:

- ▶ Windows 95 dial-up client

- ▶ Windows for Workgroups or Windows 3.1 (using RAS only)

- ▶ Windows NT 3.1 (using RAS only)

- ▶ LAN Manager (using RAS only)

- ▶ Any client using PPP

Security Considerations

A number of issues must be considered before configuring Windows 95 as a Dial-Up Networking server. These include:

- ▶ File and Printer Sharing for either Microsoft or NetWare networks must be enabled on the server.

- ▶ User-level security should be enabled on the server to provide the highest level of protection from unauthorized access to shared resources.

- ▶ You can use hardware security tools and specific authentication protocols, such as Challenge-Handshake Authentication Protocol (CHAP) or Shiva Password Authentication Protocol (SPAP) for additional security.

- ▶ When on the Internet, you should not use File and Printer sharing.

- ▶ Firewalls should be installed to separate dial-up access from the rest of the Internet.

- ▶ You can specify a list of those users who can and cannot connect remotely, even if they are valid users when connected directly to the network.

- ▶ Encrypted passwords should be used.

- ▶ Invest in an encryption program for encrypting the data you send over the Internet.

Installing Dial-Up Server

The following steps illustrate how the dial-up server can be configured to allow dial-up access to remote users. Note that the steps assume the server components already have been installed from the Microsoft Plus! Pack, and that File and Printer Sharing for Microsoft Networks and user-level security have been enabled. If all these conditions cannot be met (for example, if you are not on a Windows NT or Novell NetWare network and therefore cannot enable user-level security), you may use share-level security, but results may vary.

Install the Windows 95 Plus! Pack components, including the Dial-Up Networking Server option, using the Add/Remove Programs Wizard from Control Panel.

1. From the Start menu, choose Programs, Accessories, Dial-Up Networking. The Dial-Up Networking folder appears.

2. Choose Connections, Dial-Up Server. The Dial-Up Server dialog box appears (see fig. 9.10).

Figure 9.10

Configuring dial-up server security.

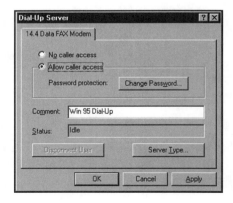

3. Select the Allow Caller Access radio button, and then choose the Add button. A dialog box appears that allows you to specify users who will have dial-up access.

4. Select users as desired, and click on OK. You return to the Dial-Up Server dialog box.

5. Choose the Server Type button, verify that Default is selected, and choose OK twice to close all open dialog boxes. You return to the Desktop and are now ready to receive incoming calls.

If you select Default, Windows 95 automatically switches to a RAS line protocol if a PPP connection fails.

Optimizing Dial-Up Networking Performance

One way in which performance over dial-up connections can be improved is by using either hardware or software compression to reduce the amount of data that must be carried over the link. The distinction between the two types of compression lies in the fact that software compression is performed by the client and server applications, whereas hardware compression is performed by the modems involved in connecting the two systems. In the case of both software and hardware compression, the client and server must be able to support the same type of compression for it to function properly. Under Windows 95, only PPP supports software compression. The setting is ignored for other line protocols.

Software compression is generally preferred, if available, because it reduces the net amount of information to be transmitted over the link.

Use the System Monitor to assist you in monitoring the performance of your Dial-Up Networking under Windows 95. After launching System Monitor, display the following items:

▶ Microsoft Client: Bytes read/second

▶ Microsoft Client: Bytes written/second

▶ Microsoft server threads to check performance of Dial-Up Server

▶ Novell server threads to check performance of Dial-Up Server

Using the Briefcase

Another tool in Windows 95 that can be used to increase the efficiency of mobile computing is the Briefcase. One of the many difficulties of mobile computing is transporting and maintaining files that, for example, are used both at a central location (an office) and with a laptop computer while traveling. The difficulty lies in ensuring that the user is always working with the latest revision of the file and is not duplicating or negating previous work.

The Briefcase addresses this problem by tracking document revisions and comparing them based on their time and date stamps. If the user chooses to synchronize objects that have been placed in the Briefcase, the Briefcase replaces unmodified revisions with modified ones. If more than one revision has been modified, Windows 95 launches the associated application for that file type so that the changes in both can be merged.

Briefcase synchronization works equally well between multiple computers attached by a network or a direct cable connection. Exercise 9.4 at the end of the chapter shows you how to use Briefcase to synchronize files. The Briefcase also can track documents used by multiple users on the same network, using the same algorithms to compare changes made by different users.

When you view the Briefcase folder, you see the files saved there for synchronization. Briefcase is a Windows System folder. Briefcase also contains the following two hidden files:

▶ **DESKTOP.INI.** Includes the OLE information for Briefcase and the settings for confirmation.

▶ **Briefcase database.** Includes date, time, size, status, and the location of the original files in the Briefcase at the last time they were synchronized.

These files are hidden so users do not accidentally delete them.

When you use Briefcase, Windows 95 uses the following files stored in the \WINDOWS\SYSTEM folder:

▶ **LINKINFO.DLL.** Tracks the path of the files to be updated. It also updates the path to create a UNC or volume name.

▶ **SYNCENG.DLL.** Looks at the files to synchronize to make sure they match.

▶ **SYNCUI.DLL.** Contains the GUI for My Briefcase.

Sometimes a file in the Briefcase becomes an orphan file. *Orphan files* are files that have been copied to the Briefcase that no longer have a master file with which to synchronize. An orphan file exists usually because the original file has been deleted, moved, or re-named. Windows 95 attempts to keep track of the link between the files if the original is moved or renamed using the link track-ing system. Sometimes, however, the tracking process fails and you must create a new link after you find the file. An orphan file also can be a new file created inside the Briefcase folder.

You can use Briefcase over a remote access connection. If you use Briefcase in this way and are synchronizing files and one or more are on a remote access site, Briefcase automati-cally connects to the remote server. You must, however, hang up (disconnect) from the remote server after the files are syn-chronized. Briefcase does not do this automatically.

Using Direct Cable Connection

Windows 95 includes the Direct Cable Connection program, which enables you to connect two computers together using a serial or parallel cable. (For serial cables, you can use standard null-modem cables or serial file transfer cables.) Both computers must be running Windows 95, the Direct Cable Connection pro-gram, and use the same parallel or serial port to communicate.

Direct Cable Connection is handy when you don't have a network established between two computers, but you need to transfer or access files from one computer to another.

To set up Direct Cable Connection, make sure the DIRECTCC.EXE file is installed in your \WINDOWS folder. From the Accessories folder, click on Direct Cable Connection. Next, designate one computer as the Host and the other as the Guest. The Host computer is the one on which the files you want to use reside. The Guest computer is the one accessing the host's resources. Click on the Next button. Select the cable type and port (which must be the same on both computers) you are using. Click on the Finish button to initiate the connection process. After you're connected to the Host computer, the Guest computer can access any files from the Host computer. The Host computer's resources appear as a drive, so Windows Explorer can be used to transfer or access files. However, the connection is only one way; the Host computer cannot access files from the Guest computer.

Exercises

Exercise 9.1: Creating a New Dialing Location

Exercise 9.1 shows how to set up a new dialing location for a modem installed under Windows 95. This exercise assumes you have a modem already installed.

1. From the Start menu, choose Settings, Control Panel, and double-click on the Modems icon.

2. In the Modems Properties sheet, select the modem for which you want to create a new location.

3. Choose Dialing Properties to open the Dialing Properties sheet.

4. Click on the New button to open the Create New Location dialog box.

5. In the Create a New Location Named field, enter a new location named **Mobile Office**.

6. Click on OK.

7. Change the settings in the Area Code field to match your area, such as 317.

8. In To Access an Outside Line, first enter **9**. For long distance, enter **1**.

9. Select the Dial Using Credit Card check box. The Change Calling Card dialog box appears. Select a calling card from the drop-down list, such as AT&T via 10ATT0. (You can delete this calling card setting after you finish with the exercise.) Fill in a calling card number in the Calling Card Number field.

10. Click on OK to return to the Dialing Properties sheet.

11. Click on OK to save your new dialing location and close the Dialing Properties sheet. This sets your selected modem to

continues

Exercise 9.1: Continued

use your new dialing location. To change it back to the previous one or to the default location, click on the Dialing Properties button and select the location name from the I Am Dialing From drop-down list.

12. Click on OK to close the Modems Properties sheet.

Exercise 9.2: Using Phone Dialer to Save and Dial a Phone Number

Exercise 9.2 shows how to use Windows' 95 TAPI application Phone Dialer to save a phone number and then use that number to dial your phone. This exercise assumes you have a modem installed under Windows 95, Phone Dialer is installed, and that you have a phone connected to the modem.

1. From the Start menu, choose Programs, Accessories, and click on Phone Dialer. The Phone Dialer application starts.

2. Click on the top blank button under the Speed Dial heading. The Program Speed Dial dialog box appears.

3. In the Name field, enter a name for someone you can call.

4. In the Number to dial field, enter a phone number of someone you can call.

5. Click on the Save button. Phone Dialer places the new name on the top button under the Speed Dial label. You can continue adding speed dial numbers.

6. Click on the top speed dial button again to initiate the phone call. Phone Dialer instructs your modem to call the number you have listed on the speed dial button. When the phone begins ringing or as soon as a person answers the phone on the other end, pick up your receiver and begin talking.

Exercise 9.3:   Installing Dial-Up Networking and Configuring for the Internet

Exercise 9.3 demonstrates the configuration of Dial-Up Networking for the Internet. This exercise assumes you have not yet configured a modem for Windows 95, but that one is physically installed in your computer and has a port associated with it in the Device Manager (for example, an internal modem configured to use COM3 should show up in Device Manager as a COM3 port). If not, you may have to use the Add New Hardware icon to allow Windows 95 to detect the port before proceeding with this exercise. The Dial-Up Networking components should already have been installed through Add/Remove Programs in the Control Panel. The TCP/IP protocol also should have been installed through the Network option in Control Panel. Finally, because this is an Internet-related exercise, if you do not have Internet access, you can substitute another connection type, but your results might vary with those of the exercise.

1. From the Start menu, choose Settings, Control Panel. Control Panel icons appear.

2. Double-click on the Modems icon. The Install New Modem Wizard appears.

3. Choose the Next button. Windows 95 searches existing modem ports to find an attached modem, and should return with the correct modem type (refer to fig. 9.8).

If your modem is not auto-detected, you may need to manually specify it, based on the supported modem types with which it is compatible. Contact your modem manufacturer or consult your documentation for this information.

4. Choose the Next button. Windows 95 installs the modem driver.

5. Choose the Finish button. The Modems Properties sheet appears.

continues

Exercise 9.3: Continued

6. Choose Dialing Properties to open the Dialing Properties sheet.

7. Select your country, area code, and dialing method, and choose OK twice to close the Modems Properties sheet.

8. From the Control Panel, double-click on the Add/Remove Programs icon and select the Windows Setup tab to display the optional Windows 95 components.

9. Double-click on Communications and select Dial-Up Networking. Choose OK twice to close the Add/Remove Programs applet and start the copying of files from the distribution media.

10. Restart the computer when prompted to initialize the Dial-Up Networking components.

11. From the Start menu, choose Programs, Accessories, Dial-Up Networking. The Dial-Up Networking folder appears, and the Make New Connection Wizard starts. Choose Next.

12. Select the modem to be used and type a name to use for the connection settings. Choose Next.

13. Type the phone number and country for the connection you want to make (you may need to get this information from your ISP). Choose Next.

14. Choose Finish to exit. The Dial-Up Networking folder will now show the new connection settings you created as an icon.

15. To verify the network-related settings for the new connection, right-click on the icon you created and choose Properties. The main properties sheet for the new connection appears.

16. Choose Server Type to view the network settings. The Server Types Properties sheet appears (refer to fig. 9.9).

By default, Dial-Up Networking is configured for a PPP connection using the TCP/IP, IPX/SPX-compatible, and NetBEUI protocols. You should deselect a protocol if it is not needed for better performance.

17. Deselect the NetBEUI and IPX/SPX Compatible protocols and click on the TCP/IP Settings button. The current settings for TCP/IP appear.

18. Enter the appropriate settings for your ISP (you need to obtain these from your provider) and choose OK three times until all properties sheets are closed. You return to the Dial-Up Networking folder.

19. Double-click on the connection icon you created. You are prompted for a user name and password.

20. Type your user name and password for your Internet account, and choose the Connect button. A connection is attempted. If successful, the connection window displays the connection baud rate and active protocols (if Details is selected). You can now use your Internet tools to access Internet resources.

If the logon process for your ISP requires more information than just the user name and password, you might have to use the Dial-Up Scripting tool to provide this information at logon time. Consult your documentation for details.

Exercise 9.4: Configuring and Using the Briefcase

Exercise 9.4 demonstrates the configuration and use of the Briefcase. The exercise assumes that the Briefcase component has already been installed and a Briefcase icon exists on the Desktop. If this is not the case, you might need to install the Briefcase component through Add/Remove Programs in the Control Panel. You also need a blank formatted floppy for this exercise.

continues

Exercise 9.4: Continued

> If the Briefcase component does not appear in the list of in-stallable components, the component probably is already installed, but the icon on the Desktop has been deleted. To recreate this icon, simply right-click on the Desktop, choose New, and click on Briefcase.

1. Right-click on an empty area on the Desktop, choose New, and then choose Text Document. You are prompted for a name for the new text document.

2. Double-click on the document. Notepad is launched and the empty document is displayed.

3. Type **REV1** on the first line; choose File, Exit; and then choose Yes to save the file. You return to the Desktop.

4. Double-click on the Briefcase icon on the Desktop. A Welcome screen briefly describes the use of the Briefcase.

5. Click on the Finish button. The Briefcase file list (currently empty) appears.

6. Using the right mouse button, drag the TEST.TXT file from the Desktop to the Briefcase window and, when prompted, choose Make Sync Copy. The file is linked to the Briefcase.

7. Close the Briefcase window. You return to the Desktop.

8. Insert a blank formatted floppy disk in drive A, right-click on New Briefcase, and choose the A drive from the Send To menu. The Briefcase is moved to the floppy.

9. Double-click on the TEXT.TXT file on the Desktop. Notepad is launched, displaying the file.

10. Type **REV2** on the second line; choose File, Exit; and then choose Yes to save the file. You return to the Desktop.

11. Right-click on the My Computer icon and choose Explore. The Exploring window appears.

12. Choose View, Details. Full file details are displayed.

13. Click on the icon for the A drive in the left panel of the Explorer window. The contents of drive A are displayed.

14. Double-click on the New Briefcase icon in the right panel of the Explorer window. The contents of the Briefcase are displayed and should be similar to figure 9.11 (note that the status of the file is Needs Updating).

Figure 9.11

The Briefcase after a file modification has been made.

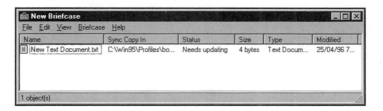

15. Double-click on the TEST.TXT file. Notepad is launched, showing that the file consists of only the line REV1.

16. Close the Notepad window. In the Explorer, choose Briefcase, Update All to open the Update Briefcase dialog box (see fig. 9.12). You are prompted to confirm the update.

Figure 9.12

Synchronizing the Briefcase contents.

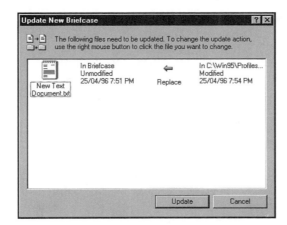

17. Choose Update. The briefcase file is replaced with the more recent file from the Desktop. When the update is complete, double-click on the TEST.TXT file inside the Briefcase. The file now contains the lines REV1 and REV2.

18. Close the Explorer window. You return to the Desktop.

Review Questions

The following questions will test your knowledge of the information in this chapter. For additional questions, see MCP Endeavor and the Microsoft Roadmap/Assessment Exam on the CD-ROM that accompanies this book.

1. Windows 95 uses line protocols to transport network protocols over a phone line. The default line protocol for Windows 95 Dial-Up Networking is _____.

    A. SLIP

    B. NRN

    C. RAS

    D. PPP

2. Jack uses Dial-Up Networking to access a remote server. He experiences problems with the connection and wants to diagnose the problem using a log file. Which two of the following are log files provided by Windows 95 Dial-Up Networking?

    A. PPP.LOG

    B. PPPMODEM.TXT

    C. MODEMLOG.TXT

    D. PPPLOG.TXT

3. You set up Windows 95 Dial-Up Networking and must choose a protocol that matches the one on the Dial-Up Server on the Windows 95 server you are dialing. Which three of the following protocols are supported over a Windows 95 PPP line connection?

    A. TCP/IP

    B. RAS

    C. IPX/SPX-compatible

    D. NetBEUI

4. You must set up your Windows 95 computer to use Dial-Up Networking. Under it, you must have multiple protocols configured because of the remote server you'll be accessing. _____ is the only line protocol that can transport multiple network protocols over a single link.

   A. NRN

   B. RAS

   C. PPP

   D. SLIP

5. You set up Windows 95 to have a direct data feed over the network. Which two of the following does Windows 95 treat as it would treat a network card?

   A. A modem

   B. ISDN

   C. A router

   D. X.25

6. Vanessa works in the company sales department and travels with a laptop computer. In her office is her main computer, which she must connect to via remote access. She asks you how much free disk space she needs for client and server software to install Dial-Up Networking. What do you tell her?

   A. 1 MB

   B. 2 MB

   C. 5 MB

   D. 10 MB

7. Which of the following statements is true?

   A. The basic Windows 95 package includes Dial-Up Networking server capability.

   B. Windows 95 is able to act as a gateway to TCP/IP resources on the Internet.

C. The basic Windows 95 package includes a Dial-Up Networking client that supports IPX/SPX.

D. Windows 95 Dial-Up Networking supports real-mode protocols.

8. Although SLIP is an older connection protocol, Windows 95 still supports it. You set up SLIP on several of your Windows 95 computers. As you configure SLIP, you need to bind it to a protocol. Which of the following protocols does a SLIP connection support?

A. NetBEUI

B. TCP/IP

C. IPX/SPX

D. Both A and B

9. You are manning the company help desk and receive a call. The caller tells you he wants to run a TAPI application under Windows 95. What does TAPI stand for?

A. Telephone Answering Programming Interchange

B. Telephony And Program Internet

C. Telephony Application Programming Interface

D. None of the Above

10. Susan needs to configure her computer to be a dial-up server using Windows' 95 Dial-Up Server software. She runs the Add/Remove Programs and clicks on the Windows Setup tab. She can't find the option for installing the server software on the list of Windows components. Why not?

A. Dial-Up Server is available only with the Microsoft Plus! Pack software.

B. Dial-Up Server is available only after you set up the Dial-Up Networking software.

    C. Dial-Up Server is listed under the Accessories components option.

    D. Dial-Up Server is part of Dial-Up Networking and is turned on by choosing Connections, Dial-Up Server.

11. Richard installs the Dial-Up Server and tries to access his computer from another computer using Dial-Up Networking. He cannot make a connection. From the following list, select two answers that may be the reason he cannot connect.

    A. He must be running Windows NT as the server.

    B. The client and server computers are not set up with the same protocols.

    C. The Allow Caller Access option is not selected in the Dial-Up Server dialog box.

    D. The Server Enabled button on the Dial-Up Server dialog box is not selected.

12. You receive a call from a user running Windows 95 with a modem installed. She reports that after making a connection, she sometimes gets prematurely disconnected. From the following list, what solution could you tell her to make that might solve her problem and still keep the modem she uses?

    A. Switch to an ISDN connection

    B. Enable caller ID on the phone line she uses.

    C. Disable call waiting on the phone line she uses.

    D. All of the above.

13. You run a pool of computers at a university on your off-hours. You have NetWare Connect software running for remote access services. Which two of the following statements are true?

    A. You can create modem-sharing pools with NetWare Connect.

    B. NetWare Connect uses the NetBEUI protocol for Novell servers.

    C. Windows 95 Dial-Up Networking can control NetWare Connect workstations remotely.

    D. You cannot dial into a Windows 95 Dial-Up Networking Server from NetWare Connect.

14. Tony runs Briefcase to synchronize his files from his laptop to his desktop computer and vice versa. When he tries to synchronize a file, he discovers one is orphaned. What is one explanation for the cause of this orphaned file?

    A. The file in Briefcase is set as read-only

    B. The original file has been renamed

    C. Briefcase automatically updated the master file attributes

    D. All of the above

15. You receive a support call from one of your users who is using Direct Cable Connection. The caller is trying to access files on his desktop computer from his laptop and vice versa. He attaches one end of a serial cable to the host's COM1 port and the other end to the guest's COM2 port. What do you tell him to do?

    A. Create a new password on his host computer only.

    B. Connect guest to COM1 and host to COM2.

    C. Use the parallel ports instead.

    D. Connect guest to COM 1 and leave host alone.

16. A Dial-Up Networking Server in your company enables users to access resources remotely. You enable these users to access files on a Windows NT server. Which of the following should you do to provide the highest level of protection from unauthorized access to these files?

A. Enable the Windows 95 Firewall program

B. Set up share-level security

C. Set up user-level security

D. None of the above

17. You give a presentation to your support group about Windows' 95 TAPI features. Which of the following are TAPI features in Windows 95? Pick two.

A. Exchange Client

B. Phone Dialer

C. Notepad

D. Modem Dialing Properties

18. Jill sets up the Windows 95 Dial-Up Networking feature so she can dial into a Windows NT 3.5 server. Which of the following is accessible through this connection?

A. Microsoft-based servers, such as Windows NT, Windows for Workgroups, and LAN Manager running NetBEUI

B. Novell NetWare servers running IPX/SPX on the Windows NT network

C. The Internet via Windows NT Internet gateway

D. All of the above

19. Phil wants to access the Internet from his workstation using a high-speed modem. Which one of the following modem types do you suggest he invest in?

A. ISDN

B. X.25

C. PSTN

D. TCP/IP

20. To decrease the amount of noise generated in the office, you ask all end-users to disable the modem speaker on their modems. How can they do this from within Windows 95?

    A. Change the sound card IRQ to 5.

    B. Set the Speaker Volume control on the Modem Properties sheet to Off.

    C. Disconnect the modem from its speakers.

    D. Set the Speaker On/Off property on the Taskbar to Off.

Review Answers

1. D	6. B	11. B C	16. C
2. C D	7. C	12. C	17. B D
3. A C D	8. B	13. A D	18. D
4. C	9. C	14. B	19. A
5. B D	10. A	15. D	20. B

Stop! Before reading this chapter, test yourself to determine how much study time you will need to devote to this section.

1. Newman and Jerry are connected by peer-to-peer network. Each runs Windows 95, but only Jerry has a fax/modem card installed. How can Newman use Jerry's fax capabilities?

2. Jerry wants to limit when Newman can access his (Jerry's) fax capabilities. Describe how Jerry can do this.

3. Charlotte sets up Microsoft Exchange under Windows 95. She wants to receive e-mail from the Internet. What must she do to configure this in Exchange?

4. What service do you need to install for Windows 95 to send and receive Microsoft Mail? Can this be done running only Windows 95 computers connected in a peer-to-peer network?

5. Instead of receiving Internet Mail, Charlotte wants to receive Compu-Serve Mail. What is the name of the directory on the Windows 95 CD-ROM you must specify to set up Exchange for CompuServe Mail support?

Answers

1. They both need to install Exchange and the Microsoft Fax information service; then Jerry needs to enable the Fax Sharing feature of the fax information service. See "Configuring Exchange to Share a Fax."

2. Jerry can set the sharing fax feature to require a password or set it to read-only access. Jerry also can disconnect from the network or shut down his computer. See "Configuring Exchange to Use the Microsoft Fax Service in a Stand-Alone Environment."

3. Make sure Charlotte has a connection to the Internet through a direct connection or through a dial-up ISP service; then, install and configure the Internet Mail information service under Exchange. See "Using Exchange to Send and Receive Internet Mail."

4. You must use the Microsoft Mail information service, which you configure by running the Mail and Fax software. Yes, but you must have a workgroup postoffice set up on a Windows 95 workstation. See "Configuring Exchange to Send and Receive Microsoft Mail."

5. \DRIVERS\OTHER\EXCHANGE\COMPUSRV. See "Configuring Exchange to Access CompuServe Mail."

Chapter 10

Microsoft Exchange

This chapter will help you prepare for the exam by covering the following objectives:

Test Objectives

- ▶ Share a fax

- ▶ Configure a fax for both stand-alone and shared situations

- ▶ Configure Microsoft Exchange to access the Internet

- ▶ Configure a Windows 95 computer to send and receive mail

- ▶ Configure a Windows 95 computer to access CompuServe Mail

This chapter looks at the Microsoft Exchange client that ships with Windows 95. Specifically, this chapter discusses the following topics:

- ▶ Exchange client architecture

- ▶ Installing the Exchange client

- ▶ Configuring the Exchange client

- ▶ Sending and receiving messages

- ▶ Using Microsoft Fax with the Exchange client

The Windows 95 Exchange client enables you to send and receive e-mail messages over a local area network, send and receive messages over a remote network (such as CompuServe), and send and receive faxes. Although many users use the Exchange client to simply send and receive e-mail, its usefulness extends far beyond that. This is because the Exchange client is built around the

Messaging Application Programming Interface (MAPI), which is a set of standard procedures used to exchange messages between Windows-based computers.

In this chapter, you learn how to install and configure the Exchange client for e-mail, how to send and receive messages, and how to use the Microsoft Fax service with Exchange. In the latter case, you also learn how to set up a shared Microsoft Fax environment, so one user can share his or her fax with other users on a network.

Don't confuse the Microsoft Exchange client that comes with Windows 95 with the Microsoft Exchange product. The Microsoft Exchange product is a client/server messaging platform that runs on Microsoft Windows NT. The Exchange client that ships with Windows 95 is simply a client application that can be used for e-mail, faxing, and other messaging services. It is not, however, a client/server platform.

Because of its use of MAPI (pronounced "mappy") and its modular, extensible architecture, the Exchange client can function as a universal inbox to receive messages from a number of services, including Microsoft Fax, The Microsoft Network Online Service (MSN), and any other MAPI-compliant services.

The Exchange client offers a wide range of features, including the following:

▶ Sending and receiving mail from other MAPI message stores, such as a Windows 95 Workgroup Postoffice, Microsoft Mail Server, Microsoft Exchange Server, or many others

▶ Sending and receiving secure faxes using the Microsoft Fax service

▶ The capability to attach electronic files or Object Linking and Embedding (OLE) objects to messages

▶ The capability to use Rich Text Formatting (RTF) to format messages with numerous fonts, colors, and other effects

> ▶ Personal address books that can contain the mail and fax addresses of frequently contacted recipients

> ▶ A hierarchical system of folders to easily keep track of your messages

Understanding the Microsoft Exchange Client Architecture

Like many Windows 95 components, the Microsoft Exchange client has a modular architecture. The two main components to the Microsoft Exchange client are as follows:

> ▶ Messaging Application Programming Interface (MAPI)

> ▶ Information services

MAPI enables multiple services to be installed that interact with the Exchange client. Windows 95 includes a number of these services, and additional third-party services can be added as well.

Messaging Application Programming Interface (MAPI)

MAPI is a set of standard commands that can be used by messaging applications to communicate with other MAPI-compliant applications and services. For example, the Exchange client uses MAPI to send mail messages to a Microsoft Exchange Server. In addition, the Exchange client can communicate with other MAPI-compliant services, such as a Microsoft Mail or the CompuServe Mail service.

The messaging architecture of Windows 95 uses a front-end client and a back-end service to send electronic messages. The MAPI specification enables electronic messages to be sent using any MAPI-aware application as a front-end and any MAPI-compliant service as the back-end portion, which is responsible for receiving and exchanging the messages (see fig. 10.1). Microsoft Word is an example of a MAPI-aware application. After a MAPI service has been configured properly, you can use Microsoft Word to send documents directly to the MAPI service using the File, Mail command. Thus, a MAPI-enabled application can send messages without requiring a full messaging client, such as Exchange client.

Figure 10.1

A diagram of how MAPI works with front-end clients and back-end services.

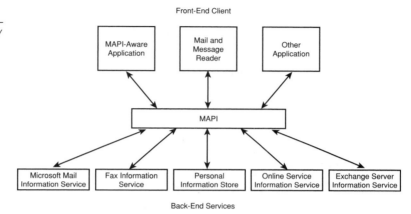

An easy way to know the difference between a front-end client and a back-end service is this: the front-end provides the user interface, and the back-end provides the instructions on how to transmit, store, and receive the data.

Information Services

The Microsoft Exchange client is sometimes referred to as a universal inbox because it can send and receive messages to and from any MAPI-compliant information service. For example, the Exchange client can receive electronic faxes or messages from Microsoft Mail, Microsoft Exchange Server, and Internet Mail post offices.

The Microsoft Exchange client uses MAPI-compliant services to communicate with other MAPI-compliant applications, such as post offices, fax services, and messaging applications. Windows 95 includes the following MAPI services that can be used by the Exchange client:

- ▶ Personal Address Book

- ▶ Personal Information Store

- ▶ Microsoft Mail (including Workgroup Post offices)

- ▶ Microsoft Fax

- ▶ CompuServe Mail

- ▶ The Microsoft Network Online Service (MSN)

- ▶ Exchange Server

The first time you start the Exchange client, the Microsoft Exchange Setup Wizard prompts you for the services you want to use with the Exchange client. You also can add and configure services at any later time by choosing Tools, Services in the Exchange client. You also can install or configure services using the Mail and Fax icon in the Control Panel.

Personal Address Book

The Personal Address Book service is installed by default with the Microsoft Exchange client. The Personal Address Book can contain the names and addresses of recipients to which an Exchange user commonly sends messages. For example, rather than type the recipient's name and fax phone number manually, you can select them from the Personal Address Book after you add the recipient to your Personal Address Book. Similarly, you can select a frequently contacted recipient from the Personal Address Book instead of by a search through a large address list of mailboxes on a Microsoft Mail Server or Exchange Server post office. Furthermore, you can use the Personal Address Book to create personal distribution lists for messages sent to multiple recipient names.

A Personal Address Book, which has the extension PAB, is stored in a file specified by the user. Thus, multiple PAB files can be created for use by different users using the same Exchange client. In addition, this allows the Personal Address Book to be located on the hard drive of the Exchange client so that the Personal Address Book can be accessible even when the client is not attached to the network or the Exchange or Mail Server. This makes it convenient to create a new message and address it to a recipient even when not connected to the Exchange or Mail Server. You might need to do this, for example, when traveling or away from the office, or if the network is currently "down" in the office.

Personal Information Store

An *information store* is a repository for electronic messages and attachments. When a message is sent to the Exchange client, it is received into the *Personal Information Store*, which is installed by default with the Exchange client. The Personal Information Store is contained in a file with the extension PST (Microsoft Personal Folder) and with a name specified by the user. This feature allows a Personal Information Store to be created for each user using the Exchange client, and for the Personal Information Store to be located on the hard drive of the Exchange client.

Personal Information Stores are referred to as Personal Folders when you configure or add a new Personal Information Store. Also, some applications create their own Personal Information Stores.

The Personal Information Store can contain a number of personal folders that can be defined by a user. By default, the Personal Information Store contains the following folders, as shown in figure 10.2:

▶ Deleted Items

▶ Inbox

▶ Outbox

▶ Sent Items

When a message is deleted from a folder, it is moved to the Deleted Items folder so it can be recovered if the message is later needed. When a user exits the Exchange client, you can set up Exchange so that all messages are removed from the Deleted Items folder and are no longer available.

Figure 10.2

The Exchange client showing a Personal Information Store.

The Inbox contains messages that have been sent to the user. These messages can be from any of the services that have been configured for the Exchange client, including Microsoft Mail, Fax, or Exchange Server.

The Outbox contains messages that have been created by the client but have not yet been sent. When a user sends the message, it is sent using the specified service and is moved to the Sent Items folder.

A user also can create a Personal Folder for organizing messages. For example, a user may want to move all messages pertaining to Top Secret Project X to a folder named "Top Secret Project X Messages." When you set up a Personal Folder like this, Exchange refers to the name you give it as a friendly name. The friendly name is *not* the PST file name; rather it is the name that appears in the Exchange window after you set it up. The PST name is the actual file name that resides on your client machine or network server.

By default, when you create a new Personal Folder, Exchange adds a Deleted Items folder in the new Personal Folder. You then can add folders to the Personal Folder as needed. You create these additional folders from within the Exchange window.

Microsoft Mail Server

If you have a mailbox on a Microsoft Mail Server, you can access the mailbox using the Microsoft Exchange client configured to use the Microsoft Mail service. Using the Exchange client instead of the Microsoft Mail client allows you to benefit from all the features of the Microsoft Exchange client. As well, unlike the Microsoft Mail client, the Exchange client is a "universal inbox," enabling you to access multiple MAPI services, such as Exchange Server and Internet Mail.

The Microsoft Mail Server is a separate server application you can purchase from Microsoft. It enables you to send, receive, store, and manage Microsoft Mail clients from a variety of platforms, including Windows NT, Windows for Workgroups 3.11, and Windows 95.

Do not confuse this server with the Microsoft Mail client you receive with Windows 95, and which you can set up with Exchange. Sometimes this is called the *workgroup edition* of Microsoft Mail. The workgroup edition enables you to set up a post office on one Windows 95 computer and let other workstations access that post office through a network or remote access connection. The other workstations can send and receive e-mail via the post office.

The workstation edition provides a powerful e-mail system, but does not offer all of the features as the full-service Microsoft Mail Server. The limitations include no access to Microsoft Mail gateways, no mail exchange with users of a different post office, and limited administration tools.

To allow the Exchange client to access a mailbox on a Microsoft Mail Server, the Microsoft Mail service is configured with the Universal Naming Convention (UNC) path of the Microsoft Mail Server post office. The UNC share name of a Microsoft Mail Server post office is commonly something like *SERVER*\\MAILDATA.

Microsoft Fax

The Microsoft Fax service can be used to send electronic faxes through a fax modem on the local computer or through a fax modem shared on the network. In addition, the Microsoft Exchange client Inbox can receive electronic faxes sent to the fax modem on the computer. Using the Exchange client, the same address book can be used to address messages to mail or fax recipients. Configuring the Microsoft fax service to be used in the Exchange client enables electronic documents and messages to be sent to fax machines in the same manner as if the destination were a mailbox. The destination for the Microsoft fax can be either a fax machine or a fax modem. To receive an electronic document attachment, the recipient must have either a Class 1 or 2 fax modem.

For information on how to install and configure the Microsoft Fax service, see the section "Configuring Exchange to Use the Microsoft Fax Service" later in this chapter.

CompuServe Mail

The CompuServe Mail service enables the Exchange client to send and receive mail directly to and from the CompuServe online service. If you have a CompuServe account, the Exchange client can be configured to dial up the CompuServe online service through a modem and exchange mail with the CompuServe service. You then can have Exchange disconnect you from CompuServe so you can read any new mail messages while offline; that is, while you are not connected to CompuServe.

To install and configure the CompuServe Mail service, see the section "Configuring Exchange to Access CompuServe Mail" later in this chapter.

As you will see in the "Configuring Exchange to Access CompuServe Mail" section, the information service for CompuServe Mail is not installed by default under Exchange. You must access the service from the Windows 95 CD-ROM when setting up the CompuServe Mail service.

Microsoft Network Online Service Mail

The Microsoft Network (MSN) is an online service similar to CompuServe. The MSN Mail service enables the Exchange client to send and receive mail to and from MSN through a modem connection. If you have an MSN account, the Exchange client can be configured to dial up MSN and send and receive mail to and from MSN.

In the section "Configuring Exchange to Access MSN Mail" later in this chapter, you learn how to install the MSN Mail service.

Exchange Server

The Microsoft Exchange Server service enables a client to send and receive messages to and from a Microsoft Exchange Server. Microsoft Exchange Server is a client/server messaging system that runs on Windows NT Server.

Do not confuse the Microsoft Exchange Server with the Exchange client software you receive with Windows 95. Exchange Server is a separate messaging program that runs only on Windows NT Server. You can, however, connect to an Exchange Server from Windows 95 using the Exchange client software that is bundled with Windows 95 and is the topic of this chapter. See the next Note about upgrading to a new Exchange client if using Exchange Server.

An Exchange Server contains such features as the following:

▶ The use of public folders in which users can post messages and use MAPI-aware applications

▶ Recipient address list replication among Microsoft Exchange Server and Microsoft Mail Server post offices

▶ The capability to send and receive mail messages using the security features of a Windows NT domain

After installing the Exchange Server service, the Exchange client will have the following functions enabled:

▶ **Inbox Assistant.** Enables an Exchange client user to set up rules that apply to new messages in the client's Exchange Server mailbox. For example, Inbox Assistant can be set to forward automatically all high-priority messages to a folder titled "Urgent Mail."

▶ **Out of Office Assistant.** Enables an Exchange user to set up rules for receiving and automatically replying to new messages. For example, an automatic response to any new messages can be sent saying that the user is out of the office until next week. In addition, new messages can be forwarded to another mailbox depending on their urgency, on who sent the messages, or even on their content (such as phrases like "you're fired").

The Microsoft Exchange Server CD-ROM contains an updated Exchange client that should be used with an Exchange Server rather than the client that comes with Windows 95. The Exchange client that shipped with Windows 95 does not have all the functionality of the version on the Exchange Server CD-ROM. For example, the client does not have the capability to post messages to public folders.

Installing the Exchange Client

Depending on the options chosen during the installation of Windows 95, the Windows 95 Exchange client may or may not have been installed. If the Windows 95 Desktop contains an icon titled "Inbox," then double-clicking on this icon starts the Microsoft Exchange client. If the Inbox is not already on the Windows 95

Desktop, then the Exchange client likely has not yet been installed from the Windows 95 distribution files.

To install the Windows 95 Exchange client from the Windows 95 distribution files, perform the following steps:

1. From the Start menu, choose Settings, Control Panel. The Control Panel appears.

2. Double-click on the Add/Remove Programs icon. The Add/Remove Programs Properties sheet appears.

3. Select the Windows Setup tab, select the Microsoft Exchange check box, and choose OK. The check box should not be gray because you will be installing all the Exchange client components. The files are installed. You are prompted for the path to the Windows 95 distribution files if they cannot be found.

4. Verify that there is now an Inbox icon on the Desktop and a Microsoft Exchange entry in the Start menu Programs.

The first time you try to use Exchange (such as double-clicking the Inbox icon), you are prompted to configure it. The Inbox Setup Wizard walks you through setting up the following items:

▶ **Information services.** You can set up Microsoft Mail, Internet Mail, and CompuServe Mail from the Inbox Setup Wizard. Later, you can set up additional services, such as the Microsoft Network (MSN) online service. Fax services is another information service Exchange supports.

▶ **Profiles.** Profiles are collections of information services that users use and that tell Exchange what type of message to create and how to create it. Users can have multiple profiles set up. You might, for example, have a profile for sending and creating messages when you work at the office and can connect to the company LAN. You might have another profile set up for when you work at home (assuming you are setting up a laptop or portable device) and don't have access to the LAN or must use remote access to connect to the LAN.

Message profiles contain the following items:

▶ **Delivery.** Instructs Exchange on where to send outgoing messages and where incoming messages are stored.

▶ **Addressing.** Instructs Exchange on where to find addresses for recipients.

▶ **Services.** Instructs Exchange on the type of message to create.

The following section discusses how to configure Exchange in more detail.

Configuring a Microsoft Exchange Client

The first time the Microsoft Exchange client is started, by double-clicking on the Inbox on the Desktop or by double-clicking on Mail and Fax in the Control Panel, the Exchange Setup Wizard is displayed. The Exchange Setup Wizard enables services to be configured for Microsoft Exchange and enables these settings to be saved in a profile. Any number of profiles can be created on the Exchange client to support multiple configurations. For example, one profile can be created that automatically connects the Exchange client to a Microsoft Mail post office on the network, and another profile can be created that prompts you to make a remote dial-up connection to the Microsoft Mail post office, using a modem. Additionally, individual profiles can be created for different users who will be using the Exchange client at different times. In short, a *profile* contains all the information necessary to connect to the appropriate services required.

The Microsoft Exchange client contains many configurable features that are explained in the online help files. For the Windows 95 certification exam, you should, at a minimum, know how to configure the Microsoft Exchange client to use information services that can be installed with Windows 95. This includes Microsoft Mail, CompuServe Mail, Internet Mail, and Fax services. You also should read the *Microsoft Windows 95 Resource Kit* for additional details on Exchange-supported information services.

The profile that the Exchange client uses when the Inbox is opened can be selected through the Mail and Fax icon in Control Panel, or through the Inbox icon Properties sheet.

When the Exchange client is first started, the Microsoft Exchange Setup Wizard asks whether Exchange has been used before or, in other words, whether you already have a profile configured for yourself. If the correct profile has already been created for you, you may select Yes and choose the profile to start Microsoft Exchange. To create a new profile, select No when prompted whether you have used Microsoft Exchange before, and choose Next. Modifications to the profile also can be made at a later time by selecting the profile, starting the Exchange client, and making the desired changes. Additional profiles can be created by choosing Show Profiles and then Add from the Mail and Fax applet in the Control Panel.

If you want to be prompted about which profile to use when starting the Exchange client, choose Tools, Options in the Exchange client and select Prompt for a profile to be used when starting Microsoft Exchange.

After a profile is created, the Microsoft Exchange Setup Wizard displays a dialog box enabling you to choose the information services to be used with the profile. For the Windows 95 certification exam, you should know how to add and configure the appropriate service to perform the following exam tasks:

▶ Configure Exchange to send and receive mail

▶ Configure Exchange to access CompuServe Mail

▶ Configure Exchange to access The Microsoft Network Online Service (MSN)

▶ Configure Exchange to send and receive Internet Mail

▶ Configure Exchange to send and receive electronic faxes

Configuring Exchange to Send and Receive Mail

To configure the Exchange client to send and receive mail, at least one mail service must be installed and configured. In general, you start setting up any information service under Exchange by using the Services dialog box. You then click the Add button and pick the information service to install. Finally, you configure specific settings for that service.

In the following sections, you learn how to set up different information services under Exchange.

Configuring Exchange to Send and Receive Microsoft Mail

You can configure Exchange to access a mailbox on a Microsoft Mail post office. Before setting up the Exchange information service for Microsoft Mail, you need to have a Microsoft Mail post office and mailbox set up. You read earlier that you can have the post office set up on a Microsoft Mail Server computer or on a Windows 95 computer running the Microsoft Mail workstation edition. Here, you are shown how to set it up on Windows 95. After you set up the post office, you need to set up mailboxes for each user who will have access to the post office. Mail messages sent to a user are stored in the post office until that user connects to the post office and receives his or her mail.

For more information on addressing messages, attaching documents, and sending mail, see the section "Sending Messages Using Microsoft Exchange Client" later in this chapter.

In the following sections, you learn how to set up a workgroup post office, create mailboxes, and then set up the Microsoft Mail client.

Setting Up a Workgroup Postoffice

If you do not have a Microsoft Mail Server post office on your network, you can use or create a Workgroup Postoffice, which is an optional component of Windows 95. The Workgroup Postoffice is similar to a Microsoft Mail Server post office except that it cannot be used to exchange mail with recipients on other post offices. To connect to an existing Workgroup Postoffice, enter the UNC path of that post office in the Microsoft Mail service setup dialog box. The UNC share name of a Workgroup Postoffice commonly takes the form *SERVER*\WGPO*????*, where *????* is an incremental number such as 0000.

A Windows 95 computer also can be used to create a Workgroup Postoffice. The following steps illustrate the necessary steps for creating a new Workgroup Postoffice on a Windows 95 computer.

1. From the Start menu, choose Settings, Control Panel. The Control Panel appears.

2. Double-click on the Microsoft Mail Postoffice icon. The Microsoft Workgroup Postoffice Admin dialog box appears.

3. Select Create A New Workgroup Postoffice and choose Next. You are prompted for the location of the post office.

4. Specify the path to the location where the Workgroup Postoffice should be created, and choose Next. For example, type **C:**. The post office files are created in a directory named WGPO0000 in the location specified, and the Enter Your Administrator Account Details dialog box appears.

5. You must enter the name of the user, the mailbox name, and a password for the administrator account. In the Name and Mailbox fields, enter **ADMIN**, for the Password field, enter **PASSWORD**, and then choose OK. A message reminds you that you must share the WGPO0000 directory with all the other users who will be using the post office.

6. If WGPO0000 is on the Windows 95 computer, start Explorer and select the WGPO0000 directory. The WGPO0000 directory is highlighted.

7. Click on the right mouse button and select Sharing from the context-sensitive menu. The Sharing tab of the WGPO0000 Properties sheet appears.

8. Give all post office members full control access to the WGPO0000 directory. If share-level security is used, assign a Full Control password to the directory and provide all post office members with this password. If user-level sharing is used, give all the post office members Full Control permissions by choosing the Permissions button and adding the user accounts to the Full Control list box.

9. Choose OK to share the WGPO0000 directory. The WGPO0000 directory folder symbol is replaced with a sharing hand symbol.

You now need to create mailboxes for your new post office.

Creating a Post Office Mailbox

To create a mailbox for each member of the Workgroup Post-office, use the following steps:

1. From the Control Panel, double-click on the Microsoft Mail Post office icon. The Microsoft Workgroup Postoffice Admin dialog box appears.

2. Select Administer an Existing Workgroup Postoffice and choose Next. You are prompted for the post office location.

3. Type the path to the Workgroup Postoffice files, such as **C:\WGPO0000**, and choose Next.

4. Enter the administrator mailbox name and password, and choose Next. The Post office Manager dialog box appears.

5. Choose Add User. The Add User dialog box opens.

6. Enter the name of the user, the mailbox name, the mailbox password, any additional information for the new user, and choose OK. The mailbox is added to the list of users with mailboxes on the post office.

7. Add other users if needed and choose Close to close the Post office Manager.

You also can use the Post office Manager dialog box to delete users, reset a user's password if the user forgets it, and compress mailbox folders to reclaim space from deleted messages.

Setting Up a Microsoft Mail Service

After you set up a workgroup post office and mailbox(es), you can configure Exchange with the Microsoft Mail information service. The following steps show you how to do this:

1. From the Control Panel, double-click on the Mail and Fax icon. The MS Exchange Settings Properties dialog box appears (see fig. 10.3).

Figure 10.3

Exchange client services.

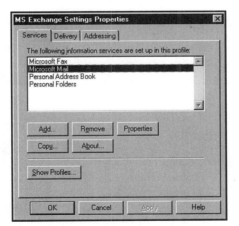

2. Choose Add to open the Add Service to Profile dialog box.

3. Select the Microsoft Mail service and choose OK. The Microsoft Mail Service Properties dialog box appears.

4. Type the path to the Microsoft Mail Server post office or Workgroup Postoffice and select Automatically Sense LAN or Remote. The Exchange client is configured for remote access if a network connection is not detected.

5. Select the Logon tab, enter your mailbox name and password, and choose OK. The MS Exchange Settings Properties dialog box again appears.

6. Choose OK to save the changes to your Exchange client profile.

7. Double-click on the Desktop Inbox icon to start Exchange. The mailbox is displayed along with some test messages.

Configuring Exchange to Access CompuServe Mail

In the following steps, you configure the Exchange client to access a mailbox located on the CompuServe online service. To perform this procedure, you must have an existing CompuServe account and have a modem configured on the Windows 95 client. You also must have the Windows 95 Setup CD-ROM.

1. Start the Exchange client, choose Tools, Services, and choose Add. The Add Service to Profile dialog box appears.

2. Choose Have Disk and enter the path to the \DRIVERS\ OTHER\EXCHANGE\COMPUSRV directory on the Windows 95 CD-ROM.

3. Choose OK. The CompuServe Mail Settings Properties sheet appears.

4. Type your CompuServe account name, ID, and password in the Name, CompuServe ID, and Password fields in the General tab.

5. Select the Connection tab and type the phone number used to connect to CompuServe in the Phone Number field.

6. Select the Advanced tab and choose the Change CompuServe Dir button. Select the path to your CompuServe software directory; for example, select C:\CSERVE. Close the services Properties sheets.

Configuring Exchange to Access MSN Mail

In the following steps, you configure the Exchange client to access your MSN mailbox. To perform this exercise, the MSN software must be installed, you must have an existing MSN account, and a modem must be installed on the Windows 95 client.

1. Choose Tools, Services in the Exchange client and choose Add. The Add Service to Profile dialog box appears.

2. If MSN has been installed on the Desktop, The Microsoft Network Online Service appears in the list of available services to add. If not, install MSN from the Windows Setup tab of the Add/Remove Programs Control Panel applet.

3. Select The Microsoft Network Online Service from the list and choose OK. The MSN service is added to the list of services.

4. Select The Microsoft Network Online Service from the list and choose Properties. The Microsoft Network Properties sheet appears.

5. Inspect the options that are available and choose OK twice to close the Properties sheet. The MSN mail service becomes available in the Exchange client.

Using Exchange to Send and Receive Internet Mail

Microsoft Exchange can be used to send and receive mail to and from other clients on the Internet who are using the Simple Mail Transfer Protocol (SMTP).

Almost all mail sent across the Internet uses the SMTP format. SMTP messages are text-only ASCII messages but they can include support for binary attachments using such protocols as MIME or UUENCODE.

To exchange mail over the Internet, you must have a service configured that has a gateway to the Internet. Examples of such services include the following:

▶ Microsoft Mail Server with an SMTP Gateway installed

▶ Netscape Mail

▶ Microsoft Plus! Pack Internet Mail

Use the following steps to set up and configure the Internet Mail information service in Exchange. To do this, you must have a direct connection to the Internet through a network, or have dial-up access to the Internet through an Internet Service Provider (ISP).

For details on the information you need from your ISP to gain Internet access, see Chapter 5, "Networking and Interoperability."

1. Choose Tools, Services in the Exchange client and choose Add. The Add Service to Profile dialog box appears.

2. Select Internet Mail from the list of information services and click on OK.

3. The Internet Mail property sheet appears. Fill in the information on the General tab. This includes the following:

▶ Full name

▶ E-mail address

▶ Internet Mail Server

▶ Account name

▶ Password

4. Click on the Connection tab and select the choice for the way in which you connect to the Internet. You can select Connect Using the Network, or Connect Using the Modem. If you select the latter, you then choose the Dial-Up Networking connection you want Exchange to use to access your ISP.

5. Click on OK to save your settings.

6. Click on OK when the Add Service to Profile dialog box displays. This dialog box tells you to log off and restart Exchange for the Internet Mail service to work.

Configuring Exchange to Use the Microsoft Fax Service in a Stand-Alone Environment

The Microsoft Fax service can be configured to access a fax modem on the local Windows 95 client or a fax modem that is shared from another location on the network. Fax messages can be sent from an Exchange client to a local fax modem on the same computer or to a shared fax modem on the network. Fax messages also can be directly received in the Microsoft Exchange client Inbox if that computer has a fax modem installed and configured.

The following steps demonstrate using the Microsoft Fax service with a Microsoft Exchange client. In the following steps, you configure Microsoft Exchange client to send and receive faxes using a local fax modem installed on the Windows 95 client.

1. Choose Tool, Services in the Exchange client and choose Add. The Add Service to Profile dialog box appears.

2. Select Microsoft Fax from the list of services and choose OK. If this option is not available, install Microsoft Fax from the Windows Setup tab of the Add/Remove Programs Control

Panel applet. You are prompted as to whether you want to configure your name, fax number, and fax modem in order to send faxes.

3. Choose Yes. The Microsoft Fax Properties sheet appears.

4. Enter your name and return fax number and any optional information in the User tab.

Enter the area code of your fax number. If you do not, the fax service fails to fax your messages after you create them. The information you provide on the User tab appears on your outgoing fax so your recipient knows who sent the message and your return fax number.

5. Select the Modem tab, select the modem to use for the fax service, and choose Set as Active Fax Modem. The Active Fax Modem field displays the modem you selected; an example is shown in figure 10.4.

Figure 10.4

The Microsoft Fax Properties sheet.

6. If no modems are available, a modem has not been set up in the Control Panel. Choose Add, select Fax Modem, and choose OK to detect or install a new fax modem.

7. From the Microsoft Fax Properties sheet Modem tab, choose Properties to configure any additional settings for the fax modem, and choose OK three times. Exit and restart Exchange client to initialize the fax service. Microsoft Exchange is ready to send and receive faxes.

Configuring Exchange to Share a Fax

You can configure the Exchange client to share a fax modem with other users on the network. This is convenient if you do not have enough fax modems (and phone lines) in your office for everyone to have one. Or, you might want to set up a dedicated fax modem workstation on which all users in your company can send and receive fax messages. This feature can optimize the hardware of a small company or department that doesn't have the resources to equip every machine with a fax modem. It also makes backing up fax messages (incoming and outgoing) easier because all messages reside on one computer.

If a user's computer is set up to share her fax modem, be sure to inform that user. This way, the user knows why her fax modem is sending and receiving messages when she did not initiate them. Also, the user knows to keep her computer running with Exchange started at all times so that other users can send or receive messages in the evening or overnight (when long-distance rates are less expensive) using the shared fax modem.

After you set up Exchange to share a fax, you can use another networked computer to access the shared network fax modem to send electronic fax messages created with the Microsoft Exchange client. You should note, however, that incoming fax messages are received in the Inbox of the computer that is directly connected to the fax modem. If the fax message is intended for another user on the network, the message must be manually forwarded to the proper recipient by a user on the computer connected to the fax modem. There is not an Exchange command to automatically route fax messages.

The following steps show you how to set up Exchange to share a fax modem:

1. Choose Tools, Services in the Exchange client. The Services dialog box appears.

2. Select Microsoft Fax from the list of services and choose Properties. The Microsoft Fax Properties sheet appears.

3. Select the Modem tab (refer to fig. 10.4).

4. Select the Let Other People on the Network Use My Modem to Send Faxes check box and choose OK.

5. Choose the Properties button next to the share name to display the shared fax directory dialog box. By default, the directory is C:\NetFax, the share name is FAX, and all users have full control permissions to the C:\NetFax directory. If desired, you can change the share name or the permissions to the shared directory.

6. Choose OK. By default, the local fax modem is shared on the network with the share name FAX under the current computer name.

In step 5, by requiring a password for the shared fax modem, you can minimize the risk that every networked user will use the shared fax. If this is not a concern, leave the required password option disabled. If you do set up a password, however, be sure to share it with those who have rights to access it. Otherwise, you could receive a call late at night or on the weekend from a frustrated user who cannot log on and use the shared fax service.

Sending Messages Using Microsoft Exchange Client

The online help in the Microsoft Exchange client contains a great deal of information on how to use all the features of the Exchange client. The following sections discuss the basics of sending electronic messages using the Exchange client, including the following topics:

- ▶ Addressing

- ▶ Rich-Text Formatting

- ▶ Attachments

- ▶ Delivery

To create a message, choose Compose, New Message in the Exchange client. Click on the To button to display the address book for addressing messages, or type the address directly if you know the exact address format.

Addressing

Select a mailbox recipient from one of the address lists in the address book to address the message. The address lists include your Personal Address Book and any address lists for services you have configured, such as the recipients list for a Microsoft Exchange Server. Selecting a mailbox name and clicking the To button adds the user to the list of recipients for that message. Choose OK when done.

Rich-Text Formatting

The body or text of the electronic message can contain ASCII text or *Rich-Text Formatting* (RTF). RTF can include multiple colors, fonts, and other attributes to spice up the display of the text. The recipient mail client must also support RTF for these attributes to be displayed correctly. If the recipient mail client does not support RTF, the text usually is displayed as unformatted ASCII text.

Attachments

In addition to text, Exchange messages can include binary file attachments. To add an attachment to a created message, select the Insert menu in the New Message composition window. You can insert either a file or an OLE object at the location of the cursor in the body of the created message. An OLE object appears as an icon that can open the proper application to view or edit the attachment.

To send attachments over TCP/IP (such as over the Internet), your TCP/IP gateway (called an SMTP gateway) must support either the UUENCODE or MIME format. Both of these formats encode the binary attachment as a series of ASCII characters. MIME-formatted messages can be automatically decoded by a MIME-enabled recipient.

Delivery

After creating a message, you can deliver it by choosing File, Send in the New Message composition window. The message is moved to your Outbox and is delivered after a periodic interval specified for the delivery service. To deliver a message immediately, select the message in the Outbox and choose Tools, Deliver Now. If you have more than one service installed that can deliver messages, you can select one or all of the services to be used to deliver the message.

Exercises

Exercise 10.1:   Installing the Exchange Client

To install the Windows 95 Exchange client from the Windows 95 distribution files, use Exercise 10.1.

1. From the Start menu, choose Settings, Control Panel. The Control Panel appears.

2. Double-click on the Add/Remove Programs icon. The Add/Remove Programs Properties sheet appears.

3. Select the Windows Setup tab, select the Microsoft Exchange check box, and choose OK. The check box should not be gray because you will be installing all the Exchange client components. The files are installed. You are prompted for the path to the Windows 95 distribution files if they cannot be found.

4. Verify that there is now an Inbox icon on the Desktop and a Microsoft Exchange entry in the Start menu Programs.

Exercise 10.2:   Creating a Workgroup Postoffice

Exercise 10.2 illustrates the necessary steps for creating a new Workgroup Postoffice on a Windows 95 computer.

1. From the Start menu, choose Settings, Control Panel. The Control Panel appears.

2. Double-click on the Microsoft Mail Postoffice icon. The Microsoft Workgroup Postoffice Admin dialog box appears.

3. Select Create a New Workgroup Postoffice and choose Next. You are prompted for the location of the post office.

4. Specify the path to the location where the Workgroup Post-office should be created, and choose Next. For example, type **C:**. The post office files are created in a directory named WGPO0000 in the location specified, and the Enter Your Administrator Account Details dialog box appears.

continues

5. You must enter the name of the user, the mailbox name, and a password for the administrator account. In the Name and Mailbox fields, enter **ADMIN**, for the Password field, enter **PASSWORD**, and then choose OK. A message reminds you that you must share the WGPO0000 directory with all the other users who will be using the post office.

6. If WGPO0000 is on the Windows 95 computer, start Explorer and select the WGPO0000 directory. The WGPO0000 directory is highlighted.

7. Click on the right mouse button and select Sharing from the context-sensitive menu. The Sharing tab of the WGPO0000 Properties sheet appears.

8. Give all post office members full control access to the WGPO0000 directory. If share-level security is used, assign a Full Control password to the directory and provide all post office members with this password. If user-level sharing is used, give all the post office members Full Control permissions by choosing the Permissions button and adding the user accounts to the Full Control list box.

9. Choose OK to share the WGPO0000 directory. The WGPO0000 directory folder symbol is replaced with a sharing hand symbol.

Exercise 10.3: Creating Workgroup Postoffice Mailboxes

You also need to create a mailbox for each member of the Workgroup Postoffice, as shown in Exercise 10.3.

1. From the Control Panel, double-click on the Microsoft Mail Post office icon. The Microsoft Workgroup Postoffice Admin dialog box appears.

2. Select Administer an Existing Workgroup Postoffice and choose Next. You are prompted for the post office location.

3. Type the path to the Workgroup Postoffice files, such as **C:\WGPO0000** and choose Next.

4. Enter the administrator mailbox name and password, and choose Next. The Post office Manager dialog box appears.

5. Choose Add User. The Add User dialog box opens.

6. Enter the name of the user, the mailbox name, the mailbox password, any additional information for the new user, and choose OK. The mailbox is added to the list of users with mailboxes on the post office.

7. Add other users if needed and choose Close to close the Post office Manager.

You also can use the Post office Manager dialog box to delete users, reset a user's password if the user forgets it, and compress mailbox folders to reclaim space from deleted messages.

Exercise 10.4: Accessing a Microsoft Mail Server Mailbox

In Exercise 10.4, you configure Exchange to access a mailbox on a Microsoft Mail workgroup post office.

1. From the Control Panel, double-click on the Mail and Fax icon. The MS Exchange Settings Properties sheet appears (refer to fig. 10.3).

2. Choose Add to open the Add Service to Profile dialog box.

3. Select the Microsoft Mail service and choose OK. The Microsoft Mail Service Properties sheet appears.

4. Type the path to the Microsoft Mail Server post office or Workgroup Postoffice and select Automatically Sense LAN or Remote. The Exchange client is configured for remote access if a network connection is not detected.

5. Select the Logon tab, enter your mailbox name and password, and choose OK. The MS Exchange Settings Properties sheet again appears.

6. Choose OK to save the changes to your Exchange client profile.

7. Double-click on the Desktop Inbox icon to start Exchange. The mailbox is displayed along with some test messages.

Exercise 10.5: Configuring CompuServe Mail Service

In Exercise 10.5, you configure the Exchange client to access a mailbox located on the CompuServe online service. To perform this exercise, you must have an existing CompuServe account and a modem on the Windows 95 client.

1. Start the Exchange client; choose Tools, Services; and choose Add. The Add Service to Profile dialog box appears.

2. Choose Have Disk and enter the path to the \DRIVERS\OTHER\EXCHANGE\COMPUSRV directory on the Windows 95 CD-ROM.

3. Choose OK. The CompuServe Mail Settings Properties sheet is displayed.

4. Type your CompuServe account name, ID, and password in the Name, CompuServe ID, and Password fields in the General tab.

5. Select the Connection tab and type the phone number used to connect to CompuServe in the Phone number field.

6. Select the Advanced tab and choose the Change CompuServe Dir button. Select the path to your CompuServe software directory; for example, select C:\CSERVE. Close the services Properties sheets.

Exercise 10.6: Installing the MSN Mail Service

In Exercise 10.6, you configure the Exchange client to access your MSN mailbox. To perform this exercise, the MSN software must be installed, you must have an existing MSN account, and a modem must be installed on the Windows 95 client.

1. Choose Tools, Services in the Exchange client and choose Add. The Add Service to Profile dialog box appears.

2. If MSN has been installed on the Desktop, The Microsoft Network Online Service appears in the list of available services to add. If not, install MSN from the Windows Setup tab of the Add/Remove Programs Control Panel applet.

3. Select The Microsoft Network Online Service from the list and choose OK. The MSN service is added to the list of services.

4. Select The Microsoft Network Online Service from the list and choose Properties. The Microsoft Network properties sheet appears.

5. Inspect the options that are available and choose OK twice to close the properties sheets. The MSN mail service becomes available in the Exchange client.

Exercise 10.7:   Sending Faxes Using a Shared-Network Fax Modem

In Exercise 10.7, you configure Exchange so you can share your fax with other users on a network. For this exercise to work, you should have a working network with Windows 95 installed, as well as file and printer sharing enabled on the computer that has the shared fax. You also need a fax/modem installed and working on this computer.

1. Choose Tools, Services in the Exchange client. The Services dialog box appears.

2. Select Microsoft Fax from the list of services and choose Properties. The Microsoft Fax Properties sheet appears.

3. Select the Modem tab (refer to fig. 10.4).

4. Select the Let Other People on the Network Use My Modem to Send Faxes check box and choose OK.

5. Choose the Properties button next to the share name to display the shared fax directory dialog box. By default, the directory is C:\NetFax, the share name is FAX, and all users have Full Control permissions to the C:\NetFax directory. If desired, you can change the share name or the permissions to the shared directory.

6. Choose OK. By default, the local fax modem is shared on the network with the share name FAX under the current computer name.

continues

Exercise 10.7: Continued

7. From another computer on the network, start the Exchange client and add the Microsoft Fax service. The Microsoft Fax service appears in the list of services under the Services option of the Tools menu.

8. Select Microsoft Fax from the list of services and choose Properties. You are prompted as to whether you want to configure your name, fax number, and fax modem to use.

9. Choose Yes. The Microsoft Fax Properties sheet appears.

10. Enter your name and return fax number and any optional information in the User tab.

11. Select the Modem tab and choose Add. The Add a Fax Modem dialog box appears.

12. Select Network Fax Server and choose OK. The Connect to Network Fax Server dialog box appears.

13. Enter the UNC path to the FAX share you created on the other computer. For example, enter **TESTPC\FAX**. The fax server appears in the list of available fax modems.

14. Select the network fax and choose Set as Active Fax Modem. The fax server is set to the active fax modem.

15. Configure any additional properties you desire, choose OK twice, and exit and restart the Exchange client. The Exchange client is ready to send faxes to the fax server.

16. Choose Compose, New Fax. The Compose New Fax Wizard appears.

17. Specify Default Location in the I'm Dialing From field. Click Next. The next Compose New Fax Wizard screen appears.

18. Type the name and fax number of the recipient and choose the Add to List button. The recipient name appears in the Recipient list.

19. Choose Next, specify whether you want a cover sheet, choose Next, specify a subject or note for the fax if desired, and choose Next again. The Add File option appears.

20. If you are sending the message to another fax modem, you can attach an electronic document in binary format, which can be detached by the recipient if the receiving fax modem and software support binary attachments. Choose Next when done, and choose Finish to send the fax. The fax is generated and sent.

Review Questions

The following questions will test your knowledge of the information in this chapter. For additional questions, see MCP Endeavor and the Microsoft Roadmap/Assessment Exam on the CD-ROM that accompanies this book.

1. You are a system administrator for your company and are asked to run MAPI-compliant applications to take advantage of Exchange's powerful features. Which three of the following are MAPI-compliant services included with Microsoft Exchange?

   A. Microsoft Fax

   B. CompuServe Mail

   C. America Online Mail

   D. Personal Address Book

2. Jill sets up Microsoft Exchange under Windows 95, but needs to call technical support for help. The technical support person asks her to read the settings stored in the _____, which is a collection of the settings used to connect to a service.

   A. information store

   B. configuration folder

   C. profile

   D. MAPI tag

3. Which of the following statements is true of Microsoft Exchange?

   A. All electronic messages must be in ASCII format.

   B. The Personal Address Book is stored in a file with a PAB extension.

   C. The Personal Information Store is stored in a file with a PIS extension.

D. You must request delivery from each mail service separately.

4. Your company standardizes on several MAPI-compliant applications and uses Exchange with them. Which two of the following statements are true of MAPI?

A. MAPI allows ASCII text-only mail to be sent to and received from any mail system.

B. MAPI helps to ensure that different mail systems can communicate.

C. A MAPI-enabled application, such as Microsoft Word, can be used to exchange documents with other users without having to use a mail application, such as Microsoft Mail.

D. A MAPI-compatible messaging client can deliver messages using more than one service at a time.

5. Exchange includes a Microsoft Mail client you can use with Windows 95. Which of the following statements is not a benefit of using a Microsoft Exchange client rather than a Microsoft Mail client?

A. An Exchange client can connect to mailboxes on multiple Microsoft Mail Servers at the same time.

B. The Exchange client uses 32-bit code.

C. The Exchange client enables multiple users sharing the same computer to connect to different mailboxes.

D. The Exchange client can be configured to send and receive Internet Mail, CompuServe Mail, or MSN Mail.

6. You are manning the company help desk and receive a call from a user who is trying to use a shared fax modem. The fax modem is on another workstation to which he is connected. The network connection is working correctly; however, he cannot access the fax modem. Pick two reasons why this may be happening.

A. The shared fax modem is out of paper.

B. The user does not have the correct password to access the shared fax modem.

C. The computer on which the shared fax modem resides is not running Exchange.

D. The phone line is busy.

7. You upgrade to Microsoft Exchange Server and connect your Windows 95 Exchange clients to it. When you run an Exchange client, which two features are now enabled?

A. Out of Office Assistant

B. Forms Assistant

C. Inbox Assistant

D. Microsoft Mail Server post office

8. You create a workgroup post office under Windows 95. Pick a correct directory name for this new post office.

A. WGP0000

B. \SYSTEM\WPGO0000

C. WGPO0000

D. None of the above

9. You create a help desk document to distribute to your users. A section on Microsoft Exchange defines some of the most common terms used in Exchange, including Personal Folder. What is another name for a Personal Folder?

A. Personal Address Book

B. Inbox Folder

C. Personal Information Folder

D. Personal Information Store

10. Wesley sends a message from Exchange to a user over the Internet. The message contains an attached document saved as a Word for Windows file. What should Wesley advise his recipient to do to ensure that he (his recipient) can read the attached document?

    A. His recipient's e-mail program must handle UUENCODED documents

    B. His recipient should use Exchange to receive the document

    C. His recipient's e-mail program must handle MIME documents

    D. All of the above

11. Tammy creates a mail message in Exchange, but she cannot locate her address book. Pick one reason why she might have this problem.

    A. She must use Word to create her mail

    B. Her address book is not stored on the local computer

    C. She can't address e-mail in Exchange

    D. All of the above

12. You set up Exchange under Windows 95. After you configure Exchange, it includes which of the following three default folders?

    A. Deleted Items

    B. Inbox

    C. Delivered Mail

    D. Outbox

13. Dave sets up a new Personal Folder in Exchange named Marketing Documents. Which default folder is added to this new Personal Folder?

A. Deleted Items

B. Inbox

C. Delivered Mail

D. Outbox

14. A user says she wants to start sharing her fax modem with other users on the network. What do you tell her she must do before this will work?

A. Disable Share-Level Security

B. Enable User-Level Security

C. Change a setting on the Modem tab of the Microsoft Fax Properties sheet

D. Enable Share-Level Security

15. After setting up Exchange under Windows 95, you want to examine the contents of the folder that is created to store Personal Address Book information. Where is this file stored?

A. \WINDOWS\SYSTEM\MAILBOX.PST

B. \EXCHANGE\MAILBOX.PST

C. \WINDOWS\MAILBOX.PAB

D. \EXCHANGE\MAILBOX.PAB

Review Answers

1. A B D	6. B C	11. B
2. C	7. A C	12. A B D
3. B	8. C	13. A
4. B D	9. D	14. C
5. A	10. D	15. D

Test Yourself

Stop! Before reading this chapter, test yourself to determine how much study time you will need to devote to this section.

1. Marie is setting up Windows 95 to work with her computer's legacy hardware. Because this hardware is not Plug and Play–compliant, Marie is not sure how resources are allocated for legacy hardware under Windows 95. What priority, after detecting legacy devices, does Windows 95 give legacy devices in allocating resources?

2. You purchase a laptop computer that has a docking station. Name the three types of docking styles Windows 95 supports. Also, what is manual, or *surprise*, style docking? How is it a potential problem to users of docking stations?

3. Eugene installs a Plug and Play device under Windows 95. He needs to modify some of the settings Windows set by default, but he doesn't want to use the Windows 95 Registry to change these values. What other option, besides reinstalling the device, does he have?

Answers

1. Windows give legacy devices first priority after detecting them. See "What Is Plug and Play?"

2. Cold, warm, and hot docking. Surprise style docking is a form of hot docking that enables users to undock a laptop without warnings regarding data loss or unsaved files. See "Docking Types."

3. He can use the Device Manager to change settings. See "Modifying Plug and Play Device Configurations Using Device Manager."

Chapter 11

Plug and Play

This chapter will help you prepare for the exam by covering the following objectives:

Test Objectives

▶ Explain how Windows 95 handles components that are not compatible with Plug and Play

▶ Explain hot docking and the potential consequences of the dynamic device changes

▶ Given a specific configuration, use Device Manager to manually reconfigure a Plug and Play device

Plug and Play technology enables the Windows 95 operating system to automatically detect and configure the devices in the Windows 95 computer. A user is usually not required to know which resource settings to assign to a particular Plug and Play device, or even the model of the Plug and Play device being used. For example, to add a Plug and Play network card in a system that fully supports Plug and Play, you insert the card in the proper adapter slot and start Windows 95. The operating system determines the model of the network card, installs the appropriate driver, and configures the driver with the appropriate resources, such as an interrupt and memory region to use.

In this chapter, the following Plug and Play topics are discussed:

▶ Resource types

▶ Viewing resource utilization

▶ Plug and Play core components

▶ Four scenarios using Plug and Play

- ▶ The hardware tree

- ▶ The Plug and Play process

- ▶ Using Plug and Play with a laptop computer

- ▶ Notes on Plug and Play for various device types

- ▶ Modifying Plug and Play device configurations using Device Manager

What is Plug and Play?

 Plug and Play, a set of hardware and software design standards, has been developed as a response to concern among computer users regarding the amount of time and technical knowledge required to properly configure a given set of hardware devices in a computer. All computers have a finite number of resources; the most common type of resources being memory regions, I/O addresses, and Interrupt Request (IRQ) lines. Allocating these resources to the hardware devices that need them is a daunting task, especially because you need to avoid hardware conflicts where two devices try to use the same resource. An internal modem is an example of a common Plug and Play device found on the market today. When you insert a Plug and Play modem into a computer running Windows 95, Windows 95 automatically recognizes the modem, the type of modem (the manufacturer and name), which drivers it uses, and which resources it needs allocated to it. Windows then sets up the modem so you can begin using the modem when Windows starts.

The objective of Plug and Play technology is to simplify the initial configuration of a computer and to simplify adding hardware devices after initial configuration. Ideally, a user should be able to buy a Plug and Play computer fully configured from the factory and, as users add or remove hardware devices (for example, a new modem) from their computer, these changes should be automatically noted by the system and reflected in the computer's configuration parameters immediately or at the next system restart, depending on the device. It therefore becomes the computer's (and not the user's) responsibility to reallocate resources to meet the needs of the currently installed devices.

The four main functions of a Plug and Play system are the following:

▶ **Device identification and specification.** Each hardware device that meets the Plug and Play specification must be able to identify both its device type and its manufacturer, as well as what types and number of resources it needs; for example, a modem might need access to one of the computer's IRQs and one of its I/O addresses to function properly. After the system gathers the resource requirements from all installed Plug and Play devices, it can properly allocate the computer's resources as needed.

▶ **Dynamic configuration changes.** A Plug and Play system must be able to detect and compensate for dynamic insertion of new Plug and Play devices. When a new device is inserted, the system is immediately notified of the device's type and resource requirements. The system dynamically reallocates the resources of the computer to accommodate the new device. Applications, if they are Plug and Play–aware, also are notified about the new device. At no point in this process is the user required to intervene, unless the system runs out of resources to allocate.

▶ **Backward compatibility with legacy components.** Legacy components include all non–Plug and Play devices. This usually refers to devices designed to existing hardware standards, such as ISA, VESA, and EISA. Each of these deals with hardware in its own way, but none has the Plug and Play capabilities described here and so cannot be dynamically configured. Thus, after a Plug and Play system identifies, it gives legacy devices first priority in resource allocation.

▶ **Operating system and hardware independence.** Plug and Play is an open architecture and is not proprietary to any one company. Thus, any hardware or software manufacturer can develop Plug and Play–compatible products, as long as their products meet the published specifications.

Resource Types

To better understand the details of the rest of this chapter, this section examines the four major resource types used in a standard computer:

- ▶ Interrupt Request (IRQ) lines
- ▶ Direct Memory Access (DMA) channels
- ▶ Input/output (I/O) ports
- ▶ Memory regions

Interrupt Request (IRQ) Line

A standard computer is designed with a certain number of communication lines that are used by peripherals when they need to contact a software process to notify it that a hardware event has occurred. These communication lines are managed by a Programmable Interrupt Controller (PIC) built onto the motherboard. The PIC can typically handle up to 16 IRQ lines, but you need to remember that many of these are reserved for use by devices on the motherboard or standard devices, such as keyboard, video, and so on. Thus, many IRQ lines are not available for use by newly introduced peripherals. For example, if you add a network card to the system, the card has to be assigned an available IRQ, such as IRQ 5 or IRQ 10, to communicate with the system.

Direct Memory Access (DMA) Channels

Computer systems typically come with eight DMA channels. These are designed to permit peripherals to access portions of the computer's RAM directly, without using the CPU. DMA speeds up the operation of a peripheral by creating buffers to accelerate redundant read/write operations involved between the peripheral and the system memory. As with IRQs, some of the channels are reserved for onboard or standard peripheral use and are not available to new devices. For example, when adding a sound card to a system, the card must be assigned one or more available DMA channels, such as DMA 1 and DMA 5.

Input/Output (I/O) Ports

I/O ports are small areas of the computer's memory that are reserved for use by peripherals to execute I/O functions. Peripherals, such as a keyboard, mouse, modem, or network card, typically use I/O ports.

Memory Regions

Many peripherals, to accelerate the processing of information, reserve a portion of the computer's memory for their own use. Generally, this memory is between 640 KB and 1 MB, although some can use the memory above 1 MB. For example, many network cards require the use of a memory region, such as D0000-DFFFF; therefore, the required region must be set aside for the exclusive use of that device. If the region is not reserved for the device that requires it, another device or application may attempt to use that memory region, which can cause the operating system to crash.

Viewing Resource Utilization

Windows provides a number of ways to view resource usage. Although you can view resource usage directly in the Registry, doing so through the Device Manager is much easier (and safer). To help you conceptualize how resources are used, open the Device Manager and view which resources have been assigned to which device. The following steps show how to open the Device Manager:

1. From the Start menu, choose Settings, Control Panel.

2. Double-click the System icon.

3. Click the Device Manager tab. A list of all your devices appears.

4. Double-click on Computer from the list of hardware devices. The Computer Properties sheet appears.

The Computer Properties sheet displays the computer's resources, including IRQ, DMA, I/O, and memory assignments.

Plug and Play Core Components

For an exercise testing this information, see end of chapter.

For a computer to be fully Plug and Play, it must have the following four core Plug and Play components:

- ▶ Plug and Play system BIOS

- ▶ Plug and Play device drivers

- ▶ Plug and Play operating system

- ▶ Plug and Play–aware applications

Plug and Play System BIOS

The main responsibility of a Plug and Play system BIOS is to notify the operating system of any insertions or removals of Plug and Play devices. In addition, the Plug and Play system BIOS passes on configuration information about devices on the motherboard to the operating system.

note

The Plug and Play system BIOS does not actually configure Plug and Play devices. That's the task of the Plug and Play operating system. A computer with a Plug and Play BIOS usually ships with its own Plug and Play software for configuring Plug and Play hardware devices. Any resource allocations initiated with this software should be detected by Windows 95 and are not altered. For example, a Plug and Play boot device would have to be configured with this software because Windows 95, which likely resides on the boot device, cannot load until the drive is properly configured.

Plug and Play Device Drivers

To dynamically activate a newly inserted Plug and Play device, the corresponding device drivers for that device must also be able to be dynamically loaded and unloaded from memory. Removing the driver from memory when the device is not present or not active enables Windows 95 to make more efficient use of memory.

Plug and Play Operating System

Windows 95 is fully Plug and Play–compatible and serves as the coordinator of the Plug and Play system. Windows 95 can receive messages from the Plug and Play BIOS about insertion or removal events, load and unload Plug and Play device drivers, and initiate the process of enumerating and allocating resources to Plug and Play hardware devices.

Plug and Play–Aware Applications

Plug and Play–aware applications are applications that can respond to Plug and Play messages sent out by the operating system. For example, if a laptop user's printer is connected to a docking station and is currently undocked, the printer at the docking station would appear grayed out in the Windows 95 Printers Folder until the next time the laptop is docked. Windows 95 can do this because the printing subsystem is a Plug and Play–aware application.

Four Scenarios Using Plug and Play

You just learned that all four of the core components must be present to fully benefit from all the features of Plug and Play. Windows 95 handles components that are not compatible with Plug and Play in four different ways. In these situations, one of the following scenarios will be present in a Windows 95 system. This list also includes a description of how each scenario can use Plug and Play.

▶ **Plug and Play system BIOS and Plug and Play devices.** In this scenario, all components are Plug and Play, making for the easiest configuration. As noted earlier, Plug and Play boot devices must be configured outside Windows 95. All other devices are configured dynamically after Windows 95 loads.

▶ **Plug and Play system BIOS and legacy devices.** The Plug and Play system configures any Plug and Play–compliant devices at boot time. If the computer contains a legacy boot device, it must be properly configured before booting Windows 95. Any other legacy devices must be found and configured using the Windows 95 hardware detection routines, initiated either during installation of Windows 95 or subsequently, in the Control Panel through the Add/Remove Hardware icon.

▶ **Legacy system BIOS and Plug and Play devices.** Because the BIOS in this case is unable to provide configuration information to the operating system, Windows 95 polls the Plug and Play devices directly at boot time and configures them dynamically. Again, any legacy or Plug and Play boot devices must be configured outside Windows 95.

▶ **Legacy system BIOS and legacy devices.** This is the scenario that existed before Plug and Play. Boot devices must be configured outside Windows 95, and all other devices are found during the hardware detection phase of installation or with Add New Hardware in the Control Panel.

The Hardware Tree

An easy way to conceptualize how a Plug and Play system sees Plug and Play devices in a computer is as a tree, which branches out from the motherboard to all installed hardware devices. Figure 11.1 shows an example of a hardware tree.

Figure 11.1

The hardware tree.

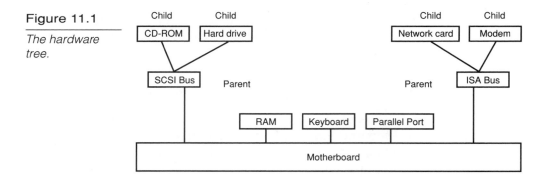

Each box on the diagram is a component that must be configured by the Plug and Play system. These components are referred to as *device nodes*. A device node can be an independent component connected directly to the motherboard (for example, the keyboard or parallel ports) or it can be connected to the motherboard through an intermediate device node. Therefore, a SCSI hard drive attached to a SCSI hard drive controller is a "child" device node to the SCSI adapter card, which acts as the "parent" device node.

To configure any device node, the Plug and Play system requires the following:

▶ A unique node ID.

▶ The type and number of resources (IRQ, DMA, I/O, memory) required by the device, known as its logical configuration.

▶ Any resources already assigned to this device (usually from a previous resource allocation); if this device is removed from the computer, the Plug and Play system will know which additional resources are now free for use.

▶ Knowing whether the node has any children attached to it.

The Plug and Play Configuration Process

When Windows 95 first boots, or when a new Plug and Play device is inserted or removed, the process of configuring all Plug and

Play devices is initiated. The major steps in this process are as follows:

1. All Plug and Play devices are put into configuration mode, which effectively deactivates them.

2. Each device is examined (also known as *enumeration*) and assigned an ID that will be used to identify it.

3. The device's resource requirements are determined. If the card has multiple functions, the resource requirements of each function are examined separately (for example, a PCM-CIA modem/network card).

4. After all resource requirements are determined, a working configuration that satisfies all these requirements is calculated. Each device is assigned its resources. These settings are stored in the current configuration section of its device node information.

5. All Plug and Play devices are reactivated.

Plug and Play Components in Windows 95

The configuration process described in the previous section is carried out in tandem by a number of Windows 95 components. These include the following:

▶ Bus enumerators

▶ Plug and Play BIOS

▶ Hardware tree and the Registry

▶ Device drivers

▶ Resource arbitrators

▶ Configuration Manager

Bus Enumerators

These agents are essentially a special type of software driver that knows how to search out and communicate with devices attached to a particular bus architecture. These drivers poll all devices on a particular bus for their device type and resource requirements, and assign each device a unique ID. When the Configuration Manager returns a working configuration, the bus enumerators pass on this information directly to the device.

Plug and Play BIOS

The Plug and Play BIOS is responsible for ensuring the correct configuration of various motherboard components, as well as the configuration of the boot device of the computer. Once established, this information is passed on to the Plug and Play operating system. The most important task performed by the Plug and Play BIOS, however, is that of notifying the operating system of insertion or removal events. This function is crucial because it prompts the operating system to reinitiate the enumeration process to accommodate the newly inserted or removed device. It also allows the operating system time to notify Plug and Play–aware applications that, for example, a network card has been removed and data loss could occur if any network activity is still in progress.

Hardware Tree and the Registry

Note that the hardware tree mentioned earlier exists only in the memory of the computer. It is re-created every time the system boots from entries stored in the Windows 95 Registry, which is a hidden file, called SYSTEM.DAT, and has a record of all devices ever installed on the computer and their last-used settings. As Plug and Play devices are enumerated, they are added as device nodes on the in-memory hardware tree, and any settings already stored for that device in the Registry are enabled. For example, if the system detects a Plug and Play network card and finds that that card has been installed previously, it will enable the workgroup name, protocol settings, and so on that were last used for that card. If a Plug and Play device is inserted or removed, the hardware tree will reflect this change. You can find most of these settings in the HKEY_LOCAL_MACHINE section of the Registry.

Device Drivers

Device drivers in a Plug and Play environment require functionality not typically found in a Windows 3.1 driver. Most important, they must be dynamically loadable and unloadable from memory as a Plug and Play device is inserted or removed. For example, keeping a driver in memory for a device that has been dynamically removed from the system would be inefficient. Therefore, to make more efficient use of available memory, Plug and Play device drivers unload whenever the device they support is not active. Also, to properly take part in the Plug and Play process, device drivers must have enhanced communication capabilities, namely to allow them to announce themselves to the Configuration Manager and to notify applications of Plug and Play events. Finally, Plug and Play device drivers have the capability to remain in memory but stay inactive (that is, take up no resources) until resources are assigned to the driver by the Configuration Manager.

Resource Arbitrators

Resource arbitrators are responsible for determining which device is allocated which particular resource. One resource arbitrator exists for each major resource type—IRQ, DMA, I/O address, and memory. The arbitrators must ensure, in finding a working configuration for their particular resource type, that no two devices are assigned the exact same resource because that would result in a device conflict, and both devices would likely be inoperative. The resource arbitrators are separate from the Configuration Manager to allow for expandability. Because of this expandability, any future resource types can be accommodated merely by adding a new resource arbitrator for that type, instead of redesigning the entire Plug and Play system.

Configuration Manager

The Configuration Manager is in charge of the entire Plug and Play enumeration/configuration process. It initiates the process both at system boot and when a Plug and Play device is inserted or removed after boot. It is responsible for passing parameters and commands between the other Plug and Play components in sequence. The Configuration Manager first makes a request to the bus enumerators to search their respective bus type for any devices that are Plug and Play–compatible. When the bus enumerators return with the type and resource requirements of each device, the Configuration Manager begins to build device nodes on the hardware tree for each of them. The Configuration Manager then loads a corresponding driver for each device (if one exists), and the driver is set to await configuration parameters. The resource arbitrators are then called into play and requested to find a conflict-free configuration for all active devices. When this is complete, the resource arbitrators return the parameters to the Configuration Manager, which passes the information to the bus enumerators to configure their enumerated devices.

Using Plug and Play with a Laptop Computer

Because laptops are one of the areas of computing most likely to benefit from Plug and Play technology, noting a few issues related to laptops and Plug and Play is worthwhile.

Windows 95 supports the creation of hardware profiles, which can be used to maintain different hardware configurations for a system. This feature is especially useful for a laptop that is used in a docking station, because different components are available to the system depending on whether the laptop is in the docking station.

Second, Windows 95 supports various methods of docking and undocking a laptop, such as cold docking, warm docking, or hot docking. The type of docking that can be performed with a laptop depends only on the limitations of the hardware.

Hardware Profiles

Most laptops are now available with an optional component called a *docking station*. The docking station enables users to "plug in" to additional computing power or hardware functionality with their laptop by adding a nonportable desktop station that may contain additional hardware, such as a regular monitor, a CD-ROM drive, a sound card, a network card, or additional ports, which are not available when the laptop is not docked at the station. Due to this fact, you must account for this additional hardware when configuring the laptop for its docked and undocked states. A feature of Windows 95 that addresses this issue is the capability to store multiple hardware profiles or configurations for a single computer. Figure 11.2 shows the hardware profile dialog box.

Figure 11.2

The Device Manager hardware profile selection for a network card.

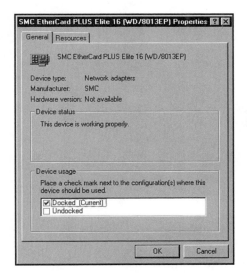

By using this feature, you can create a docked and undocked hardware profile for the laptop; for example, when you have the laptop at the office and docked, you could use a profile that has drivers for a regular monitor, a CD-ROM, network, sound, and so on, whereas the undocked profile would have these devices disabled or unchecked in the Device Manager.

If the laptop has Plug and Play functionality, the task of creating docked and undocked profiles is greatly simplified. When you boot for the first time in a docked state, Plug and Play enumeration occurs. Then you simply save this state as your docked hardware profile. Similarly, the next time you boot in an undocked state, enumeration will occur again, and you can save that state as your undocked hardware profile. From this point on, the laptop should be able to automatically determine, based on the devices present in each profile, whether the laptop is docked or undocked.

If the laptop has any legacy devices, either in the system or in the docking station, the system should be booted in both the docked and undocked states before creating the respective hardware profiles. This ensures that all legacy devices have been detected and can be included in both the docked and undocked hardware profiles.

Docking Types

The three docking styles supported by Windows 95 are as follows:

▶ Cold docking

▶ Warm docking

▶ Hot docking

These styles are described in the following sections.

Cold Docking

Cold docking dictates that the laptop must be completely turned off to be able to remove or insert it into the docking station. In this scenario, Plug and Play functionality is most often used at boot time because the hardware in the docking station cannot be removed while the laptop is on. Therefore, very few dynamic events will occur.

Warm Docking

Warm docking entails removing or inserting the laptop into the docking station while the laptop is in a suspended state. In this scenario, Plug and Play enumeration occurs after the laptop resumes full-power operation.

Hot Docking

Hot docking enables the laptop to be docked or undocked while running at full power. Any insertion or removal event immediately prompts a Plug and Play re-enumeration. Note that two types of hot docking systems exist. The first is *Auto-Eject* or "VCR style," in which a software interface is used to eject the laptop automatically from the docking station. This interactive approach allows Windows 95 to analyze the possible consequences of ejecting the laptop. For example, if you have open files on the network, Windows 95 warns you that ejecting the laptop could cause data loss, and that it would be wise to close all open files before ejecting the laptop.

The second type of hot docking is called *Manual* or "Surprise Style." In this type of hot docking, ejection is completely at the user's discretion. No warnings are given regarding open files or data loss because the computer has no way of determining when the user might eject the laptop. Therefore, ensuring that all relevant files and applications have been closed before ejection occurs is the user's responsibility. A consequence of using manual docking is that users may lose unsaved data.

Notes on Plug and Play for Various Device Types

The following sections include technical notes regarding Plug and Play functionality on various bus architectures and device types, including the following:

- ▶ PCMCIA

- ▶ SCSI

- ▶ PCI and VESA Local Bus

- ▶ IDE

- ▶ MicroChannel Architecture (MCA) and EISA

PCMCIA

Primarily designed to enhance the portability of peripherals for laptops, the *Personal Computer Memory Card International Association* (PCMCIA) specification describes a set of standards for developing the software and hardware required to manufacture credit card–sized peripherals for laptops. Although the specification was originally intended to be used for memory cards, it has been expanded to include almost any device type imaginable, from sound cards to modems to SCSI adapter cards. This specification supports the key features of Plug and Play, including the capability to insert or remove a PCMCIA device and have the system automatically enumerate and reconfigure without rebooting the system.

In a traditional PCMCIA configuration, two software components are required: Card Services and Socket Services. These components are responsible for coordinating resource allocation for all PCMCIA cards and for enabling communication between the cards and the rest of the computer. In a Plug and Play environment, many of the functions performed by these services are handled by the Configuration Manager and a special PCMCIA bus enumerator. The Configuration Manager and PCMCIA bus enumerator ensure that PCMCIA devices are enumerated and configured in a fashion compatible with other Plug and Play devices.

SCSI

SCSI (pronounced *scuzzy*), which stands for Small Computer Standard Interface, is a bus architecture known for its capability to chain a number of devices, such as CD-ROM drives and hard drives, on one SCSI cable. In the past, configuring SCSI devices to work together properly was a technical challenge, to say the least. Although most SCSI adapters do not presently support Plug and Play, a Plug and Play specification for SCSI has been developed and is slated for future implementation.

SCSI configuration must occur in two distinct phases:

1. Configuring the SCSI adapter card for appropriate IRQs, DMAs, and so on.

2. Configuring the SCSI bus and its devices, determining what SCSI ID to assign to which device, and ensuring termination of the bus.

Although the current SCSI-II standard does not support automating the latter of these two phases, the emerging Plug and Play SCSI standard will allow automatic termination and ID assignment, as well as the dynamic configuration of the SCSI host adapter.

PCI and VESA Local Bus

Of the standard bus architectures, *Peripheral Component Interconnect* (PCI) is the most compatible with Plug and Play. It has the built-in capability to query PCI devices for identification and resource requirements. Most computers that are PCI-compatible (mostly Pentiums and late-model 486s), however, have a mixture of PCI slots and ISA (standard computer) slots. Having a "PCI computer" does not mean the Plug and Play functionality of the PCI bus is passed on to the ISA slots as well. ISA devices still must be identified and configured through the standard hardware-detection routines of Windows 95.

Remember that PCI devices can share IRQs, whereas ISA devices cannot. For that reason, you should configure the BIOS on PCI system IRQs that are used by ISA devices in the system. To do this, you must reserve an IRQ for the ISA devices that require them in the BIOS, usually by using a system configuration utility (SCU).

Video Electronics Standards Association (VESA) Local Bus, mostly present on older model 486s, is a high-speed bus architecture that is much less compatible with Plug and Play specifications than PCI. VESA Local Bus devices are treated like ISA devices in terms of their identification and configuration.

Windows 95 does not ship with a VESA Local Bus enumerator. However, ISA devices connected to the VESA Local Bus can still be detected by the ISA enumerator.

IDE

Integrated Drive Electronics (IDE) is primarily a standard for communication with hard drives and CD-ROM drives. Although some standard IDE hard drive controllers can sometimes auto-detect IDE hard drive parameters (heads, cylinders, sectors per track), the controller itself is not Plug and Play. It must be identified and configured using standard hardware detection routines. On systems with IDE or Enhanced IDE (EIDE) controllers, however, both the IDE drives and the controller normally are automatically detected by the Plug and Play system.

Micro Channel Architecture (MCA) and EISA

Micro Channel Architecture (MCA) is a bus architecture developed by IBM and introduced in the PS/2 line of computers. *Enhanced Industry Standard Architecture* (EISA) is a competing standard. Both of these architectures can automatically identify and configure devices attached to their bus. To integrate with Windows 95 Plug and Play functionality, an appropriate bus enumerator for the type of bus used must be present. The bus enumerator then passes on configuration information to the operating system by taking over most of the functions formerly provided by a separate proprietary configuration utility. For example, Configuration Manager would replace the EISA Configuration Utility.

Windows 95 does not ship with a Micro Channel enumerator. If necessary, you must obtain it from the OEM.

Modifying Plug and Play Device Configurations Using Device Manager

Although modifying the settings assigned to a Plug and Play device is not required under normal conditions, it might be necessary at times. These settings are stored in the Registry, and can be edited manually using the Registry Editor. It is recommended, however, that the Device Manager be used instead, because incorrect parameters entered into the Registry can leave the system inoperative.

The Device Manager is located in the Windows 95 Control Panel (see fig. 11.3). It is an upgrade to a utility found in Windows 3.1 called the *Microsoft Diagnostic* (MSD) tool. MSD, which you ran at the DOS command line, gave a record of all the devices and resources installed on your system. MSD was helpful, but did not provide a way to change or remove device settings. With Device Manager, however, you can view and edit hardware settings, including reconfiguring Plug and Play devices.

Figure 11.3

The Device Manager changes resource allocations for Plug and Play devices.

You can open the Device Manager by double-clicking on the System icon in the Control Panel. From the System Properties page, click on the Device Manager tab. You can display devices in the Device Manager in one of two ways. You can list them by type, such as CD-ROM controllers, Hard disk controllers, Mouse, and so on. Or, you can list them by connection, which displays devices under the hardware to which they are connected. A modem, for example, would be listed under a heading named Computer, whereas SCSI devices would be listed under a heading for the SCSI controller to which they are connected.

To get a view of the resource allocation on your system, click on Computer in the Device Manager and click on the Properties button. The View Resources tab of the Computer Resources dialog box appears (see fig. 11.4). On this tab, you can view (but not change) allocations for IRQ, I/O, DMA, and memory resources. If a device setting needs to be changed, click on OK, double-click on the device in the Device Manager, and click on the Resources tab. Exercise 11.3 at the end of the chapter shows an example of changing a resource setting for a device.

Figure 11.4

The View Resources tab displays system resource allocations.

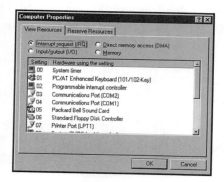

Some devices display a Driver tab when you display its properties. If this is the case, you can use the Device Manager to change the device driver for that device. This is useful if you download a new driver from a manufacturer or from Microsoft and don't want to use the Add New Hardware Wizard to install the new driver.

One way to troubleshoot hardware problems is to use the Hardware Conflict Troubleshooting help topic. To start this, from the Start menu, choose Help. From the Help window, click on the Contents tab. Double-click on the Troubleshooting item and click on the If You Have a Hardware Conflict topic. In the Windows Help window that appears, click on the Start the Hardware Conflict Troubleshooter item and follow the step-by-step instructions.

Exercises

Exercise 11.1:   Viewing Resource Utilization

Exercise 11.1 demonstrates how to view which resources have been assigned to which device. The exercise also demonstrates how to reserve a resource so it is not used by the Plug and Play system.

1. From the Control Panel, double-click on the System icon (alternatively, right-click on the My Computer icon and choose Properties). The System Properties sheet appears.

2. Select the Device Manager tab. A list of all hardware devices currently installed appears.

3. Double-click on Computer from the list of hardware devices. The Computer Properties sheet appears, showing the computer's resource usage viewable by IRQ, DMA, I/O, or memory.

4. Select the Direct memory access (DMA) radio button. You can see that DMA 2 and DMA 4 are used by the floppy controller and the DMA controller, respectively. Additional DMA resources may be used by other devices, if present.

5. Write down the number of a DMA channel that is not being used. You will use the number later in the exercise.

6. Click on the other resource types to see what IRQs, I/O addresses, and memory ranges are in use. The usage map for each resource type appears.

7. Click on the Reserve Resources tab. The list of reserved resources appears; it is blank.

8. Click on the Direct memory access (DMA) radio button. The list of reserved DMA channels appears; it is blank.

9. Choose the Add button. The Edit Resource Setting dialog box appears.

continues

Exercise 11.1: Continued

10. Use the arrows to increment the DMA to the value you wrote down earlier. Choose OK twice to close the Properties sheets. You are prompted to restart your computer.

11. Choose Yes. Your computer restarts.

12. When Windows 95 has booted, go back to Device Manager and view the DMA channel usage. The DMA channel you noted earlier now lists as System Reserved; this indicates that the DMA resource is not included in the pool of resources that can be assigned to a device.

Exercise 11.2: Examining Hardware Settings in the Registry

Exercise 11.2 demonstrates how the Windows 95 Registry stores information gathered by the various Plug and Play components.

Be sure not to change any of the values in the Registry, because your computer might not function properly following those changes.

1. From the Start menu, select Run. The Run dialog box appears.

2. Enter **REGEDIT.EXE** in the Open box. The Registry Editor loads and displays the various keys of the Registry.

3. Click on the plus sign (+) next to HKEY LOCAL_MACHINE. A number of subkeys appear.

4. Click on the + next to the Enum subkey; additional subkeys appear.

5. Click on the + next to the Root subkey. The subkeys of Root represent device classes.

6. Click on the + next to one of the starting subkeys beginning with "PNP." Subkeys numbered at "0000" appear.

7. Click on the subkey numbered "0000." A description of the device and its various configuration parameters appears,

similar to the sample shown in figure 11.5. Note that some of the values are in hexadecimal notation and therefore are not readable.

Figure 11.5

An example of detected Plug and Play device parameters.

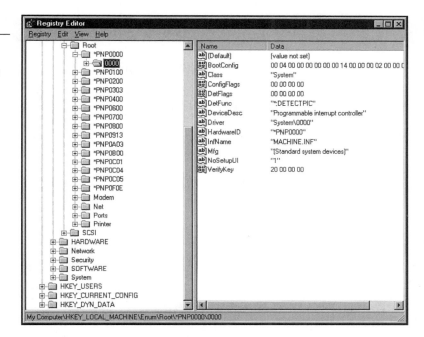

8. Click on the other PNP device subkeys as well as the subkeys with user-friendly names, such as "Ports" or "Printer." You will find configuration settings for most if not all the devices in your computer.

9. When finished, select Exit from the Registry menu. You return to the Desktop.

The name assigned to a device class is determined by the way it was identified. Devices enumerated by the Plug and Play system or by standard hardware detection are given a name beginning with "PNP" and ending in a four-digit hex code determined by the type of device detected. Any devices added manually through the Add New Hardware icon in the Control Panel are given friendly names, such as "Ports" or "Printer."

Exercise 11.3: Modifying Plug and Play Device Settings Through Device Manager

In Exercise 11.3, you use the Device Manager to alter Plug and Play configuration settings. The steps also demonstrate how to reserve a resource so it is not used by the Plug and Play system.

1. From the Control Panel, double-click on the System icon (alternatively, right-click on the My Computer icon and choose Properties). The System Properties sheet appears.

2. Select the Device Manager tab. A list of all hardware devices currently installed appears.

3. Click the plus sign (+) next to the Ports icon. The tree expands to show all installed ports, including serial and parallel.

4. Double-click on COM1. The Communications Port (COM1) Properties sheet appears.

5. Select the Resources tab. The resources currently assigned to the port appear.

6. Remove the X from the Use Automatic Settings check box and click on the drop-down arrow in the Settings Based On drop-down box. A number of alternate configurations appear.

7. Choose one of the alternate configurations. The resource settings change.

8. Double-click on Interrupt Request under Resource Settings. The Edit Interrupt Requests dialog box appears.

9. Increase or decrease the interrupt value using the spin controls. As you move through the values, the Conflict Information dialog box notifies you of any conflicts with another device currently using that interrupt value.

10. Choose a non-conflicting new interrupt value and click on OK twice to close the Properties sheets. You are prompted to restart your computer.

11. After restarting the computer, go back to the Properties sheet of COM1 and verify the Interrupt Request setting. If no other device has requested the IRQ you chose, it should still be displayed.

12. Set the interrupt request back to 4 and click on OK twice to close the Properties sheets. You are again prompted to restart your computer.

Review Questions

The following questions will test your knowledge of the information in this chapter. For additional questions, see MCP Endeavor and the Microsoft Roadmap/Assessment Exam on the CD-ROM that accompanies this book.

1. Windows 95 supports devices that conform to the Plug and Play specifications. When a new Plug and Play device is installed under Windows 95, resources are distributed to these devices automatically. Which three of the following are major resource types used in a standard computer?

   A. IRQs

   B. Memory regions

   C. DMA channels

   D. IDE drives

2. Mindy is setting up a hardware device under Windows 95. The device is not Plug and Play–compliant, so she must configure the device manually. The device calls for a specific DMA address. With all her other devices installed, Mindy is not sure she has enough DMA channels. Computers typically come with _____ DMA channels.

   A. 2

   B. 6

   C. 8

   D. 16

3. You purchase a Plug and Play hardware device to work with Windows 95. Which three of the following are core Plug and Play components?

   A. Plug and Play hardware device and device drivers

   B. Plug and Play protocols

   C. Plug and Play operating system

   D. Plug and Play system BIOS

4. James migrates to Windows 95 and purchases all new hardware that is Plug and Play–compliant. He does this so he will not have to manually configure his devices. However, all _____ must be configured outside of Windows 95 regardless of the level of Plug and Play compatibility.

   A. modems

   B. tape drive

   C. CD-ROM devices

   D. boot devices

5. A client calls asking how the Windows 95 Registry stores information about his system. Among other features about the Registry, you tell him that the _____ is created from entries stored in the Registry every time the system boots.

   A. PNP Registry

   B. hardware tree

   C. device map

   D. device tree

6. When Windows 95 detects a new device installed on your computer, it attempts to allocate resources to it. The _____ is responsible for determining which resource is allocated to which particular device.

   A. Configuration Manager

   B. Plug and Play BIOS

   C. resource controller

   D. resource arbitrators

7. Dirk installs Plug and Play devices under Windows 95. Because of certain tasks he performs at his job, he must remove and insert different devices routinely. The _____ is responsible for tracking the insertion and removal of Plug and Play devices.

    A. Configuration Manager

    B. Plug and Play BIOS

    C. resource controller

    D. resource arbitrators

8. At a training class for the sales team, you discuss the topic of docking. The sales team members use laptops in a docking environment and are concerned about accidentally removing hardware while using their laptops. You tell them that in a _____ docking environment, hardware cannot be removed while the laptop is on.

    A. hot

    B. warm

    C. cold

    D. manual

9. Windows 95 uses bus enumerators to search out and communicate with devices attached to a particular bus architecture. Which two of the following bus enumerator types do not ship with Windows 95?

    A. VESA

    B. PCMCIA

    C. SCSI

    D. MCA

10. Nick upgrades to Windows 95. His hardware is a mixture of new hardware and legacy devices. He wants to make sure all his hardware will work together. Which of the following statements is true?

    A. PCI devices can share IRQs but ISA devices cannot.

    B. The SCSI-II standard is fully Plug and Play–compliant.

    C. The IDE standard is fully Plug and Play–compliant.

    D. PCMCIA devices should not be inserted into or removed from a system while the system is running, unless the system supports warm or hot docking.

11. You receive a call from a client who wants to modify the resources Windows 95 allocates to her devices. Before she changes them, however, she wants to view how Windows has them currently set up. Which two tools new in Windows 95 let her do this?

    A. MSD and Control Panel

    B. Configuration Manager and Device Manager

    C. Device Manager and the View Resources tab

    D. Registry and Plug and Play

12. Nina uses hot docking to connect her laptop to her docking station. When the laptop is not docked, the printer set up for the docking station is grayed out. Why is the printer grayed out when the laptop is not docked?

    A. The printer driver uninstalls each time the laptop is undocked.

    B. Windows 95's printing subsystem is a Plug and Play–aware application.

    C. Windows 95 does not support hot docking of printers.

    D. The printer is a legacy device.

13. Roger wants to view his hardware settings in the Registry. How can he do this, and in what section are these settings located?

    A. Use Registry Editor and look in HKEY_LOCAL_MACHINE

    B. Use Registry Editor and look in HKEY_CLASSES_ROOT

    C. Use Policy Editor and look in HKEY_CURRENT_USER

    D. Use Device Manager and look in HKEY_LOCAL_MACHINE

14. When you set up a laptop that is part of a docking environment, you usually have two different configurations. One configuration is used when the laptop is docked to the docking station. The other configuration is used when it is not docked. Where does Windows 95 store these different configurations?

   A. In the Plug and Play BIOS

   B. In the enumeration manager

   C. In hardware profiles

   D. In RAM

15. You are asked to diagram the hardware tree for a training class you are conducting for your company's help desk. What three components are part of the Windows 95 hardware tree?

   A. motherboard

   B. RAM

   C. ISA bus

   D. printer

Review Answers

1. A B C	6. D	11. C
2. C	7. B	12. B
3. A C D	8. C	13. A
4. D	9. A D	14. C
5. B	10. A	15. A B C

Test Yourself

Stop! Before reading this chapter, test yourself to determine how much study time you will need to devote to this section.

1. Describe the six general steps to troubleshooting problems in Windows 95.

2. Windows 95 has many built-in tools you can use for both optimizing and troubleshooting. Name four of these utilities.

3. In such an environment as Windows 95, a need for careful management of the system's resources exists. When two processes request the use of a device at the exact same moment, how does Windows 95 arbitrate such requests?

4. You want to optimize Windows' 95 file system. What are two ways to maximize the use of 32-bit drivers under Windows 95?

5. As more and more companies migrate their technical resources to the Internet, locating new drivers and finding technical data on software products is increasingly easy. Name three sources Microsoft recommends for finding technical information.

6. By pressing the F8 key when Windows 95 boots, you can access the Boot menu. Name at least five of the options on this menu.

7. WIN.COM includes support for a number of error-isolation switches. These switches are as follows: f, m, n, s, v, x. Name what each of these switches does.

8. If you are presented with the problem of not being able to print to a network printer from a Windows 95 computer, what are two possible solutions for correcting it?

9. Discuss the function of the System Monitor.

10. Windows 95 provides ways to optimize the file system. Name three ways you can ensure the highest file system performance.

Answers

1. You can follow a number of steps when attempting to isolate technical problems. Some are specific to Windows 95; others are simply part of a logical approach to any problem. See the six general ones in "General Troubleshooting Guidelines."

2. System Monitor, Net Watcher, System Resource Meter, and ScanDisk. See "Select Appropriate Windows 95 Tools for Optimization and Troubleshooting."

3. Virtual machines. See "Virtual Machines."

4. Update any non-Microsoft disk compression to a 32-bit driver from the manufacturer. Verify that the Performance tab in the My Computer Properties sheet shows all 32-bit components for the file system and for virtual memory. See "Optimize the System to Use Windows 95 Drivers."

5. Microsoft TechNet; the Internet; and Online Help. See "Resolve Problems Using Available Technical Resources."

6. Answers can include the following: Normal mode, Logged mode, Safe mode, Safe mode with network support, Step-by-Step confirmation, Command-Prompt-Only mode, Safe mode command prompt, and previous version of MS-DOS. See "The Boot Menu."

7. f: disables 32-bit file system drivers; m: starts Windows 95 in Safe mode; n: starts Windows 95 in Safe mode with network support; s: excludes the ROM address space between F000 and 1 MB from use by Windows 95; v: disables virtualization of hard disk interrupts; x: disables use of upper memory by Windows 95. See "WIN.COM Switches."

8. Ensure that File and Printer Sharing is enabled at the remote computer; verify that you have correct network protocols configured. See "Troubleshooting Other Specific Scenarios."

9. System Monitor provides real-time monitoring of system activities, both locally and at remote computers, to determine the effect of configuration changes and to identify potential system performance bottlenecks. See "Use System Monitor to Monitor System Performance."

10. Remove SHARE.EXE and SMARTDRV.EXE from AUTOEXEC.BAT; Check the IOS.LOG for any real-mode drivers that might be causing Windows 95 not to use 32-bit file system drivers; Use Windows' 95 Disk Defragmenter regularly. See "Optimizing the File System For Desktop Performance."

Chapter 12

Troubleshooting

This chapter will help you prepare for the exam by covering the following objectives:

Test Objectives

- ▶ Resolve problems using appropriate resources

- ▶ Select appropriate tools for troubleshooting

- ▶ Audit access to a Windows 95 local resource

- ▶ Monitor Windows 95 performance and resolve performance problems

- ▶ Optimize the system to use the Windows 95 drivers

- ▶ Optimize a computer for desktop performance

- ▶ Optimize a computer for network performance

- ▶ Choose the appropriate course of action when file system problems occur

- ▶ Discriminate between a process and a thread

- ▶ Discriminate between preemptive and cooperative multitasking

- ▶ Predict the consequences to the operating system when MS-DOS–based applications, WIN16-based applications, and WIN32-based applications fail to respond to the system while running under Windows 95

- ▶ Explain Windows 95 multitasking of WIN16-based applications and WIN32-based applications

- ▶ Choose the appropriate course of action when an application fails

- ▶ Explain how Windows 95 performs memory paging as compared to Windows 3.x

- ▶ Optimize printing

- ▶ Choose the appropriate course of action when a print job fails

- ▶ Choose the appropriate course of action when Dial-Up Networking problems occur

- ▶ Choose the appropriate course of action when the installation process fails

- ▶ Choose the appropriate course of action when the boot process fails

- ▶ Use the startup disk to repair a faulty network setup

- ▶ Discriminate between resource usage in Windows 3.1, Windows 95, and Windows NT

In a complex operating system environment, troubleshooting technical problems or optimizing for performance is never an exact science. Although the number of possible hardware and software combinations (and resulting conflicts and configuration issues) on any given computer is virtually limitless, you can narrow the scope of any problems that may arise and, with luck, isolate the offending component(s), whether internal or external to Windows 95. Often, the problems are a combination of both internal and external factors. Troubleshooting and optimization are very closely related because, in a sense, poor performance is itself a serious technical problem.

This chapter looks at the following topics:

- ▶ Available technical resources

- ▶ Windows 95 tools for optimization and troubleshooting

- ▶ Using 32-bit drivers

- ▶ Optimizing the file system

- ▶ Optimizing printing

- ▶ Troubleshooting

note

The Troubleshooting section of the Windows 95 "Implementing and Supporting Microsoft Windows 95" exam contains many objectives. For that reason, this chapter includes information introduced and discussed in previous chapters in this book. Further, this chapter includes passages from some earlier chapters. This way you can find in this chapter every objective listed at the beginning of the chapter, making it easier for you to prepare.

Resolve Problems Using Available Technical Resources

Countless sources of information exist to guide you in solving technical problems. They include the following:

- ▶ Online help

- ▶ Microsoft TechNet

- ▶ The Internet

- ▶ The Windows 95 Resource Kit

- ▶ Technical support by phone

- ▶ Hardware and software compatibility lists

- ▶ Online discussion forums

Online Help

The online help facility in Windows 95 contains a great deal of technical information, and it includes several interactive troubleshooting tools that can resolve many common problems.

Microsoft TechNet

Microsoft TechNet is a CD-ROM publication and is an invaluable tool that contains vast amounts of technical data on all Microsoft products, including electronic versions of various resource kits, driver updates, and databases of known problems.

The Internet

As more and more companies migrate their technical resources to the Internet, locating new drivers and finding technical data on software products is increasingly easy. Finding that a hardware or software manufacturer is not accessible through the Internet is rare. If new or updated drivers are required to resolve a problem, or sending a technical question through e-mail is acceptable, the Internet is the first place to go. You also can find many Windows 95 discussion groups where technical questions can be posted.

The Windows 95 Resource Kit

This is the A-to-Z compendium of Windows 95 technical information. Although you can obtain the Resource Kit electronically either from the Internet, through Microsoft's WWW site, or on the TechNet CD-ROM, reading large amounts of information from a book rather than from a computer screen is much easier. You can find additional support tools and utilities on the disks bundled with the *Windows 95 Resource Kit*. You should acquire a copy.

Technical Support by Phone

If you're looking for help on a technical problem and you're in a situation in which intuition is more important than information, you may find contacting Microsoft Product Support directly by phone to be productive. In addition to an in-depth knowledge of the product, the technical representatives have access to a great deal of technical data that is not available to the consumer.

Hardware and Software Compatibility Lists

These lists, which are on the TechNet CD-ROM or can be downloaded from Microsoft's WWW site, contain all the hardware and software that have been tested and are known to work with Windows 95 (you may find notes on how to make them work better as well). Although not seeing a product on the list does not mean it does not work, seeing a product on the list gives you affirmation that you should continue troubleshooting, because the product is supposed to work with Windows 95.

Online Discussion Forums

If you have access to online services, such as CompuServe, America Online, or Microsoft Network, you can get access to a number of very useful Windows 95–related discussion groups. You also can usually directly contact Microsoft Product Support from these groups; Microsoft and other companies assign a certain number of technical support representatives to monitor the groups.

Select Appropriate Windows 95 Tools for Optimization and Troubleshooting

Windows 95 has many built-in tools you can use for both optimizing and troubleshooting. You can access these tools by choosing Start, Programs, Accessories, System Tools. The available utilities include the following:

- ▶ System Monitor

- ▶ Net Watcher

- ▶ System Resource Meter

- ▶ Disk utilities, such as ScanDisk and Disk Defragmenter

If one of the preceding tools is not present in the System Tools group, you can add it using the Add/Remove Programs applet by selecting the tool from Accessories in the Windows Setup tab.

Use System Monitor to Monitor System Performance

Windows 95 is equipped with a tool for monitoring various performance-related factors of the operating system environment. This tool is called the *System Monitor*. You can use it to provide real-time monitoring of system activities both locally and at remote computers, to determine the effect of configuration changes and to identify potential system performance bottlenecks.

Performance information, such as how much the processor is being used, how many programs are currently running, or how many bytes are being written to a hard disk per second, can be displayed in one of three formats: as a bar chart, as a line chart, or as numbers. By observing this information over time, as various operations are performed by the operating system or applications, you can see how a certain operation affects a given performance parameter and tune the system to minimize any negative effects on performance.

To monitor a remote computer, the owner of that computer must have enabled remote administration and have specified you as an authorized user.

Tips for Using System Monitor

The following are some guidelines for using System Monitor to identify technical problems or bottlenecks:

- ▶ Run System Monitor during normal activity at first, to get a sense of how certain values change when certain actions are performed.

- ▶ Identify which items in System Monitor are applicable to the problem (for example, monitor swap file size to determine whether more memory is needed in the system) and then set up specific tests.

Use Net Watcher to Audit Access to the System

You can use the Net Watcher utility to create or delete shared resources on remote computers, as well as monitor access to those resources. The following factors are important when considering remote administration using Net Watcher:

- ▶ The remote computer must have File and Printer Sharing enabled.

- ▶ You can access only remote systems that use the same security model you are using on your computer (share-level security computers cannot access user-level security computers).

- ▶ You can connect only to remote systems that use the same type of file and printer sharing (Microsoft or NetWare).

For more information on the Net Watcher utility, refer to the section "Net Watcher" in Chapter 4, "Editing User and System Profiles."

Use System Resource Meter to Monitor System Performance

 You can use the System Resource Meter utility to monitor dynamic changes in system resources. Many Windows 3.1 applications fail to release the resources allocated to them when they unload from memory, which causes the total system resource pool of the system to decrease. If you suspect an application of this behavior, it is advisable to activate the System Resource Meter and observe whether subsequently closing the suspected application restores the resources to their previous levels. If this is not the case, the application may not be releasing all its allocated resources back to the operating system.

Disk Utilities

You can use the utilities ScanDisk and Disk Defragmenter to increase performance and, especially in the case of ScanDisk, to help detect potential problems with hard drives. These utilities are discussed in more detail in Chapter 6, "Managing Disk Resources and Utilities."

Optimize the System to Use Windows 95 Drivers

 One of the main ways in which you can enhance performance and compatibility in Windows 95 is by using 32-bit protected-mode device drivers. These drivers are designed to be faster and work more efficiently in relaying data than older 16-bit drivers. As manufacturers begin updating their product lines for Windows 95 compatibility, obtaining native Windows 95 drivers for most hardware devices will become easier. A Windows 3.1 driver or MS-DOS–based driver should be used only if no 32-bit driver ships with Windows 95 and the manufacturer has not yet developed one.

A number of ways exist to maximize the use of 32-bit drivers:

▶ Verify that the Performance tab in the My Computer Properties sheet shows all 32-bit components for the file system and for virtual memory.

▶ If you're using non-Microsoft disk compression, that compression is operating in Real mode (unless you have obtained a 32-bit compression driver since the release of Windows 95) and should be updated with a 32-bit driver from the manufacturer.

▶ Ensure that disk partitioning software is not being used. If a local hard drive employs nonstandard or software-based partitioning, it likely will not be able to function with the 32-bit file system drivers of Windows 95.

Optimizing the File System for Desktop Performance

You can take a number of actions to ensure the highest file system performance, including the following:

▶ Remove SHARE.EXE and SMARTDRV.EXE from the AUTOEXEC.BAT because these files are not needed in Windows 95 and take up memory needlessly.

▶ If the Performance tab of the My Computer Properties sheet indicates that the file system is not using 32-bit drivers, check the IOS.LOG to find the file name of the Real-mode driver that may be preventing the use of 32-bit file system drivers.

▶ Use Windows' 95 Disk Defragmenter regularly to ensure that system performance does not degrade due to fragmentation of data on your hard drive.

Optimizing the File System for Different Roles

Because computers can be optimized for different roles, including network performance, Windows 95 allows the configuration of certain performance-related file system parameters according to what role the computer is expected to play. The three possible configurations are as follows:

▶ Desktop computer

▶ Mobile computer

▶ Network server

The following parameters are keyed to these configurations:

▶ The number of most recently accessed folders that are tracked

▶ The number of most recently accessed files that are tracked

The settings are calculated based on each configuration's needs. For example, in the case of a network server, due to its intensive file processing needs, both the listed settings would be at their maximum to increase efficiency in retrieving files. Figure 12.1 illustrates how Windows 95 can be optimized for a particular role using the File System Properties sheet.

Figure 12.1

Optimizing for typical computer roles.

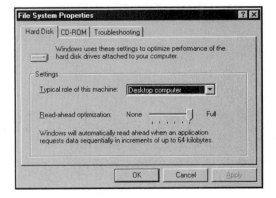

Choose the Appropriate Course of Action when File System Problems Occur

 If you encounter difficulty with any applications and you suspect the file system might be involved, you can disable a number of file system features using the Performance tab of the My Computer Properties sheet to isolate the problem. You can disable the following features:

- ▶ File sharing

- ▶ Long file name preservation for old programs

- ▶ Protected-mode hard disk interrupt handling

- ▶ 32-bit protected-mode disk drivers

- ▶ Write-behind caching

Disabling File Sharing

You can disable file sharing for applications that are incompatible with the way Windows 95 typically implements file sharing (use SHARE.EXE until the application is updated to support Windows 95 file sharing).

Disabling Long File Name Preservation for Old Programs

If an application requires the directory space used by LFNs in Windows 95, you might have to disable this support for older applications.

Disabling Protected-Mode Hard Disk Interrupt Handling

The Disable Protected-Mode Hard Disk Interrupt Handling option disables Windows' 95 normal practice of intercepting all MS-DOS–level disk I/O requests and handling them with a 32-bit protected-mode driver. Disk performance is degraded, but compatibility with older applications is enhanced.

Disabling All 32-Bit Protected-Mode Disk Drivers

If a hard drive is experiencing problems reading or writing information while Windows 95 is running, you can disable all 32-bit disk drivers to enhance compatibility with older applications. Once again, disk performance is degraded.

Disabling Write-Behind Caching

The Disable Write-Behind Caching for All Drives option is useful when data integrity is crucial and you cannot risk losing data due to it being in the write-behind cache when a power failure occurs. Write-behind caching causes Windows to wait until idle time to write disk changes, which may be too late if a power failure occurs and all cache items are lost. When write-behind is disabled, all write operations are performed immediately. Yet again, performance likely will be degraded.

Understanding Multitasking, Processes, and Threads in Windows 95

A clear understanding of Windows' 95 architecture is needed to do well on the "Implementing and Supporting Microsoft Windows 95" exam. If you have reservations about your knowledge and understanding of the architecture, be sure to read Chapter 2, "Architecture and Memory," and Chapter 8, "Running Applications," prior to taking the test. Also, the following sections provide an overview of virtual machines, multitasking, process, and threads in Windows 95. You also learn about how WIN16-based applications multitask under Windows 95.

Virtual Machines

Windows 95 is capable of running three types of applications:

▶ MS-DOS 16-bit applications

▶ Windows 3.1 16-bit applications (also known as WIN16 applications)

▶ 32-bit Windows applications (also known as WIN32 applications; includes most Windows NT software)

Windows 95 can run these varying applications because of a number of architectural design factors, the most important being the idea of virtual machines (VMs). In a single-tasking, single-threaded environment, such as MS-DOS, in which only one application at a time is requesting the operating system's resources, managing those resources is much easier. In such an environment as Windows 95, which is intended to manage multiple applications that might be operating simultaneously, a much greater need for careful management of the system's resources exists, because the computer remains primarily a single-task machine (one processor equals one task at a time, no matter how fast it performs those tasks). In this single-task environment, two processes requesting the use of a device at the exact same moment would be very problematic. Clearly, a procedure in place to arbitrate such requests is necessary.

Windows 95 implements this procedure through VMs. A VM is designed so that every application executed in the Windows 95 environment is executed from within a specialized container created especially for that application (or type of application). This container is intended as much as possible to keep applications separate from each other, thus minimizing the chance that they might not work together. Because some applications (MS-DOS applications) were not designed to function in a multitasking environment, the operating system must deceive them into thinking they are the only process running on the computer (or they would fail to operate properly).

Multitasking: Preemptive and Cooperative

Two types of multitasking are used in Windows 95, depending on the type of application involved: preemptive multitasking and cooperative multitasking. *Preemptive multitasking* involves dividing the processor's capacity into time slices that are allocated equally among processes requiring them. Thus, one application processes for x number of milliseconds, then it is suspended, and another application processes for the same amount of time, and so on.

Cooperative multitasking is different in that it allows a given process to engage the processor until it voluntarily cedes its control to another process. The disadvantage of this type of multitasking is that a misbehaving application can monopolize the processor's time and effectively stop other processes from executing.

Multithreading

Windows 95 is an operating system. That is, an application designed to take advantage of multithreading is able to submit multiple independent requests to the processor simultaneously. Thus the application can have two separate execution processes multitasked by the processor, creating the impression that the application is itself performing two tasks simultaneously. For example, Word can repaginate a document and allow the user to type at the same time. All multitasking is done at a thread level, with applications submitting either single or multiple threads, depending on the application type.

Hardware Virtualization

Another important component in the creation of VMs is hardware virtualization. Especially in the case of legacy MS-DOS and (to a lesser extent) Windows 3.1 applications, simulating the hardware environment in which the application is accustomed to running is necessary. It must seem that all devices are available when needed. This is implemented through software drivers called VxDs (Virtual Device Drivers), which are responsible for arbitrating requests (often simultaneous) from running processes and queuing them so they do not conflict with each other or cause the device in question to fail because it is trying to do two things at once.

Internal Messaging

A message is generated each time a key is pressed or the mouse is clicked, effectively asking an application to do something. In a single-tasking environment, there is no question which application the keyboard or mouse input is intended for. In a multitasking environment, a more complex system of determination and delivery is required. Because you can have multiple applications on-screen simultaneously, where the mouse is clicked or what window is active when a key is pressed determines which application the message is intended for. After the intended application is targeted, the message is placed in the appropriate message queue to be processed.

16-Bit Applications Resource Usage

WIN16 applications generally are those created for Windows 3.1. You need to remember the following when dealing with WIN16 applications:

▶ Windows applications (including WIN32 applications) exist in the System Virtual Machine, which is a special VM designed to provide one hardware virtualization layer for all Windows software.

▶ Within this VM, WIN16 applications share a common address space (this is necessary to maintain backwards compatibility with the way Windows 3.1 applications are designed to interact).

▶ WIN16 applications operate on a cooperative multitasking basis (this also is due to the way applications were designed for Windows 3.1, which did not support preemptive multitasking).

▶ A single message queue is used for all WIN16 applications.

▶ All WIN16 applications are single-threaded, because Windows 3.1 does not support multithreading.

▶ WIN16 applications generally load themselves into the virtualized space between 3 and 4 GB, and some use a space between 0 and 4 MB to be able to share data with other WIN16 applications.

▶ WIN16 applications do not access the Registry because they are designed to use INI files for their stored settings. However, Windows 95 can migrate certain settings from the

INI files into the Registry. The WIN16 applications can continue to access and modify the INI files, and these modifications then can be migrated to the Registry.

▶ 16-bit applications are not designed to recognize or use LFNs because LFNs are not implemented in Windows 3.1.

▶ Whereas under Windows 3.1 system resource stacks are 64 KB, these have been converted to 32-bit stacks in Windows 95, dramatically decreasing the likelihood of running out of system resources.

32-Bit Applications Resource Usage

Windows 95 is designed to support and best interact with 32-bit applications specifically designed for Windows 95 or for Windows NT. These applications are best suited to take advantage of the new architectural design features of Windows 95. These design features include the following:

▶ The capability to take advantage of Windows' 95 flat 32-bit, 4-GB memory address space (WIN32 applications typically load into the 4-MB to 2-GB range of memory)

▶ The capability to pass more information in a single 32-bit programming call than is possible with a single 16-bit programming call, thus increasing processing performance

▶ The capability to submit multiple simultaneous threads for processing, allowing greater user productivity within the 32-bit application because the user does not need to wait for one task to finish to start another

▶ The capability to take advantage of Windows' 95 preemptive multitasking, which is more efficient and runs more smoothly than Windows' 3.1 cooperative multitasking

▶ More comprehensive protection from other applications because each WIN32 application is assigned its own separate address space that is not visible to other applications

▶ A separate message queue for each thread in a WIN32 application, which prevents other applications from interfering with the receipt or processing of system messages

▶ The capability to use the Registry to store all application settings on a generic or per-user basis

▶ The capability of the application to uninstall itself more easily than previous application types, because all changes to the Registry can be tracked and rolled back in the case of uninstallation

Predicting Problems When Running Applications Under Windows 95

Although applications should normally run without interruption, situations do arise when, due to either programming errors or incompatibilities, applications cease to function properly. The two main problems that occur with applications are General Protection Faults and application hangs.

Recognize General Protection Faults and How They Are Caused

A General Protection Fault (GPF) typically is caused by an application that attempts to violate system integrity in one of a number of ways:

▶ By making a request to read or write to a memory address space owned by another application

▶ By attempting to access the system hardware directly

▶ By attempting to interact with a failing hardware driver (drivers operate at Ring 0 and so can seriously impact the operating system)

The GPF is generated when the operating system shuts down an offending application to prevent a system integrity violation. How the offending application is specifically handled depends on its application type.

Because MS-DOS applications reside in their own VM and have their own message queue, if they cause a GPF, a message is displayed and the application is simply terminated without impacting the rest of the operating system.

In the case of WIN16 applications, the procedure is somewhat more complex. Because WIN16 applications share both a common address space and a common message queue, when one application creates a GPF, all others are suspended until the offending application is terminated. After this is done, the remaining applications resume processing.

Finally, with 32-bit applications, the procedure is quite straightforward. Because 32-bit applications exist in their own separate address space, and each has a separate message queue, a GPF in one 32-bit application in no way impacts any other 16- or 32-bit programs. The offending program is simply terminated.

Choose the Appropriate Course of Action When an Application Fails

An application is said to be "hung" when it is running but is not responding to messages from the operating system. Much improved support exists in Windows 95 for a local reboot of the application in question, which permits the application to be terminated without impacting other currently running processes. A local reboot is performed by pressing Ctrl+Alt+Delete once, which opens a Close Program dialog box. Listed in this dialog box are all currently running tasks (including system processes not otherwise listed on the Taskbar). You must then select a process ("Not Responding" usually is indicated in brackets next to the process name) and click on the End Task button. The operating system then attempts to terminate the process (which might take several seconds). Depending on the reason why the application is hung, you also might be presented with the option to wait a few seconds for the application to respond, and then to terminate the application if no response is received.

The following sections describe some considerations you should make when an application hangs, based on the application type:

▶ MS-DOS

▶ Windows 16-bit Subsystem (Win16)

▶ Windows 32-bit Subsystem (Win32)

MS-DOS Application

A normal local reboot as described previously should work on an MS-DOS session because the MS-DOS application exists in its own VM and has its own message queue—a hung MS-DOS session does not impact the operation of any other process.

> An MS-DOS session also can be terminated from the Properties sheet of the session if the session is in a window.

16-Bit Windows Subsystem

As stated earlier, because WIN16 applications share a common memory address space and a common message queue, if a WIN16 process hangs while in the foreground, all other WIN16 processes cease to receive messages from the operating system and also appear hung.

This is due to a flag that is set for WIN16 processes, known as the *WIN16 mutex* (mutually exclusive). Because 16-bit code is considered nonreentrant (it cannot be used by more than one process at a time), a system must be in place to ensure that no two processes attempt to use the same piece of 16-bit code simultaneously. Under Windows 95, this is done by enforcing the rule that only the process that currently owns the rights to the WIN16 mutex is able to make requests to 16-bit API functions. When the given process is finished using the 16-bit code, it hands the mutex to the next process.

If an application hangs while it owns the WIN16 mutex, no other application can access 16-bit API functions. Thus, all 16-bit applications appear to be hung. In addition, any 32-bit application that requires the use, through thunking, of a 16-bit API function (such as writing to the screen) also appears to be hung. The application is still running but cannot make any updates to the screen, and thus appears to be inactive or unresponsive.

To remedy this situation, the 16-bit application that currently holds the mutex must be locally rebooted through the means described previously. After this is done, the mutex should be reset and available for use by other processes.

32-Bit Windows Subsystem

Just testing to see whether you have been paying attention! A 32-bit application will not hang the system, because it will be preemptively multitasked. In other words, control will be taken away from a misbehaving WIN32 application even if does not want to relinquish control.

Understanding Windows 95 Memory Paging

Windows 95 uses two types of memory: physical and virtual memory. The Windows 95 operating system uses a *flat memory model,* which leverages off the Intel 386 or greater processor's capability to handle 32-bit addresses. This flat memory model provides a logical address space range of up to 4 GB. Although current computer hardware does not yet handle up to 4 GB of physical memory, some file servers can now run with up to 1 GB of RAM. Virtual memory bridges the gap between physical memory and logical memory.

The 4 GB of addressable space used as virtual memory under the flat memory model is implemented through the use of both RAM and a swap file. The Windows 95 operating system performs memory management, called *demand paging*, whereby code and data are moved in 4-KB pages between physical memory and the temporary Windows 95 swap file on the hard drive. The Virtual Memory Manager controls paging and maintains a page table. The *page table* tells which pages are swapped to the hard drive, and which remain in RAM, and to which system process or application they belong.

Application programs are allocated a virtual memory address space, which is the set of addresses available for use by that program. Both WIN32- and MS-DOS–based programs are allocated private virtual memory address space. All WIN16-based programs share a single, common virtual memory address space. Windows 95 allocates the 4 GB of virtual memory to each address space. Each process is allocated a unique virtual address space of 4 GB. The upper 2 GB is shared with the system, whereas the lower 2 GB is private to the application.

The virtual memory is allocated as follows:

- ▶ **0–640 KB.** If not used for a Virtual DOS Machine (VDM), this memory is made available for any Real-Mode device drivers and terminate-and-stay-resident (TSR) programs.

- ▶ **0–1 MB.** In a VDM, this memory is used to execute MS-DOS programs. If a shared, common, WIN16 VM is used, then WIN16 applications operate much as they do under Windows 3.1.

- ▶ **1–4 MB.** Normally this memory is unused. Windows 95 does not use this space, nor do WIN32 applications. If this memory is needed by WIN16 applications, it is available.

- ▶ **2 MB–2 GB.** This memory is used by WIN32 applications and some WIN16 applications. Each WIN32 application has its own address space, whereas WIN16 applications all share a common address space.

- ▶ **2–3 GB.** This memory is used to run all Core System Service components, shared DLLs, and other shared objects. Those components are available to all applications.

- ▶ **3–4 GB.** This memory is reserved for all Ring 0 components, such as the File Management subsystem and the Virtual Machine Manager (VMM) subsystem. Any VxDs are loaded in this address space.

Virtual memory and virtual addresses enable you to have more memory available to programs than actually exists on the computer in physical RAM. The Windows 95 swap file implementation is much improved over that from Windows 3.1.

With Windows 3.1, you can have either a temporary or permanent swap file. Windows 3.1 recommends how much hard disk memory to allocate to the swap file. If the hard-disk controller is compatible with 32-bit disk access, running 32-bit disk access will improve performance. A temporary swap file that does not need to be on contiguous hard disk space is created when Windows 3.1 starts. This same temporary swap file is released when the user exits Windows. Although a permanent, contiguous swap file provides better performance than a temporary swap file, because it is a static file, hard disk space is not freed up when the user exits Windows.

In Windows 95, the swap file configuration is much easier. The best features of temporary and permanent swap files are combined through improved virtual memory algorithms and 32-bit access methods. By default, Windows 95 uses a dynamic swap file, which shrinks and grows based on the needs of the operating system and the available hard disk space. A permanent swap file has little benefit in Windows 95.

Optimizing Printing

The main factor in ensuring print performance is spool settings. Windows 95 spools, by default, using a proprietary internal page description format called *Enhanced Metafile* (EMF), which is discussed in more detail in Chapter 7, "Managing Printers." When printing across a network, the translation into EMF format, and ultimately into a printer-specific format called *raw*, is performed differently, depending on the operating system installed at the print server. If the print server has Windows 95 installed (which can interpret EMF format), then most of the rendering of the print job from EMF format into raw format is done at the server. If the print server has any other operating system installed, the EMF and raw format rendering must be done at the client, which increases the client's processing load. When printing locally, both types of rendering are done at the local computer.

A second consideration is how quickly control is returned to the user after a print job is submitted. You can configure the print subsystem of Windows 95 to return control to the user after the first page of a print job is spooled or after the last page is spooled.

This parameter can be configured from the Spool Settings dialog box (click on the Spool Settings button on the Details tab of the Properties sheet for the printer in question). Figure 12.2 illustrates the parameters available from the Spool Settings Properties sheet.

Figure 12.2

Spool settings.

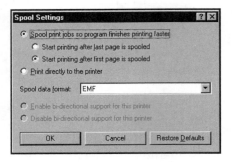

Choosing to return control after the first page shortens wait time but increases printing time and consumes more disk space; the inverse is true if control is returned after the last page is spooled.

Troubleshooting Printing

One way to remedy a printing problem is to use the Print Troubleshooter, which is available from the Windows 95 Help utility. You also can use the following guidelines to help clear up printer problems:

- ▶ Make sure the printer is turned on, full of paper, and is online.

- ▶ Check the printer cable and parallel port to make sure the printer is connected to the computer.

- ▶ Open the Printers folder, right-click the printer, and choose Properties. Make sure the settings are correct for your printer.

- ▶ Turn off metafile spooling. It may not work properly for all printers.

▶ Make sure you have the latest printer driver installed. Sometimes reinstalling the same printer driver fixes the problem. Contact the printer manufacturer to obtain a new printer driver for Windows 95, if available.

▶ Download a PostScript error handler to the printer if the problem is with a PostScript printer.

▶ View your resources, such as free disk space and free memory. For each print job you need some free disk space for temporary files to be stored. Likewise, free memory address space is needed to process the print job. Close an idle application to free up some memory, if necessary.

▶ Attempt to print to the printer from another application. A quick test is to open Notepad, create a line of text, and print the file. If this works, the original application that failed to print may need to be configured for printing. If this does not work, you may need to reinstall the printer.

▶ Print to a file; next, copy the file to a printer port to see if the file prints to the printer. If this works, the problem is due to spooler or data transmission problems. If this does not work, the program or printer driver is at fault.

▶ Shut down and restart Windows 95. Similarly, turn off and on your printer. Sometimes this clears memory buffers on the computer and printer.

A good habit to develop is to document printer problems and distribute copies of the document to other users in your company or organization. Because most end-users send a job to the printer sooner or later, the rate at which they experience a printer problem far outweighs the frequency of many other problems they encounter. Having a document that end-users can refer to might decrease the number of support calls you get for printer problems.

Troubleshooting Dial-Up Networking Problems

To troubleshoot Dial-Up Networking problems, the first places to start looking for the problem are in the Network Properties sheets for the Dial-Up Adapter, the Dial-Up Networking connection, the modem, and the application you want to use over the connection. This isolates your troubleshooting to the client computer. You then can start looking at problems that may be affecting the phone line connection, such as a busy signal on the other end, dead phone line, or whether the modem is connected to the outgoing phone line. Finally, you can isolate the problem to the server side computer. In this case, you may not have physical access to that computer and may need to rely on someone local to that computer to diagnose and fix any problems on the server.

Some of the problems you may encounter with Dial-Up Networking (DUN) include the following:

- ▶ **Modem problems.** Be sure your modem is installed properly to work with Windows 95. If the modem is external, make sure it is turned on. Also, be sure it is plugged in to the phone line.

- ▶ **Phone numbers.** Double-check the phone number you're dialing to be sure your modem is correctly dialing that number. If you need to enter a number for an outside line, be sure to enter it. If you have call waiting on your phone line, disable it. If you need to dial a long distance number, be sure the entire number, including 1 + area code, is being dialed. Also, make sure the number you are dialing is for a modem or fax modem.

- ▶ **Protocol issues.** Make sure the Dial-Up Adapter is configured to use the same protocol as the server-side computer. If, for example, you use DUN to connect one Windows 95 computer to another using the Dial-Up Networking Server software, use the same protocol, such as NetBEUI or IPX/SPX. Also, if you use TCP/IP to connect to the Internet, make sure your DNS, IP address, host names, and other configurations are correct. These values cannot be wrong by one character; they must be exact.

▶ **Access rights.** If you are able to connect to a remote server but cannot access user resources on that site, you may not have proper access privileges. Make sure you enter the correct password and that the server side is set up to allow you access to it.

▶ **Server problems.** A common problem with the Dial-Up Networking Server is that it is not enabled. Enable it by opening the Dial-Up Networking folder and choosing Connections, Dial-Up Server. Choose the Allow Caller Access option. Also, the computer on which the server software resides must be turned on, running Windows 95, and connected to a phone line.

▶ **Application problems.** If your application does not function properly over Dial-Up Networking, you may have a slow connection, a bad connection, or your application is not intended to function as remote access software. Read the application's documentation to make sure it can operate as remote software, or contact its manufacturer for specific steps on making it work with Windows 95.

When you attempt to use an application that does not work with Windows 95 TAPI architecture and you have the Dial-Up Server enabled, your application will not be able to call out. If, for example, you use CompuServe WinCIM 2.01 or earlier software to dial CompuServe, you receive a Cannot Initialize Port message when Dial-Up Server is running. You may forget you have Dial-Up Server running in these cases (Windows 95 does not display a message or indicator that it is on).

General Troubleshooting Guidelines

You can follow a number of steps when attempting to isolate technical problems. Some are specific to Windows 95; others are simply part of a logical approach to any problem:

1. Determine whether the problem is intermittent or occurs with regularity. If the problem is regular, your next step is to look for patterns and the factors that are common to each

occurrence of the problem. If the problem is intermittent, it becomes more difficult to diagnose. You should note that, although a problem seems to occur randomly, it often is, in fact, occurring regularly—but the factors linking each occurrence may be very obscure. It is rare for computers to behave erratically for no apparent reason, except in the case of intermittent hardware failures, when the laws of physics are dictating system behavior.

2. Determine whether the problem began after a particular change was made to the configuration of the operating system, such as a driver update, the addition of a new modem, or a new video resolution setting. If this is the case, try to determine how the new configuration and the problem may be related.

3. Use binary logic to isolate one variable at a time in your search for the failing component. For example, if the operating system is suspect, turn off all its advanced features simultaneously. If the problem goes away, refine your search, turning the features back on one at a time until the problem reoccurs. If turning off all the features does not solve the problem, you can likely look elsewhere.

4. Determine as precisely as possible whether the problem seems to be clearly internal to Windows 95 or includes external software and/or hardware. Generally, installing Windows 95 on a new computer will not cause many problems, unless those problems are related to hardware incompatibilities. The situation always becomes more complex when an existing system's software and hardware are migrated to Windows 95, because Windows 95 is then likely to inherit any existing problems with the computer as well as some potential new problems, such as Windows 3.1 applications that do not work properly under Windows 95. The best example of this methodology is booting into Safe mode, because this disables many if not all special features, drivers, and software of the operating system. If the problem goes away in Safe mode, the problem probably is limited to a few key configuration parameters.

5. Determine whether sequence is important to the problem. Is it a matter of the order in which things happen in the operating system? This can point out conflicts between different applications, for example. Does one application fail only after another particular application has loaded?

6. Is this a known or common problem? Does it occur on other computers, or is it an isolated event? To find known problems, consult your available technical resources (see "Available Technical Resources") to learn potential solutions or to determine whether a known solution exists. Obviously, this is much easier to do if you can produce the problem on demand.

Troubleshooting Setup and System Startup

The Windows 95 installation is usually successful; but on occasion there can be problems. These problems are usually due to hardware configuration and software difficulties. This section is directed toward helping you troubleshoot both the Windows 95 installation and normal system startup. Some basic troubleshooting techniques also are discussed in much finer detail in Chapter 35 on general troubleshooting in the *Windows 95 Resource Kit*. You should review it.

I use a simple approach to problem solving, which you can adopt (or adapt) for your own use as well. This simple approach can be characterized as making the solution "FIT" the problem. The following shows how this particular problem-solving approach works:

▶ **F.** Find the problem by drawing a box around it. Collect the symptoms of the problem, under what conditions it occurs, and when it happens. Draw a box around the problem to determine and narrow the scope. Consult any technical resources to see if it is a known problem. If the problem is a known problem, it might already have a known solution or work-around.

▶ **I.** Isolate and diagnose the problem. Make an assumption about what is causing the problem. Don't overlook the obvious. Ask what has recently changed, and why.

▶ **T.** Test the solution to the problem. By eliminating recent changes or by controlling the number of variables, you can methodically test each modification to see if it solves the problem. Return the computer to the original state after each test. If you change three things and this somehow fixes the problem, which change was the effective one? Document your solution for the next time, or for the next person.

Choose the Appropriate Course of Action When the Installation Process Fails

The Windows 95 Setup program creates several log files (SETUPLOG.TXT, DETLOG.TXT, and DETCRASH.LOG) during hardware detection failure, and other files (NETLOG.TXT and BOOTLOG.TXT) as Windows 95 starts up the first time. The following list looks at these files in detail:

▶ **SETUPLOG.TXT.** This is an ASCII text file that contains the Windows 95 Setup information created during installation. As Windows 95 is being installed, entries are written into this text file for each step in sequence. This file will show any error conditions encountered. It is used by the Windows 95 Setup program in case of setup failure, and you can use it to troubleshoot errors during the installation process.

The Windows 95 Setup program uses the information contained within SETUPLOG.TXT to ensure that the Windows 95 Setup program does not fail twice on the same problem. When you restart the Windows 95 Setup program after a failure, the contents are reviewed to see which process started, but did not complete successfully. These processes are skipped, and the next process in sequence is run. The DETLOG.TXT and DETCRASH.LOG files, discussed next, are used to skip any hardware detection modules that failed.

note

Buried on the CD-ROM version of Windows 95 is a helpful program called LOGVIEW.EXE, which enables you to examine all the text files mentioned in this list in a manner similar to the

SYSEDIT.EXE program found in earlier versions of Windows. To find this program, look in the OTHER\MISC\LOGVIEW directory.

SETUPLOG.TXT is stored as a hidden file on the computer's root directory. Information is added to this file in the same order as the installation process. If you need to determine what caused the Windows 95 Setup program to fail, look at the entries at the bottom of this file before restarting.

▶ **DETLOG.TXT.** This is an ASCII text file that contains a record of all devices found during the hardware detection phase of installation. If a device is found, the detected parameters are identified and recorded.

If the hardware detection phase should cause the computer to stall or lock up, a binary file named DETCRASH.LOG is created. While DETLOG.TXT is an ASCII file for you to read, the Windows 95 Setup program reads the binary information in DETCRASH.LOG to determine what steps successfully completed.

DETLOG.TXT is stored as a hidden file on the computer's root directory. Information is added to this file in the same order as the hardware detection phase. If you need to determine what caused the Windows 95 Setup program to fail or lockup, look at the entries at the bottom of this file before restarting again.

▶ **DETCRASH.LOG.** This is a binary file that only exists during the hardware detection phase. It tracks the entire process in case of errors for the Windows 95 Setup program. You need to be aware of its existence, but you would use the DETLOG.TXT ASCII file to do any troubleshooting.

▶ **NETLOG.TXT.** This is an ASCII text file that contains a record of all detected network components found during installation. There are four parts to the network detection phase. These correspond with the four class types of network configuration: network clients, network protocols, network adapters, and network services (such as file and print sharing).

This file is stored as a nonhidden file on the computer's root directory. Information is added to this file in the same order as the network detection phase. If you need to determine what caused the Windows 95 Setup program not to communicate across the network, look at the entries in this file.

▶ **BOOTLOG.TXT.** This is an ASCII text file that contains a record of the current startup process when starting Windows 95. When Windows 95 is started for the first time, this file is created automatically. This file records the Windows 95 components and drivers as they are loaded and initialized, and records the status of each step.

The information in BOOTLOG.TXT is written in sequence during startup. You might need to examine it closely to determine which error occurred. The Windows 95 Resource Kit has a good description of the sections within this file. You also can create this file by pressing F8 during the "Starting Windows 95" startup and then selecting menu option 2—normal with a boot log.

This file is stored as a hidden file on the computer's root directory. Information is added to this file during the Windows 95 startup process. If you need to determine what caused Windows 95 to fail or lockup, look at the entries within this file before restarting again.

The three key files used to troubleshoot the Windows 95 Setup process are the SETUPLOG.TXT, DETLOG.TXT, and BOOTLOG.TXT ASCII text files. The Windows 95 Resource Kit provides code for a batch file you can create that looks at these key files and extracts information.

Choose the Appropriate Course of Action When Startup and Boot Processes Fail

A large majority of the technical problems that arise under Windows 95 can be traced back to the configuration files and how these files control the boot process. Especially in upgrade situations, many settings that were necessary and that worked properly in a Windows 3.1 environment are either redundant or incompatible in a Windows 95 environment. Isolating which of these settings are redundant or incompatible with Windows 95 can be difficult. Windows 95 provides a number of tools and configuration parameters that can aid in this task:

> Also see the "Troubleshooting Scenarios" section in Chapter 1, "Planning and Installation." That section lists and describes some of the most common installation and startup errors received under Windows 95.

- ▶ Safe Recovery mode of Setup

- ▶ The Boot menu

- ▶ The Verify install procedure

- ▶ The Startup disk

- ▶ WIN.COM switches

Safe Recovery Mode of Setup

To avoid having to restart the entire installation procedure in the event of a system crash or other mishap during setup, Windows 95 implements an automatic Safe Recovery mode that, when the computer is restarted following the crash, and Setup is rerun, restarts the Setup procedure at the point at which it was interrupted.

The Boot Menu

By pressing the F8 key when Windows 95 boots, you can access the Boot menu, which provides a number of different modes in which Windows 95 can be booted. The menu options depend in part on what parameters are specified in the MSDOS.SYS file, but generally consist of the following:

- ▶ Normal mode

- ▶ Logged mode

- ▶ Safe mode

- ▶ Safe mode with network support

- ▶ Step-by-step confirmation

- ▶ Command-prompt-only mode

- ▶ Safe mode command prompt

- ▶ Previous version of MS-DOS

Normal Mode

This is the normal operation mode of Windows 95. If you decide to complete the boot process to start Windows 95 under normal conditions, select this mode.

Logged Mode

When you select Logged mode, the entire boot process is logged to a file called BOOTLOG.TXT, which catalogs VxD initializations, driver loads, and various other boot-related events.

Safe Mode

Safe mode is likely the single most important troubleshooting tool available in Windows 95. In this mode, a number of key Windows 95 components and settings are disabled, including the following:

- ▶ CONFIG.SYS and AUTOEXEC.BAT

- ▶ The [Boot] and [386Enh] sections of SYSTEM.INI

▶ The Load= and Run= parameters of WIN.INI

▶ The Startup group in Windows 95

▶ The Registry

▶ All device drivers except the keyboard, mouse, and standard VGA video driver

Disabling these items allows the separation of fundamental operating system problems from those caused by a combination of software factors. For example, in a situation in which the display is not functioning properly in Normal mode, if the problem does not appear in Safe mode, the problem probably is video driver–related and is not due to a defective video card.

Similarly, you can use Safe mode to troubleshoot scenarios, such as the following:

▶ GPFs

▶ Application hangs

▶ A hang during the boot process

▶ A blank screen at boot time

In some instances, you cannot use the Safe mode boot option because certain drivers in the CONFIG.SYS or AUTOEXEC. BAT are necessary for booting the system (such as partitioning software drivers). In these cases, you can boot to a Command-prompt-only mode (which processes CONFIG.SYS and AUTOEXEC.BAT) and then, using the command WIN /d:m, you can continue the remainder of the Safe mode boot process.

Safe Mode with Network Support

This mode is similar to Safe mode but enables Real-mode Net-BEUI networking support. This mode also processes some Registry information needed to enable network support. This mode can be useful when the following problems occur:

▶ The computer hangs during a network operation

▶ Network print operations fail

▶ The computer is using a shared install of Windows 95, requires access to the shared files, and networking in Normal mode is not functioning

Step-by-Step Confirmation

This boot mode is similar to the F8 function of previous versions of MS-DOS; it permits the user to step through the various stages of the boot process and specify whether each should or should not be completed. This mode can be very useful when you're trying to isolate boot stages to determine which may be causing a given problem. It also can be used to view system responses to various parameters in CONFIG.SYS and AUTOEXEC.BAT, which otherwise are displayed far too quickly to read.

Command-Prompt-Only Mode

Command-prompt-only boot mode is similar to a normal boot of MS-DOS. Only CONFIG.SYS, AUTOEXEC.BAT, COMMAND.COM, and the Registry are processed (along with any necessary disk compression drivers). This mode is useful in troubleshooting problems running MS-DOS applications in a VM under Windows 95. If the application functions in this mode but not inside Windows 95, the problem is likely due to a compatibility issue. If the application does not function in Command-prompt-only mode, the problem is likely a configuration problem in CONFIG.SYS or AUTOEXEC.BAT, or the application may be corrupt.

Safe Mode Command Prompt

This mode functions similarly to Command-prompt-only, except that CONFIG.SYS and AUTOEXEC.BAT are not processed (disk compression drivers are still loaded). This mode can be useful in situations in which even Safe mode does not function properly.

Previous Version of MS-DOS

Although the Previous version of MS-DOS boot mode is not primarily for troubleshooting, it can be used in situations in which particular MS-DOS–related functions worked in previous versions of MS-DOS but do not seem to function properly under Windows 95. This boot mode can be used to test that functionality in both environments.

The Verify Install Procedure

If you suspect that some Windows 95 files or Registry information has become corrupted, you can have Windows 95 examine all installed components to determine whether this is the case and, if so, recopy or reconstitute the component. If Setup is rerun after installation, Windows 95 prompts the user as to whether installation should be rerun or components should be verified. If verification is chosen, the following occurs:

▶ A validity check is performed on all required files. If the check fails, the file is recopied from the Windows 95 installation media.

▶ The VMM32.VXD file is rebuilt.

▶ Incorrect Registry entries are overwritten.

The Startup Disk

You can create the Startup disk at installation time or later through the Add/Remove Programs option in the Control Panel. The disk serves as an emergency boot disk should the operating system fail to load. The disk also contains FDISK, FORMAT, and several other MS-DOS–based file and disk utilities that may be useful in diagnosing and repairing system problems.

When you install Windows 95 in a shared network situation, the Startup disk includes information for that shared environment. In this situation, the Startup disk can be a floppy disk, a remote-boot disk image on a server, or a local hard disk. It

continues

includes real-mode software that is needed to start the computer and attach it to the shared Windows folder on the server. It also includes a copy of the mini-Registry Windows 95 uses to start the computer.

WIN.COM Switches

WIN.COM includes support for a number of error-isolation switches. Although some are available from within Windows 95, you may have to specify them from the command prompt in situations in which Windows 95 fails to load. These switches are specified in the format

win /d:[f] [m] [n] [s] [v] [x]

The switches function as follows:

Switch	Function
[f]	Disables 32-bit file system drivers
[m]	Starts Windows 95 in Safe mode
[n]	Starts Windows 95 in Safe mode with networking
[s]	Excludes the ROM address space between FOOO and 1 MB from use by Windows 95
[v]	Disables virtualization of hard disk interrupts
[x]	Disables use of upper memory by Windows 95

You can use these switches independently or together as part of a single command.

Troubleshooting Other Specific Scenarios

Although you cannot anticipate every potential problem that a system may encounter when Windows 95 is installed, certain courses of action are recommended for particular troubleshooting scenarios. These suggestions neither are exhaustive nor guaranteed to work in the given situation, because every technical problem is in many ways unique to its operating environment. Table 12.1 shows some possible solutions for common problems. These solutions are intended to provide examples of applicable methodologies.

Table 12.1

Troubleshooting Examples

Problem	Possible Solution
Cannot print to a local printer	Verify that the correct driver is installed, ensure that the printer's buffer is clear, try printing directly to the LPT port from a DOS prompt
Cannot print to a network printer	Ensure that File and Printer Sharing is enabled at the remote computer; verify that you have correct network protocols configured
Print jobs are not spooling properly	Disable spooling in the Properties sheet of the printer, which will indicate whether spooling is in fact the problem; verify that enough disk space is available to hold the spooled print jobs
Print jobs are garbled	Disable EMF spooling; check whether Windows 3.1 printer drivers are being used
Fatal Exception errors and GPFs	Try Safe mode; try a standard VGA driver; run ScanDisk with a full surface scan to check for corrupted files
Message that communications port is already in use when attempting to use a terminal program	Verify that no fax manager software is running in the background, waiting for calls, because this ties up the communications port
A newly installed ISA device is not functioning	Check the Device Manager for conflicts with existing devices (designated by a yellow exclamation mark)
CD-ROM drive is not listed as a drive in the Explorer or the Device Manager	Most likely not a supported brand; install Real-mode driver support

continues

Table 12.1 Continued

Problem	Possible Solution
A device is malfunctioning, but when it is removed from Device Manager and redetected, the problem persists	Edit the Registry, delete the associated key under HKLM\Enum\Root\, restart the computer, and run hardware detection again

Discriminate Resource Usage in Windows 3.1, Windows 95, and Windows NT

For an exercise testing this information, see end of chapter.

As you prepare for the Troubleshooting section of the exam, you need to be able to discriminate the resource usage in Windows 3.1, Windows 95, and Windows NT. You need a clear understanding of the Windows 95 system architecture. Chapter 8 discusses the details of running applications under Windows 95. Table 12.2, however, compares and contrasts the memory usage of a Microsoft MS-DOS–based application, a WIN16 application, and a WIN32 application operating in Windows 95. Also, complete Exercise 12.2 at the end of the chapter to refresh your memory on how to count virtual machines using System Monitor.

Table 12.2

Comparing Memory Usage	
Application	Memory Usage
MS-DOS	Each runs in a private Virtual DOS Machine (VDM). No message queue. Loaded in the lower 1 MB of virtual memory.
Windows 16-bit	All run in a common address space and share a single message queue. Loaded in the lower 2 GB of virtual memory.
Windows 32-bit	Each runs in a private address space, and each thread has its own message queue. Loaded in the 4 MB to 2 GB range of virtual memory.

Exercises

Exercise 12.1: Configuring and Using System Monitor

Exercise 12.1 demonstrates how to configure and use the System Monitor. This exercise assumes you have installed the System Monitor component through the Add/Remove Programs option in the Control Panel.

1. From the Start menu, choose Programs, Accessories, System Tools, System Monitor. The System Monitor window appears.

2. Choose Edit, Remove Item. Select all listed items and choose OK. The System Monitor window should now be empty of tracked items.

3. On the View menu, verify that Line Charts is selected, and then choose Edit, Add Item. A list of system-related counter categories appears.

4. Select the Kernel category and the Processor Usage (%) item. Kernel: Processor Usage (%) now appears as a line chart.

5. Choose Options, Chart; increase the Update interval to 1 second; and choose OK. The chart now updates more frequently.

6. Choose View, Bar Chart. Kernel: Processor Usage (%) now appears as a bar chart.

7. Close the System Monitor. You return to the Desktop.

Exercise 12.2: Counting Virtual Machines

To illustrate the point about how Windows 95 manages virtual machines, follow Exercise 12.2 to count the number of virtual machines running on your Windows 95 computer.

1. From your computer, start Windows 95.

2. If you installed Windows 95 on your computer with the Typical Setup option, the System Monitor program might not be installed, because it is an optional component.

continues

Exercise 12.2: Continued

To determine whether the System Monitor utility program is installed, from the Start menu, choose Programs, Accessories, System Tools, System Monitor. If System Monitor is not available, you must add it to your computer by following these steps:

   a. From the Start menu, choose Settings, Control Panel. From the Control Panel program group, choose the Add/Remove Programs icon.

   b. Click on the Windows Setup tab, double-click on Accessories, and select the System Monitor check box. Press Enter or choose OK. Press Enter or choose OK again to install the System Monitor.

3. From the Start menu, choose Programs, Accessories, System Tools, System Monitor. The System Monitor utility program displays key system information in either a Line Chart, Bar Chart, or Numeric Chart format.

4. Any items previously selected are displayed when the System Monitor utility program starts. When you run the System Monitor utility program for the first time, the Kernel: Processor Usage (%) appears in a Line Chart.

5. You need to remove all current items to run this exercise. Highlight any items you want to remove, and choose Edit, Remove Item.

6. Choose Edit, Add Item to open the Add Item dialog box. From the Category list, click on Kernel to display the list of Kernel items.

7. Choose Virtual Machines from the Item list. If you need an explanation of each item, choose Explain to see that this shows the number of virtual machines present in the system. Press Enter or choose OK to add the item Virtual Machines as a selection.

8. Choose View, Numeric Charts to obtain the number of virtual machines that currently are active. Normally this value is 1, because the Windows 95 computer has just been started. It could be higher.

9. Open some Windows program applications or the Windows Explorer. Has the number of virtual machines changed? The number of active virtual machines should not change when Windows programs are started.

10. Start an MS-DOS command prompt by choosing Start, Run to open the Run dialog box, or choose Start, Programs, MS-DOS Prompt. Has the number of virtual machines changed? It should change, because each MS-DOS application will start another virtual machine.

11. Start another MS-DOS command prompt, and then a third. What happens to the count of virtual machines after you start each new MS-DOS command prompt? Each time another MS-DOS command prompt is started, the number of virtual machines should increase by a count of 1. If the initial count was 1, then starting three MS-DOS command prompts increases the number to 4.

12. Close all three MS-DOS command prompts. How many virtual machines are currently active? The count of virtual machines should be back down to 1, or the starting number in step 8.

   Based on what you know about virtual machines, explain why the count changes during the exercise.

   All the Windows 16-bit and 32-bit applications run in a single system virtual machine. But each MS-DOS application runs in its own Virtual DOS Machine. Opening a new MS-DOS command prompt causes the virtual machine count to increase by 1.

13. When you finish viewing the System Monitor utility information, close the System Monitor.

Exercise 12.3: Rebuilding the Default Program Groups

Exercise 12.3 shows how to rebuild the default program groups. When you do this, you do not affect any new groups or shortcuts you've created.

1. From the Start menu, choose Run.

2. In the Open field of the Run dialog box, type **GRPCONV**.

3. Click on OK. The default program groups are rebuilt.

Review Questions

The following questions will test your knowledge of the information in this chapter. For additional questions, see MCP Endeavor and the Microsoft Roadmap/Assessment Exam on the CD-ROM that accompanies this book.

1. Your boss comes to you and asks if you want to belong to Microsoft TechNet. What is Microsoft TechNet?

    A. a CompuServe forum

    B. an Internet forum

    C. a CD-ROM publication

    D. a users group

2. You set up Windows 95 on 10 computers in your company. You want to set up optimization and troubleshooting tools on all these computers. Which three of the following are Windows 95 optimization and troubleshooting tools?

    A. System Resource Monitor

    B. Net Watcher

    C. System Monitor

    D. System Resource Meter

3. Which two of the following statements are true?

    A. System Monitor cannot monitor a remote computer.

    B. A share-level computer cannot monitor a user-level computer using Net Watcher.

    C. System Monitor is located in System Tools in the Accessories group.

    D. System Monitor is located in the System Control Panel applet.

4. You want to optimize all printers connected to your Windows 95 computers. From what you know about Windows 95 printer support, what is the main factor in ensuring print performance?

    A. spool settings

    B. driver compatibility

    C. queue management

    D. font management

5. Frank prints several documents from the same application and wants to know how Windows' 95 spooling affects his wait time. Choosing to return control after the first page is spooled _____ Frank's wait time.

    A. increases

    B. shortens

    C. doesn't change

    D. eliminates

6. At the help desk, you receive a call from a user who wants to start Windows 95 from a Boot menu item. He doesn't know how to display the Boot menu. You tell him to press _____ while Windows 95 boots.

    A. Ctrl+Alt+Delete

    B. Alt+Tab

    C. F6

    D. F8

7. Which two of the following would be disabled in Windows 95 Safe mode?

    A. A 256-color display driver

    B. Control Panel applets

    C. AUTOEXEC.BAT

    D. A non-Microsoft mouse

8. You create a troubleshooting document to circulate around the IT department. One of the issues is about error-isolation switches. Which of the following includes support for a number of error-isolation switches?

    A. BOOT.COM

    B. WINCHK.COM

    C. WIN.COM

    D. WIN95.COM

9. Abby wants to record her boot process to isolate problems with devices not setting correctly. If she uses the Logged mode to log the entire boot process, which file is created?

    A. BOOT.LOG

    B. BOOTLOG.TXT

    C. BOOT.TXT

    D. LOGBOOT.TXT

10. Pierre runs several types of applications under Windows 95, but is having problems with some of them. He asks you what types of applications Windows 95 can run. You tell him which of the following two?

    A. All OS/2 applications

    B. MS-DOS and 16-bit Windows applications

    C. 24-bit Windows applications

    D. 32-bit Windows applications (also known as WIN32 applications; includes most Windows NT software)

11. Windows 95 has many built-in tools you can use for both optimizing and troubleshooting. Which of the following are Windows 95 utilities?

    A. System Monitor

    B. System Resource Meter

    C. Net Connector

    D. Speed Disk

12. In such an environment as Windows 95, a need for careful management of the system's resources exists. When two processes request the use of a device at the exact same moment, what does Windows 95 use to arbitrate such requests?

    A. WIN95.COM

    B. Virtual memory

    C. Virtual Machine Manager

    D. None of the above

13. When Peter attempts to use WinCIM 2.01 to dial into CompuServe, he receives an error telling him the port is already busy. He checks and no other applications are running. What could be causing this problem?

    A. Dial-Up Networking Server caller access is enabled

    B. His modem is not plugged in

    C. CompuServe's phone line is busy at the moment

    D. Registry Editor is running

14. After setting up Windows 95 on a shared networked server, you need to run the Startup disk for it. Where can the Startup files exist for this situation?

    A. On a floppy disk

    B. On a local hard drive

    C. On a remote-boot disk image on a server

    D. A and C only

15. You want to optimize the Windows 95 file system. Which two are ways to maximize the use of 32-bit drivers under Windows 95?

A. Delete all TMP files on your system under Windows 95.

B. Set the virtual memory settings on the Performance tab of the My Computer Properties sheet to 0% or disable it.

C. Update any non-Microsoft disk compression to a 32-bit driver from the manufacturer.

D. Verify that the Performance tab of the My Computer Properties sheet shows all 32-bit components for the file system and for virtual memory.

16. WIN.COM includes support for a number of error-isolation switches. What does the m switch do?

A. disables 32-bit file system drivers

B. starts Windows 95 in Safe mode

C. starts Windows 95 in Safe mode with network support

D. excludes the ROM address space between F000 and 1 MB from use by Windows 95

17. Karen starts a print job to a local printer. The print job comes out garbled. What are two possible solutions to fixing this problem?

A. Resend the print job until it comes out correctly

B. Check whether Windows 3.1 printer drivers are being used and update to Windows 95 drivers

C. Reduce font size on the document

D. Disable EMF spooling

18. James is using an application that does not work with the Windows 95 TAPI architecture. He discovers that when he tries to use that application with an installed modem, he gets an error message telling him the requested port is still open. What could be causing this error message?

A. The Dial-Up Server application is enabled on his system

B. The serial cable is not tightened to the serial port

C. The Enable-TAPI switch is turned on

D. None of the above

19. When diagnosing Dial-Up Networking (DUN) problems, you tend to concentrate on protocol issues. Pick the best reason why this is so.

A. Because DUN cannot use the TCP/IP protocol

B. Because the Dial-Up Adapter automatically synchro-nizes protocols on the client and server sides

C. Because the Dial-Up Adapter needs to be configured to use the same protocol as the server-side computer.

D. All of the above

20. Normally, memory in the 1–4 MB range is not used by Win-dows 95. What is this memory range used for?

A. MS-DOS applications that need it

B. Networking applications running as 32-bit applications

C. TSRs

D. 16-bit applications that need it

Review Answers

1. C	6. D	11. A B	16. B
2. B C D	7. A C	12. C	17. B D
3. B C	8. C	13. A	18. A
4. A	9. B	14. A B C	19. C
5. B	10. B D	15. C D	20. D

Appendix

Overview of the
Certification Process

To become a Microsoft Certified Professional, candidates must pass rigorous certification exams that provide a valid and reliable measure of their technical proficiency and expertise. These closed-book exams have on-the-job relevance because they are developed with the input of professionals in the computer industry and reflect how Microsoft products are actually used in the workplace. The exams are conducted by an independent organization—Sylvan Prometric—at more than 700 Sylvan Authorized Testing Centers around the world.

Currently Microsoft offers four types of certification, based on specific areas of expertise:

▶ **Microsoft Certified Product Specialist (MCPS).** Qualified to provide installation, configuration, and support for users of at least one Microsoft desktop operating system, such as Windows 95. In addition, candidates may take additional elective exams to add areas of specialization. MCPS is the first level of expertise.

▶ **Microsoft Certified Systems Engineer (MCSE).** Qualified to effectively plan, implement, maintain, and support information systems with Microsoft Windows NT and other Microsoft advanced systems and workgroup products, such as Microsoft Office and Microsoft BackOffice. The Windows 95 exam can be used as one of the four core operating systems exams. MCSE is the second level of expertise.

▶ **Microsoft Certified Solution Developer (MCSD).** Qualified to design and develop custom business solutions using Microsoft development tools, technologies, and platforms, including Microsoft Office and Microsoft BackOffice. MCSD also is a second level of expertise, but in the area of software development.

▶ **Microsoft Certified Trainer (MCT).** Instructionally and technically qualified by Microsoft to deliver Microsoft Education Courses at Microsoft authorized sites. An MCT must be employed by a Microsoft Solution Provider Authorized Technical Education Center or a Microsoft Authorized Academic Training site.

You can find complete descriptions of all Microsoft Certifications in the Microsoft Education and Certification Roadmap on the CD-ROM that comes with this book. The following sections describe the requirements for each type of certification.

For up-to-date information about each type of certification, visit the Microsoft Training and Certification World Wide Web site at http://www.microsoft.com/tran_cert. You must have an Internet account and a WWW browser to access this information. You also can call the following sources:

▶ Microsoft Certified Professional Program: 800-636-7544

▶ Sylvan Prometric Testing Centers: 800-755-EXAM

▶ Microsoft Online Institute (MOLI): 800-449-9333

How to Become a Microsoft Certified Product Specialist (MCPS)

Becoming an MCPS requires you pass one operating system exam. Passing the "Implementing and Supporting Microsoft Windows 95" exam (#70-63), which this book covers, satisfies the MCPS requirement.

Windows 95 is not the only operating system you can be tested on to get your MCSP certification. The following list shows the names and exam numbers of all the operating systems from which you can choose to get your MCPS certification:

- ▶ Implementing and Supporting Microsoft Windows 95 #70-63

- ▶ Implementing and Supporting Microsoft Windows NT Workstation 4.02 #70-73

- ▶ Implementing and Supporting Microsoft Windows NT Workstation 3.51 #70-42

- ▶ Implementing and Supporting Microsoft Windows NT Server 4.0 #70-67

- ▶ Implementing and Supporting Microsoft Windows NT Server 3.51 #70-43

- ▶ Microsoft Windows for Workgroups 3.11–Desktop #70-48

- ▶ Microsoft Windows 3.1 #70-30

- ▶ Microsoft Windows Operating Systems and Services Architecture I #70-150

- ▶ Microsoft Windows Operating Systems and Services Architecture II #70-151

How to Become a Microsoft Certified Systems Engineer (MCSE)

MCSE candidates need to pass four operating system exams and two elective exams. The MCSE certification path is divided into two tracks: the Windows NT 3.51 track and the Windows NT 4.0 track. The "Implementing and Supporting Microsoft Windows 95" exam covered in this book can be applied to either track of the MCSE certification path.

Table A.1 shows the core requirements (four operating system exams) and the elective courses (two exams) for the Windows NT 3.51 track.

Table A.1

Windows NT 3.51 MCSE Track

Take These Two Required Exams (Core Requirements)	Plus, Pick One of the Following Operating System Exams (Core Requirement)	Plus, Pick One of the Following Networking Exams (Core Requirement)	Plus, Pick Two of the Following Elective Exams (Elective Requirements)
Implementing and Supporting Microsoft Windows NT Server 3.51 #70-43	Implementing and Supporting Microsoft Windows 95 #70-63	Networking Microsoft Windows for Workgroups 3.11 #70-46	Microsoft SNA Server #70-12
AND Implementing and Supporting Microsoft Windows NT Workstation 3.51 #70-42	*OR* Microsoft Windows for Workgroups 3.11–Desktop #70-48	*OR* Networking with Microsoft Windows 3.1 #70-47	*OR* Implementing and Supporting Microsoft Systems Management Server 1.0 #70-14
	OR Microsoft Windows 3.1 #70-30	*OR* Networking Essentials #70-58	*OR* Microsoft SQL Server 4.2 Database Implementation #70-21
			OR Microsoft SQL Server 4.2 Database Administration for Microsoft Windows NT #70-22
			OR System Administration for Microsoft SQL Server 6 #70-26
			OR Implementing a Database Design on Microsoft SQL Server 6 #70-27

Take These Two Required Exams (Core Requirements)	Plus, Pick One of the Following Operating System Exams (Core Requirement)	Plus, Pick One of the Following Networking Exams (Core Requirement)	Plus, Pick Two of the Following Elective Exams (Elective Requirements)
			OR Microsoft Mail for PC Networks 3.2-Enterprise #70-37
			OR Internetworking Microsoft TCP/IP on Microsoft Windows NT (3.5–3.51) #70-53
			OR Internetworking Microsoft TCP/IP on Microsoft Windows NT 4.0 #70-59
			OR Implementing and Supporting Microsoft Exchange Server 4.0 #70-75
			OR Implementing and Supporting Microsoft Internet Information Server #70-77
			OR Implementing and Supporting Microsoft Proxy Server 1.0 #70-78

Table A.2 shows the core requirements (four operating system exams) and elective courses (two exams) for the Windows NT 4.0 track. Tables A.1 and A.2 have many of the same exams listed, but there are distinct differences between the two. Make sure you read each track's requirements carefully.

Table A.2

Windows NT 4.0 MCSE Track			
Take These Two Required Exams (Core Requirements)	Plus, Pick One of the Following Operating System Exams (Core Requirement)	Plus, Pick One of the Following Networking Exams (Core Requirement)	Plus, Pick Two of the Following Elective Exams (Elective Requirements)
Implementing and Supporting Microsoft Windows NT Server 4.0 #70-67	Implementing and Supporting Microsoft Windows 95 #70-63	Networking Microsoft Windows for Workgroups 3.11 #70-46	Microsoft SNA Server #70-12
AND Implementing and Support- Microsoft Windows NT Server in the Enterprise #70-68	*OR* Microsoft Windows for Workgroups 3.11-Desktop	*OR* Networking with Microsoft Windows 3.1 #70-47	*OR* Implementing and Supporting Microsoft Systems Management Server 1.0 #70-14
	OR Microsoft Windows 3.1 #70-30	*OR* Networking Essentials #70-58	*OR* Microsoft SQL Server 4.2 Database Implementation #70-21
	OR Implementing and Supporting Microsoft Windows NT Workstation 4.02 #70-73		*OR* Microsoft SQL Server 4.2 Database Administration Microsoft Windows NT #70-22
			OR System Administration for Microsoft SQL Server 6 #70-26

Take These Two Required Exams (Core Requirements)	Plus, Pick One of the Following Operating System Exams (Core Requirement)	Plus, Pick One of the Following Networking Exams (Core Requirement)	Plus, Pick Two of the Following Elective Exams (Elective Requirements)
			OR Implementing a Database Design on Microsoft SQL Server 6 #70-27
			OR Microsoft Mail for PC Networks 3.2–Enterprise #70-37
			OR Internetworking Microsoft TCP/IP on Microsoft Windows NT (3.5–3.51) #70-53
			OR Internetworking Microsoft TCP/IP on Microsoft Windows NT 4.0 #70-59
			OR Implementing and Supporting Microsoft Exchange Server 4.0 #70-75
			OR Implementing and Supporting Microsoft Internet Information Server #70-77
			OR Implementing and Supporting Microsoft Proxy Server 1.0 #70-78

How to Become a Microsoft Certified Solution Developer (MCSD)

MCSD candidates need to pass two core technology exams and two elective exams. Unfortunately, the "Implementing and Supporting Microsoft Windows 95" (#70-63) exam does NOT apply toward any of these requirements. Table A.3 shows the required technology exams, plus the elective exams that apply toward obtaining the MCSD.

The "Implementing and Supporting Microsoft Windows 95" (#70-63) exam does NOT apply toward any of the MCSD requirements.

Table A.3

MCSD Exams and Requirements

Take These Two Core Technology Exams	Plus, Choose from Two of the Following Elective Exams
Microsoft Windows Operating Systems and Services Architecture I #70-150	Microsoft SQL Server 4.2 Database Implementation #70-21
AND Microsoft Windows Operating Systems and Services Architecture II #70-151	*OR* Developing Applications with C++ Using the Microsoft Foundation Class Library #70-24
	OR Implementing a Database Design on Microsoft SQL Server 6 #70-27
	OR Microsoft Visual Basic 3.0 for Windows–Application Development #70-50
	OR Microsoft Access 2.0 for Windows–Application Development #70-51
	OR Developing Applications with Microsoft Excel 5.0 Using Visual Basic for Applications #70-52

Take These Two Core Technology Exams	Plus, Choose from Two of the Following Elective Exams
	OR Programming in Microsoft Visual FoxPro 3.0 for Windows #70-54
	OR Programming with Microsoft Visual Basic 4.0 #70-65
	OR Microsoft Access for Windows 95 and the Microsoft Access Development Toolkit #70-69
	OR Implementing OLE in Microsoft Foundation Class Applications #70-25

Becoming a Microsoft Certified Trainer (MCT)

To understand the requirements and process for becoming a Microsoft Certified Trainer (MCT), you need to obtain the Microsoft Certified Trainer Guide document (MCTGUIDE.DOC) from the following WWW site:

http://www.microsoft.com/train_cert/download.htm

On this page, click on the hyperlink MCT GUIDE (mctguide.doc) (117 KB). If your WWW browser can display DOC files (Word for Windows native file format), the MCT Guide displays in the browser window. Otherwise, you need to download it and open it in Word for Windows or Windows 95 WordPad. The MCT Guide explains the four-step process to becoming an MCT. The general steps for the MCT certification are as follows:

1. Complete and mail a Microsoft Certified Trainer application to Microsoft. You must include proof of your skills for presenting instructional material. The options for doing so are described in the MCT Guide.

2. Obtain and study the Microsoft Trainer Kit for the Microsoft Official Curricula (MOC) course(s) for which you want to be certified. You can order Microsoft Trainer Kits by calling 800-688-0496 in North America. Other regions should review the MCT Guide for information on how to order a Microsoft Trainer Kit.

3. Pass the Microsoft certification exam for the product for which you want to be certified to teach.

4. Attend the MOC course for which you want to be certified. This is done so you can understand how the course is structured, how labs are completed, and how the course flows.

You should use the preceding steps as a general overview of the MCT certification process. The actual steps you need to take are described in detail in the MCTGUIDE.DOC file on the WWW site mentioned earlier. Do not misconstrue the preceding steps as the actual process you need to take.

If you are interested in becoming an MCT, you can receive more information by visiting the Microsoft Certified Training (MCT) WWW site at http://www.microsoft.com/train_cert/mctint.htm; or by calling 800-688-0496.

Appendix

Study Tips

B

Self-study involves any method that you employ to learn a given topic, with the most popular being third-party books, such as the one you hold in your hand. Before you begin to study a certification book, you should know exactly what Microsoft expects you to learn.

Pay close attention to the objectives posted for the exam. The most current objectives can always be found on the WWW site http://www.microsoft.com/train_cert. This book was written to the most current objectives, and the beginning of each chapter lists the relevant objectives for that chapter. As well, you should notice a handy tear-out card with an objective matrix that lists all objectives and the page you can turn to for information on that objective.

If you have taken any college courses in the past, you have probably learned which study habits work best for you. Nevertheless, consider the following:

▶ Study in bright light to reduce fatigue and depression.

▶ Establish a regular study schedule and stick as close to it as possible.

▶ Turn off all forms of distraction, including radios and televisions; or try studying in a quiet room.

▶ Study in the same place each time you study so your materials are always readily at hand.

▶ Take short breaks (approximately 15 minutes) every two to three hours or so. Studies have proven that your brain assimilates information better when this is allowed.

Another thing to think about is this: there are three ways in which humans learn information: visually, audially, and through tactile confirmation. That's why, in a college class, the students who took notes on the lectures had better recall on exam day; they took in information both audially and through tactile confirmation—writing it down.

Hence, use study techniques that reinforce information in all three ways. For example, by reading the book, you are visually taking in information. By writing down the information when you test yourself, you are giving your brain tactile confirmation. And lastly, have someone test you outloud, so you can hear yourself giving the correct answer. Having someone test you should always be the last step in studying.

Pre-testing Yourself

Before taking the actual exam, verify that you are ready to do so by testing yourself over and over again in a variety of ways. Within this book, there are questions at the beginning and end of each chapter. On the accompanying CD-ROM, there are a number of electronic test engines that emulate the actual Microsoft test and enable you to test your knowledge of the subject areas. Use these over and over and over again, until you are consistently scoring in the 90 percent range (or better).

This means, of course, that you can't start studying five days before the exam begins. You will need to give yourself plenty of time to read, practice, and then test yourself several times.

The New Riders' TestPrep electronic testing engine, we believe, is the best one on the market. Although it is described in Appendix D, "All About TestPrep," here it's important for you to know that TestPrep will prepare you for the exam in a way unparalleled by most other engines.

Hints and Tips for Doing Your Best on the Tests

In a confusing twist of terminology, when you take one of the Microsoft exams, you are said to be "writing" the exam. When you go to take the actual exam, be prepared. Arrive early, and be ready to show two forms of identification and to sit before the monitor. Expect wordy questions. Although you have 90 minutes to take the exam, there are 70 questions you must answer. This gives you just over one minute to answer each question. That might sound like ample time for each question, but remember that most of the questions are lengthy word problems, which tend to ramble on for paragraphs. Your 90 minutes of exam time can be consumed very quickly.

It has been estimated that approximately 85 percent of the candidates taking their first Microsoft exam fail. It is not so much that they are unprepared and unknowledgeable. It is more the case that they don't know what to expect and are immediately intimidated by the wordiness of the questions and the ambiguity implied in the answers.

For every exam Microsoft offers, there is a different required passing score. The "Implementing and Supporting Windows 95" required score is 714, or 71.4 percent. Because there are 70 questions on the exam (randomly taken from a pool of about 150), you must correctly answer 50 or more to pass.

Things to Watch For

When you take the exam, look closely at the number of correct choices you need to make. Some questions require that you select one correct answer; other questions have more than one correct answer. When you see radial buttons next to the answer choices, remember that the answers are mutually exclusive; there is only one right answer. On the other hand, check boxes indicate that the answers are not mutually exclusive and there are multiple right answers. On the "Implementing and Supporting Windows 95" exam, as opposed to several others, the number of correct choices is always stated on-screen. Be sure to read the questions closely to see how many correct answers you need to choose.

Also, read the questions fully. With lengthy questions, the last sentence often dramatically changes the scenario. When taking the exam, you are given pencils and two sheets of paper. If you are uncertain of the meaning of the question, map out the scenario on paper until you have it clear in your mind. You're required to turn in the scrap paper at the end of the exam.

Marking Answers for Return

You can mark questions on the actual exam and refer back to them later. If you get a wordy question that will take a long time to read and decipher, mark it and return to it when you have completed the rest of the exam. This will save you from wasting time and from running out of time on the exam. Remember, there are only 90 minutes allotted for the exam and it ends when those 90 minutes expire—whether or not you are finished with the exam.

Attaching Notes to Test Questions

At the conclusion of the exam, before the grading takes place, you are given the opportunity to attach a message to any question. If you feel that a question was too ambiguous, or tested on knowledge you did not need to know to work with the product, take this opportunity to state your case. Microsoft has never changed a test score as a result of an attached message; however, it never hurts to try—and it helps to vent your frustration before blowing the proverbial 50-amp fuse.

Good luck.

Appendix

What's on the CD-ROM

C

This appendix is a brief rundown of what you'll find on the CD-ROM that comes with this book. For a more detailed description of the newly-developed TestPrep test engine, exclusive to New Riders, please see Appendix D, "All About TestPrep."

New Riders' Exclusive TestPrep

A new test engine was developed exclusively for New Riders. It is, we believe, the best test engine available, because it closely emulates the actual Microsoft exam, and it enables you to check your score by category, which helps you determine what you need to study further. For a complete description of the benefits of TestPrep, please see Appendix D.

New Riders' Exclusive FLASH! Electronic Flash Card Program

You can use the FLASH! Electronic Flash Card program to convert some of the questions in the test engine database to a fill-in-the-blank format. Run the FLASH! program and select the categories on which you want to be tested. The engine then goes through the database in sequential order and tests your knowledge without multiple choice possibilities.

Transcender Corporation's Certification Sampler

The Transcender Corporation Certification Sampler test engine is the best-selling free-standing self-study certification product on the market today. This demonstration sampler will familiarize you with Transcender's products and help you further prepare for the exam.

MCP Endeavor

This is a testing application that helps you prepare for MSCE Certification.

Microsoft's Roadmap to Education and Certification

This application helps you define goals for Microsoft certification or for improving your on-the-job skills. Use this program to map your route to achieving these goals.

Microsoft TechNet Sampler

Microsoft TechNet is a comprehensive information resource for technical professionals. The sampler provides an interactive look at content delivered to Microsoft TechNet subscribers.

Exclusive Electronic Version of Text

Use the electronic version of this book to help you search for terms or areas that you need to study. It comes complete with all figures as they appear in the book.

Copyright Information and Disclaimer

New Riders' TestPrep test engine: Copyright 1997 New Riders Publishing. All rights reserved. Made in U.S.A.

FLASH! Electronic Flash Cards: Copyright 1997 New Riders Publishing. All rights reserved. Made in U.S.A.

MCP Endeavor: Copyright 1995 VFX Technologies, Inc. All rights reserved. Made in the U.S.A.

Microsoft Roadmap to Education and Certification: Copyright 1994-1995 Microsoft Corporation. All rights reserved. Made in the U.S.A.

The included software programs are provided "as is" without warranty of any kind, either express or implied, including, but not limited to, the implied warranties of merchantability and fitness for a particular purpose, or any warranty of noninfringement. Microsoft shall not be liable for any consequential, incidental, or special damages arising out of use of the enclosed software programs.

Some states/jurisdictions do not allow the exclusion of implied warranties, so the above exclusion may not apply to you. Your legal rights vary from state/jurisdiction to state/jurisdiction.

Microsoft TechNet Sampler: Copyright 1995 Microsoft Corporation. All rights reserved.

The included software is licensed to the user. Use of the software constitutes acceptance of the terms of the online Microsoft License Agreement included in the Setup procedure.

Appendix

All About TestPrep

The electronic TestPrep utility included on the CD-ROM accompanying this book enables you to test your Windows 95 knowledge in a manner similar to that employed by the actual Microsoft exam. When you first start the TestPrep exam, select the number of questions you want to be asked and the objective categories in which you want to be tested. You can choose anywhere from one to 70 questions, and from one to 12 categories, of which the real exam consists.

Although it is possible to maximize the TestPrep application, the default is for it to run in smaller mode so you can refer to your Windows 95 Desktop while answering questions. TestPrep uses a unique randomization sequence to ensure that each time you run the program you are presented with a different sequence of questions—this enhances your learning and prevents you from merely learning the expected answers over time without reading the question each and every time.

Question Presentation

TestPrep emulates the actual Microsoft "Implementing and Supporting Microsoft Windows 95" exam (#70-63), in that radial (circle) buttons are used to signify only one correct choice, while check boxes (squares) are used to signify multiple correct answers. Whenever more than one answer is correct, the number you should select is given in the wording of the question.

You can exit the program at any time by choosing the Exit key, or you can continue to the next question by choosing the Next key.

Scoring

The TestPrep Score Report uses actual numbers from the "Implementing and Supporting Microsoft Windows 95" exam. For Windows 95, a score of 714 or higher is considered passing; the same parameters apply to TestPrep. Each objective category is broken into categories with a percentage correct given for each of the 12 categories.

Choose Show Me What I Missed to go back through the questions you answered incorrectly and see what the correct answers are. Choose Exit to return to the beginning of the testing routine and start over.

Non-Random Mode

You can run TestPrep in Non-Random mode, which enables you to see the same set of questions each time, or on each machine. To run TestPrep in this manner, you need to create a shortcut to the executable file, and place the CLASS parameter on the command line calling the application, after the application's name. For example:

```
C:\TESTENG\70_63.EXE CLASS
```

Now, when you run TestPrep, the same sequence of questions will appear each and every time. To change the sequence but stay in Non-Random mode (for example, if you're in a classroom setting, where it is important that everyone see the same questions), choose Help, Class Mode on the main screen. This lets you enter a number from 1 to 8 to select a predefined sequence of questions.

Instructor Mode

To run TestPrep in Instructor mode (seeing the same set of questions each time, or on each machine), create a shortcut to the executable file, and place the INSTR parameter following CLASS on the command line calling the application, after the application's name. For example:

```
C:\TESTENG\70_63.EXE CLASS INSTR
```

Now, when you run TestPrep, the same sequence of questions will appear each and every time. Additionally, the correct answer will be marked already, and the objective category from which the question is coming will be given in the question. To change the sequence of questions that appear, choose Help, Class Mode on the main screen. This prompts you to enter a number from 1 to 8 to select a predefined sequence of questions; increment that by 100 and the sequence will be presented in Instructor mode.

Flash Cards

As a further learning aid, you can use the FLASH! Electronic Flash Cards program to convert some of the questions in the database into a fill-in-the-blank format. Run the FLASH! program and select the categories on which you want to be tested. The engine then goes through the database in sequential order and tests your knowledge without multiple choice possibilities.

I n d e x

Symbols

X - Y - Z

MACMILLAN COMPUTER PUBLISHING USA

A VIACOM COMPANY

 ---- Support:

If you need assistance with the information in this book or with a CD/Disk accompanying the book, please access the Knowledge Base on our Web site at **http://www.superlibrary.com/general/support**. Our most Frequently Asked Questions are answered there. If you do not find the answer to your questions on our Web site, you may contact Macmillan Technical Support **(317) 581-3833** or e-mail us at **support@mcp.com**.